A Network Architect's Guide to 5G

Syed Farrukh Hassan
Alexander Orel
Kashif Islam

Boston • Columbus • New York • San Francisco • Amsterdam • Cape Town
Dubai • London • Madrid • Milan • Munich • Paris • Montreal • Toronto • Delhi • Mexico City
São Paulo • Sydney • Hong Kong • Seoul • Singapore • Taipei • Tokyo

ISBN-13: 978-0-13-737684-1
ISBN-10: 0-13-737684-7

ScoutAutomatedPrintCode

Trademarks

Microsoft and the trademarks listed at http://www.microsoft.com on the "Trademarks" webpage are trademarks of the Microsoft group of companies. All other marks are property of their respective owners.

Warning and Disclaimer

Every effort has been made to make this book as complete and as accurate as possible, but no warranty or fitness is implied. The information provided is on an "as is" basis. The authors, the publisher, and Microsoft Corporation shall have neither liability nor responsibility to any person or entity with respect to any loss or damages arising from the information contained in this book or from the use of the programs accompanying it.

Special Sales

For information about buying this title in bulk quantities, or for special sales opportunities (which may include electronic versions; custom cover designs; and content particular to your business, training goals, marketing focus, or branding interests), please contact our corporate sales department at corpsales@pearsoned.com or (800) 382-3419.

For government sales inquiries, please contact governmentsales@pearsoned.com.

For questions about sales outside the U.S., please contact intlcs@pearson.com.

Editor-in-Chief
Mark Taub

Director, ITP Product Management
Brett Bartow

Executive Editor
Nancy Davis

Development Editor
Christopher A. Cleveland

Managing Editor
Sandra Schroeder

Project Editor
Mandie Frank

Copy Editor
Bart Reed

Indexer
Erika Millen

Proofreader
Donna E. Mulder

Technical Reviewers
Dave Hucaby
Rehan Siddiqui

Editorial Assistant
Cindy Teeters

Designer
Chuti Prasertsith

Compositor
codeMantra

Pearson's Commitment to Diversity, Equity, and Inclusion

Pearson is dedicated to creating bias-free content that reflects the diversity of all learners. We embrace the many dimensions of diversity, including but not limited to race, ethnicity, gender, socioeconomic status, ability, age, sexual orientation, and religious or political beliefs.

Education is a powerful force for equity and change in our world. It has the potential to deliver opportunities that improve lives and enable economic mobility. As we work with authors to create content for every product and service, we acknowledge our responsibility to demonstrate inclusivity and incorporate diverse scholarship so that everyone can achieve their potential through learning. As the world's leading learning company, we have a duty to help drive change and live up to our purpose to help more people create a better life for themselves and to create a better world.

Our ambition is to purposefully contribute to a world where

- Everyone has an equitable and lifelong opportunity to succeed through learning.

- Our educational products and services are inclusive and represent the rich diversity of learners.

- Our educational content accurately reflects the histories and experiences of the learners we serve.

- Our educational content prompts deeper discussions with learners and motivates them to expand their own learning (and worldview).

While we work hard to present unbiased content, we want to hear from you about any concerns or needs with this Pearson product so that we can investigate and address them.

Please contact us with concerns about any potential bias at https://www.pearson.com/report-bias.html.

Credits

Cover	Blue Planet Studio/Shutterstock
Figure 2-14, Figure 5-29a	Andrei_M/Shutterstock
Figure 4-2, Figure 4-6	International Telecommunication Union (ITU)
Figure 9-7a	Cisco Systems, Inc
Figure 9-7b	Juniper Networks, Inc

I would like to dedicate this book to my late grandfather, my mentor, and my teacher—Dr. Syed Enam-ul-Haque. He always encouraged and inspired me to share knowledge and learnings with others, and it was with him that I started working on our first book. I want to thank my lovely wife, Sameera, and my children—Omer, Ammaar, and Emaad—for their love and their strong support of me while writing this book. I would also like to acknowledge the support of my parents. I couldn't achieve what I have without their encouragement and the guidance they continue to give through their wisdom.
—Syed F. Hassan

I would like to dedicate this book to my beloved wife, Tatiana Orel, for her endless patience, understanding, encouragement, and tremendous support, which helped me continue with this endeavor and provided much needed inspiration.
—Alexander Orel

To my wonderful parents, Khurshid and Shakila, who instilled in me the value of hard work and perseverance from a very young age; to my wife, Sara, my north star who inspires me to be a better person every day; and to my kids—Aleena, Rayan, and Faaris—who motivate me to do my part in building a better tomorrow.
—Kashif Islam

Contents at a Glance

Contents

Chapter 7: Essential Technologies for 5G-Ready Networks: DC Architecture and Edge Computing   250

Foreword

4G LTE was about broad-reaching, universal connectivity and coverage. However, 5G is about an immersive experience, led by new services-enhanced mobile broadband access everywhere, massive Internet of Things (IoT), tactile Internet, higher user mobility, ultra-reliable communications, and enterprise use cases. These services have divergent latency, scale, and throughput requirements requiring network transformation in addition to 5G New Radio (NR) evolution. However, 5G is not just about radio; it is genuinely a network and services evolution. The promise of 5G services looks to be simultaneously an evolutionary and revolutionary opportunity.

The opportunity comes from new applications, business models, innovative new revenue streams, and leaner operational efficiency for mobile operators—all directly contributing to a more profitable set of offerings and robust business. However, the evolution of the mobile operator's network is a significant financial (current ARPU being flat or declining) and engineering undertaking that must be thought through from end to end. The new network infrastructure must simultaneously satisfy 2G/3G/4G requirements and 5G's exploding bandwidth demands, massive logical scale, and the incredibly low-latency needs of new applications and services in an efficient, automated, programmable manner.

The traditional network design will not address these divergent 5G service requirements since services need to be placed closer to the edge to deliver ultra-low latency. Massively scalable, low-latency–enabled applications at the edge will open up new ecosystems and business models across every industry's enterprise and residential markets. Hence, programmable network fabric, packet core evolution to Control Plane and User Plane Separation (CUPS), Multi-access Edge Computing (MEC), and network slicing will be the critical enablers for 5G architecture.

Mobile network operators have built large-scale LTE/LTE-Advanced networks that are mostly centralized today. Now they need to evolve their networks to accommodate 5G requirements. However, 5G is not only about mobile operators. Alternate access vendors (AAV) will also need to evolve their network and services to cater to 5G service delivery needs. Enterprises will deploy private 5G.

Along with the significant technological change to the mobile core and radio access network (RAN), operators will also need to evolve their transport networks to cost-effectively deliver a satisfying mobile broadband experience while simultaneously meeting the scale requirements for massive IoT and the ultra-low-latency requirements for real-time applications. With the evolution of Centralized RAN to Cloud RAN, RAN decomposition (that is, the breaking down of baseband unit to virtualized centralized unit (CU) and distributed unit (DU)), virtual packet core to CUPS, and new services, IP transport will need to enable seamless connectivity and reachability, and support the flexible placement of mobile functions. 5G will also help the convergence of wireline and wireless architectures to support a broad range of SLAs for service and transport, starting with the stringent latency, bandwidth, and timing requirements. RAN densification (sub-6 GHz and mmW) in 5G, either by adding a new spectrum or by adding antennas, sectors, and/or carriers in the existing sites, will result in a massive number of service endpoints. The only way to avoid operational complexity is to reduce touchpoints for service enablement.

All that being said, we need to manage the financial impact in 5G, meaning we need to reduce CapEx/OpEx. The only way to achieve that would be stat-muxing using IP/Ethernet to reduce access costs instead of TDM technology.

It is therefore critical to invest in a 5G transport network that will underpin the worldwide adoption of 5G technologies and delivery of applications.

I had the opportunity to work with network operators globally to help them in their 5G transformation journey. Most of them had similar questions: Will their network accommodate 5G network requirements of increased bandwidth, large scale, and low latency? How would they address the placement of the 5G cloud-native RAN network functions centralized unit (CU) and distributed unit (DU) and the packet core's control and user plane functions? Is O-RAN ready for their deployment use case? Do they need to upgrade their cell site routers as well as pre-aggregation and aggregation routers for their existing and new C-band and mmW spectrum? How will they address low-latency edge use cases? What will be the requirements for the new far-edge, edge, and regional data centers? Can they place the user-plane function on the public cloud? How will they place compute at cell sites? What are the benefits of Cloud RAN, and what percentage of their RAN architecture will be fronthaul, midhaul, or backhaul? How can they deliver packet-based fronthaul? What are their dark fiber requirements? How can they monetize their network architecture to provide enterprise services? What are the network slicing requirements? How can they be ready for 5G and beyond? What is private 5G?

Besides network evolution questions, 5G network also requires changes in the network operator's organizational structure due to a lack of clear responsibility demarcation. It involves transport, mobile core, virtualization, and RAN teams to understand the requirement of their adjacent areas.

A Network Architect's Guide to 5G takes a holistic approach of providing an end-to-end mobile network evolution overview, starting with legacy 2G/3G and 4G LTE network architectures. It then introduces the promise of 5G with 5G fundamentals, followed by an in-depth coverage of 5G network transport, data center, edge data center, clocking, and 5G network design. It has done a great job of addressing the preceding questions and concerns by the network operators.

It may be the first book covering the mobile core, transport, RAN technology fundamentals, and network design details. I would highly recommend this book for anyone who is already working on 5G transformation or is in the planning phase or for anyone who wants to understand end-to-end 5G network technologies and design.

—Waris Sagheer
Chief Technology Officer,
Service Provider, Cisco Systems

Preface

This book introduces the mobile network evolution toward 5G from a network architect's perspective as well as provides an in-depth view of the concepts and technologies required to design and deploy 5G-ready networks.

When the topic of 5G comes up, the focus is typically on the mobile core and radio technologies, often overlooking the underlying data network's needs. The mobile core, radio access, and transport data networks have historically had well-defined boundaries, thus remaining fairly siloed throughout recent mobile evolutions. However, with 5G, these previously co-dependent yet segregated networks are becoming tightly integrated and encroaching on each other's domains.

The essential fundamentals of mobile networks, along with advanced data network technologies, are therefore stitched together in this book to provide a comprehensive learning experience for network engineers, designers, and architects.

Motivation for Writing This Book

The authors of this book have been involved in designing and implementing complex service provider networks for a couple of decades. When tasked with designing a 5G network, however, the authors came to the realization that the knowledge and experience accumulated over the years while designing and deploying 3G and 4G mobile backhaul networks are no longer enough. As 5G network architects, the authors had to acquire deeper knowledge of mobile technologies to have meaningful dialogue with mobility and radio architects to be able to translate 5G requirements into an actionable transport network design.

With the rapid proliferation of 5G technology, more network engineers and architects will face similar challenges. These network professionals may be up to date with advanced networking technologies such as software-defined networks, Segment Routing, EVPN, and others, yet they are likely to find themselves in a position where they will need to be proficient in mobile technology to create sophisticated and architecturally robust next-gen mobile transport networks that could satisfy 5G requirements.

The goal of this book is to bridge the knowledge gap for the traditional network engineers with an understanding of 5G technology and its implications on underlying transport networks. It also aims to enable these network architects to interpret the design requirements for the next generation and correlate those with the emerging and essential network technologies required to implement transport networks for 5G. Simultaneously, this book also provides radio network engineers and mobility architects a peek into enabling technologies for the networks supporting 5G.

Acknowledgments

We would like to say a very special thanks to Waris Sagheer, Rehan Siddiqui, Shahid Ajmeri, Muhammad Faraz, Ali Bokhari, Nouman Jaferi, Steve Mailey, Valentin Filippov, and Milan Stolic, who shared their knowledge and experience, helping shape this book. We especially extend our thanks to the technical reviewers, Dave Hucaby and Rehan Siddiqui, who took up the challenge of reviewing and correcting the technical inaccuracies and shared their expert opinions by providing us with helpful recommendations. Their expertise, suggestions, and guidance helped us to navigate presenting the content in the right way and keep it at an appropriate level.

We would also like to thank Nancy Davis, Chris Cleveland, and others at Pearson for bearing with us throughout the process of putting this book together and guiding us through each step.

About the Authors

Syed Farrukh Hassan has been designing and deploying networks for over 20 years. In his current role as principal telecommunications architect at Red Hat, Syed provides consultancy services to global 5G customers. Prior to that, Syed worked as a senior solutions architect in the Cisco professional and consulting services organization, providing guidance, strategy, and planning support to various Internet, cloud, and mobile service providers in their adoption of innovating networking technologies and transformation of their networks to new architectures. Syed co-authored one of the first books on NFV and SDN, has been a regular speaker in public forums and conferences, and is recognized as a Cisco Live Distinguished Speaker. Syed is a double CCIE in Service Provider and Data Center technologies (#21617), Google Certified Professional Cloud Networking Engineer, and Certified Kubernetes Administrator (CKA). He holds a bachelor's degree in engineering from NED University (Pakistan) and a master's degree in engineering from the University of Florida, Gainesville (USA).

Alexander Orel has more than 20 years of experience in designing, deploying, and supporting large-scale transport networks for major Internet and mobile service providers. He has worked as a lead network engineer and senior network designer in various system integration companies and Internet service providers. Alexander spent a significant part of his career as a solutions architect in the Customer Experience New Product team at Cisco Systems, where he specialized in IOS XR-based platforms, NFV technologies, Segment Routing, application-driven networks, EVPN, and other bleeding-edge technologies. Recently, Alexander joined the Global Networking team at Google, where he continues to apply and expand his knowledge of large-scale networks. Alexander has a master's degree in applied mathematics and physics from Moscow Institute of Physics and Technology and holds CCIE certification #10391 in R&S and DC. Alexander has been a frequent presenter at various technology conferences such as Cisco Live and Cisco Connect and was recognized as a Cisco Live Distinguished Speaker.

Kashif Islam is a 20+ year veteran in the IT industry and has architected several complex, large-scale networks for some of the largest wireline and mobile service providers across the world. He is currently a Principal Telecommunication Architect in Red Hat's consulting organization and is tasked with helping service providers transform their existing mobile infrastructure into next-generation, cloud-native 5G networks. Prior to his work with Red Hat, Kashif was a senior solutions architect at Cisco Systems. During his tenure at Cisco, he devised strategies and provided technical leadership to service providers in modernizing and transforming their existing mobile backhaul networks into xHaul to support Cloud RAN architectures and new 5G services. Kashif is a Distinguished Speaker at industry events such as Cisco Live, Society of Cable and Telecommunication Engineers (SCTE), and others. He has also co-authored Open RAN (O-RAN) Alliance's xHaul Packet Switched Network Architecture Specification. Kashif is a double CCIE (#14300) and holds a Bachelor of Computer Engineering from Sir Syed University of Engineering and Technology in Karachi, Pakistan, as well as a Master of Engineering in Internetworking from Dalhousie University, Canada. Kashif lives in Raleigh, North Carolina, with his family and, when not working, enjoys hiking in the Blue Ridge mountains.

Introduction

Who Should Read This Book

This book introduces all essential aspects of a mobile communication network and thus assumes no prior knowledge of cellular networking concepts. It is primarily meant for network architects, designers, and engineers; therefore, knowledge of foundational networking concepts such as routing and switching technologies, quality of service mechanisms, Multi-Protocol Label Switching–based traffic forwarding, and so on is expected from the reader.

Following are some of the audience groups for this book:

- IP network engineers, consultants, and architects involved in planning, designing, deploying, and operating mobile transport networks

- Networking students as well as early and mid-career professionals looking to expand into service provider networking

- Senior networking professionals setting strategic goals and directions for a mobile service provider and looking to evolve their current networks for 5G and beyond

- Mobile core and radio access network (RAN) architects looking to understand how the transport network will need to adapt to the changes imposed by 5G

- Large enterprise IT professionals looking to leverage services offered by 5G (for example, private 5G networks) for their organizations

- Inquisitive minds trying to understand what 5G is all about

How This Book Is Organized

To allow technical and nontechnical audiences to consume the material in an effective manner, this book approaches the topic of architecting 5G networks using four key learning objectives.

Learning Objective I: Understanding the Evolution of Cellular Technologies from Pre-cellular to Today's 4G LTE Networks

The first three chapters build the foundational knowledge necessary for network architects to understand mobile communication networks.

Chapter 1, "A Peek at the Past": The book starts with a historic view of the pivotal changes in mobile communication. This chapter takes into consideration the technological shifts in both data and mobile networks, while presenting a bird's-eye view of mobile communication evolution from pre-cellular to 1G and the enhancements offered by 2G, 2.5G, and 3G mobile networks.

Chapter 2, "Anatomy of Mobile Communication Networks": This chapter takes a closer look at distinct yet tightly interconnected domains that constitute an end-to-end mobile communication network: radio access network (RAN), mobile core, and mobile transport. It discusses the composition of all three domains in detail and introduces key concepts such as radio frequency (RF) spectrum allocation, types of cell sites, mobile backhaul networks, as well as the distinction between circuit switched and packet switched mobile cores.

Chapter 3, "Mobile Networks Today": Currently deployed mobile technology is covered in this chapter, with a focus on 3GPP releases leading up to 4G LTE and Evolved Packet Core. This chapter also explores the use of Seamless MPLS for scalable backhaul architectures and brings in the concepts of Centralized RAN (C-RAN), fronthaul, and xHaul networks.

Learning Objective II: Foundational Concepts and Market Drivers for 5G

Chapters 4 and 5 introduce the 5G market drivers and use cases, followed by a deep dive into the 5G architecture and technologies.

Chapter 4, "The Promise of 5G": Before diving into the details of 5G technology fundamentals, it is important to understand the value proposition presented by 5G. This chapter does exactly that by going over the market demands and the services offered by 5G to address those demands. This will enable the reader to better grasp the technological changes required to fulfill the promise of 5G.

Chapter 5, "5G Fundamentals": This chapter explains the concepts and technologies imperative to designing and deploying 5G mobile networks. The chapter continues to focus on the evolution of RAN, mobile core, and transport to offer the full range of 5G services. It goes deeper into the 5G New Radio's advanced antenna functions, virtual RAN architectures, the importance of Open RAN design as well as the decomposition and cloudification of 5G Core to enable Control and User Plane Separation (CUPS) and Service-Based Architecture (SBA). By the end of this chapter, the reader is expected to have gained a clear and solid understanding of the 5G architectural evolution and its impact on mobile transport networks.

Learning Objective III: Essential and Emerging Networking Technologies for 5G-Ready Networks

Chapters 6 through 9 go over the details of networking technologies necessary for architecting 5G-ready mobile networks.

Chapter 6, "Emerging Technologies for 5G-Ready Networks: Segment Routing": This chapter describes Segment Routing as well as its role in simplifying traditional MPLS-based networks and paving the path toward a software-defined network (SDN). It covers the mechanics of Segment Routing Traffic Engineering (SR-TE), the use of external controllers such as the Path Computation Element (PCE), rapid traffic restoration through Topology Independent Loop Free Alternative (TI-LFA), and Flexible Algorithms for transport network slicing. The chapter also introduces Segment Routing for IPv6 (SRv6).

Chapter 7, "Essential Technologies for 5G-Ready Networks: DC Architecture and Edge Computing": Technologies covered in this chapter enable the reader to understand the design and architecture of data centers (DCa) in a 5G network. It focuses on DC technologies as well as their evolution, integration, and positioning in the 5G transport networks. The chapter also goes over typical DC design and deployment considerations such as the Clos fabric, routing and switching within a DC, and the Data Center Interconnect (DCI) function. It briefly touches on the optimization of compute resources for applications hosted in data centers.

Chapter 8, "Essential Technologies for 5G-Ready Networks: Transport Services": This chapter goes further into the essential networking technologies, focusing on the virtual private network service required for end-to-end (E2E) connectivity between various components of the mobile communication network. It covers traditional Layer 2 VPN (L2VPN), Layer 3 VPN (L3VPN), and the newer Ethernet VPN–based services and their use across fronthaul, midhaul, and backhaul networks.

Chapter 9, "Essential Technologies for 5G-Ready Networks: Timing and Synchronization": Timing and synchronization are often overlooked, yet they are critical aspects of an efficient mobile network architecture. This chapter covers the basics of timing and synchronization, including the concepts of phase, frequency, and time of day (ToD) synchronization as well as their relevance and importance in a 5G network. The chapter expands on synchronization sources and timing acquisition along with the protocols and architectures required to distribute highly accurate timing information in a mobile communication network.

Learning Objective IV: Architecting and Designing a 5G Network

This part of the book (a single chapter) guides you in forging a cohesive 5G network architecture by amalgamating the principles of mobile radio communications with advanced transport network technologies.

Chapter 10, "Designing and Implementing 5G Network Architecture": This chapter blends together all the knowledge shared in the previous chapters and applies that knowledge toward the design and implementation of a 5G-capable mobile communication network. The chapter covers end-to-end design considerations such as domain-specific requirements in xHaul networks, device selection criteria, routing design simplification, QoS modeling, and vRAN deployment scenarios. It also covers the use of a private cloud infrastructure as well as augmenting it with a public cloud to deploy 5G mobile communication networks. The chapter concludes with a hypothetical conversation between a network architect and radio engineers, the mobility team, and deployment specialists, highlighting the blurring of boundaries between the RAN, mobile core, and xHaul networks, as well as the skills expected from the network designer to extract critical information required to build 5G transport networks.

It's worth mentioning that this book is written with a vendor-neutral approach and does not give recommendations on what vendor should be deployed. If anything, the book sometimes calls out the reluctance of incumbents in creating an open mobile ecosystem. This is done to provide the reader with an honest assessment of the complexities in mobile networking as well as the challenges faced by new entrants in the industry.

Register your copy of *A Network Architect's Guide to 5G* on the InformIT site for convenient access to updates and/or corrections as they become available. To start the registration process, go to informit. com/register and log in or create an account.

Chapter | **1**

A Peek at the Past

From social media check-ins during a beach vacation to geo-tagging and uploading photos of a trekking adventure or answering a critical call from your mobile device during a desert safari, it is expected that *the network* will always be there, providing continuous connectivity to fulfill what are now considered to be regular, everyday tasks.

Ubiquitous mobile connectivity is not just a requirement but rather an expectation in today's mobile services landscape. The flexibility and usability enjoyed by a vast majority of mobile users daily have been a result of multiple decades of innovation in mobile communication technologies as well as the underlying network infrastructure that supports it. Over the past few decades, multiple generations of mobile technologies have been adopted globally, each one of them enabling new possibilities for the mobile users. This chapter briefly looks at the pivotal changes in mobile communication over time to understand how the mobile services were shaped through various generations.

Brief History of Pre-Cellular Mobile Networks

Starting from the initial systems using circuit-switched analog voice, mobile communication systems have gone through multiple generations of evolution—from 1G all the way to 5G. That's an average of a generational leap every decade, compared to a century-long initial leap from fixed-line to mobile communications. Each generation brought revolutionary changes and enabled new use cases that catalyzed rapid embrace of the technology, slowly laying the foundation of what we know today as 5G. To truly appreciate 5G, and more importantly to understand the technology, it's essential to take a look at the evolution in the previous generations of mobile telephony.

The very first mobile telephony networks were built using the well-known concepts of a broadcast radio network. The goal of these mobile communication networks was to be able to provide the ability to make and receive phone calls while on the move. The pioneers of the mobile telephony service followed the seemingly straightforward approach of using a single service area—inline with radio broadcast methods.

Mobile Telephone Service (MTS), introduced in 1946, can be considered the very first mobile communication system. MTS was deployed using a single omnidirectional transmitter that covered the whole service area. The service was limited by the technology of its time, with the central transmitter's location, power, and usable frequency spectrum restricting the coverage distance and capacity. Additionally, the mobile radio telephone units had limited power at their disposal for transmitting back to a central receiver. The mobile telephone units used at the time were not the miniaturized, technically sophisticated devices that we use today, but rather a bulky piece of equipment, weighing several pounds and drawing power from the car or truck they were typically installed in.

To accommodate for this lack of transmitting power in the mobile telephone units, multiple receiving antennas were strategically placed to improve the stability of signal reception from mobile users. The mobile telephone unit would receive the signal from the main transmission tower; however, return signals were relayed back through the receiver closest to the end user.

Frequency Spectrum and Channels

The air interface of a mobile network uses specific frequencies for communication. Because frequencies available for communication are limited, their use has been regulated. To avoid interference, mobile operators need to have a specific frequency range allocated to them for their dedicated use. A *frequency spectrum* refers to the range of frequency available for a system to transmit and receive on.

Mobile operators may internally split the frequency spectrum into sub-ranges, to allow multiple simultaneous communication to take place. These frequency ranges are referred to as *channels*.

Due to the limited number of channels available in the frequency spectrum, MTS allowed just a handful of simultaneous calls from subscribers in the service area. MTS did not allow two-way speech either, and only one person on the voice call could talk at a time by pressing and holding the talk button. Despite its shortcomings, MTS systems were widely used due to the attractive nature of mobile communication. The air interface provided by MTS was merely an extension of the Public Switched Telephone Network (PSTN). When an MTS subscriber wanted to make a call, they would first have to manually check for mobile channel availability to reach the operator. The operator would then use the PSTN to connect the MTS call. Figure 1-1 provides a high-level overview of MTS. As shown in the figure, multiple MTS service areas could connect to each other using PSTN as their backbone. Within each MTS service area, the user's mobile device communication was split between the central transmitter (Tx) and the receiver (Rx) closest to the device. In the central exchange, an operator would assist in completing the call through PSTN.

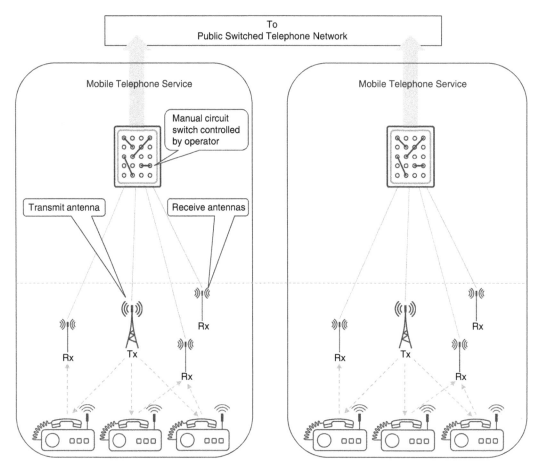

FIGURE 1-1   Mobile Telephone Service (MTS) Overview

MTS left a lot to be desired, and during the 1950s and 1960s, many incremental improvements were made. The Improved Mobile Telephone Service (IMTS) was introduced in 1964,[1] which allowed more simultaneous calls by using additional frequency channels that were made available as well as introduced auto-dialing capability. IMTS also brought auto-trunking, which meant that subscribers no longer had to manually search for an available voice channel. While IMTS allowed for higher subscriber scale, it was still very much limited. By the mid-1970s, Bell's IMTS offering in New York City consisted of 543 paying customers, with a waiting list of 3,700 people.[2]

The mobile service offering had proved its market viability, but technology limitations severely handicapped widespread adoption of mobile services. Some of the challenges were as follows:

- Geographically limited service area due to the use of a single transmitter for a whole service area.

- Small number of channels in the available frequency spectrum, resulting in a limited number of subscribers.

- Mobile telephone units required a significant amount of power to transmit radio signals. Nearly all IMTS mobile units were automobile based and used large batteries to provide the desired power levels, making true mobility harder and more cumbersome to achieve.

These limitations, among others, required a fundamental change to the underlying principles of mobile networks. A new approach to arranging the service area into small *cells* promised to change the mobile telephony landscape, introducing the concept of *cellular* service as we know it today.

The Very First Cellular Networks: 1G

While MTS and IMTS were gaining a foothold in the mobile telephone market during the 1950s and 1960s, major telecommunication service providers were working on developing techniques to expand their service area and increase capacity. Figure 1-2 shows an overview of 1G network architecture, outlining major components such as the Mobile Switching Center (MSC), which provided call processing, as well as the Home Location Register (HLR) and Visitor Location Register (VLR), which were used to store information about local and visiting mobile subscribers. These components are discussed in greater detail later in this chapter.

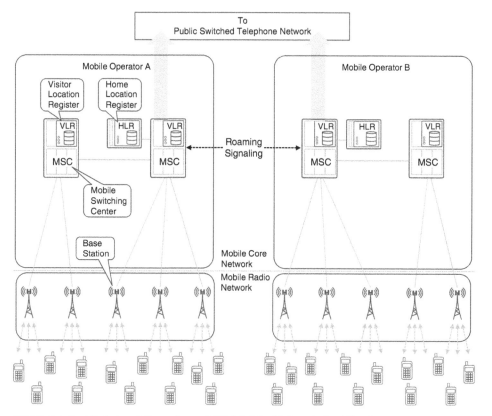

FIGURE 1-2   High-level Overview of 1G Mobile Network Architecture

The 1G cellular network for North America was developed and marketed as the *Advanced Mobile Phone Service (AMPS)* system, whereas the European equivalent was labeled *Total Access Communication System (TACS)*. TACS was further adopted as *European TACS (ETACS)* in select European markets and as *Japan TACS (JTACS)* in Japanese markets.[3] Both AMPS and TACS were virtually similar in architecture and principles but used different frequency spectrums and carrier channels, as discussed in the "Choosing the Right Frequency" section in Chapter 2, "Anatomy of Mobile Communication Networks."

Another 1G analog mobile communication network worthy of mention is the *Nordic Mobile Telephone (NMT)* system. Originally developed by and used in Scandinavian countries in the early 1980s, it quickly expanded to the rest of the Nordic region, the Baltics, the rest of Europe, Turkey, and Russia. NMT was one of the most widely adopted 1G networks outside of North America and a precursor to the development of 2G specifications.

From a network engineer's perspective, 1G network architectures introduced three main functional domains:

- Mobile Radio Networks
- Mobile Transport
- Mobile Switching Center (MSC)

Innovations in Radio Access

As mentioned in the previous section, a single mobile transmitter and large service areas impeded the progress of the mobile telephone service. To address this challenge, AT&T Bell and other telecommunication providers introduced the concept of using multiple antenna towers within a geographical service area.[4] Each antenna tower provides transmit and receive functions for a smaller coverage area, dubbed a "cell." The antenna tower, known in 1G as a *base station (BS)*, is at the heart of each of these cells, and multiple BSs could be placed strategically to form a cellular network throughout the desired service area. Figure 1-3 illustrates this concept.

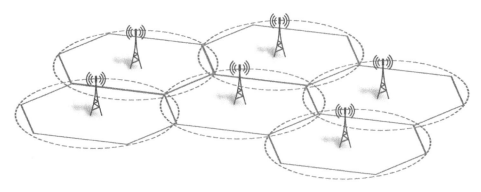

FIGURE 1-3   Cellular Radio Network Representation

Figure 1-3 shows multiple transmission stations, each covering a smaller area (or "cell"), which provided a simple, scalable, and extensible solution to the limitations of MTS and IMTS. Now mobile (or rather cellular) service subscribers were more likely to be in close proximity of a base station (BS) throughout the coverage zone. Using this approach, more "cells" could be added to the network, thus easily expanding the service coverage area if required.

While this cellular approach addressed some of the problems in the original MTS-based mobile design, it introduced the problem of radio wave interference between neighboring cells. The pictorial representations of a cellular network give an illusion of clean radio coverage boundaries between cells, but the reality is not so. Radio waves transmitted from base stations travel through the cell coverage area, but they do not magically stop at theoretical cell boundaries. The cell boundaries are rather amorphous, where cellular signal from adjacent base stations overlap each other (as shown by circular shapes in Figure 1-3). This results in signal interference, thus distorting the signal and sometimes making it harder for the user handset to extract meaningful information from it.

Cellular vs. Mobile

Because the use of cells is a foundational concept in land-based mobile networks, starting from the very first generation, the terms *cellular network* and *mobile network* are often used interchangeably when describing mobile communication networks.

Adjusting the transmission power could help minimize this interference but does not eliminate it. The problem was solved by using non-overlapping frequency ranges in neighboring cells. The solution encompassed dividing the available frequency spectrum into smaller ranges, and then using one of these subdivided frequencies in each cell. The same subdivided frequency spectrums can be reused in multiple cells, provided the cells have sufficient geographical separation among them to avoid service-impacting interference from neighboring cells. Figure 1-4 shows the various frequency reuse patterns, where each unique frequency range is represented by a number. Clusters of 4, 7, or 12 frequencies are commonly used frequency reuse patterns. These patterns can be repeated over a larger geography, thus allowing for expanded coverage area using the same frequencies.

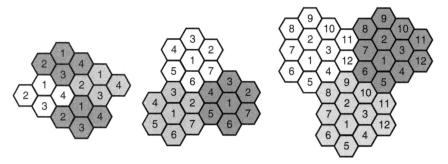

FIGURE 1-4   Frequency Reuse Examples

It must be noted that *Code Division Multiple Access (CDMA)*, an air-interface access method, uses a different principle. CDMA uses special codes that allow reuse of the same frequency across all cells. CDMA is further explained later in the section, "Third Generation (3G)."

An Introduction to Mobile Transport

While the cellular network concept made it easier for the user equipment to communicate with geographically disperse base stations, it also highlighted the need for a robust mobile transport. The system now required a transport mechanism to connect these *distributed* cellular base stations to the central exchange. In the case of early 1G networks, all base stations within the coverage area were directly connected to the central exchange, typically using analog leased lines. Virtually all the 1G network systems were developed independently and used proprietary protocols over these leased lines for communication between the base station and MSC. This could be considered the very first mobile transport network, and although the underlying protocols and communication mechanisms have evolved significantly over the years, the fundamental concept of a mobile transport originated from these very first 1G networks.

Emergence of a Mobile Core

The base stations used a point-to-point connection to the exchange or central office within the coverage area. This central office, referred to as the Mobile Switching Center (MSC), provided connectivity services to cellular subscribers within a single market. The MSC performed its functions in conjunction with other subsystems located in the central office, including the following:

- **Home Location Register (HLR):** A database that contained the information of all mobile users for the mobile operator.

- **Visitor Location Register (VLR):** A database that temporarily stored the subscriber profile of mobile users currently within the coverage area serviced by the MSC.

- **Authentication Center (AuC):** This subsystem provided security by authenticating mobile users and authorizing the use of mobile services.

The MSC was responsible for all functions in the 1G cellular network, including the following:

- **User authentication and authorization:** Done through the AuC subsystem using the HLR.

- **Security and fraud prevention:** Done by comparing locally stored phone data in the AuC's Equipment Identity Register (EIR) with equipment information received. This helped the MSC deny services to cloned or stolen phone units.

- **Cellular subscriber tracking and mapping to base station within its coverage area:** Each base station would provide the MSC with this information for subscribers associated with that base station.

- **Voice call connectivity, including local and long-distance calls:** Any calls between cellular subscribers within the coverage area were connected directly through the MSC, while call requests to cellular subscribers in other coverage areas or to traditional PSTN subscribers were routed through the PSTN network. Using PSTN as the backbone ensured universal connectivity between all cellular and traditional land-line subscribers.

- **Subscriber handoff between different base stations:** This was assisted by the MSC, which constantly kept track of subscriber signal strength received through base station(s). When the MSC determined that the subscriber signal was stronger from a base station different from the one that subscriber was currently registered to, it switched the subscriber to the new base station. In cellular terminology, this process is known as a *handoff*. In 1G networks, cellular handoff was initiated by the MSC, as shown in Figure 1-5.

- **Roaming between different MSCs:** This refers to both roaming within the mobile provider coverage zone (intra-operator roaming) and roaming between different mobile providers (inter-operator roaming). Initially, inter-operator roaming and registration was a manual process, but it was subsequently replaced by automatic registration.

- **Billing:** Billing was also managed by the MSC as it kept track of all subscribers, their airtime usage, and call type (such as local or long distance).

Figure 1-5 shows a local cellular handoff within an MSC service region as well as a subscriber roaming between different MSC regions, including both inter-operator and intra-operator roaming.

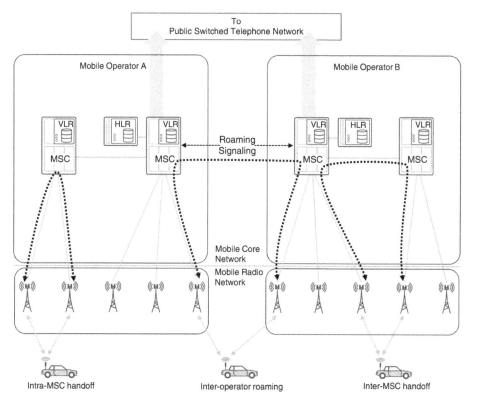

FIGURE 1-5 Subscriber Handoff and Mobile Roaming

1G cellular networks provided a robust framework for scalable mobile telephony services. Cellular radio access network, mobile transport from base station to MSC, and modular functional blocks within the MSC provided an architecture that laid the foundation for subsequent generations to build upon. Because the MSC was handling all the major functions of managing and monitoring of user devices as well as call control functions, it limited the overall scalability of the mobile system. Second generation (2G) mobile architecture aimed to address these limitations.

Second Generation (2G) Cellular Networks

The first generation cellular network was a great success, but its wide-scale adoption was limited by several factors, including the following:

- 1G used analog voice modulation inherited from land-line telephony, which resulted in higher transmit power requirements for the handset as well as higher bandwidth requirements. The consequences were the need for bigger, bulkier handsets with limited talk time and a limited number of available voice channels through the air interface.

- The MSC was handling call processing, inter- and intra-operator roaming, as well as base station management, which created a resource bottleneck.

- Initially the focus had been on voice-based communication. Though data transmission was not a pressing need at that time, the interest to be able to transmit non-voice information was definitely there.

- The information in the user handset was hard-coded and didn't give the user flexibility to switch devices easily. For vendors, that meant a barrier to a market opportunity.

As digital voice encoding and transmission were replacing analog voice in telephony networks, the mobile industry saw the huge benefits it could bring. There was also a desire to offload some of the MSC functionalities to remove the resource bottleneck and achieve better scale. These motivations resulted in the evolution toward the second generation (2G) of cellular mobile communication, which introduced enhancements in every functional domain of the cellular network.

Different geographies and markets ended up with different variations of 2G implementations. *Digital AMPS (D-AMPS), Global System for Mobile Communications (GSM)*, and *Interim Standard 95 (IS-95)* were some of the 2G implementations in the early and mid-1990s.

2G Innovations in Radio Access

2G introduced a number of technical enhancements over its 1G counterpart, primarily focused on providing ease of use and scaled services through digital modulation, multi-access, enhanced security, and handset flexibility.

Use of Digital Voice

2G systems were designed to use digital encoding of voice and digital modulation for transmission. Use of digital transmission not only improved voice quality significantly but also increased spectral efficiency through encoding and compression.

The air interface in 2G was designed to use Common Channel Signaling (CCS). CCS could "steal" some of the bits from the encoded voice and use it for signaling between the user and the base station. This made it possible for a user to be on a voice call while still being able to exchange information with the base station for providing value-added services such as call waiting.

Improved Multi-Access Scale

North American and European 2G efforts adopted different techniques for multi-access—that is, allowing multiple mobile users to communicate at the same time. The European implementations favored Time Division Multiple Access (TDMA) techniques by offering separate time slots to the mobile devices. Global System for Mobile Communications (GSM) emerged as the predominant European standard and was built on TDMA.

North American implementations were split between use of TDMA (for D-AMPS implementations) and Code Division Multiple Access (CDMA) based deployments. CDMA was also a popular choice in the Asia-Pacific region.[5]

Handset Flexibility

GSM introduced the subscriber identity module (SIM) card—a small memory card that could store key information related to a mobile user's identity. SIM cards made it possible for a user to change their handset while porting the identity and credentials to the new device. The handsets no longer needed to be tied to a mobile provider but could now be a generic device made to GSM specifications. The handset could communicate with the GSM network by using the information stored in the SIM card. The use of SIM cards opened up a new market opportunity to handset manufacturers as well as offered subscribers the flexibility to change their handset as often as desired.

Security Considerations

Privacy and security had always been a concern in mobile communication. The communication through air interface could easily be sniffed without the sender and recipient learning about it. Setting up a "man in the middle" (MitM) and hijacking a communication was also not very difficult either. The shift from analog to digital voice made it slightly harder to sniff the communications but didn't make it any more secure. 2G standards, especially GSM, started to implement key-based encryption of the encoded voice. This offered some level of privacy to the mobile communication.

2G Mobile Transport

In order to provide a more efficient and scalable network, 2G introduced the concept of a base station controller (BSC). Now, instead of a direct point-to-point connection from each base transceiver station (BTS) to MSC, multiple BTSs would connect to a BSC that provides connectivity to MSC. The BTS in 2G was the equivalent of a base station (BS) in 1G. Figure 1-6 provides an overview of the end-to-end 2G mobile network.

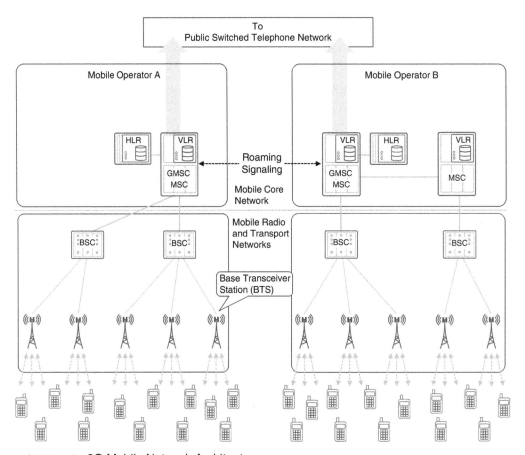

FIGURE 1-6   2G Mobile Network Architecture

As shown in Figure 1-6, multiple BSCs acted as an aggregation point for a group of BTSs. The physical link between the BTS and BSC was a full or fractional T1 or E1 link, with specialized protocols for communication between the two. The control functions of the BTS, such as frequency channel allocation, user signal level measurement, and cellular handoff between BTSs (previously the responsibility of MSC), were now handled by the BSC.

> ### Visitor MSC (V-MSC) and Gateway MSC (G-MSC)
>
> MSCs in 2G networks have the responsibility to manage multiple BSCs. These MSCs are interconnected and can route calls to and from the mobile handsets that are registered to it. For calls that originate from or terminate at networks outside the mobile provider's network (for example, PSTN or other mobile providers), a small subset of these MSCs has connectivity to external networks and act as a *gateway* to those networks. Consequently, these MSCs are referred to as the Gateway MSC (G-MSC), as shown in Figure 1-6. The MSC where a mobile subscriber is registered is referred to as the Visited MSC (V-MSC) for that subscriber. The G-MSC still serves as the V-MSC for the BSCs it manages, but it performs the additional function of acting as a gateway to external networks.

Modular transport provided extensibility to add a new BSC and/or BTS when desired. As the BSC acted as an aggregator for multiple BTSs, the architecture allowed the MSC to scale better by controlling more BTSs using the same number of links. Additionally, depending on the vendor, the BSC also provided switching center capabilities, thus further reducing the load at the MSC. BSCs were connected to the MSC using Frame Relay over full or fractional T1/E1 links.

2G Mobile Core

With the introduction of the BSC, some 2G networks, such as GSM, started to distinguish between the radio network and the switching network. The terms *base station subsystem (BSS)* and *network switching subsystem (NSS)* were introduced to highlight this architecture. The BSC and BTS functions belonged to the BSS, while MSC and the databases it used collectively comprised the NSS, performing all validation and switching functions. This distinction led to how the mobile networks are architected today; NSS evolved into the *mobile core*, and BSS evolved into *radio access network (RAN)*. The transport network providing the connectivity between the RAN and mobile core evolved into what is commonly known as the *mobile backhaul*.

The 2G mobile core offered a number of key enhancements over the previous generation in terms of efficiency, interoperability, and services, some of which are covered here.

An Efficient Mobile Switching Center

2G improved MSC scalability and operational efficiency by splitting some of the MSC functions and moving them to the newly introduced BSC. As previously explained, the role of BSC was to communicate with a group of BTSs, facilitating their functioning and coordination, as well as to work with the MSC for authorization, billing, and voice communications. Functions such as HLR, VLR, and PSTN connectivity stayed within the MSC.

One of the functions that BSC offloaded from MSC was the capability to perform most of the handoffs between base stations. Because multiple BTSs were connected to the same BSC, if a mobile user moves between BTSs connected to the same BSC, the handoff is handled locally at the BSC. However, a handoff between a BTS controlled by different BSCs was still handled by the MSC. These BSC-based handoffs helped the network perform better by reducing handoff times and saving resources on the MSC.

Step Toward Standardization

With the architectural changes and introduction of new components (such as BSC), there was also a subtle move toward standards-based communication between network components. As such, the MSC-BSC interfaces were standardized—a small but significant step toward vendor interoperability and multivendor networks.

In Europe, the market size and geography didn't make it practical for each country to develop its own mobile communication systems. The *European Telecommunication Standards Institute (ETSI)* helped develop a common communication standard across Europe under the marketing name Global System for Mobile Communications (GSM). This was a significant step toward standardizing communication protocols across countries.

New Text and Data Services

GSM allowed the use of voice channels for low-rate-data transmission as well. Just like PSTN dialup, 2G GSM handsets would use a built-in modem to establish a data connection over the voice circuit. While this was not very efficient (it would take time to establish the connection, the subscriber couldn't use voice service while the data session was active, and data rates were awfully low), it was still an improvement compared to the "voice-only" capability in 1G.

Another popular service was Short Message Service (SMS), which could allow exchange of short (up to 160 characters) messages between the users. SMS used control channels between existing network components, and hence no new messages/protocols were required for this value-added service. This provided a monetization opportunity for operators by offering SMS add-on service to their subscribers.

2G Technology Summary

2G development was an interesting time in mobile standardization and adoption, as multiple technologies were competing in standard bodies as well as in the marketplace. GSM quickly emerged as the dominant market force owing to its widespread adoption in the European market. GSM emerged as the major 2G mobile standard; its users could get "roaming service" in multiple countries and could easily switch handsets using SIM cards. All these "features" propelled GSM to frontrunner status in the race for mobile dominance.

At the turn of the century, GSM had more than two-thirds of the market share compared to rest of the mobile technologies, with over 788 million subscribers in 169 different countries.[6]

Generation Two and a Half (2.5G)

As previously mentioned, 2G/GSM used time-based multiplexing, in which a timeslot is allocated for a user's communication. These timeslots, over the duration of the call, create a logical channel for this user called the *traffic channel (TCH)*. The end-to-end connection was established by using a TCH on the shared air interface. Figure 1-7 shows the mapping of a TCH to allocated timeslots for the duration of a call.

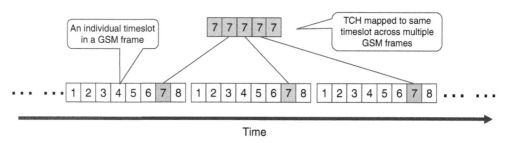

FIGURE 1-7   Timeslot-to-TCH Mapping

Even though 2G/GSM had made it possible to establish a data connection, it was at the cost of sacrificing the user's entire TCH. The TCH would remain occupied for the entire duration of the connection, thus making the underlying timeslots unavailable for any other use. While both data and voice kept the TCH circuit occupied for that particular user only, the fundamental difference between the nature of voice versus data calls made dedicated TCH not an optimal choice for data connections. Most voice calls tend to be brief, and the TCH/timeslots would then be freed up for use by other subscribers. On the other hand, a data connection might be for a much longer duration, making underlying timeslots unavailable for users to establish a new TCH.

In the mobile core, a data connection is established using a circuit switched network that was originally meant for voice. This *circuit switched data* inherited the same problems as PSTN dialup in terms of speed and connectivity. This combination of circuit switched data with dedicated TCH made it inefficient for activities such as email and web browsing, which work best with always-on connectivity. Besides, a single timeslot could offer only 14.4Kbps of data transmission rate, which by modern standards is, well, slow. 2G/GSM did allow concatenation of multiple timeslots to provide a single high-speed communication channel of up to 57.6Kbps per mobile station. This offered slightly higher speeds; however, the drawback was that these concatenated timeslots were now consumed by a single user exclusively, resulting in others being starved of resources for voice and/or data calls. As one can guess, a single user utilizing multiple dedicated timeslots for data was rather impractical and couldn't satisfy growth.

2.5G enhanced GSM standards by adding a new functionality called *General Packet Radio Service (GPRS)* in the year 2000. This was meant to facilitate packet transmission (that is, data transmission) over a mobile network. Instead of allocating all the timeslots for voice channels, as was originally done in GSM, GPRS allowed for carving out a small number of timeslots for data transmission purposes. Instead of occupying timeslots for the whole duration of the session, these data timeslots were made available to users only when they had data to transmit or receive, thus taking advantage of statistical multiplexing. As a consequence, users could now be charged for the data exchanged and not based on the duration of the connection. With flexible and on-demand use of timeslots, users could now get the "always-on" data experience.

GPRS also introduced new functions in the mobile core to facilitate direct connectivity to the packet switched data network. Note that in the case of 2G, data was being circuit-switched through PSTN. GPRS brought direct integration with the data network (referred to as the *packet data network*, or *PDN*) to contrast it with PSTN. Examples of PDNs include the Internet as well as private corporate networks (or intranets). To connect mobile users directly with the PDN, GPRS introduced entities called *GPRS support nodes (GSN)*. Figure 1-8 provides an architectural overview of 2.5G.

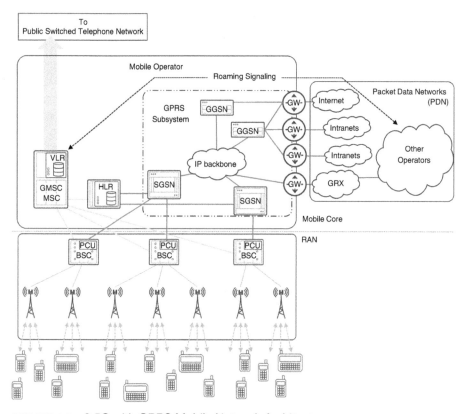

FIGURE 1-8   2.5G with GPRS Mobile Network Architecture

As Figure 1-8 illustrates, the collection of new entities introduced in the mobile core network by GPRS was called the GPRS Subsystem, or GSS. The key element of the GSS is the pair of *Serving GPRS Support Node (SGSN)* and *Gateway GPRS Support Node (GGSN)*. Collectively, these two nodes bring mechanisms and protocols required to enable efficient packet-switched-based data transmission. The SGSN was the subscriber-facing node, while the GGSN interfaced with the PDN to complete the data connectivity for the subscriber. The functions of these nodes will be discussed in detail in the next chapter.

As seen in the figure, BSCs were also retrofitted with additional capability implemented by a *Packet Control Unit (PCU)* to identify and redirect data traffic toward the GSS, whereas the voice traffic continued to be sent to the MSC. The GGSN could forward subscriber traffic to the public Internet, various different intranets, or another mobile provider through a *GPRS roaming exchange (GRX)*. The role of a GRX was critical in implementing 2G roaming across multiple mobile providers. Chapter 2 covers GRX extensively.

Enhanced Data Rates for GSM Evolution (EDGE)

With the growing need for data transmission over mobile networks, the GRPS subsystem continued to evolve. Without a major system redesign, new modulation and link adaptation methods were introduced that increased the efficiency of frequency use and timeslots utilization for packets. The changes, introduced to the market as EDGE (Enhanced Data Rates for GSM Evolution), were limited to the radio access network. Optimization in modulation and encoding provided a slightly higher data speed. As a result, EDGE offered a maximum data transmission speed of 384Kbps with all eight TDMA slots concatenated.[7] EDGE was first deployed in the early 2000s, shortly after the introduction of GRPS.

Third Generation (3G)

Although EDGE, also sometimes referred to as 2.75G, did bring some improvements in data transmission speeds, it still could not keep up with the growing demands for data consumption. The industry forerunners envisioned rapid growth in both the subscriber base as well as the data volume pushed through the mobile network. The mainstream vision at that time pictured many additional services the next generation network would provide along with voice and data transmission, such as video telephony, digital video and audio delivery, advanced car navigation, collaborative applications, and others.[8] Some of these services did gain momentum, while others had to wait until later generations of mobile networks.

At the same time, the proliferation of higher-speed Internet access with cable and DSL lines boosted adoption of applications offering voice and video calls, such as Skype and others. In many cases, the quality of voice over Internet using broadband exceeded the voice quality that mobile networks offered natively, thus putting competitive pressure on mobile network operators to improve call quality.

A new generation of mobile systems was needed to address these gaps. In the late 1990s, a few major mobile vendors and operators in North America started work on defining third generation mobile network principles. Many other mobile vendors and operators from around the world joined this initiative. This consortium, later called *3rd Generation Partnership Project (3GPP)*, released the first

3G mobile network specification called Release 99 in the year 2000. Release 99 defined the *Universal Mobile Telecommunications System (UMTS)* that forms the basis of 3G networks.

3GPP Standardization Efforts

3GPP, or 3rd Generation Partnership Project, is currently the de facto standardization body for the mobile industry. Although named after third generation, its standardization efforts extend into the fourth and fifth generations of mobile networks. 3GPP is a consortium uniting a number of national and regional standard development organizations. Major telecom vendors, wireless service providers, and national standard developing bodies contribute to the development of new mobile system architectures under the 3GPP umbrella. The three Technical Specification Groups (TSGs)—Radio Access Networks (RAN), Services and Systems Aspects (SA), and Core Network and Terminals (CT)—within 3GPP are further subdivided into Working Groups (WGs). All TSGs and WGs work together to create technical specifications called "releases," with Release 99 being the first one.

The UMTS consisted of two key components: *UMTS Terrestrial Radio Access Network (UTRAN)* and *UMTS Core Network (CN)*. The CN components and flows defined in Release 99 were very similar to GSM/GPRS network but evolved significantly over the next few 3GPP releases. In contrast, the UTRAN specification introduced many technological advances from the very beginning.

3G Innovations in Radio Access

The frequency resource was still a significant constraint in meeting the growing bandwidth demand. In addition to adding more frequency bands, 3G also offered more efficient air interface sharing among a growing number of subscribers and services.

Improvements in digital signal processing made it possible to consider more complex media access technologies than Frequency Division Multiple Access (FDMA) and Time Division Multiple Access (TDMA). This resulted in the acceptance of Wideband Code Division Multiple Access (WCDMA) as a standard for 3G. WCDMA is a flavor of CDMA that was used in some mobile networks of second generation, such a IS-95. WCDMA and CDMA are both multi-access technologies based on the same principle of separating user transmissions using codes. Compared to CDMA, WCDMA uses higher code rates, wider channel widths of 5MHz instead of 1.25MHz, and some other differences.

Unlike previous generation radio access, WCDMA does not assign a separate frequency or a timeslot to different users. Instead, their signals are transmitted at the same time and using the same frequency. This media access technology is based on a counterintuitive approach of transmitting a signal using substantially more bandwidth than would be necessary with other modulation techniques. Each bit or group of bits (a symbol) of an original digital signal is encoded by a few rectangular pulses (called "chips"), based on a special sequence of bits, called a "spreading code." When an original digital signal is multiplied by such a code, it could be said that the signal is being spread over the spectrum, as a higher rate signal of rectangular pulses occupies a wider frequency spectrum compared to a similar but lower rate signal. The spectrum of an original signal becomes wider, and the energy of the original symbols is also distributed over the wider frequency band. Figure 1-9 illustrates the use of spreading codes over a digital signal in WCDMA.

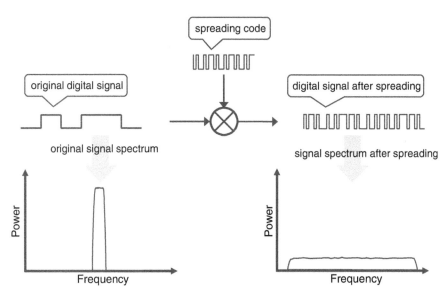

FIGURE 1-9   Digital Signal Modulation Using Spreading Codes

The reverse operation, or de-spreading, requires exactly the same code to recover the original signal. The energy of each original symbol is combined during de-spreading operations and results in the recovery of the symbol. This process is also referred to as "correlation."

Spreading codes are generated in such a way that they maintain a mathematical property of orthogonality. When a de-spreading operation is done with a code different from the one used for spreading, it results in recovery of nearly zero energy for each symbol that appears as negligible noise. Different spreading codes are used to encode different data channels, making it possible to distinguish them at the receiver. Therefore, these are also referred to as "channelization codes."

When both transmitter and receiver use the same code, the de-spreading operation recovers the original signal while effectively filtering out any other signals. This allows simultaneous transmission of multiple signals encoded with different orthogonal spreading codes using the same frequency band. Figure 1-10 illustrates the signal transmission and de-spreading operation in WCDMA.

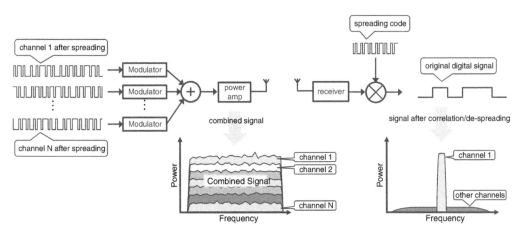

FIGURE 1-10   Multiple Signals Transmission and De-spreading Operation

The spreading codes used in WCDMA have a fixed rate of 3.84M chips per second, which is related to the width of a radio channel (5MHz). The number of chips used to encode a single bit (or more strictly, a symbol) of the original signal is known as "spreading factor" and may vary in WCDMA transmissions between 4 and 512.

When spreading codes don't start at the same time, they might have decreased orthogonality. This becomes a challenge in WCDMA due to asynchronous mode of base stations operation. To cope with that, WCDMA uses an additional code, called a "scrambling code." An already spread signal is further encoded by a scrambling code without increasing the rate of the signal. This operation ensures better orthogonality and helps to better distinguish transmissions from different mobile devices and base stations. Different scrambling codes are used by each individual transmitter in a cell.

WCDMA transmissions use *Quadrature Phase-Shift Keying (QPSK)* modulation in the downlinks and *dual-channel QPSK* in the uplinks. Without going into the complexity of modulation theory, suffice to say that QPSK modulation converts 2-bit symbols into a radio signal with four distinguishable phase shifts. Thus, each 2 bits of a downlink channel in UMTS are modulated by a single-phase shift of QPSK. In the uplink direction, however, 2 bits comprising a single symbol for QPSK are provided by two separate channels: control and data, hence the name dual-channel QPSK. Multiplexing of two uplink channels into a single transmission improves air interface efficiency when significant asymmetry of the traffic patterns exists between uplink and downlink.

Microdiversity and Macrodiversity in 3G

Use of expanded signal bandwidth in WCDMA has another benefit for UTRAN. The signal fading due to interfering multiple propagation paths can be compensated with so-called *rake receivers*. A typical rake receiver can be viewed as a collection of many radio receiver sub-units (fingers), which apply different delays to the signal and process it independently. The results are then combined, harvesting more of the signal's energy that's otherwise wasted. This concept is also known as *microdiversity combining*. UMTS introduced the use of rake receivers in both base stations and mobile devices.

Along with microdiversity combining, UMTS also employs *macrodiversity combining*, where a signal received by two adjacent cells is compared and combined at the Radio Network Controller (RNC). When a signal from an adjacent cell becomes substantially better, the mobile device might experience *soft handover* to an adjacent cell if it is controlled by the same RNC. Soft handovers reduce the amount of signaling required in UTRAN and prevent gaps in communication resulting from this.

When adjacent cells participating in macrodiversity are controlled by different RNCs, UTRAN defines a special interface for RNC-to-RNC communication.

The very foundational principle of WCDMA, that all mobile devices within the cell transmit on the same radio frequency, can lead to a situation where a single powerful transmission jams all other (weaker) signals. This is also known as "near-far problem" in CDMA systems. To address this problem, it is critical to control power of each mobile device transmitting in the cell. Each radio node constantly evaluates radio signal parameters, such as signal-to-interference ratio (SIR), and instructs each device to reduce or increase its power level.

In addition to these, there were many other innovations such as Adaptive Multi-Rate (AMR) codecs for voice, switching off transmissions during voice silence or gaps in data streams with discontinuous transmissions (DTX), and so on, but their details fall outside the scope of this book. Collectively, these innovations helped to create a robust, efficient, and fast UMTS air interface, reaching the peak speeds of 2Mbps in the downlink and 768Kbps in the uplink; however, later 3GPP releases boosted achievable data rates significantly.

3G Mobile Transport

3G UMTS introduced the concept of NodeB, which terminates the air interface from mobile devices and is considered the demarcation point between radio access networks and the mobile backhaul network. Similar to its predecessor (BTS) in 2G, NodeB required connectivity to its controller in the mobile core. In 3G, the controller is called the *Radio Network Controller (RNC)*, and NodeB relies on the mobile transport to provide robust connectivity between the two.

Initial 3G implementations used a similar approach for mobile transport as their predecessor (that is, point-to-point T1/E1 links between the NodeB and RNC). As bandwidth consumption continued to grow, however, the 1.5/2Mbps capacity offered by T1/E1 links quickly became saturated. The use of 5MHz channels, along with the efficient coding techniques, significantly increased the bandwidth requirements in the mobile backhaul (that is, from the cell site to the mobile core). One of the solutions was to use multiple T1/E1 links; another option was an upgrade to higher capacity T3/E3 links. This was a costly proposition, however, given the dedicated use of such point-to-point links, and the industry moved toward higher capacity yet cost-effective alternates such as Asynchronous Transfer Mode (ATM) and IP in the mobile backhaul.

Around the same time when the first 3G networks were being deployed, Internet providers and network operators were also deploying high-speed data networks to meet the growing Internet bandwidth requirements. One of the leading technologies for such networks was ATM, which provided higher speeds (155Mbps or more), traffic prioritization through quality of service (QoS), and predictable traffic delay. These properties made ATM a suitable transport mechanism for mobile traffic, where voice required careful handling due to its time-sensitive nature and data required higher bandwidth.

With 3GPP standardizing the use of ATM, and subsequently Internet Protocol (IP), for mobile transport, this presented service providers with an opportunity to consolidate their Internet and mobile transport networks. The potential to use a single transport network tempted the service providers and network operators to embrace a common technology for mobile and Internet transport in the hopes of optimizing operation, reducing operational expenses, and extracting maximum return on investment on their deployments. For mobile communication networks (MCNs), this meant that instead of using purpose-built, mostly point-to-point links, base stations and NodeBs could utilize general-purpose high-speed data networks to connect to the mobile core. While this concept of a "single converged network" was introduced in 3G, it did not see significant adoption in most service providers until well into the 2010s. Some service providers preferred to maintain separate physical networks for mobile and traditional data networks, while many others made substantial strides towards consolidating the two. 3G heralded the arrival of the mobile backhaul (MBH) era for MCNs. Whereas, previously, transport was simply a collection of dedicated point-to-point links from a base station to the mobile core, MBH networks provided a blueprint for robust, reliable, multiservice connectivity within and between the radio access network and the mobile core. MBH networks are discussed in more detail in the next chapter.

3G Mobile Core

As previously mentioned, the 3GPP definition of the core network in Release 99 did not feature many changes to the GSM/GPRS standards. Although new interfaces were defined to interact with UTRAN, the main constituents of the core network remained largely unchanged: MSC, GMSC, HLR, SGSN, GGSN, and so on. However, scalability challenges in the circuit switched domain became a reality due to mobile networks' expansion and consolidation over large geographic areas. Major core network changes were therefore introduced in 3GPP Release 4 to address these challenges by splitting the functions of MSC into two entities: *MSC server (MSC-S)* and *media gateway (MGW)*. Figure 1-11 shows an overview of the 3G/UMTS architecture and components.

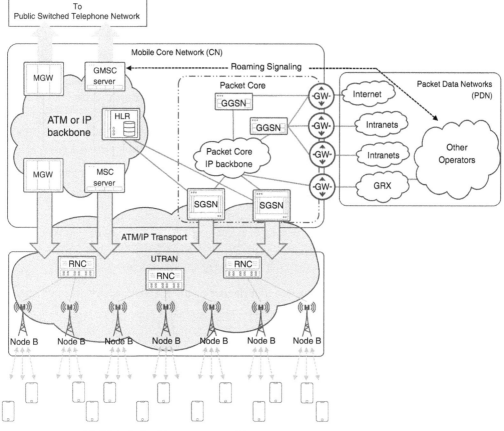

FIGURE 1-11   3G/UMTS Architecture at a Glance

The MSC-S is sometimes also referred to as a "call server" and implements call control and signaling. Put simply, MSC-S takes care of call routing decisions and negotiating voice bearer requirements when a mobile subscriber makes or receives a circuit switched voice call. MSC-S is also responsible for HLR interrogation, maintaining VLR, and the generation of call detail records for the billing system. An MSC-S connecting its mobile networks with other networks is called Gateway MSC-S (GMSC-S).

While MSC-S and GMSC-S implement call control and signaling, the actual circuit switching is performed by media gateways (MGWs). In other words, MGWs provide bearers for circuit switched voice, perform media conversion between TDM and ATM or IP-based voice, transcoding, and other call-related functions such as echo cancellation.

Both ATM and IP were defined by 3GPP as acceptable transport for MGW and MSC connectivity. The signaling between MSC-S, which was originally done using a protocol called Signaling System 7 (SS7), can now be carried over ATM or IP. When carried over IP, it is referred to as SIGTRAN, short for *signaling transport*.

Although some significant changes were introduced in the circuit switched part of 3G CN, the packet switched domain remained largely unchanged. The functional split between SGSN and GGSN allowed for scaling the packet switched domain efficiently by adding more SGSNs and/or GGSNs where and when needed. SGSNs and GGSNs were retrofitted with new interfaces to communicate with RNCs in the UTRAN over ATM or IP.

The terms *circuit switched core* and *packet switched core* also emerged to distinguish between two major functional domains of 3G CN, with the latter further simplified to just *packet core*. Even though the circuit switched core could now use an ATM or IP backbone for connectivity, interestingly enough it remained separate from the packet-switched core's IP backbone in most implementations.

3G Enhancements

Though 3GPP had originally defined its Release 99 for the third generation mobile wireless specifications, the consortium continued to define new specifications in the subsequent years. Unlike Release 99, where the number "99" was influenced by the year (1999) when most of it was developed, the subsequent releases were simply given a sequential name, starting with Release 4.

These released specifications had varying degrees of influence on the RAN, transport, and mobile core of 3G mobile systems. These influences will be discussed in this section.

3GPP Release 4

As mentioned in the previous section, Release 4 brought a major change to the packet core with a very significant step of specifying the MGW and MSC-S. The use of the IP network to communicate between these was the first step toward the transition away from circuit switched voice.

While 3G networks based on Release 99 were mostly limited to proof of concepts, lab trials, and few early deployments, the 3GPP Release 4 was the first release of 3G specifications that was practically deployed. Release 99 standards, however, were widely used in production deployment as part of 2G, 2.5G, and EDGE networks.

3GPP Release 5

Release 5 of 3GPP was more focused toward defining new radio specifications to improve bandwidth. For this reason, Release 5 and its subsequent releases are collectively referred to as *High Speed Packet Access (HSPA)*.

In Release 5, the downlink speed (cell tower to mobile user) was the focus, hence it's called *High Speed Downlink Packet Access (HSDPA)*. The specifications made it possible for the theoretical maximum speed to be increased to 14.4Mbps, through the use of a new modulation technique. It was a big increase compared to the previous theoretical maximum of Release 99.

On the mobile core, Release 5 specified the *IP Multimedia Subsystem (IMS)* with the goal of moving to packet switched voice communication; however, IMS didn't see any real traction until much later. IMS will therefore be discussed in more detail in Chapter 3, "Mobile Networks Today."

3GPP Release 6

As Release 5 had enhanced downlink speeds, Release 6 (which is also part of HSPA) provided specifications to enhance uplink speeds and hence was known as *High Speed Uplink Packet Access (HSUPA)*. HSUPA bumped up uplink speeds to 5.8Mbps under ideal radio conditions.

3GPP Release 7

The predominant change that Release 7 of the 3GPP specifications brought was once more focused on improving the data speeds over the air interface. Using more sophisticated modulation techniques and multiple simultaneous transmissions, the theoretical downlink speed was increased to 28Mbps, while the uplink speeds were brought up to 11Mbps. These speeds still required ideal conditions, and the realistically achievable speeds were somewhat lower. Regardless, these speeds offered a great amount of improvement compared to 2G speeds. To distinguish these changes from HSPA, the Release 7 data rate enhancements are referred to as HSPA+.

Release 7 also brought some improvements to the connectivity mechanism used by the mobile devices. Previously, devices experienced excessive battery drain in the idle state before they went into sleep mode. When waking up from the sleep state, they faced a significant lag in connectivity. New specifications in Release 7 brought major improvements in this area and thus improved the battery power consumption for devices. The details of these techniques, known as Continuous Packet Connectivity (CPC), are beyond the scope of this book.

3GPP Release 8 and Beyond

After 3GPP Release 4, which had brought significant changes to the mobile core, all the releases were more focused on improving the air interface data rates. However, Release 8 once again specified major changes to the mobile core using the new specifications called *Evolved Packet Core (EPC)*. On the radio side, it specified *Enhanced Universal Terrestrial Radio Access Network (E-UTRAN)*.

These enhancements, known as *Long-Term Evolution (LTE)*, paved the path for 4G networks, which are covered in Chapter 3.

Figure 1-12 shows a progression of uplink and downlink speeds across various 3GPP releases.

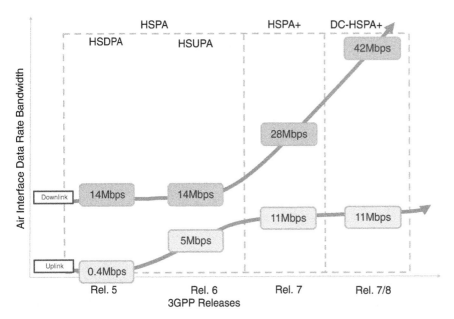

FIGURE 1-12   3GPP Releases and Corresponding Theoretical Speeds

3G Technology Summary

2G passed the baton to the third generation of mobile networks at a critical turning point in mobile networking history.

3G enhanced mobile services on two major fronts. Early 3GPP releases focused on major changes in the radio access technologies with the use of WCDMA, establishing a solid foundation for air interface evolution. Through the separation of MSC functions into MSC-S and MGW, 3G kickstarted the adoption of ATM/IP transport in the mobile core and eventually in the mobile transport. The transition from TDM to ATM/IP promised operational expense reduction and maximization of the return on investment on future deployments.

Later 3GPP releases introducing HSPA provided tangible benefits to end users through higher upload and download speeds. The result was a massive growth in the subscriber base. By the end of 2008, the number of mobile subscriptions surpassed 4 billion globally.[9]

Summary

This chapter covered the evolution of mobile services from pre-cellular mobile networks through the third generation. Many key concepts were covered, including the following:

- The three domains of mobile communication networks: radio access network, mobile transport, and mobile core

- Building blocks of each of these domains across multiple generations

- The concept of a cell and frequency spectrum reuse

- The limitations of each mobile generation and the solution adopted to overcome those in the next generation

- Industry adoption for every generation of mobile communication

Knowledge of these topics and their historical context play a key role in understanding the principles of mobile communication. The next chapter will explore the three distinct domains of the mobile communication network in more detail and will discuss how these domains interact together to provide end-to-end services.

References

1. https://www.britannica.com/technology/mobile-telephone#ref1079045 (last visited: Mar 2022)

2. Theodore S. Rappaport, *Wireless Communications: Principles and Practice, 2nd Edition* (Upper Saddle River, N.J.: Prentice Hall PTR, 2002), Chapter 1.

3. Op. cit., Chapters 2 and 11.

4. Op. cit., Chapter 1.

5. https://www.qualcomm.com/news/releases/1998/09/02/qualcomm-awarded-first-cdmaone-technology-type-approval-and-quality (last visited: Mar 2022)

6. https://www.itu.int/itunews/issue/2003/06/thirdgeneration.html

7. https://www.3gpp.org/technologies/keywords-acronyms/102-gprs-edge

8. http://www.itu.int/osg/spu/ni/3G/workshop/Briefing_paper.doc

9. https://www.itu.int/itunews/issue/2008/10/30.html

Chapter | **2**

Anatomy of Mobile Communication Networks

Various individual components and interconnected systems come together to make an end-to-end mobile communication network (MCN). The previous chapter introduced the evolution of mobile generations in the context of three distinct MCN domains, namely:

- **Radio access networks (RANs):** These networks comprise discrete interconnected components that collectively provide the air interface to connect the end user of the mobile services to the mobile network.

- **Mobile transport and backhaul:** The network infrastructure that provides connectivity between RANs and the mobile core.

- **Mobile core:** The brain of an MCN. The mobile core enables and implements services for the end users.

Mobile services rely on each of these domains working together in cohesion. A deeper understanding of the anatomy of these domains, as well as the interaction within and between them, is critical for designing effective mobile network architectures. This chapter will take a closer look at these distinct yet tightly interconnected domains that make up an end-to-end mobile communication network.

Understanding Radio Access Network

The RAN is perhaps the most prominent component of the mobile communication network. It is also the interface between a mobile operator and its subscriber. A vast majority of mobiles users remain completely oblivious to the rest of the network's components, typically equating the quality of their overall service to an operator's RAN performance. Mobile operators obviously seem to be aware of this and use slogans like "Can you hear me now?" (Verizon) or "More bars in more places" (AT&T)—a nod to the performance and reliability of their RAN—in an effort to win market share.

While the perceived key measure of RAN performance is cellular coverage, there are actually many factors that contribute to an efficient RAN design. Mobile operators spend a lot of effort, time, and money ensuring optimal operations and continued RAN enhancements. Although radio frequency (RF) planning and optimization might be an apt topic for a book on its own, this section provides a brief overview of key RAN concepts.

> ## Units of Radio Frequency
>
> When Heinrich Hertz proved the existence of electromagnetic waves through his experiments between 1886 and 1889, nobody, including Hertz, believed that there could be any real-life applications for them. Initially referred to as *Hertzian waves* and later commonly called *radio waves*, these electromagnetic waves were measured in cycles per second (CPS). The cycles represent the frequency of oscillations per second, with higher frequency waves being measured in kilocycles (kc) and megacycles (mc). As an honor to Heinrich Hertz, cycles per second was replaced with Hertz (Hz) as the unit of frequency measurement in 1920 and was officially adopted by the International System of Units in 1933.

How the RF Spectrum Is Allocated

When electromagnetic waves propagate, they don't directly affect each other. Yet, a receiver detects the superposition of electromagnetic waves as they appear in certain points in space. This phenomenon, called *interference*, restricts the receiver's ability to reliably detect radio waves emitted by a specific transmitter. When two transmitters, in close proximity to each other, emit radio waves in the same direction and at the same frequency, it is very hard or sometimes impossible to detect individual transmission. To avoid this scenario, the concept of "right to use" was introduced to regulate the use of radio frequencies within a geographical area.

As part of the right-to-use process, the "usable" frequency ranges would first be defined by the standard bodies. Based on these standards, the regulatory bodies (that is, government agencies) would then auction off the rights to use these frequencies within a geographical area to various operators. New frequency ranges are sometimes made available, either due to technological enhancements or through the repurposing of a previously allocated spectrum, kicking off a new round of auctions. The right is to a frequency range in a particular market is a valuable commodity, one which mobile operators spend hundreds of millions, if not billions, of dollars to acquire and use. One such example is FCC Auction 107, where a mere 280MHz spectrum attracted bids upward of $80 billion.[1]

Mobile operators are not the only users of the radio frequency spectrum. Public services (law enforcement, fire departments, first responders, hospitals), broadcasting (radio and television), as well as government and military services are all consumers of the radio spectrum. As such, government bodies tasked with regulating the RF spectrum set aside various frequency ranges for specialized use. For instance, in the United States, radio frequencies in the 535–1705KHz range are reserved for AM radio broadcast, 88–108MHz are reserved for FM radio, and 54–72MHz, 76–88MHz, 174–216MHz, and 512–608MHz are reserved for TV broadcast.[2, 3]

In addition to auctioning off frequency ranges for exclusive use of mobile operators, some frequency ranges are made available to operators for unlicensed usage. One such example is the *Citizens Broadcast Radio Service (CBRS)* in the U.S. CBRS and its equivalent around the world, such as *Licensed Shared Access (LSA)* in Europe, provide specific frequency spectrum ranges to new and incumbent mobile providers as well as to private entities for various uses, including deploying mobile networks. This is done, in part, to foster competition and to lower the cost of entry for startups. CBRS and other free-to-use spectrums are an important part of mobile standards.

Choosing the Right Frequency

Radio waves operating at different frequencies have different characteristics in terms of their applicability for mobile services. For instance, radio waves in lower frequency ranges are less susceptible to absorption and reflection by obstacles. These radio waves tend to bend easily around corners, a phenomenon called *diffraction*, and would therefore penetrate buildings and structures better, thus providing superior signal propagation. Conversely, higher frequency radio waves tend to be more susceptible to obstacles and have far worse penetration within buildings and structures.

Another factor affecting radio transmission is the way antennas emit and receive radio waves. Although many different antenna types exist and are used for different purposes, mobile communication systems usually rely on omnidirectional antennas in their mobile devices. The size of a typical omnidirectional antenna is a function of its operational frequency and becomes proportionally smaller for higher frequencies. This has a profound effect on the reception of radio waves by omnidirectional antennas. Due to its smaller *effective area*, a high-frequency omnidirectional antenna collects less energy compared to its lower-frequency counterpart at the same distance from the transmitter. In other words, smaller high-frequency omnidirectional antennas produce weaker electrical signals at the inputs of a receiver. Hence, this effectively reduces the usable distance of a higher-frequency transmission even in the absence of obstacles. This dependency is routinely included in the equations used by radio engineers designing transmission systems and is often referred to as *free space path loss*. Despite its utility in radio engineering, the free space path loss equation and concepts can be somewhat misleading, as this effect is not inherent to higher-frequency radio waves themselves and is rather caused by the omnidirectional antennas' operational principles. High-frequency radio transmissions can be successfully implemented over great distances with the use of directional antennas (for example, dish antennas). Mobile devices, however, are typically designed with omnidirectional antennas for better usability, but there are trade-offs in terms of effective coverage area for higher-frequency bands.

If signal propagation was the only goal, a provider would use lower-frequency ranges in locations with more buildings and structures such as a metro downtown. In that case, higher-frequency ranges would then be reserved for suburbs and open spaces such as along stretches of highways. Signal propagation is just one of the factors in a provider's RF strategy, however. There are other factors to consider as well, such as the width of the frequency range.

The radio frequency range, known as a *frequency band*, is akin to highway traffic lanes. The wider the highway, the more individual traffic lanes that can be fit in either direction. The more traffic lanes there are, the more cars that can simultaneously use the highway. The same is true of radio waves and mobile traffic. The individual highway lanes are the "channels" in a mobile radio network that carry mobile traffic. An individual channel, also called *carrier channel*, is a range of frequencies within the available spectrum. Generally speaking, the *channel width* and the total number of channels in a defined frequency spectrum determine overall traffic capacity.

Simply put, a frequency band is a range of frequencies, and a carrier channel is a subset of a frequency band used for mobile communications. Channels are characterized by their width and central frequency, also called the *carrier frequency*. In mobile communications, it is the carrier frequency that is then modulated to produce the resulting signal.

Each mobile generation has defined the carrier channel width as well as the supported frequency spectrum. For instance, 1G AMPS networks used a channel width of 30KHz, while their European counterpart, ETACS, used 25KHz channels. AMPS used frequency bands in the range of 824–849MHz for user-to-base-station communication (referred to as *reverse link* in the mobile world and *upstream frequency* from a network's perspective) and 869–894MHz for base-station-to-user communication (referred to as *forward link* or *downstream frequency*). ETACS had defined 890–915MHz as upstream and 935–960MHz as downstream frequency bands. With defined channel widths of 30KHz and 25KHz, AMPS and ETACS allowed for 832 and 1000 channels, respectively, in each direction.

Correlating Frequency Ranges and Capacity

Recent advances in electronics have unlocked the use of higher frequency ranges (24GHz and higher). These higher frequency ranges have wider bands available, providing the capability for not only more channels but also wider channel widths. For instance, between 900 and 910MHz, there is 10MHz or 10,000,000Hz available, whereas between 2.4 and 2.5GHz, there is 100MHz available that can be utilized for various channels. Hence, it should be kept in mind that when frequencies are listed in GHz, a small delta in the numbers would reflect a large step when compared to MHz. This is a subtle distinction that is easy to overlook.

Newer generations introduced higher channel widths (for example, 200KHz for GSM, 5MHz for most 3G implementations) as well as new frequency ranges. 1G and 2G networks primarily used the frequencies below 1GHz, whereas 3G and 4G defined and used additional higher-frequency ranges between 1 and 6GHz. Recently, 3GPP Release 16 extended this range to 7.125GHz. Today, the frequencies below 1GHz (also called sub-1GHz frequencies) are referred to as *low-band*, whereas the frequencies in the 1–7.125GHz range (also called sub-7GHz frequencies) are called *mid-band* frequencies. These low-band and mid-band frequency ranges are collectively referred to as *Frequency Range 1 (FR1)*.

More recently, the use of frequencies higher than 24GHz has been defined for mobile communication as well. These frequencies are classified as *high-band* frequencies and referred to as *Frequency Range*

2 (FR2). These ultra-high frequencies are also called *millimeter wave (mmWave)* frequencies, due to their wavelengths being a few millimeters. Figure 2-1 shows various frequency band classifications, their relative spectrum availability, and their propagation efficiency characteristics.

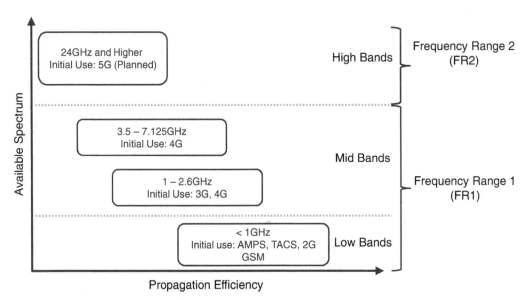

FIGURE 2-1   Frequency Band Classifications

Going back to the analogy of highway traffic lanes, larger frequency bands represent highways that can now fit more and wider traffic lanes, thus providing higher capacity. From a transport network perspective, the use of higher-frequency ranges, where wider channels are more readily available, results in greater overall bandwidth requirements to adequately support all services.

The frequency range used by a provider is dependent on three primary factors:

- Whether the frequency range has been introduced for use by standard bodies such as 3GPP

- Whether the regulatory authorities have made the frequency spectrum available

- Whether the provider has the rights to use that particular frequency band for a given geographical area

As long as the preceding three criteria are met, a provider could use a frequency range for their 2G, 3G, 4G, or 5G service offerings. Frequency spectrum is not tied to a single generation, and a provider may repurpose a previously used band, assigning it for a newer generation of mobile service. In reality, low-band frequencies that have been available since 1G and 2G networks were the first ones to be repurposed and used in 5G networks. Figure 2-2 illustrates this frequency use and reuse across generations.

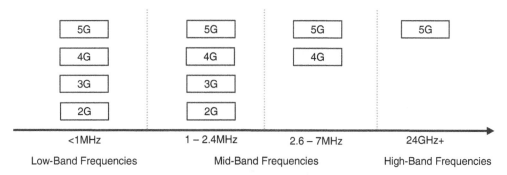

FIGURE 2-2   Typical Frequency Band Usage Across Mobile Generations

To summarize, frequencies in low bands have better propagation efficiency than higher ones, while mid and high bands offer more and wider available channels, which translates into higher overall system capacity. Using high bands might require direct line of sight or close proximity to the radio tower to provide adequate coverage. In that context, mid-band frequencies (below 7GHz) provide a good balance of coverage and capacity, and hence attract extremely high bids for acquiring right of use.[4] The highly sought-after *C-Band* frequencies fall under this category. For example, in the year 2021 Verizon Wireless spent about $53 billion to acquire an average of 161MHz of C-Band spectrum for nationwide use in the USA. C-Band spectrum is the higher end of mid-band frequencies (that is, above 3GHz) which has been allocated for cellular use.

Mobile operators typically use a mix of various frequency bands. Due to their propagation properties, low-frequency bands are often better suited for suburban and rural areas, whereas higher bands might be preferred in dense urban areas. In reality, multiple frequency bands are used within the same cell to provide a mix of coverage and speed to as many mobile users as possible.

RF Duplexing Mechanisms

All radio transmissions are simplex (that is, unidirectional) in nature. This means that for the mobile phone and antenna on the cellular tower to communicate in both directions, duplexing techniques are required. The two primary techniques used to achieve duplex communication in mobile systems are Frequency Division Duplex (FDD) and Time Division Duplex (TDD).

FDD uses two separate frequencies for uplink and downlink communications. In this case, both the mobile phone and cell tower would transmit and receive at the same time, albeit on different frequencies. When an FDD schema is used, the uplink and downlink frequency bands are separated by what is called a *guard band*. This guard band is an unused frequency channel that provides a buffer between the uplink and downlink channels to minimize interference between the two. An example of an FDD guard band would be the 20MHz channel between the 1850–1910MHz uplink and 1930–1990MHz downlink frequencies specified for operating band number 2.[5]

Operating Band Numbers

Supported frequency ranges are typically identified by a *band number* and a common name. There is no direct correlation between a band number and its frequency range, as the ranges are added as and when it becomes feasible to do so. Hence, band 1 (commonly called 2100) defines 1920–1980MHz for upstream and 2110–2170MHz for downstream, while band 2 (called PCS 1900) identifies 1850–1910MHz and 1930–1990MHz. The specification also defines if an operating band uses FDD or TDD as the duplexing mechanism.

In 5G specifications, the previously defined band numbers are prefixed with *n* (for example, band 1 becomes n1) and new operating bands are specified as well. Before 5G, a total of 88 operating bands were defined.[6] 5G NR Base Station (BS) radio transmission and reception specification by 3GPP currently specifies operating bands n1 though n96 in the FR1 frequencies and addition band in FR2 frequency ranges.[7]

TDD is another mechanism used to provide duplex communications between a cell tower and mobile equipment. In TDD, a single frequency is used in both upstream and downstream directions, but it uses different timeslots to achieve duplex communication. With this approach, there is no need for a guard band; however, the timeslots are now separated by a *guard interval* that ensures transmit and receive timeslots do not overlap. The guard interval should be long enough to accommodate for signal propagation time between transmitter and receiver. The use of a guard interval introduces inefficiencies in spectral usage, as no signal transmission can occur for the duration of the guard interval. Likewise, inefficiencies also exist in FDD transmission in cases where a frequency band is left unused in order to provide the guard band function. Figure 2-3 provides an overview of TDD and FDD mechanisms in mobile systems.

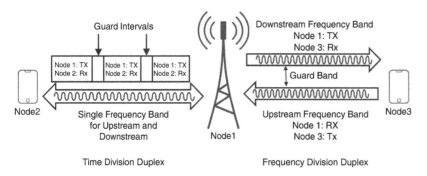

FIGURE 2-3   TDD and FDD Duplexing Mechanisms

There are pros and cons to both duplexing techniques. FDD has been in use since the early days of mobile communications, making it a proven and more widely deployed technology. With dedicated upstream and downstream frequencies, FDD offers traffic symmetry and continuous communications in either direction. On the other hand, FDD contributes to spectral wastage due to the need of allocating frequencies in pairs and setting aside a guard band to separate upstream and downstream frequencies. The hardware costs for FDD-based systems are typically higher than their TDD counterparts due to the use of *diplexers*—passive devices to separate upstream and downstream bands using frequency-based filtering.

TDD systems adjust well to asymmetrical traffic distribution, as is typically the case with consumer data traffic. With timeslots allocated for transmit and receive over the same frequency band, it is possible to adjust timeslot allocation to match traffic distribution. Using a single frequency band also results in similar channel propagation characteristics in either direction. This *channel reciprocity* is useful in implementing advanced antenna features, some of which will be discussed in Chapter 5, "5G Fundamentals." TDD requires strict synchronization between cell towers and mobile phones to ensure all entities adhere to their timeslots. The guard interval also plays a role in terms of the coverage area for TDD-based mobile systems. For smaller cell coverage zones, the signal travel time between a cell tower and mobile phones can be relatively shorter, resulting in a smaller guard interval. For larger cell coverage zones, a longer guard interval might be required, introducing significant spectral inefficiencies and overhead. For this reason, TDD systems might be more suited to smaller coverage zones. While TDD systems are cheaper than FDD in terms of hardware, their coverage shortcomings result in more cell towers being deployed in a geographical region, potentially resulting in higher overall deployment and subsequent management costs.

To summarize, FDD has the following characteristics:

- Dedicated upstream and downstream frequency bands (that is, all channels within a given band are used for either upstream or downstream communications).

- Symmetric upload and download capacity due to dedicated frequency bands.

- Guard band between upstream and downstream channels contributes to spectral wastage.

- Slightly higher capital cost due to diplexer-based antenna systems.

TDD characteristics can be summarized as follows:

- Uses the same frequency band for upstream and downstream. All channels within the frequency band are used for both upstream and downstream communication.

- Allows reassignment of upstream and downstream timeslots to match traffic asymmetry.

- Guard interval contributes to spectral wastage. This wastage increases with larger geographical coverage, as the guard interval proportionally increases with distance.

Using either FDD or TDD techniques, modern communication systems achieve duplex communications over the radio interface. The choice of duplexing mechanism is completely transparent to the end user; however, network architects need to be aware of RF duplexing mechanism to ensure proper network synchronization and bandwidth utilization planning.

Cell Splitting and Sectoring

Each cell in a cellular network contains RF antennas and transceivers to provide mobile service throughout the cell's coverage zone. As cells in densely populated areas start to experience a higher number of subscribers, the resulting congestion creates capacity and connectivity challenges.

Cell splitting and cell sectoring are the two common mechanisms that address these challenges, and they are extensively utilized today.

Cell splitting is the process of dividing an existing cell into multiple smaller cells, each with its own base station location and frequency carriers. The result is a statistical distribution of subscribers over multiple cells, thereby increasing overall cellular system scale and capacity. Cell splitting could be an expensive option for an operator, as it requires site acquisition and installation of new base stations as well as managing connectivity to the mobile core. Although it's sometimes necessary, an operator would typically avoid cell splitting due to the complexities and cost associated with the process.

Another option is *cell sectoring*, where multiple *directional antennas* are used instead of an omni-directional antenna. These directional antennas are mounted on the same antenna tower without the need for an additional base station site, with each one providing RF coverage within its own *sector*. A multisector cell site, therefore, scales better and can provide services to a larger number of subscribers. Most common sectoring configurations are three, four, or six sectors per cell with the use of either 120-degree, 90-degree, or 60-degree directional antennas, respectively. Figure 2-4 provides a high-level overview of cell sectoring for various directional antenna configurations.

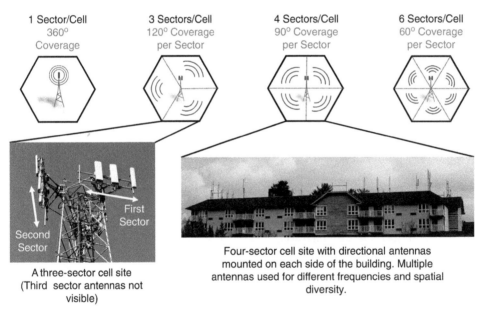

FIGURE 2-4   Cell Sectoring Examples

Variations in terrain, building structures, and obstacles might cause higher RF signal attenuation and degradation in certain directions. In such cases, it might be necessary to boost signal strength in a particular direction to compensate for geographical considerations. Cell sectoring, with its directional antennas, makes it easier to adjust transmission power to match the terrain in a given sector. This would not be possible with omnidirectional antennas, as adjusting transmission levels can increase interference with neighboring cells.

> **Spatial Diversity Within a Sector**
>
> *Spatial diversity* is a commonly used technique to increase RF performance and reliability within a sector or cell. Multiple antennas are mounted for the same sector, but with enough physical separation among them to ensure that radio signals between each antenna panel and the mobile device take different physical paths. Figure 2-4 shows different sectors within a cell, as well as multiple spatially diverse antennas in each sector. In doing so, spatial diversity provides increased reliability for subscribers through multiple signal paths.
>
> Spatial diversity also has a utility in implementing advanced antenna features such as Multiple Input, Multiple Output (MIMO). Chapter 5 covers advanced antenna features in more detail.

Each sector, through the use of its own set of antennas and frequencies, is considered an independent cell by the mobile network. As a result, cell sectoring increases the overall capacity without significant costs; however, sectors result in an increase in the number of handoffs as mobile users move across different sectors within the same cell. The *cell site* also has to account for additional radio antennas and corresponding equipment.

Today, almost all cellular deployments take advantage of multiple sectors to not only increase capacity and scale but also RF efficiency by adjusting transmit power in directions where it is most needed.

What's a Cell Site?

A cell site is the demarcation point between radio access and mobile transport networks. It houses the necessary radio and transport equipment to provide an air interface to mobile subscribers as well as connects the radio network to the mobile backhaul. A mobile operator can have thousands, if not tens of thousands, of cell sites throughout its cellular coverage area.

The most prominent part of the cell site is a *cell tower*—a tall structure that mounts antenna panels. While certainly noteworthy and significant, cell towers and antennas are not the only components of a cell site. Each antenna panel is connected to a *radio unit (RU)* that has historically been placed at the base of the cell tower in a weatherized cabinet or shelter, along with other equipment such as the *baseband unit (BBU)*, DC power batteries, and routers or switches. Together, the RU and BBU provide radio signal modulation and demodulation, power amplification, frequency filtering, and signal processing. Depending on the RAN equipment manufacturer, the RU and BBU could be separate devices or implemented in a single modular chassis, but historically co-located in the cell site cabinet.

Due to the placement of antennas and the RU, the coaxial cable connecting the two is dozens of feet or sometimes over 100 feet (30+ meters) long. When traveling such a distance over coaxial cable, the RF signal experiences significant attenuation that degrades the signal quality. One of the earlier workarounds implemented involved placing amplifiers near the antennas to compensate for signal attenuation.

In later deployments, the RU functionally is moved away from the BBU and implemented in smaller form factor that can be mounted on top of the cell tower alongside antenna panels. This *remote radio unit (RRU)*—also called *remote radio head (RRH)*—connects to the antenna panels using jumper cables that are just a few feet long, typically 3–5 feet (1–2 meters). The reduction in length of the cable ensures significantly less attenuation between the antenna and RRH, eliminating the need for an external amplifier. The resulting RF efficiency, along with the technically advanced RRH hardware, opens up the possibilities for new and advanced antenna functions, some of which will be discussed in later chapters.

> ### Integrated Antenna and Remote Radio Head
>
> While current deployments use a remote radio head (RRH) and antenna connected by a jumper cable, there are some integrated antenna–RRH devices available for deployment. The adoption of such integrated devices stems from a desire to simplify antenna deployments as well as to reduce the wear and tear on jumper cable connections overtime.

Figure 2-5 provides a pictorial view of the placement of the antenna, RRH, and BBU.

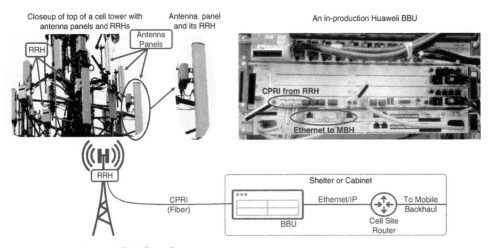

FIGURE 2-5   Typical Cell Site Components

While the RU relocated to the top of the cell tower as RRH, the BBU remained at the base of the cell tower. As the RRH became remote to the BBU, there was a need to define an interface and protocols between the two. This led to RAN equipment manufacturers—Ericsson, Huawei, Alcatel (now Nokia), and NEC—to come together to define the *Common Public Radio Interface (CPRI)*, a publicly available specification using optical fiber for RRH-to-BBU communications.[8] In reality, however, the RAN equipment vendors created proprietary CPRI implementations with little to no vendor interoperability between RRH and BBU. The motivation for a proprietary CPRI implementation was as much an effort to offer a differentiated product as it was to protect market share and deter competition. As a result, the mobile operator would be locked in to the same vendor for its RRH and BBU needs.

Base Station or Cell Sites?

Described for the first generation of mobile networks, the expression *base station* has now become synonymous with a generation-neutral description of RAN equipment and its related functionality at the cell site. Although 3GPP has defined explicit generation-specific terminologies, the use of *base station* has persisted and continues to this day.

The combination of antenna, RU or RRH, and BBU, along with the RAN functions these devices provide, is referred to as *base transceiver station (BTS)* in 2G, *NodeB* in 3G, *evolved NodeB (eNodeB or eNB)* in 4G, and *gNodeB (gNB)* for 5G. Going forward, this book will use the generic terms *cell site* and *cell tower*, except when referring to generation-specific mobile terminologies.

Who Owns the Cell Site?

A mobile operator typically owns the equipment at a cell site, but they might not own the physical site itself. Depending on the location, a cell site can be established on a dedicated piece of land or on the roof of a building structure. Whatever the case may be, it is very likely that the physical cell site location is owned by a different company that leases the site to the mobile service provider.

The cell site owner might lease parts of the site to multiple mobile operators. Such an arrangement would include a place at the cell tower for antenna panels and RRUs as well as dedicated shelter and/or cabinet(s) at the base of the tower for BBU and other equipment.

This business model offers many benefits to a mobile operator, including cost savings, access to cell sites at favorable locations, and minimizing operational expenses. Mobile operators are increasingly moving toward a leased cell site model instead of owning their own cell sites.[9]

Types of Cell Sites

A mobile operator deploys different types of cell sites depending on the desired coverage area, location, and population density. The most commonly deployed cell type is a *macrocell* or a *macrosite*—a high-powered cell site providing mobile coverage over several kilometers. A macrosite is typically a multi-sector site that requires a large footprint to accommodate cell tower and shelter space. However, such dedicated spaces might not always be possible for specialized venues such as shopping malls, sports stadiums, or densely populated urban areas. In those scenarios, a mobile operator might deploy *small cells* in lieu of, or in addition to, macrocells.

Small cell is an umbrella term used to define multiple types of cell sites. For all intents and purposes, a small cell is functionally equivalent and has all the components of a macrocell—antennas, RU, and BBU—just at a smaller scale. Small cells are likely to be single sector sites that provide mobile coverage over a limited geographical area. Some examples of small cells include *microcells*, *metrocells*, *picocells*, and *femtocells*, each one being differentiated primarily by the service area and the number of subscribers. Depending on the scenario, a small cell can be deployed as an indoor site (shopping mall, hospital, stadium, house, and so on) or as an outdoor site (university campus, densely populated downtown, and so on).

Given the propagation characteristics of mmWave frequencies, small cells play an increasingly important role in providing adequate bandwidth and coverage in high-density areas. Figure 2-6 shows some sample cell site types.

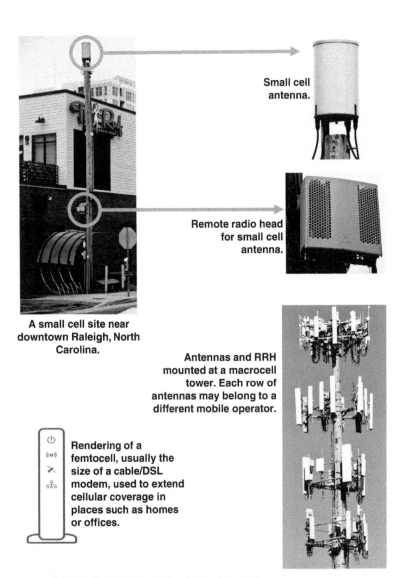

Small cell antenna.

Remote radio head for small cell antenna.

A small cell site near downtown Raleigh, North Carolina.

Antennas and RRH mounted at a macrocell tower. Each row of antennas may belong to a different mobile operator.

Rendering of a femtocell, usually the size of a cable/DSL modem, used to extend cellular coverage in places such as homes or offices.

Shelter and cabinets, likely for different mobile operators, at the base of a macrocell site.

FIGURE 2-6   Cell Site Examples

Some small cell devices, especially the ones designed for residential use, such as femtocells, have the BBU functionality embedded into the device itself. This implementation, defined in 3GPP Release 9,[10] is called a *home NodeB (HNB)* in 3G and *home eNodeB (HeNB)* in 4G. Other small cells do require an external BBU that could be placed in a centralized location if there is no room for a BBU at the small cell site. The mobile architecture, with a BBU in a central location, is called *Centralized RAN (C-RAN)* and is discussed in Chapter 3, "Mobile Networks Today." Some small cell deployments use a *distributed antenna system (DAS)*. Primarily used indoors, a DAS environment usually consists of a centralized radio unit with antennas distributed within the building. A coaxial cable, with splitters, is used to connect the radio equipment to multiple antennas.

Table 2-1 provides an overview of common cell site types and their deployment scale.

TABLE 2-1 Commonly Used Cell Site Types

Cell Type	Deployment Type	Coverage Area	Subscribers per Sector
Macrocell	Outdoor	5+ kilometers (3+ miles)	Few thousand
Microcell	Outdoor	~3 kilometers (2 miles)	Around a thousand
Metrocell	Outdoor	~1 kilometer (<1 mile)	Few dozen
Picocell	Outdoor/indoor	~ 500 meters (0.3 miles)	Couple of dozen
Femtocell	Indoor	~ 50 meters (0.03 miles)	Less than a dozen

A mobile operator would use a combination of macrosites as well as indoor and outdoor small cells, creating a *heterogenous network (HetNet)* of multiple types of cell sites. The use of different site types is aimed at providing adequate coverage and bandwidth for its subscribers.

Mobile Transport and Backhaul

When talking about mobile communication networks (MCNs), the mobile industry focuses primarily on two domains—RAN and the mobile core—as these interact closely to provide mobile services. As such, the mobile industry by and large considers the transport networks as just a pipe connecting these two mobile domains. Perhaps this disregard is a holdover from the early days of mobile networks, when transport was an ordinary point-to-point link from base stations to the central office. The transport network, however, plays a vital role in the implementation of MCNs. With the exponential growth of mobile subscribers, the scale and complexity of the transport network have grown as well, requiring sophisticated and efficient transport design. This transport network, connecting the RAN and mobile core in an MCN, is called a *mobile backhaul (MBH)* network. Figure 2-7 shows a snapshot of a typical mobile communication network comprising these three domains.

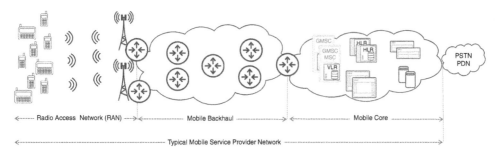

FIGURE 2-7   A Typical Mobile Communication Network

Historically, mobile and data services were offered by different service providers. In cases where mobile operators don't own the transport infrastructure, they would lease it from a network provider. For early mobile deployments, these were point-to-point T1/E1 links, but they gradually evolved to include ATM, IP, or Frame Relay after 3GPP defined IP and ATM as acceptable transport mechanisms.

Ethernet, standardized in the 1980s for use in local area networks (LANs), kept evolving by introducing higher speeds (1Gbps, 10Gbps, and higher) as well as providing the capability to be deployed over larger geographical distances. Moreover, IP and Ethernet made significant strides in quality of service (QoS) mechanisms, chipping away at the advantages of technologies offering strict service level agreements (SLAs), such as ATM. By the mid-2000s, Ethernet had started replacing T1/E1, Frame Relay, and similar technologies and established itself as a cheap and effective technology, offering superior bitrates in campus, metro, and wide area networks.

Mobile operators also saw these benefits and (slowly) started to make a similar transition toward IP. This made Ethernet and IP the de facto standards, instead of TDM and ATM, for mobile backhaul as well.

What Constitutes Mobile Backhaul Networks?

Traditionally, data networks have been organized in a three-layer hierarchy:

- **Access:** Provides network connectivity to end users or hosts
- **Aggregation (sometimes called distribution):** "Aggregates" multiple access networks (also called access domains)
- **Core:** Connects multiple aggregation networks (also called aggregation domains) to provide end-to-end connectivity

This layered network concept emerged from the early days of local and campus area networks as an effective, extensible, and scalable network architecture.

Service providers adopted a similar architecture for high-speed wide area transport networks as well. The roles of aggregation and core domains largely stayed the same as their campus network counterparts, but the access domain now provides the last mile for residential and/or business connectivity. As such, the access domain can be considered a collection of various smaller networks with a multitude of last-mile access technologies. Data Over Cable Service Interface Specifications (DOCSIS, commonly called *cable* for simplicity), Digital Subscriber Line (DSL), passive optical network (PON), and Ethernet are the most commonly used last-mile technologies in access networks.

The consolidation of Internet and mobile service providers in the early 2000s meant that the newly created, larger telecom companies now owned the RAN, MBH, and the mobile core, along with the high-speed data and Internet networks. This ownership of multiple networks created an opportunity for consolidated service providers to, over time, merge their networks for operational simplicity and cost savings.

The mobile transport networks from 3G onward, which used IP as the transport, were modeled very similar to high-speed data networks in terms of layered hierarchy. However, despite growing similarity between the mobile transport and data networks and the mergers between Internet and mobile providers, the mobility networks remained separate. The reason for keeping two parallel networks was simple—merging these was a complicated task, and the mobile networks were a source of considerable revenue, so the old "if it ain't broke, don't fix it" mentality prevailed.

Mobility and data network architects have their own unique perspectives on transport architectures. Data network architects view transport as distinct access, aggregation, and IP core domains. For these architects, MBH is just another access domain. The mobility architects, on the other hand, view the whole IP network as mobile backhaul, discounting the access, aggregation, and core boundaries. This perception is understandable given that data and mobility architects have considerably different focus areas. Figure 2-8 gives a pictorial representation of networks from a mobility architect's perspective and a network architect's perspective.

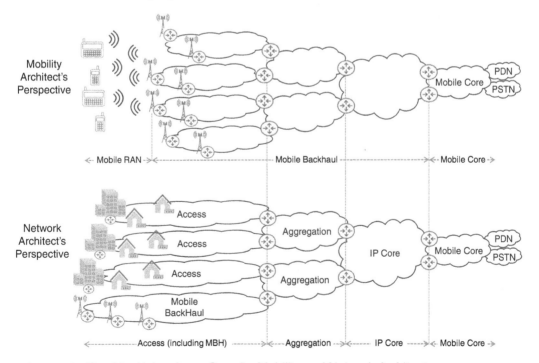

FIGURE 2-8   Provider Networks as Seen by Mobility and Network Architects

As shown in Figure 2-8, MBH networks can be considered another type of access network. As such, various connectivity models could be applied to create a robust and efficient MBH network.

Cell Site Connectivity Models

By some estimates, the United States had over 395,000 cell sites in 2019. This number was up from 104,000 in 2000 and 253,000 in 2010.[11] Most mobile operators have thousands, if not tens of thousands, of cell sites in their network, with some operators exceeding 100,000 sites. For instance, as of 2021, Reliance Jio in India has over 170,000 cell towers with tens of thousands more planned.[12] The scale of the MBH network connecting these cell sites is in stark contrast with the scale of IP core and aggregation networks where the typical device count is in the tens or hundreds of devices. Given the size of the MBH network, it typically consumes the biggest chunk of the overall mobile transport network deployment budget. Hence, an efficient and cost-effective cell site backhaul connectivity model is of paramount importance. In addition to the scale, another aspect that complicates the deployment and connectivity models for MBH networks is the geographical distribution of cell sites. These cell sites are usually deployed over large areas with varying terrain, and any connectivity model must take location diversity into account.

Considering these complications, perhaps it's not too surprising that mobile network operators utilize various connectivity models for MBH networks, as shown in Figure 2-9. The section that follows explores these connectivity models in more detail.

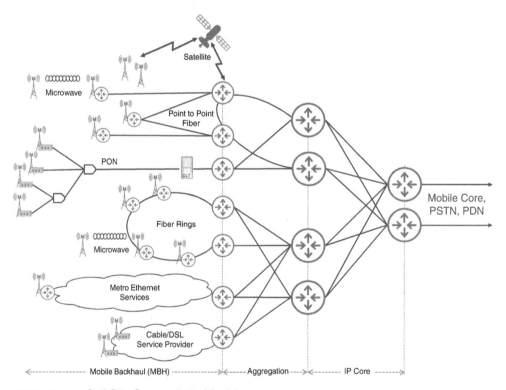

FIGURE 2-9 Cell Site Connectivity Models

Point-to-Point Fiber Connectivity

With the capability to carry massive amounts of data over longer distances, optical fiber has always been the preferred medium for transport networks. This also holds true for mobile backhaul networks where fiber connectivity could be extended from aggregation nodes to each cell site. The use of point-to-point fiber from each cell site to aggregation node is perhaps the best, albeit expensive, option to accomplish this task.

The dedicated fiber between the cell site and aggregation node(s) offers the highest bandwidth availability to and from the cell site, thus alleviating any scalability concerns resulting from increased data use from mobile subscribers. At the same time, it's easier to upgrade to a higher capacity interface (for example, 10Gbps or 100Gbps), provided the transport devices at both the aggregation and cell sites support high-capacity interfaces. Additionally, any failures such as fiber cuts or cell site router failures are also localized between the two devices and do not impact other parts of the network.

The aggregation node, however, represents a single point of failure in the access domain for all cell sites connected to it. To alleviate this, as a best practice, aggregation nodes are deployed in pairs, and cell sites can be dual-homed to both aggregation nodes for redundancy. Both single-homed and dual-homed cell sites with point-to-point fiber links were previously shown in Figure 2-9.

The two aggregation nodes to which the cell sites are dual-homed are often, but not necessarily, co-located. The dual-homed connections from the cell sites to the aggregation nodes create a Clos architecture, creating an access fabric of dual-connected nodes. The same concept could be applied in the aggregation and IP core networks (see Figure 2-10).

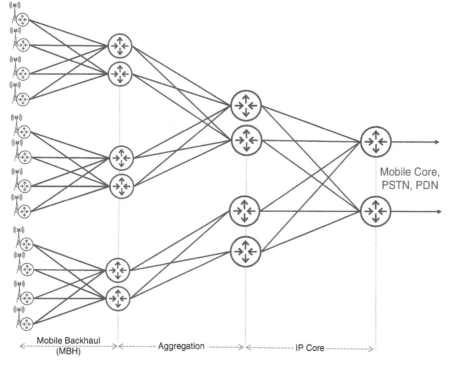

FIGURE 2-10 Clos Fabric for Mobile Backhaul Networks

> ### Clos Fabric
>
> The term *Clos fabric* refers to a hierarchical, point-to-point connectivity design that creates a partial mesh topology between, and across, different network layers. Clos fabric offers a deterministic number of hops between various devices. It is extensively used in data center architectures and is covered in detail in Chapter 7, "Essential Technologies for 5G-Ready Networks: DC Architecture and Edge Computing."

Point-to-point fiber to each individual cell site provides unparalleled architectural simplicity, flexibility, and scalability. However, the downside of such fabric-style, point-to-point fiber connectivity is its significant cost. The dedicated link for each site also requires a dedicated network interface on the aggregation node. This not only adds to the overall cost of the aggregation node(s), but also requires a larger, bulkier chassis (to accommodate a network port per cell site) that in turn needs more real estate for installation and consumes more power. This option also requires abundant fiber availability from aggregation nodes to every cell site, which could be challenging for large geographical areas. Oftentimes the projected cost of fiber deployment for an access fabric for MBH makes this option impractical.

To better balance cost and benefits, mobile operators have been exploring other options for MBH network design. One of these alternatives is to use fiber rings instead of point-to-point connections between cell site and aggregation nodes.

Fiber Rings

Fiber rings provide a healthy mix of cost and functionality in comparison to a point-to-point topology. In a ring-based deployment model, a number of cell sites are chained together, with each end of the chain connected to an aggregation node. The two aggregation nodes, marking the ends of this chain, may have a direct link between them, making it a *closed ring* as opposed to an *open ring*, where there is no link between the aggregation nodes. Both open and closed ring models are acceptable and widely deployed options, and both provide a redundant path to aggregation in case of a link failure on the ring. The ring topology depicted in Figure 2-9 is an open ring.

A ring-based topology operates with significantly fewer fiber links as compared to a point-to-point fiber connectivity model. Fiber rings also reduce the span of each fiber link, as the neighboring cell sites tend to be closer to each other than the aggregation node site. Therefore, rings allow the mobile service provider to connect a significantly higher number of cell sites with a lower fiber deployment cost. The cost savings, coupled with geographical coverage and built-in redundancy, make fiber ring topologies a favorite among mobile service providers for backhaul connectivity.

Fiber ring-based mobile backhaul deployments are not without their compromises. First and foremost, higher-capacity interfaces are required on the ring, as a plurality of cell sites share the same connection. Latency is another concern, as traffic from a cell site router now traverses more devices, and potentially longer distances, before getting to the aggregation node. The increased latency could have an impact on latency-sensitive services.

It's hard to estimate how many cell sites are currently deployed using fiber rings, as providers tend not to publish this level of design and deployment choices, but it's fair to say that ring-based topologies are overwhelmingly preferred by service providers for their MBH deployments.

Passive Optical Networks (PONs)

Developed as a last-mile access technology, passive optical networks (PONs) provide fiber access to the end user, who could be a residential subscriber, an enterprise, or, in the case of MBH, a cell site.

A PON operates as a two-device solution, consisting of an *optical line termination (OLT*, sometimes called an *optical line terminal*) and an *optical network termination (ONT*, also called an *optical network unit*, or *ONU*). The OLT resides at the aggregation site, whereas the ONT or ONU is the user-side device that, in the case of MBH, resides at the cell site.

ONT vs. ONU

The terms *ONT* and *ONU* are frequently used interchangeably, the difference being that ONT is used in ITU-T defined standards, while ONU is used by IEEE. An ONT was initially considered more feature-rich than an ONU, but that distinction is almost negligible today.[13]

This book will refer to the user-side equipment of a PON as ONT.

The optical network that connects the OLT and ONT, called the *optical distribution network (ODN)*, uses a single strand of fiber with different wavelengths for upstream and downstream communication. An optical splitter, a passive mechanical device, splits this single strand of fiber from the OLT into 2, 4, 8, 16, or more branches to create point-to-multipoint connectivity between the OLT and ONT. The technology gets its name from the *passive* nature of the splitter; that is, it does not require any power to operate. Multiple optical splitters can be cascaded, resulting in flexible topologies to match a provider's fiber availability. An OLT has multiple PON interfaces, with each one connecting to multiple cell sites, as shown in Figure 2-11.

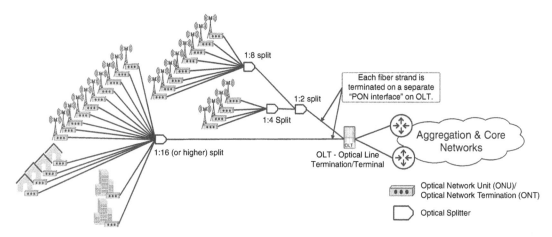

FIGURE 2-11   Passive Optical Networks for Mobile Backhaul

There is a one-to-many relationship between the OLT and the ONT, where upon bootup, every ONT registers with its respective OLT and downloads its configuration. PON is a TDM-based technology, where an OLT acts as a "controller" for all the ONTs registered with it, providing each one with a timeslot for upstream and downstream communication.

PON has been an effective technology that brings fiber access to consumers and businesses at a reasonable cost to network operators. PON standards have evolved over the years to keep up with growing adoption and demands. Some of the popular PON variations are *Gigabit PON (GPON)*, *XGPON (10 Gig PON), Next Generation PON (NG-PON)*, and its subsequent evolution, *NG-PON2*. Each one of these standards extends the bandwidth available per PON port as well as the total number of subscribers that can be connected over a single port. GPON, for instance, offers 2.4Gbps downstream and 1.2Gbps upstream bandwidth with up to 64 nodes (128 in some cases) on a single GPON interface. NG-PON2, by contrast, offers 40Gbps downstream and 10Gbps upstream with a split ratio of up to 1:256 (that is, a single NG-PON2 port could support 256 ONTs).

The lower cost of the solution comes from the use of flexible fiber layout, as well as the cost of the equipment itself. The passive optical splitter is a low-cost, compact device that could be installed anywhere without having to worry about power availability. The ONT is an inexpensive optical-to-electrical converter with limited functionality that can often be implemented on a pluggable transceiver. A single PON interface on the OLT can terminate dozens of ONTs, further reducing the overall cost of a PON-based solution.

The total bandwidth of a PON interface is shared among all the ONTs connected to that interface. A higher split ratio means a larger number of ONTs connected on the same PON port, resulting in less bandwidth for each individual ONT. In an MBH network, this means the cell site's throughput is dependent on the split ratio, with an inverse relationship between the split ratio used and total bandwidth available.

Microwave Links

All the mobile backhaul models discussed thus far require fiber connectivity all the way to the cell site. In many cases, however, getting fiber to a cell site might not be possible or feasible. Difficult terrain, unusually long distances to remote cell sites, high cost of deployment, challenges in obtaining necessary permits for fiber trenching, and meeting time to market goals are some of the reasons why a mobile network operator may forgo wired connectivity to cell sites in favor of wireless options.

One of the wireless options is *microwave*, a line-of-sight technology that uses *directional* antennas to transmit and receive traffic between two fixed locations. Using microwaves, the cell sites could either be connected directly to the aggregation nodes or daisy chained. Figure 2-12 shows sample mobile backhaul topologies using fiber and microwave.

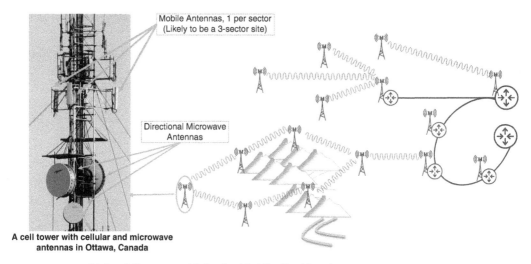

Mobile Antennas, 1 per sector
(Likely to be a 3-sector site)

Directional Microwave
Antennas

A cell tower with cellular and microwave
antennas in Ottawa, Canada

FIGURE 2-12 Using Microwave Links for Mobile Backhaul

While fiber is the preferred connectivity option for MBH networks, microwave links offer an opportunity to extend connectivity to cell sites quickly and often at a lower cost. Microwaves do have considerable drawbacks in terms of link speed and stability. Because microwave requires direct line of sight, careful planning is essential to ensure there are no obstacles (natural or man-made) between microwave sites, taking into account future vegetation growth and construction plans. Microwave links are also susceptible to atmospheric conditions, and link performance could deteriorate in unfavorable weather conditions. Nonetheless, due to shortened deployment timelines and cost savings, microwave is a popular backhaul connectivity choice for mobile operators, even though microwave links provide significantly lower bandwidth compared to fiber links. A combination of fiber and microwave offers a mobile operator flexible options to create a backhaul topology. As of 2017, microwave links accounted for more than 56% of all MBH links due to widespread adoption of the technology in developing regions.[14]

Metro Ethernet Services

As Ethernet gained popularity, it created a growing need for standardized Ethernet services for metro and wide area networks. Metro Ethernet Forum (MEF), a nonprofit consortium of network operators and equipment vendors, was created in 2001 with an objective of expanding Ethernet from a LAN-based technology to a "carrier class" service over long distances.

MEF Certification

To help Ethernet become a reliable and robust form of WAN communication technology, MEF created standardized service definitions, established common terminologies, and devised service attributes. MEF also created a certification program, where equipment vendors and network operators can get their products and service offerings certified. The certification ensures that both the Metro Ethernet products as well service offerings adhere to the various service guidelines and attributes defined by MEF.

The services defined by MEF are commonly referred to as *MEF services, Metro Ethernet services,* or *Carrier Ethernet Services* and are broadly classified into three categories:

- **Ethernet Line (E-Line) services:** *Point-to-point* services between two sites, similar to a leased line such as T1/E1.

- **Ethernet LAN (E-LAN):** *Multipoint* services between multiple sites, similar to how multiple individual nodes communicate in a LAN.

- **Ethernet Tree (E-Tree):** *Rooted multipoint services* where multiple end nodes communicate with a few select "root" nodes. The end nodes are not allowed to communicate between themselves directly, similar to legacy Frame Relay services.

MEF services operate independently of the underlying physical medium and topology and can be implemented over fiber rings, fabric, PON, or wireless technologies such as microwave. Figure 2-13 shows a view of these E-Line, E-LAN, and E-Tree services.

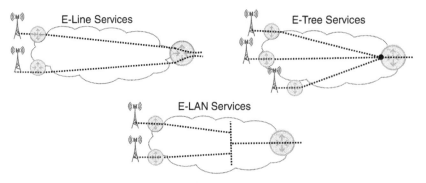

FIGURE 2-13   Metro Ethernet Services for Mobile Backhaul

Metro Ethernet services play a significant role in providing backhaul connectivity. Mobile operators that do not own their own transport can purchase Metro Ethernet services from data service providers, whereas the ones that do may implement MEF services to provide connectivity from cell sites to the rest of the network. A detailed implementation of MEF services is covered in Chapter 8, "Essential Technologies for 5G-Ready Networks: Transport Services," and its application in mobile networks is discussed in Chapter 10, "Designing and Implementing 5G Network Architecture."

Cable and DSL

Commercial Internet services such as cable and Digital Subscriber Line (DSL) are additional low-cost cell site connectivity options for backhaul networks. These technologies were originally designed to provide Internet access for residential and business subscribers and are geared toward best-effort quality of service with relatively low bandwidth.

Cable and DSL might be good connectivity options for smaller cell sites catering to a limited number of mobile subscribers but are not suitable for typical macrocell sites that offer mobile services over a larger geographical area. The use of cable and DSL in mobile backhaul has been steadily declining and being replaced with fiber or microwave.

Satellite

In rare cases, satellite-based communications from cell sites can be used for mobile backhaul. Traditionally, satellite backhaul has been a costly connectivity mechanism, offering lower speeds and higher latency, when compared to most of its terrestrial counterparts. Recent advancements in satellite technology have, to some extent, addressed the cost challenges. Latency, however, continues to be a major concern with satellite-based backhaul communications. Depending on the satellite orbit (low-earth, mid-earth, or geosynchronous), the round-trip latency from cell sites may range from tens to hundreds of milliseconds, which might not be feasible for latency-sensitive applications.

Satellite-based backhaul might be useful for some outlying cell sites due to their isolated or remote locations. Providers might also use satellites as a temporary, stopgap measure while building out their microwave or wired networks. Satellite links make up less than 2% of total backhaul links and are expected to remain a niche option for backhaul connectivity.[15]

Mobile Core Concepts

What started as a then-sophisticated mobile switching center in the first generation of mobile communication slowly transformed into a set of individual devices implementing multiple functions to provide the mobile services. These devices perform functions such as mobile device registration, processing and switching mobile traffic (both voice and data), implementing and managing subscriber policies, usage tracking, and billing support—essentially acting as the brain of the mobile network. This brain of the mobile communication network (MCN) is called "mobile core."

The evolution of mobile core's individual functional blocks has been extensively discussed in the previous chapter. This evolution of functionality was accompanied by changes to how mobile core devices are physically deployed and connected. For someone designing or implementing the RAN and

MBH, the mobile core appears as a monolithic block that they are connecting to. However, in reality, the mobile core is geographically spread out.

In the initial days of cellular services, the mobile core (just the MSC and some databases at that time) served small geographical regions where they were deployed. Though these MSCs were initially connected using PSTN, data technologies such as Frame Relay, ATM, and eventually IP/Ethernet started to dominate this connectivity landscape over subsequent years. Mergers of many data network providers and mobile service providers further bolstered this transition through reduced cost of long-haul data links that could meet the growing bandwidth demands of inter-MSC communication. Mobile providers therefore started using leased (or owned) data links to connect the geographically spread mobile core devices.

The distributed nature of this mobile core resulted in higher deployment, management, and maintenance costs. To lower that expense, mobile operators found it attractive to try consolidating the data centers hosting mobile core devices and reducing the devices' footprint. There were a few key challenges that initially hindered such consolidation:

- The subscriber scale supported by the mobile core devices would limit the coverage area per device.

- The cost associated with backhauling the traffic from the cell site to mobile core would increase with distance.

- Due to their higher serialization delays, the lower capacity links would result in higher latency and degraded user experience.

Over the years, multiple factors and innovations contributed to overcoming these challenges. The multifold increase in devices' capacity and performance allowed a fewer number of mobile core devices to serve subscribers over a larger geographical region. At the same time, technological improvements resulted in higher-bandwidth links with lower serialization delays, which made it possible to cover larger distances within the same latency budget. Business mergers yet again supported the transition as the cost of backhaul connectivity decreased with network consolidations. The resulting reduction in mobile core footprint and its geographical consolidation still required an optimal balance between backhaul cost, device scalability, and network latency to be considered. Therefore, the RAN-facing devices had limited room for consolidation due to these limiting factors. On the other hand, devices, such as databases and authentication servers, implementing functions internal to the mobile core could be consolidated even further into a few central locations.

The resulting architecture is a geographically distributed mobile core, with some devices in centralized data centers, with other devices in data centers forming the periphery of this distributed mobile core. PSTN, PLMN, and PDN gateways were also consolidated to select locations on this periphery—determined based on requirements and traffic load of the various geographical markets. Figure 2-14 shows this geographical deployment layout of the mobile core.

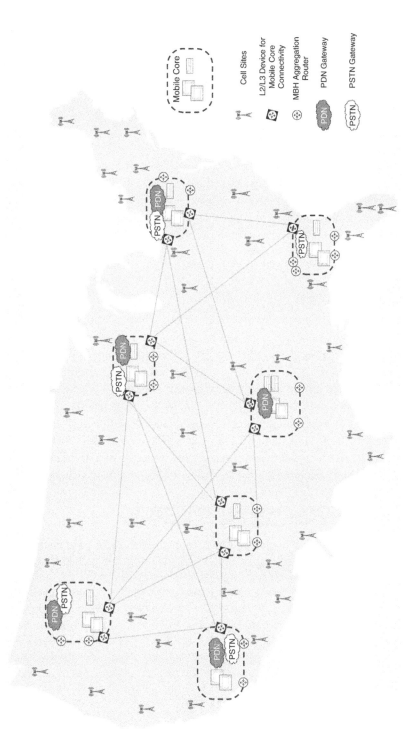

FIGURE 2-14 A Geographical Layout of a Mobile Core

By the third generation of mobile networks, the functions within the mobile core could be broadly placed into three categories:

- Voice traffic signaling, processing, and switching

- Data traffic signaling, processing, and forwarding

- Databases to store subscriber information and usage details

As voice traffic was historically handled using circuit switched networks, the part of the mobile core performing those functions was dubbed *circuit switched core*. On the other hand, starting with 2.5G, the data traffic functions were implemented as a packet switched network and consequently dubbed *packet switched core*, or simply *packet core*. The databases supporting the functions such as user registration and authentication continued to be part of the circuit switched core, even though the packet core also made use of them.

Circuit Switched Core

Up until 3G, the voice traffic in mobile networks was circuit switched, with the MSC performing the functions of user registration, call routing and establishment, switching the voice circuit between end users, intra- and inter-provider roaming, and so on. For calls that originated or terminated outside the provider network, Gateway-MSC (G-MSC) were used—which would perform all the regular MSC functions and additionally connect with the PSTN. In later releases of 3G, the MSC was split into MSC-Server (MCS-S) and Media-Gateway (MGW). The MSC-S inherited the signaling responsibilities of the MSC, while the voice circuit was established via MGWs. In 3G, IP started to take center stage to interconnect MSCs, or rather their 3G equivalents—MGW and MSC-S. This resulted in new frameworks such as SIGTRAN that defined the use of SS7 protocols over IP transport. However, the use of circuit switched voice continued to exist and hence the name "circuit switched core."

> ### Visited MSC (V-MSC) and Gateway MSC (G-MSC)
>
> All MSCs in the 2G network have the responsibility to manage multiple base station controllers. These MSCs are interconnected and can route calls to and from the mobile handsets that are registered to it. For calls that originate or terminate from networks outside the mobile provider's network (for example, PSTN and other mobile providers), a small subset of these MSCs has connectivity to external networks and acts as a gateway to those networks. Consequently, these MSCs are referred to as *Gateway MSC (G-MSC)*. The MSC where a mobile subscriber is registered is referred to as *Visited MSC (V-MSC)* for that subscriber. The G-MSCs still serve as V-MSCs for the BSCs they manage but perform the additional functions of gateways to external networks.

Identifiers and Databases in Mobile Networks

The user registration and communication flow makes use of various identifiers. The identifiers used are stored in various databases as well as the SIM card and mobile handset.

Subscriber Identification Module (SIM) Card

GSM introduced the concept of the SIM card, which is a small card with a microcontroller and memory built into it. SIM cards are meant to securely store the user's identifying information and provide that information to the mobile service provider when authenticating and registering the user. A subscriber can therefore use the mobile service by plugging their SIM card into any compatible mobile device.

Figure 2-15 shows where these identifiers were originally stored.

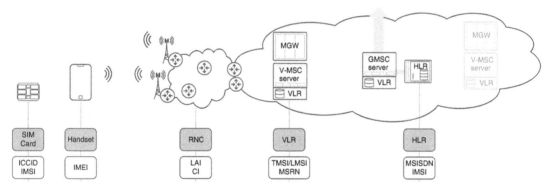

FIGURE 2-15   Owners of Key Identifiers in a Mobile Network

Table 2-2 summarizes the identifiers and their use.

TABLE 2-2   Summary of Identifiers Used in Mobile Communication Network

Identifier	Description and Purpose
Integrated Circuit Card Identifier (ICCID)	The ICCID is used to uniquely identify a SIM card. It's up to 22 digits long—starting with "89," representing the Telecom Industry. The ISSID is followed by Mobile Country Code (MCC), Mobile Network Code (MNC), a provider-generated serial number, and a single-digit checksum (C).
International Mobile Subscriber Identity (IMSI)	IMSI uniquely identifies a mobile subscriber and is assigned upon signing up for the mobile service. IMSI is typically 16 digits long, comprising the MCC, MNC, a unique serial number generated by the provider called the mobile subscriber identification number (MSIN), and finally a single-digit checksum. IMSI is securely stored within the SIM card's memory as well as the mobile provider's databases.
International Mobile Equipment Identity (IMEI)	IMEI is a unique 15-digit number associated with a mobile device. The first eight digits of IMEI, referred to as the type allocation code, encodes information about the device manufacturer and model number. These are followed by a serial number specific to the manufacturer (six digits) and finally a check digit to verify the integrity of the other values. IMEI can be used to track and/or block stolen and grey market devices from connecting to the mobile network.
Home Network Identity (HNI) or Public Land Mobile Network (PLMN)	The service provider is uniquely identified using the combination of MCC and MNC values. This value is referred to as HNI or PLMN.
Mobile Station International Subscriber Directory Number (MSISDN)	The MSISDN is what the mobile subscribers generally refer to as their phone number. It is mapped to the IMSI in the mobile provider's database. The MSISDN comprises a country code (up to three digits), a national destination code (up to three digits), and a subscriber number that can be up to 10 digits long.
Mobile Station Roaming Number (MSRN)	To facilitate the routing of calls within the mobile core, the visiting MSC assigns a temporary number to the subscriber, called the MSRN. It is locally significant within the network of the provider and uses the same format as the MSISDN.
Temporary Mobile Subscriber Identity (TMSI)	TMSI is a temporary identity assigned to the mobile subscriber to use in lieu of the IMSI, which is kept secret and used only during registration to secure the privacy of the subscriber from eavesdroppers.
Local Mobile Station Identity (LMSI)	LMSI is another temporary value assigned to the subscriber with the purpose of acting as a pointer to the database for faster IMSI lookup.
Cell Identification (CI) value	CI is a byte value that uniquely identifies a cell site.
Location Area Code (LAC) and Location Area Identifier (LAI)	The cells in the mobile network are grouped together into location areas, and a 16-bit identifier called the LAC is used to represent that area. The LAC, MCC, and MNC are broadcasted as a single value referred to as the LAI.

Figure 2-16 illustrates the format of these identifiers.

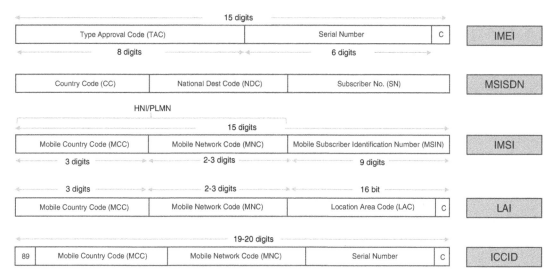

FIGURE 2-16   Formats for Key Identifiers in a Mobile Network

In the mobile core, the four mentionable databases where these identifiers are stored are the HLR, VLR, AuC, and EIR, as described in the sections that follow.

Home Location Register (HLR)

The Home Location Register (HLR) was introduced in the previous chapter as a database containing information of all the mobile users. Expanding that definition further, the HLR is the mobile service provider's master database where a subscriber's information is populated upon signing up for the service. This information includes the subscriber's phone number (MSISDN), the IMSI value allocated, types of services subscribed, permissions and privileges, and authentication information. Additionally, the HLR also stores some runtime information about the subscriber, such as knowledge of the MSC currently serving the subscriber.

There are usually just a handful of HLR nodes across the mobile provider's network, and these are geographically distributed. All MSCs communicate with HLR in their network to pull subscriber information.

Visited Location Register (VLR)

In contrast to HLR, the Visited Location Register (VLR) databases are individually associated with each MSC. In fact, VLRs have been typically bundled within the MSC hardware instead of being implemented as separate database servers. When a user enters any MSC's coverage area, making it the Visited MSC (V-MSC), that V-MSC queries its local VLR for information to authenticate, register, and authorize the user. The VLR entries are temporary and will contain information only about the subscribers that are either currently or were recently registered with its associated MSC. If the user information does not already exist in the VLR, it reaches out to the HLR and copies over the subscriber information to its own database. This makes the VLR a sort of cache database for HLR, hence reducing the number of queries that V-MSCs would need to send toward the HLR. Regardless of whether the user information is already present in the local VLR or needs to be fetched from the HLR, the V-MSC always informs the HLR when it registers the user. This helps the HLR to keep track of which MSC is serving as the subscriber's V-MSC. When any other MSC, including the G-MSC, receives a call meant for that user, it can consult the HLR for the V-MSC information to route the call to that V-MSC.

VLR also allocates some local temporary parameters to the user, some of which are copied to HLR. Figure 2-17 shows a high-level view of the information stored in the HLR database and VLR databases as well as the permanent fields that are copied from HLR to VLR upon user registration.

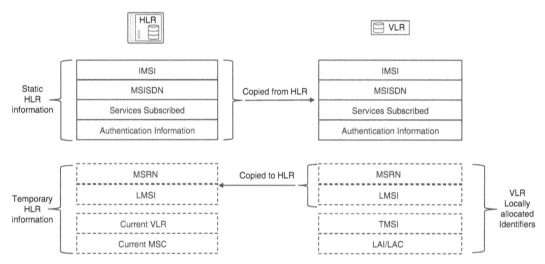

FIGURE 2-17   HLR and VLR Entries at a Glance

Among the identifiers mentioned previously, the TMSI, LMSI, and LAI/LAC are allocated by the V-MSC locally and stored in its own VLR, as depicted in Figure 2-17. MSRN is also locally assigned, but because the rest of the network needs to be made aware of this number being assigned to the subscriber (for calls to be routed to the V-MSC), the MSRN value is copied over to the HLR as a temporary piece of information mapped to the IMSI of that subscriber.

Authentication Center (AuC)

The Authentication Center was previously mentioned as the database that facilitates authentication and authorization of mobile subscribers. Specifically, it stores unique key values mapped to each subscriber's IMSI. A copy of that key is also safely stored in the user's SIM card. When validating the subscriber's identity, the VLR queries the HLR, which then communicates with the AuC. The AuC uses the key stored against the user's IMSI to authenticate the user. This key is also used by the mobile device and the AuC to generate a cipher for encrypting radio communication.[16]

Equipment Identity Register (EIR)

This purpose of the Equipment Identity Register (EIR) is to verify the equipment being used by the subscriber. The EIR stores the devices' IMEI that may be explicitly allowed or restricted on an operator network. Some of the information in EIR may include the IMEI values for mobile devices that have been reported as lost, stolen, fraudulent, or illegal. During the authentication process, the IMEI of the user's device is cross-checked against the EIR stored values to ensure that the device should be allowed to register with the mobile network.

User Registration and Call Flow

The subscriber information initially exists only in three places—the HLR and AuC of the service provider as well as the SIM card provided to the subscriber. Once the subscriber plugs the SIM card into a mobile device and turns it on, the device scans its supported frequencies for carrier information broadcasts, which includes, among other parameters, the PLMN (MCC+MNC) of the service provider. The mobile device will also read the SIM card's ICCID and match the PLMN values from the SIM card to the PLMN values in the broadcasts. If a match is found, the device continues to the registration process. If a match is not found (that is, the subscriber is not within the coverage area of its service provider), the selection process randomly chooses other available PLMN values and attempts the registration process. For a selected PLMN, the mobile handset sends the IMSI (extracted from the SIM card) and the IMEI of the device as part of the registration request.

The MSC that receives this information (V-MSC) checks if its VLR records contain information about this IMSI. If it doesn't, the HLR is consulted to verify that the IMSI value is authorized to use cellular services. The HLR ensures that the IMSI belongs to an existing subscriber and then passes the IMSI to its corresponding AuC to authenticate the user. At the same time, it checks the EIR to ensure that the IMEI of the user's device is not in any list that is not allowed to register.

AuC looks up the subscriber's secret key using the IMSI value and then performs a 128-bit hash on a randomly generated number using that key. It passes the result of that encryption back to the HLR along with the random number used. This random number is sent to the subscriber as a challenge, where the hash is now performed by the SIM card using the key stored on it. Results of both hash calculations—the one performed by AuC and that performed on SIM card—should be identical as long as the key values match. Hence, the hash calculations from the SIM are sent to the V-MSC, which compares these values and completes the authentication process if there is a match.

Once the subscriber is authenticated, the subscriber's static information from the HLR is copied over to the local VLR. Additionally, the HLR is updated about the MSC where the subscriber is registered (that is, the V-MSC). The V-MSC will also allocate the TMSI identifier (to be used for subsequent communication with the mobile handset) and notify the device about its current TMSI value. The MSRN is also allocated and populated in the VLR and HLR databases.[17]

To complete the registration, the mobile handset updates the V-MSC about its selected LAI and CI values. This helps the V-MSC keep track of the cell tower being used. At this point, the device is ready to make and receive phone calls. Interestingly, the device doesn't need to know its own phone number (MSISDN). Instead, the IMSI/TMSI values identify the subscriber to the MSC, which then maps these to the subscriber's MSISDN for outgoing calls. Figure 2-18 summarizes this subscriber registration process.

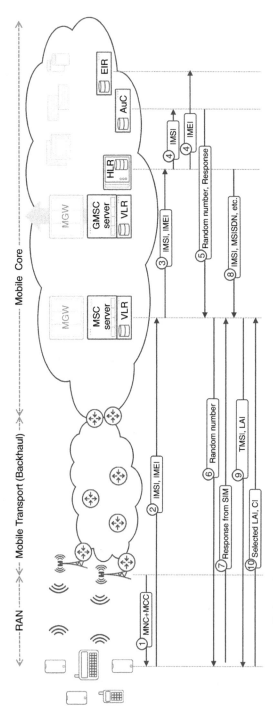

FIGURE 2-18   Subscriber Registration Process

Once the subscriber is registered with the network, the HLR keeps track of the V-MSC/VLR serving this subscriber. For any incoming call for this subscriber's MSISDN number, whether originating within or outside the mobile provider's network, the G-MSC will be consulted to route the call. For calls within the network, the G-MSC notifies the caller's MSC about the called subscriber's MSRN. The MSRN can then be used to route the call to the V-MSC. If the call has originated in a different telephony network, the G-MSC will use the MSRN to route the call to the V-MSC. At the same time, a bearer channel is established between the V-MSC and the caller's MSC (or G-MSC, if the call originated from outside the PLMN). In both cases, the V-MSC will send a call-setup message to the subscriber's TMSI, within the currently known area of the subscriber (using the LAI value stored in the VLR). Once the call is confirmed by the callee's device, a bearer channel is established over the air interface between the callee's device and the V-MSC. Figure 2-19 shows this call-setup process.

For calls made by the subscriber, initially the mobile device requests allocation of a bearer from the mobile network. Once the bearer is provided, the caller's V-MSC determines reachability to the dialed number by consulting the G-MSC. If this number is outside the network, the call is routed to the G-MSC, which can then route externally. If the number is registered with the network, the previously described steps take place.

Packet Switched Core

Although the first two generations of mobile networks were voice-centric and did not offer dedicated data transmission service, it was still possible to use data by establishing a modem connection to a remote fax machine or email server. The data rates for such modem connections were much lower compared to dial-up over PSTN.

Data speeds were slightly improved by making 2G networks aware of data transmission within a circuit switched connection. Indeed, a 2G mobile device didn't feature a real modem. The mobile devices used a traffic adaptation function instead to fit the data transmission into a digital traffic channel while the actual modulation and demodulation happened at the MSC. Although this helped to achieve data transmission speeds of 14.4Kbps over a single traffic channel or even 57.6Kbps over multiple concatenated timeslots, a significant innovation was needed to boost data transmission rates and capabilities of the mobile network. It was inevitable that circuit switched data would be replaced by packet switched data communication in the mobile core.

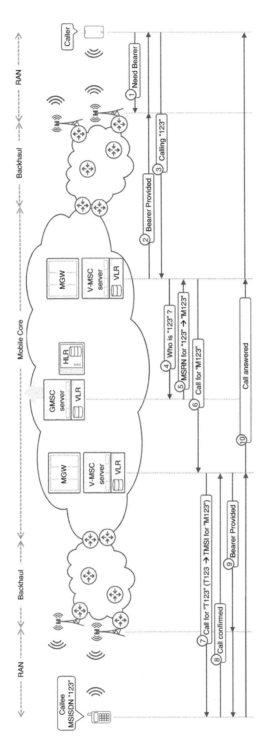

FIGURE 2-19   End-to-End Call Flow

Packet Switched Data

The technological jump from circuit switched data communication to packet switched required significant mobile core innovations and new functions. These new functions were separated from MSC in second-generation (2G) mobile networks and implemented as new nodes for scalability and efficiency. These nodes were collectively called the General Packet Radio Service (GPRS) sub-system (GSS) and became the foundation of what was later dubbed a "packet core" in 3G networks. In addition to GSS, a typical packet core uses other supplementary components such as Domain Name System (DNS) servers, Dynamic Host Configuration Protocol (DHCP) servers, and Authentication Authorization Accounting (AAA) servers.

The GPRS sub-system did not significantly change in 3G, save for some enhancements to allow 3G-specific interfaces and flows. Even in the fourth-generation (4G) mobile networks (which will be discussed in the next chapter), many GSS components can be easily identified, albeit with some changes in node names and certain functions redistributed.

GPRS Sub-System (GSS)

GSS comprises two GPRS support nodes (GSNs) called the *Serving GPRS Support Node (SGSN)* and *Gateway GPRS Support Node (GGSN)*. Collectively, the GSN implement functions critical for packet switched data services such as preparation of data packets for transmission over the air interface, routing, traffic management, data encryption/decryption, and IP address allocations. This is in addition to other mobile functions (for example, subscriber tracking across different cells or roaming to other networks, billing, and lawful intercept).

SGSN's primarily role is to control the subscriber's session and data packet delivery between the mobile phone and mobile core. GGSN, on the other hand, is responsible for grooming and routing data packets to and from the Internet, intranets, or other external packet networks and mobile core. In other words, whereas SGSN is the mobile-phone-facing node, GGSN is a gateway between external packet networks and the mobile core. Simply put, SGSN provides session management, whereas GGSN provides connectivity to the Internet and other data networks.

While physically SGSN looks more like yet another rack with modules and various interfaces, it is common for a GGSN to be implemented using an IP router with specialized modules and interfaces to communicate with the rest of mobile core.

SGSN, GGSN, and PDP Context

Before a mobile subscriber can use data service, a series of exchanges has to take place between the mobile phone, GPRS sub-system, and other components of the mobile core. A mobile device's request for data service triggers an SGSN inquiry into the HLR to authenticate and authorize use of network resources by the subscriber. SGSN also notifies the HLR about the subscriber's location.

Once the subscriber is attached to the network, the mobile device has to negotiate additional parameters to access data services. These include the type of PDN it is allowed to access (public vs. private), QoS policies, and IP address allocation. Collectively, these parameters along with the assigned billing profile comprise a subscriber-specific *Packet Data Protocol (PDP) context.*

Note

The PDP context may be perceived as a subscriber's data profile, defining what PDNs can be accessed and how. The PDP context is an essential construct to bring data connectivity to the mobile device.

The request for PDP context activation is sent by a mobile device to its serving SGSN, and the SGSN must forward this request to a GGSN. A typical mobile network has a number of GGSNs deployed, with each GGSN providing access to one or more PDNs. Depending on the request, the SGSN selects the appropriate GGSN to forward this request.

Among other parameters, a PDP context activation includes an *access point name (APN)*, which is akin to a fully qualified domain name (FQDN) in data networks. An APN serves as a reference to a particular GGSN and a specific PDN connection within that GGSN. The APN scope is limited to the collection of PLMN networks bound by roaming agreements and has no meaning outside of it.

Access Point Name (APN)

A typical APN might look like the following string: *internet.operatorname.gprs*. It can be viewed and changed in the mobile device settings and, in most cases, is automatically pulled from a subscriber's SIM card. It is not uncommon for a phone to have more than one APN configured and used.

SGSN resolves the requested APN to a GGSN's IP address using PLMN internal DNS servers and sends the request to activate PDP context to this GGSN. In turn, GGSN may consult with AAA server to ensure a user is authorized to use a particular PDN and, upon successful authorization, allocates an IP address to the mobile device using a local or external DHCP server. Once the PDP context is created, the GGSN responds back to the SGSN with the PDP context, including the IP address, and is ready to route packets between mobile device and the respective PDN. GGSN also maps the session to QoS profiles and ACLs. Figure 2-20 shows the PDP context activation process and GPRS data flows.

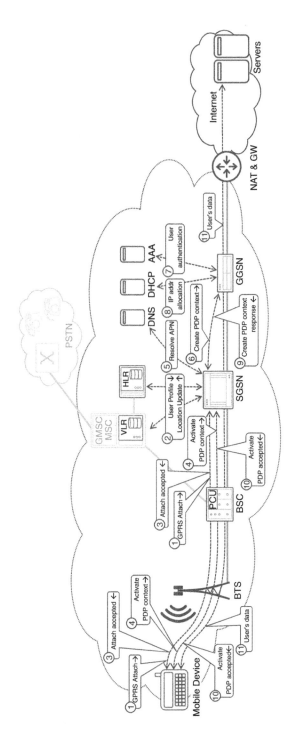

FIGURE 2-20 GPRS Data Flows

The PDP context in the SGSN–GGSN pair remains active as long as the GPRS subscriber is attached and reachable. When a mobile device roams into another SGSN serving area, the "new" SGSN pulls the existing PDP context from the "old" SGSN and updates the HLR with the new location. The parameters associated with the PDP context (such as the IP address) stay the same, even though the subscriber is now being served by a new SGSN.

With PDP context activated, the network is now ready to provide data services. When the subscriber starts exchanging data with the PDN, both the SGSN and GGSN generate charging tickets and supply usage data to the billing system. Additionally, the SGSN and GGSN can be a point of lawful intercept functions.

If a mobile device moves out of reach and remains unreachable for a certain time duration, it is detached from the GPRS network and the PDP context is deactivated. A mobile device can also voluntarily request a GPRS detach, and once this is completed, it can no longer send or receive data until it reattaches to the GRPS network.

GPRS Interfaces

These sophisticated series of communications between multiple mobile core entities require a number of interfaces and protocols. Earlier mobile core entities were not IP-enabled and used many legacy protocols and interfaces from the circuit switched world. Being new and based on packet switching, the GPRS sub-system adopted IP for communications between SGSN, GGSN, and supplemental DNS AAA and DHCP servers. Yet, they needed to support other interfaces and protocols to communicate with other mobile core nodes.

> **Note**
>
> In the mobility world, the term *interface* is also used to define connectivity reference points, as defined by 3GPP. These are meant to standardize communication between various functions.

Figure 2-21 provides a view of GPRS interfaces with their relation to mobile core nodes. The shaded area represents the packet core.

The few mentionable interfaces are Gi and Gn/Gp. Gi is an IP interface and connects the GGSN to the external PDN, such as the Internet or intranets. Gn and Gp interfaces connect the SGSN and GGSN and are very similar in nature. While the Gn interface connects the SGSN and GGSN belonging to the same PLMN, the Gp interface provides connectivity between the SGSN and GGSN in different PLMNs. These interfaces used IP over ATM as the transport in some early implementations but have since moved to IP over Ethernet.

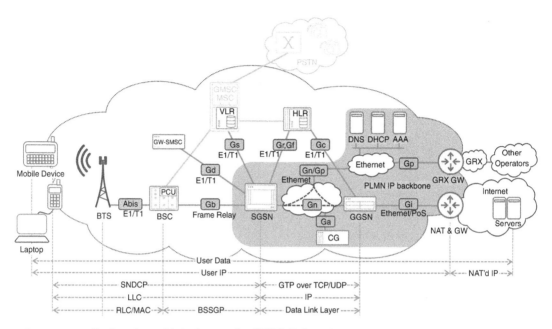

FIGURE 2-21   Protocols and Interfaces of a GPRS Subsystem

The figure also highlights some of the protocols used in GPRS. Base Station Subsystem GPRS Protocol (BSSGP) is used to transport data units of upper protocols and layers between SGSN and PCU components of the BSC. These data units are then relayed by the PCU/BSC to mobile phones using Radio Link Control/Medium Access Control (RLC/MAC) over the air interface. Upper layer protocols used over BSSGP are SubNetwork Dependent Convergence Protocol (SNDCP) and Logical Link Control Layer (LLC). This tandem is used to reliably transport data units belonging to different subscribers, all the way to their mobile phones, as these layers extend from the SGSN beyond the BSC and reach the mobile phones.

GPRS Tunneling Protocol (GTP)

Despite both the subscriber's data and GGSN-SGSN communication happening over IP, it is not feasible to use a subscriber's IP address for routing inside the packet core for several reasons. Instead of using IP natively, the subscriber's IP packets are transported in a tunnel between the SGSN and GGSN, using GPRS Tunneling Protocol (GTP) to provide traffic isolation. GTP tunnels also help avoid routing complications within the packet core and shield the subscriber's data sessions from changes when a user moves between different SGSNs. When a serving SGSN changes, it pulls the existing PDP context details from the "old" serving SGSN and updates the corresponding GGSN. This way, no changes are required in the packet core IP transport routing protocols, and the subscriber's IP address can stay unchanged during handovers. Figure 2-22 shows GTP tunnels established between GSNs.

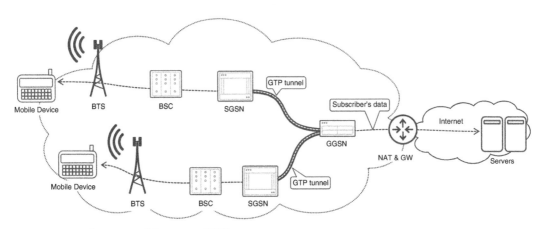

FIGURE 2-22   GTP Tunnel Between GSNs

GTP is a TLV-based protocol, and besides transporting user data it is also used to deliver many types of control messages to establish and tear down tunnels, exchange information between GSNs, and so on. GTP also supports keepalive messages between GSN nodes to verify if their counterparts are alive and responsive.

A new GTP tunnel between the SGSN and GGSN is created each time a PDP context is activated. A subscriber might have multiple GTP tunnels and certain fields within the GTP frame (such as Flow Label and Tunnel Identifier, or TID), which can be used to uniquely identify the tunnel, subscriber, and the PDP context for transported data.

The initial release of the GPRS specification defined version 0 of GTP, which supported transport over both TCP and UDP with a well-known port of 3386. Because the same port number is used for all GTP communications in version 0, the only way to distinguish whether the GTP packets are carrying encapsulated subscriber datagrams, or signaling messages, is to look at the TLV values and the reference interface a packet belongs to (the Gn, Gp, or Ga interface).

In Release 99, GTPv1 was defined as a new version of GTP, bringing additional TLVs for signaling and replacing TID with Tunnel Endpoint ID (TEID). GTPv1 also distinguishes GTP-C for control plane traffic and GTP-U for data. UDP and TCP port numbers were also changed to 2123 for GTP-C and 2125 for GTP-U.[18] Even though GPRS was defined in 2G with GTPv0, today GTPv1 is used in 2G, 3G, and partially in 4G networks. 3GPP introduced GTPv2 in Release 8, which included enhancements in the control plane (that is, GTPv2-C), while leaving the user plane intact.[19]

Although earlier releases specified support for GTP over both TCP and UDP, the majority of implementations favored UDP. This resulted in the removal of TCP support for GTP-C and GTP-U protocols from 3GPP specifications.[20]

With the evolution of mobile networks through the third and fourth generations, the amount of data traffic consumed by mobile subscribers grew exponentially, resulting in much higher bandwidth requirements within the mobile core. The GTP traffic awareness becomes critical for mobile core transport, as it often relies on load-balancing mechanisms over link bundles to provide the required bandwidth. A network gear's ability to peek inside GTP packet headers and extract flow information allows for an even distribution of traffic over multiple links.

GSN Enhancements in 3G Core

Packet core composition did not significantly change in third-generation mobile networks. SGSN and GGSN preserved their key role in handling subscribers' data traffic, keeping a number of G reference interfaces (Gn/Gp, Ga, and so on) untouched. Those G interfaces, used to interconnect packet core and circuit switched core entities, expanded their physical transport options with Ethernet and adopted use of the SIGTRAN (SS7 over IP) signaling framework. Otherwise, changes in the packet core were limited mainly to the new interfaces between UTRAN (the RAN component for 3G) and packet core. 3GPP initially proposed the use of ATM as a transport for new interfaces in UMTS specifications, with IP transport being added in later releases. Figure 2-23 shows interfaces interconnecting various components of the packet core (shaded area) and other mobile network entities as well as new interfaces introduced in UMTS.

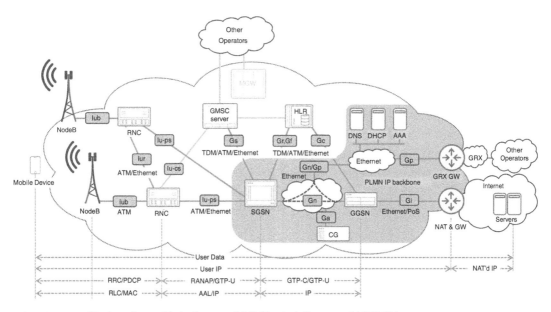

FIGURE 2-23   Protocols and Interfaces of 3G Packet Core and UTRAN

Two notable interfaces defined to connect UTRAN to the mobile core were Iu-CS (for RNC-to-MSC/MGW connections) and Iu-PS (for RNC-to-SGSN connections). These two interfaces carry both control and user traffic. The control plane uses a protocol named Radio Access Network Application

Protocol (RANAP), which runs on SS7 over ATM. Use of SIGTRAN also became an option later. The user plane of Iu-CS either uses ATM or RTP over IP transport.

Particularly significant is the use of the GTP-U protocol for user traffic by the Iu-PS interface. Although it might seem like the GTP-U tunnel extends all the way from GGSN to RNC, in reality SGSN acts as a relay between GGSN–SGSN and SGSN–RNC GTP-U tunnels. Later 3GPP releases provided an option to establish a direct GTP tunnel between GGSN and RNC. It must be noted that a direct GTP tunnel can only be established within an operator's network and cannot be used in inter-operator roaming scenarios. More details on GPRS roaming are covered in the next section. Figure 2-24 shows GTP-U tunnels with and without the direct tunneling option.

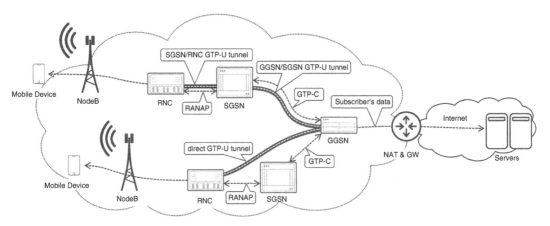

FIGURE 2-24   GTP-U Tunnels With and Without Direct Tunneling Option

For the sake of completeness, it is worth mentioning the Iur and Iub interfaces of UTRAN. The Iur interface is used to support handover and signal macrodiversity features (briefly described in Chapter 1, "A Peek at the Past"). Iub is the interface that connects RNC and NodeB and transports necessary signaling and subscribers' voice and data. Both interfaces are primarily implemented over Ethernet today.

GPRS Roaming eXchange (GRX)

If allowed by the operators' agreement and the subscriber's profile, a mobile user can get data services on a visited network, and GTP plays an essential role in it. The process of registration on the visited GPRS network is very similar to what was described in the previous sections; however, a few important distinctions exist. When a roaming mobile device requests a PDP context activation, the SGSN on a visited network establishes a GTP tunnel to the home network's GGSN. It is the home network's GGSN responsibility to provide the subscriber with an IP address and access to the requested PDN. In other words, if a subscriber from North America accesses the Internet while roaming on a European mobile network, this subscriber's IP packets appear to an Internet server as if they were coming from North America.

An operator's SGSN can establish a GTP tunnel to another operator's GGSN as long as the packet cores of both operators are interconnected. *GPRS Roaming eXchange (GRX)* is the most common way to establish such a connection. The concept of a GRX is similar to what Internet service providers use to interconnect their networks via transit networks and Internet peering exchanges. The GRX is usually operated by a private company and provides IP prefix information exchange, transit of IP traffic between different mobile operators, and root DNS service for GPRS.

IP Addressing and GRX

For security reasons, GRX networks are isolated from the Internet, which naturally reduces the risk of various attacks on GPRS nodes. Despite this isolation, GSN interfaces in the packet core typically use globally routable IP addresses to prevent IP address overlap between multiple operators. The GRX gateway connects the GSN's Gp interfaces as well as DNS to the GRX networks and advertises some of the packet core's IP subnets to the GRX network using Border Gateway Protocol (BGP). IP subnets and BGP autonomous system numbers are allocated to the mobile service providers by regional Internet registries in exactly the same manner and from the same IP addressing space used by the Internet.

DNS operation is essential for GPRS roaming, as it resolves the APN supplied by a roaming mobile device during PDP context activation request. The DNS on the visited network queries a root DNS server, which normally resides on the GRX operator's network. The root DNS server then returns a referral to an authoritative DNS. Finally, the authoritative DNS resolves the APN to an IP address of the GGSN server in the home network.

Figure 2-25 illustrates a typical data roaming scenario. Notice that the DNS on the GRX is completely isolated from the DNS on the Internet for security purposes.

Evolving mobile services have diversified inter-operator traffic, which now includes packet voice and signaling, data traffic between mobile subscribers and content providers, and bulky GPRS roaming traffic. Inter-operator exchange of new traffic types requires improved security, services isolation, and differentiated SLAs. Naturally, a new type of inter-operator traffic exchange service emerged to meet new demands: IP eXchange (IPX). IPX is similar to GRX in many respects, but unlike its predecessor, it supports multiple SLAs for different traffic types, end-to-end QoS, improved security, and traffic separation. In fact, GRX traffic is defined as just one of the traffic types for an IPX. Nevertheless, it is not uncommon to see exchange providers advertising transit services as GRX/IPX. Most of inter-operator traffic today is transported over GRX/IPX exchanges.

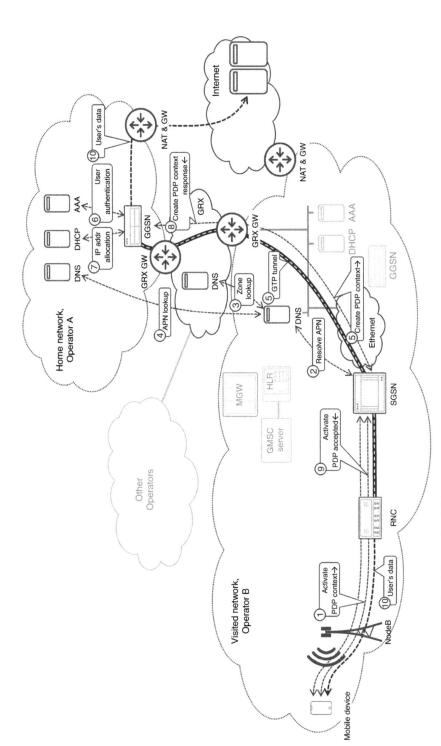

FIGURE 2-25   Data Roaming Flows via GRX

Summary

This chapter expanded on the composition of the three mobile communication network domains: radio access networks, mobile backhaul, and mobile core.

For the radio access network (RAN), the following key factors were covered:

- RF spectrum, various band properties, and optimal band selection
- RF duplexing mechanisms
- Cell splitting and sectoring
- Key components of a cell site and cell site types

Mobile backhaul focused on the following key factors:

- The role of mobile backhaul networks from the perspective of data network and mobility network architects
- Historical insights and transition to Ethernet/IP-based backhaul
- Various connectivity models for mobile backhaul networks

Mobile core's concepts and details were discussed with an emphasis on the following:

- Main elements of a mobile core and distinction between circuit switched core and packet core
- Identifiers and databases used in mobile core
- Packet core entities, interfaces, and important communication flows

The next chapter will discuss how the mobile communication networks have evolved across all three domains to create a more cohesive, efficient, and scalable end-to-end network.

References

1. https://auctiondata.fcc.gov/public/projects/auction107 (last visited: Feb 2022)

2. https://www.ntia.doc.gov/files/ntia/publications/2003-allochrt.pdf (last visited: Feb 2022)

3. https://transition.fcc.gov/oet/spectrum/table/fcctable.pdf (last visited: Feb 2022)

4. https://auctiondata.fcc.gov/public/projects/auction107 (last visited: Feb 2022)

5. https://www.etsi.org/deliver/etsi_ts/136100_136199/136101/16.07.00_60/ ts_136101v160700p.pdf, Table 5.5-1 (last visited: Feb 2022)

6. Ibid.

7. https://www.etsi.org/deliver/etsi_ts/138100_138199/138104/16.05.00_60/ ts_138104v160500p.pdf, Table 5.2-1 (last visited: Feb 2022)

8. http://www.cpri.info/downloads/CPRI_v_7_0_2015-10-09.pdf (last visited: Feb 2022)

9. https://www.businessinsider.com/reliance-jio-tower-asset-sale-indicative-of-industry-trend-2019-12 (last visited: Feb 2022)

10. https://portal.3gpp.org/desktopmodules/Specifications/SpecificationDetails. aspx?specificationId=910 (last visited: Feb 2022)

11. https://www.statista.com/statistics/185854/monthly-number-of-cell-sites-in-the-united-states-since-june-1986/ (last visited: Feb 2022)

12. https://www.businessinsider.com/reliance-jio-tower-asset-sale-indicative-of-industry-trend-2019-12 (last visited: Feb 2022)

13. James Farmer, Brian Lane, Kevin Bourg, and Weyl Wang. *FTTx Networks: Technology Implementation and Operation* (Cambridge, MA: Morgan Kaufman, 2017), Chapter 1

14. "GSMA Mobile Backhaul Options: Spectrum analysis and recommendations," https://www.gsma.com/spectrum/wp-content/uploads/2019/04/Mobile-Backhaul-Options.pdf (last visited: Feb 2022)

15. Ibid.

16. https://portal.3gpp.org/desktopmodules/Specifications/SpecificationDetails. aspx?specificationId=1692 (last visited: Feb 2022)

17. Martin Sauter. *From GSM to LTE-Advanced Pro and 5G: An Introduction to Mobile Networks and Mobile Broadband, Third Edition* (Hoboken, NJ: Wiley, 2021), Section 1.8.2

18. https://www.3gpp.org/ftp/Specs/archive/29_series/29.060/29060-330.zip (Last visited: Feb 2022)

19. https://portal.3gpp.org/desktopmodules/Specifications/SpecificationDetails. aspx?specificationId=1692 (last visited: Feb 2022)

20. https://www.3gpp.org/ftp/Specs/archive/29_series/29.060/29060-3a0.zip (last visited: Feb 2022)

Chapter | 3

Mobile Networks Today

The past few years have seen dramatic changes in mobile communication networks. Although the domains and their functions have mostly stayed the same, there has been amalgamation, redistribution, and rebranding of various device roles within each domain. The initial generations of mobile technology had been easy to classify and identify, with each generation bringing distinct changes in one or more domains of the mobile communication network (MCN). For example, 2G brought digital voice, 2.5G signified data communication and introduced packet core, 3G brought a major shift toward using IP/Ethernet-based technologies as well as a new air interface. However, after 3G, the boundaries between generations were somewhat blurred. This blurring is a combined effect of gradual and continued improvements brought through each subsequent release of 3GPP standardization as well as the marketing campaigns by mobile service providers who often jumped ahead and offered "new" generation networks while simply implementing a new 3GPP release or a subset of it. In reality, the move from 3G to 4G or from 4G to 5G is not a single leap but rather a series of transitions across the MCN domains.

Mobile providers have often kept the previous generations intact when they moved parts of the system to the new standards. It was neither feasible nor compelling to completely replace those networks, especially when they were still generating revenue. New technology and generations start off in the major markets (cities, downtowns, and so on), and in many cases, especially in underdeveloped countries, those network upgrades do not generate enough return on investment for remote locations with small numbers of subscribers. Standards have also been supportive of this; for example, the 3GPP releases associated with 4G have also specified interworking, handoff, and message exchanges between 4G- and 3G-based mobile cores.

As a consequence, most mobile networks today are a combination of the recent generations. In most developed countries, 4G networks are prevalent in urban areas, with a fall back to previous generation networks when needed. As of 2019, it was estimated that millions of devices still use 2G/2.5G networks, and many providers across the globe are likely to keep their 2G/2.5G networks functioning until 2025.[1, 2] More recently, some mobile providers have started boasting of 5G network availability, especially in areas with a high population density, but in reality, many such implementations are some aspects of 5G implemented on a predominantly 4G-based network architecture.

3GPP Releases and Evolved Packet System

The most noticeable contributions by 3GPP Releases 4 through 7 were toward improvements in the uplink/downlink speeds of the mobile network; however, there were other subtle innovations that were also part of these releases and played a significant role in the way 4G networks are implemented today. Noticeable among these were the introduction of *IP Multimedia Subsystem (IMS)* in Release 5 with enhancements in Releases 6 and 7 as well as the introduction of *policy and charging control (PCC)* in Release 7. Hence, the overall architecture of the mobile communication system remained unchanged until Release 7, under the 3G tag.

Release 8 of the 3GPP specifications was, however, a major turning point. It took the initial step toward a revolutionary set of changes to RAN and mobile core that consequently affected the mobile backhaul networks as well. These architectural transformations are referred as *Evolved Packet System (EPS)* by 3GPP. EPS proposed transformations spanned across both the mobile access and air interface architecture as well as the mobile core. The changes toward the mobile air interface were referred to as *Long Term Evolution (LTE)*, while the new mobile core architecture was discussed as *System Architecture Evolution (SAE)*. Although revolutionizing separate domains, these transformations through EPS had a common set of mutually supporting goals, some of which were the following:[3]

- Offer higher data rates for mobile traffic to match the ever-growing (and now dominating) demand for data traffic.

- Improve user experience by reducing latency as well as providing more granular quality of service (QoS) for the user traffic, hence enabling various applications to offer the desired level of service to a subscriber.

- Reduce the complexity of the architecture and hence lower the capital expenses (by consolidating the device roles and improving scale) as well as operational expenses (by simplifying operations and system management).

- Make a smooth transition to the new architecture without disrupting (and, in fact, continuing to utilize and interoperate with) the existing 3G systems.

3GPP considered the EPS goals to be met through evolution over the subsequent years (hence the use of the word *evolved*). The next few 3GPP releases continued to bring changes and enhancements in line with EPS, such as extending support to new cell types and spectrums (Release 9), enhancing carrier aggregation (CA) and multiple-input multiple-output (MIMO) performance to radio access technology (Release 10/11), security and emergency services (Release 12/13). These air interface enhancements are discussed later in this chapter. The most mentionable among these is Release 10, dubbed as *LTE-Advanced (LTE-A)*, offering the possibility of air interface downlink speeds of up to 1Gbps and accredited by the International Telecommunication Union (ITU) as *4G*.

When Did 4G Start?

Although ITU doesn't define the mobile generations, such as 3G, 4G, and 5G, it does publish guidelines that indicate what a certain generation has to offer. ITU published the *International Mobile Telecommunication-Advanced (IMT-Advanced)* specifications in early 2012, and defined the expectations from fourth-generation (4G) mobile technology. Among other things, this specification suggested a 1Gbps downlink speed for slow-moving or static users.

The LTE specifications in Release 8 of 3GPP didn't meet the IMT-Advanced definitions, and hence fell short of being called 4G. Nevertheless, many providers started marketing LTE as 4G, using the two terms interchangeably. Later, when LTE-A was specified in 3GPP Release 10, it was officially accepted as 4G.[4]

Providers who had previously marketed LTE as 4G continued their marketing strategy by using tags like 4.5G or 4G+ for LTE-A, creating further ambiguities regarding the terminologies.

Long Term Evolution (LTE)

LTE defined many significant changes to the air interface of the evolved packet system. The resulting architecture based on LTE was officially called the *Enhanced-UTRAN (E-UTRAN)* since it represented significant enhancements to 3G's UTRAN architecture. Air interfaces implemented today in most mobile deployments use E-UTRAN specifications. LTE/E-UTRAN is discussed in detail later in this chapter. As interoperability with 3G systems was a major consideration for EPS, special interfaces were defined for the E-UTRAN network to seamlessly work with the 3G-based circuit switched core. In fact, many deployments of 4G initially continued to rely on the 3G-based core for voice communication while providing only data services through the 4G-based core—an implementation that is commonly known as *Circuit Switched Fallback (CSFB)*.

System Architecture Evolution (SAE)

SAE's focus was on the mobile core. It redefined the packet core architecture with new consolidated device roles and new interfaces for them to communicate. The new packet core, known as *Evolved Packet Core (EPC)*, defined the use of Internet Protocol (IP) for signaling within the packet core. Interestingly, SAE didn't include any definition for the new circuit switched core. Instead, the EPC design incorporated the use of packet switched voice communication, hence finally weaning mobile networks off the legacy circuit switching techniques. SAE was designed to interop with previous generation networks by interfacing with both the 4G-based (that is, E-UTRAN) and 3G-based (that is, UTRAN) radio access network. Figure 3-1 depicts the transformation of the 3G mobile network as a result of EPS.

> **Note**
>
> The architectural evolution started with 3GPP Release 8 was officially called EPS, with LTE referring to only the evolution of the air interface. The common reference to these transformations, however, is LTE, which is used synonymously with 4G.

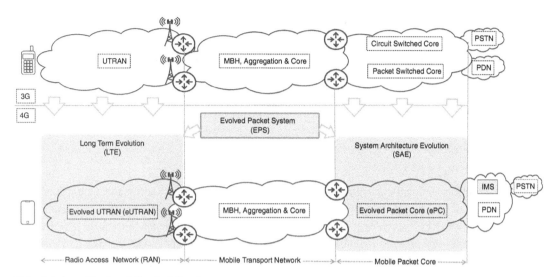

FIGURE 3-1 Evolved Packet System

Evolved Packet Core (EPC) Architecture

While the EPC was the evolution of the packet core, there wasn't any parallel evolution of the circuit switched core. That was a conscious decision by 3GPP, as part of the complete transition to use of IP for all services. Voice over IP (VoIP) was a mature technology by that time and commonly used for voice communication over the public Internet and intranets. Hence, voice signaling and traffic in a mobile network could leverage these technologies on a packet switched network. This removal of the circuit switched core resulted in the simplification of the mobile core's architecture. Now, instead of maintaining the devices and managing the functions belonging to two pseudo-independent portions of the core (namely, circuit switched core and packet core), the mobile service providers had to deploy and manage only a single set of devices in the form of EPC.

EPC Functions

Aside from an "all IP" core, the other driving force behind the EPC architecture was the separation and regrouping of control plane and user plane functions, designating those roles to individual devices. This was done to achieve the scalability desired by EPS—as these control and data plane devices could now be scaled and deployed independently of each other. The new nodes that emerged from the EPC evolution were called Mobility Management Entity (MME), Serving Gateway (SGW), Packet Data Network Gateway (PGW), and Home Subscriber Server (HSS). Figure 3-2 provides an overview of these EPC nodes and their interaction within and outside the EPC domain. These EPC building blocks will be discussed next.

Mobility Management Entity (MME)

With SAE, separation of the control and data planes in the packet core was accomplished by consolidating all the user management and other control functions into a single device in the evolved packet core, called the *Mobility Management Entity (MME)*. The MME, therefore, inherited the user management role of the MSC (or MSC-Server to be more specific) as well as the control plane functions of the Serving GPRS Support Node (SGSN). However, unlike the SGSN, the MME doesn't play any role in the forwarding of user traffic. In addition to these two roles, some of the functionalities of the Radio Network Controller (RNC) were also delegated to the MME. This included the RNC's roles of allocating radio resources as well as facilitating some handoff scenarios.

With the subscriber and call control roles from MSC, the data path setup and management functions from SGSN, and the mobile device management from the RNC, the MME became the centralized control node in the EPC. Some of the main functions that MME was meant to perform include user registration, facilitating establishment of the GTP tunnel between the user and the serving gateway, and interoperating with previous generation cores (Universal UMTS and GSM) for services such as CSFB. Note that the establishment of a voice call and the setting up of a voice circuit, which were functions of the MSC, are not performed by the MME. Those roles were eliminated in EPC with the deprecation of the circuit switched core.

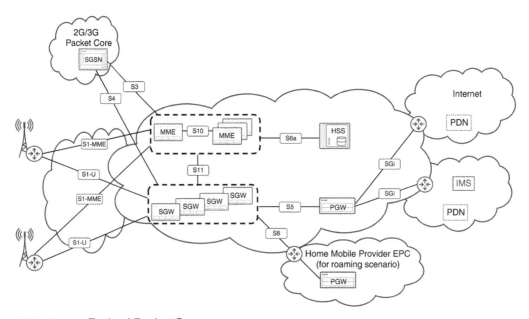

FIGURE 3-2   Evolved Packet Core

An *Evolved NodeB (eNodeB or eNB)*, an LTE equivalent of 3G NodeB, has connectivity to a pool of MMEs that helps with load balancing, scalability, and redundancy. eNodeB is discussed in detail later in this chapter. A mobile user may therefore connect with any of these MMEs in the pool and continue using it unless they roam into an eNB being served by a different MME pool. In such a roaming scenario, the MME performs a handover of the user to the new pool.

3GPP has defined the EPS interfaces to start with *S*, to contrast with the GPRS's *G* interfaces and UMTS's *I* interfaces. Therefore, the interface defined for communication between eNB and EPC is called *S1*, with two subtypes defined: namely, *S1-MME* (for control plane communication) and *S1-U* (for data). As the MME and eNB communication is only for control plane, only S1-MME is used between these two entities. A different interface, called *S10*, is defined for inter-MME communication during an MME handover, within and outside its pool. Another mentionable MME interface is *S3*, which is defined for interoperability with 2G/3G packet core SGSN. This interface exchanges control plane information for handover between the packet cores.

Serving Gateway (SGW)

With MME inheriting the control plane and signaling functions of the SGSN, the forwarding of the user traffic was delegated to a new function called the *Serving Gateway (SGW)*. The SGW, therefore, acts as a simple aggregation point terminating the GTP tunnel from the user's device, and starting a new GTP tunnel toward the PDN Gateway. It acts as the *anchor point* for user traffic, similar to how SGSN would in a UMTS network. The separation of the control functions and data functions through the MME and SGW enables scaling of these devices independently.

SGWs are also implemented as a pool, where each SGW in the pool connects directly to the eNodeBs the pool is "serving." The geographical areas served by the MME pool and SGW pool are independently defined and don't have to be identical. As a result, if the user roams to a different eNB area, it's possible that the user's device may switch over to a different MME pool while staying connected to the same SGW, and vice versa. As long as the user stays connected to the same SGW, the GTP tunnel between the SGW and PDN Gateway doesn't need to be torn down and re-established, even if the MME pool is switched. In such a situation, only the connectivity between the MME and eNB will be re-established.

Note that even though the 3GPP standards define SGW and MME as separate functions, these could be implemented in separate devices or collapsed and implemented in the same device.[5]

3GPP has defined a couple of interfaces for SGW. The data plane part or the S1 interface, *S1-U*, is defined to carry the user traffic between the eNB and SGW. The GTP-U protocol is used over this interface, and the connectivity established is commonly referred to as *S1 Tunnel*. Meanwhile, for control information exchange with MME, both SGW and MME connect using the *S11* interface. This interface uses the GTPv2C protocol for all its messages. Two other interfaces, called *S5* and *S8*, are used between the SGW and PDN Gateway. Similar to the MME, an interface, called *S4*, is defined between the SGW and 2G/3G SGSN for interoperability.

It's worth highlighting that there isn't any interface defined for communication between SGWs within or between pools, as such communication is not needed—all SGW signaling communication is with MME or SGSN, while all data communication goes from the SGW to either the PGW or the subscriber, depending on the direction of the traffic.

Public Data Network Gateway (PGW)

In EPC, the role of the packet core's gateway to the packet data network was rebranded to Packet Data Network Gateway, or simply *PDN Gateway (PGW)*. This is similar to the *Gateway GPRS Support Node's (GGSN)* role of gateway in the 3G/UMTS network, and just like GGSN, the PGW is reachable using access point name (APN) resolution performed by the MME using DNS internal to the EPC. PGW allocates the IP address to the user's device and provides the user with appropriate and allowed connectivity to the PDN network based on the APN, user profile, and type of subscribed services. Additionally, the PGW keeps track of the usage and data consumption by each user and provides that information to the billing system. Other functions the PGW performs include lawful intercept, packet filtering firewall functions, and deep packet inspection. Whether the mobile user is connected to their home network or is roaming into a different provider's network, the home provider's PGW is typically used. The SGW and PGW functions, although independently defined, can also be implemented together and referred to as *SAE-Gateway (SAE-GW)*.

3GPP defines different *S* interfaces for PGW connectivity to other EPC components and to the PDN. The interface between SGW and PGW is called *S5* when both the SGW and PGW are in the same network. However, in a roaming scenario where the SGW is in a visited network and connected to the PGW in the home provider network, a different interface called *S8* is used to provide connectivity through the IP eXchange (IPX) network. Because S8 is initiated over IPX, the SGW and PGW use globally routable IP addresses for connectivity across mobile providers. The interface defined for PGW and PDN connectivity is called *SGi*.

Other mentionable interfaces for PGW are the Gx and Gy interfaces used to communicate with the Policy Charging and Rule Function (PCRF) and Online Charging System (OCS), respectively.

PCRF

The PCRF predates EPS, as it was introduced in Release 7 of 3GPP. However, it's now considered a key building block of EPC. The PCRF is queried by the PGW to determine the services permitted for the user. While policy enforcement is still done by the PGW, a function referred to as Policy and Charging Enforcement Function (PCEF), it's the PCRF that determines the policy to be enforced. More precisely, the Gx interface is defined between the PCEF (which is part of PGW) and the PCRF. There are other Gx interfaces (for example, Gxa) defined for PCRF to communicate with entities such as SGW; however, the use and implementation of these have not been hugely popular in practical deployments.

Home Subscriber Server (HSS)

The last of the EPC building blocks is the Home Subscriber Server, or HSS. Although this is a newly defined entity, it's actually a consolidation of the HLR and AuC databases from previous generations. Just like its predecessors, the HSS is consulted for user authentication, authorization, session establishment, and so on. The HSS interfaces with the MME using an interface called *S6a*. For interoperability with previous generations, an additional interface called *S6d* is defined between the HSS and SGSN. In either case, these HSS interfaces use a protocol called *Diameter*, which is an enhancement of the AAA protocol RADIUS.

Figure 3-3 summarizes these functions of the EPC and how they map as the evolution of similar functions in the 3G mobile core. As shown in the figure, some 3G functions map partially to their 4G equivalent, while in other cases multiple 3G functions are mapped to a single 4G counterpart. For example, the MSC-Server's role of user authentication and registration is passed on to the MME, while the comparable function to its voice call establishment role is performed by the IP Multimedia Subsystem (IMS), a new entity outside of the EPC. IMS is yet another PDN meant to provide VoIP services for mobile subscribers and is described later. Similarly, the MSC-Gateway's role of transcoding and PSTN connectivity is also performed by the IMS. Lastly, the SGSN's control plane function is inherited by the MME, and the data plane functions are performed by the SGW.

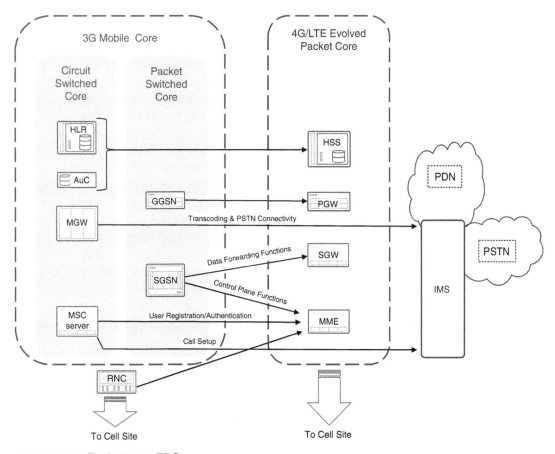

FIGURE 3-3   Evolution to EPC

Data over EPS

The subscriber registration process (called the *network attach*) to the EPS network has a flow similar to that of the previous generation networks. However, it's worth revisiting that process due to the renaming of some identifiers (with their purpose almost unchanged), the architectural change with EPC, and, especially, the deprecation of the circuit switched core. The biggest contrast between EPS registration and 2G/3G registration is that in the latter, the mobile subscriber will need to register for voice and data services separately with the circuit switched core and packet core. Once registered in the 2G/3G network, a voice path for the subscriber is created when making or receiving a voice call, or a data path is created when data is exchanged. However, in the case of EPS, because voice connectivity is provided through a PDN-based service (namely, IMS), the registration with EPC is only for data connectivity. Voice services registration happens outside of the EPC, directly with the IMS. A user registered with the network always has a data path established and IP address allocated as part of the registration process, and it stays allocated for as long as the device is registered.

Network Attach Process

Like previous generations, the user devices in 4G/LTE also use Universal SIM (USIM) and the information built into it. When the device is turned on, it uses the ICCID to scan through the available PLMN identifiers. After selecting the advertiser of the matching PLMN (or a random one, if there isn't any match), the device attempts to register by sending the IMSI stored in the SIM card to the base station (that is, the eNB in the case of LTE). The eNB then selects an MME to perform user authentication and registration. MME selection is based on the MME's advertised weight factor[6] and considerations to minimize possible MME handover for the user device. The selected MME looks up its own database, similar to what MSC would have done in previous generations, by looking up the Visitor Location Register (VLR) for any existing information for the mobile user. If none is found, the MME consults with the HSS to identify the user. Just as the combination of HSS and AuC was used previously for authenticating the user through a challenge-response procedure, now the HSS and MME perform a similar set of steps. In the case of roaming, the MME reaches out to the HSS of the subscriber's home mobile service provider. It also retrieves the APN that the subscriber shall use. The subscriber can also request a specific APN, but that will be accepted only if the HSS user's profile permits it.

USIM vs. SIM

What was originally called a SIM card was the combination of the physical card and the application embedded within. However, starting with 3G, there was a differentiation between the physical card and the authentication algorithms running on it. The physical card was called the Universal Integrated Circuit Card (UICC), while the application was referred to as the Universal Subscriber Identity Module (USIM). Compared to SIM's software, there were security enhancements and additional features included in the USIM. In colloquial terms, this combination is still called a "SIM card," though technically it's more accurate to distinguish between the two.

Upon authentication, the MME allocates a 32-bit temporary identifier for the user called *SAE Temporary Mobile Subscriber Identity (S-TMSI)*. This S-TMSI substitutes the IMSI in subsequent communication and is stored in the MME as well as communicated to the mobile subscriber. The S-TMSI uniquely identifies the subscriber as well the serving MME within the mobile provider's network. Another parameter that's provided to the mobile device is the Tracking Area Identifier (TAI). This is similar to the Location Area Identifier (LAI) used in 3G, and just like the LAI, the TAI comprises the MNC, MCC, and Tracking Area Code (TAC).

The MME then selects an optimal SGW for the mobile subscriber based on criteria such as the user device location, minimizing the probability of switching the SGW at a later time and load-balancing between SGWs.[7] It then informs the subscriber of the SGW's IP address for it to create the S1-U connection. Using the APN value previously received from the HSS, the MME now performs a DNS lookup to determine the appropriate PGW. This information is provided to the SGW to set up S5 or S8 connectivity with the PGW. The PGW now assigns an IP address to the subscriber.

To complete the attachment process, the MME instructs the eNB to reserve the radio resources for data exchange, referred to as the *radio access bearer (RAB)*. At this point, an end-to-end packet path is established between the subscriber device and the PGW. Finally, to allow the PDN access to the subscriber, the PGW queries the PCRF to determine the type of access this subscriber is allowed and then subsequently provides that connectivity. PGW also keeps the PCRF informed about the type and amount of network usage by the subscriber for compliance, billing, and accounting purposes. Figure 3-4 summarizes the network attachment process.

EPS Bearer

The tunnel established over S1-U and S5/S8, as well as the allocated data channel over the radio link, is referred to as an *EPS bearer*, or simply a *bearer*. 3GPP uses this term to represent a bidirectional data path with specifically defined characteristics. A bearer's characteristics include prioritization and treatment for quality of service (QoS), allowed bandwidth, acceptable error rate, and so on for the traffic using that bearer. Bearers are established using tunneling protocols such as GTP-U over IP. The end-to-end EPS bearer comprises three separately established bearers—that is, from the mobile device to the eNB over radio link, the eNB to SGW using the S1-U interface, and between the SGW and PGW using an S5/S8 interface. These have common characteristics defined for them (or replicated between them) based on the service type.

E-UTRAN Radio Access Bearer (E-RAB)

While the S1 bearer and S5/S8 bearer carry only data traffic, the bearer over the radio link, called the *radio access bearer (RAB)*, can carry both signaling traffic (belonging to the S1-MME interface and also for eNB), called the *signaling radio bearer (SRB)*, and data traffic that will end up in the S1-U bearer, called the *data radio bearer (DRB)*. The combination of the DRB and S1 bearer therefore carries the data traffic from the mobile user's device to the SGW and is referenced as *E-UTRAN radio access bearer (E-RAB)*.[8]

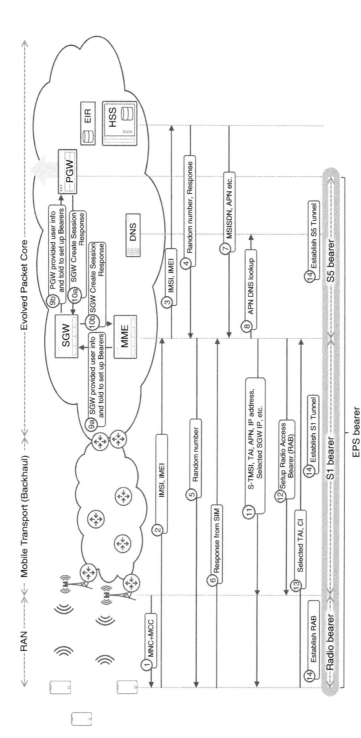

FIGURE 3-4 EPS Subscriber Registration Process

Multiple bearers can be established by a user device while using the same or different APNs. At least one bearer, called the *default bearer*, is established when the subscriber connects to any new APN. A subscriber connects to at least one APN during the attach process, but might later connect to multiple other APNs, each with its own default bearer. The first default bearer established during the subscriber's attach process to the EPS network uses best-effort connectivity for the mobile device to reach the PDN. Additional bearers with different characteristics can be established while using the same APN. The request for those can be triggered by the user's device, originate in the EPC, or be requested by an external application. The last of these scenarios is of particular importance because it's used for setting up a dedicated bearer for voice calls.

Ensuring Quality of Service

LTE architecture was developed with the focus on subscriber's *quality of experience (QoE)*. It is a compounded parameter, with some contributing factors beyond the operator's control, such as web resource responsiveness. However, it is possible to improve other QoE contributing factors such as end-to-end delay within the mobile network, delay variations, and overall packet loss. To ensure best possible service for various application types, it is important to differentiate various flows on the network. Enhancing *quality of service (QoS)* mechanisms from previous generation networks, 3GPP defined a range of QoS classes for LTE.

Various service flows might get different forwarding treatment based on their bearer's *QoS class identifier (QCI)*. Originally, QCI values were defined as "a" through "i" in Release 7, and later changed to use a number from 1 to 9 in Release 8. Additional QCI values continue to be added in later releases as needed for new services. These additional QCIs start from 65 and are defined for services such as push-to-talk services used in public safety, mission-critical video, and others.

Each QCI has different characteristics in terms of end-to-end delay budget, packet scheduling priority, and packet error loss on radio interface. For example, conversational voice uses bearers with QCI 1, and it is expected to experience no more than 100ms end-to-end delay, with a packet error loss rate of less than 10^{-2}. QCI 1 is also a guaranteed bitrate class with a packet scheduling priority of 2. The only QCI with a higher packet priority scheduling is QCI 5, which is used for IMS voice signaling, but it's a nonguaranteed bitrate class. Interestingly enough, QCIs 8 and 9, normally used for best-effort browsing traffic and for video-on-demand, require no more than 10^{-6} packet error loss rate, which is significantly stricter compared to conversational voice. Nevertheless, these are best-effort, lowest packet scheduling priority classes, with an acceptable end-to-end delay of up to 300ms. QCI values are defined in 3GPP TS23.203[9] and can be mapped by the mobile network operator to transport network QoS parameters for classifying, prioritizing, and shaping traffic based on its QoS design. Chapter 10, "Designing and Implementing 5G Network Architecture," covers the detailed QCI values to transport network QoS parameters, such as DSCP, CoS, and EXP bits.

Voice over EPS

The attach process described earlier provides the mobile subscriber with a default bearer offering data connectivity through PDN. Essentially, the only services available to the user at this point are access to the Internet and/or intranet(s), depending on the APN used and the services allowed in the subscriber's profile. However, the user isn't able to make or receive any voice calls at this point. Considering the maturity of VoIP technology and the benefits it could bring through network simplification, value-added features, and cost-effectiveness, EPS adopted the use of IP Multimedia Subsystem (IMS), originally defined in Release 7, to offer voice services based on VoIP.

IMS acts as a special-purpose PDN providing voice calling on the data-only EPS architecture. It therefore meant to provide few foundational capabilities of a voice call gateway—namely, it has to be able to register a mobile subscriber for voice services as well as reach other IMS systems and the PSTN based on a dialed phone number, route, and optionally transcode packetized voice, as needed. Such capabilities were already available in the VoIP world through protocols such as *Media Gateway Control Protocol (MGCP)*, ITU's H.323, the IETF-defined *Session Initiation Protocol (SIP)*, and *Real-Time Protocol (RTP)*. 3GPP chose SIP as the protocol to implement voice services and built IMS features and capabilities on top of it. Additionally, RTP was chosen for transporting packetized voice. This implementation is commonly referred to as *Voice over LTE (VoLTE)*.

IMS is not a part of the EPC, however. It connects to the EPC as a regular PDN network using the SGi interface with the PGW. Just like other PDNs, reaching the IMS is not possible using the default APN but rather requires the appropriate APN. This reachability has to be allowed by the policy defined for the subscriber.

Once a mobile device has an established default data bearer as a result of the attach process, it requests access to the IMS's APN. Once this APN connectivity is authorized, a new default bearer is created, and a new IP address is allocated by the PGW to the mobile device to access IMS's APN services. The default bearer is used for signaling messages with the IMS. Using this newly assigned IP address, the mobile device initiates SIP registration messages with the IMS. It's worth noting that there are two separate default bearers established at this point, each for a different APN, and hence two different IP addresses are in use by the mobile device. The SIP registration process uses the user's IMSI, the device's IMEI, and other such information to authenticate and authorize the user. For this purpose, IMS connects with the HSS system in the EPC through the "Cx" interface and uses the Diameter protocol for queries. Although the detailed registration steps and messages exchanged are beyond the scope of this book, suffice it to say that after successful registration, the device is now ready to make and receive voice calls using IMS as the SIP proxy.

The default bearer, typically established using a QCI value of 5, is for signaling messages with IMS and is not meant for voice data. When the subscriber initiates a voice call, the IMS requests a new bearer (typically with QCI 1 or 2) to carry the packetized voice. To establish this voice bearer, IMS uses PCRF's "Rx" interface. Because this voice bearer is given a guaranteed bandwidth across the entire EPS network, keeping it active for longer than needed can strain the network's resources. Therefore, when the voice call ends, the IMS signals the PCRF to terminate this dedicated voice bearer. Figure 3-5 illustrates the different bearers used by the mobile device.

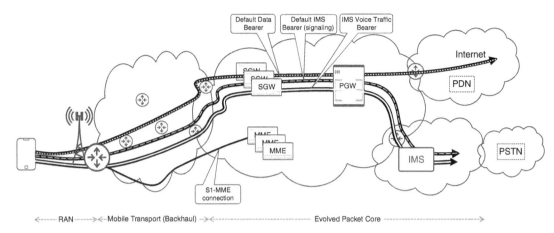

FIGURE 3-5   Data, IMS Signaling, and Voice Bearers

PCRF's Rx Interface

The Rx interface allows applications in the PDN to interact with the EPC. IMS uses this interface to request the bearer with voice-appropriate QoS parameters toward the correct destination IP address and UDP port and so on. The PCRF then initiates the bearer creation from the IMS to the subscriber's device.

RAN Evolution

Rethinking of the radio access architecture to accommodate the fourth-generation mobile network requirements resulted in a number of innovations and changes introduced into the RAN domain. New media access method, reduced RAN complexity, and distributed intelligence of RAN components were aimed at reduced latency, higher scale, and better user experience. These RAN architectural shifts also affected cell site connectivity models, with more effective and optimized approaches proliferating further into the network, driving down complexity and reducing operational expenses.

Evolved UTRAN

Like many things in EPS architecture, the Long Term Evolution in RAN is called *Evolved UTRAN*, or simply *E-UTRAN*. The foremost change distinguishing E-UTRAN from older mobile technologies is the media access method. Other changes include removal of RNC and simplification of RAN architecture. RNC intelligence moved into *evolved* NodeB, allowing for the use of more sophisticated methods for intercell interference control for improved spectral efficiency.

OFDMA

Although WCDMA used in UMTS provided many benefits over simple TDMA and FDMA approaches, increasing data rates using this media access method is difficult. WCDMA is a single-carrier media access technology with a fixed 5MHz channel width and a chip rate of 3.84M chips per second (refer to Chapter 1, "A Peek at the Past," for more details on WCDMA technology). This translates into WCDMA's maximum transmission rate of 3.84M symbols per second. Higher data rates can be achieved by transmitting multiple bits per symbol using complex modulation methods such as quadrature amplitude modulation (QAM). While QAM encoding increases the effective bit rates for end users, the WCDMA 5MHz channel width imposes a limit on the data improvements that could be achieved. The most obvious way to increase data rates would be to increase the channel width from 5 to 10, 15, or 20MHz or more, but doing this with WCDMA would worsen the inter-symbol inter-ference (ISI) problem.

Inter-Symbol Interference (ISI)

In the real world, a radio signal propagates between transmitter and receiver using many different paths. While one path might be just a direct line of sight, the other might involve reflection from a distant building. The reflected signal takes a longer path; hence, it arrives at the receiver with some delay. If this delay is comparable with the symbol duration, the next symbol being received via a shorter path might overlap and interfere with the previous symbol, still propagating over the longer path. This phenomenon is called inter-symbol interference (ISI). With a 5MHz WCDMA channel, the symbol duration is 0.26μs at the highest symbol rate.

A radio signal can travel less than 100m (33 feet) in that time, yet a path difference in multi-path propagation in a typical cell can be much more than that. Mitigation of ISI requires sophisticated approaches, such as the use of rake receivers. Rake receivers were briefly covered in Chapter 1.

Demand for higher data rates in LTE propelled the optimal RF modulation technology search beyond WCDMA and resulted in the selection of *Orthogonal Frequency-Division Multiple Access (OFDMA)* for downlink in the LTE air interface in 3GPP Release 8.[10]

OFDMA is an application of Orthogonal Frequency-Division Multiplexing (OFDM) modulation for multiuser media access. The basic principle of OFDM is to break down a single wide channel into a number of relatively narrow subchannels or subcarriers, each transmitting data at a lower speed. The subcarrier spacing is carefully selected such that transmissions on different subcarriers do not interfere with each other. The non-interfering property of frequencies is also referred to as *orthogonality*, thus the name of modulation and media access techniques. When analyzed in the frequency domain, each orthogonal frequency or subcarrier has a peak amplitude and power exactly where other subcarriers' power and amplitude are zero. This way, the subcarriers do not cause interference with each other. Figure 3-6 illustrates the principle of orthogonal subcarriers in OFDMA.

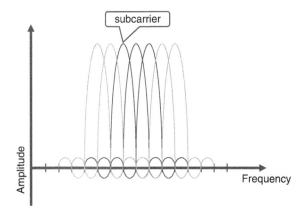

FIGURE 3-6 Orthogonal Subcarriers in OFDMA

Such dense spacing of subcarriers makes OFDM a very efficient modulation technology that performs quite close to the theoretical maximum of achievable data rates over a given channel bandwidth. The choice of orthogonal subcarriers also depends on symbol rate, as this rate defines the width of each subcarrier. The selected subcarrier spacing in LTE is 15KHz; thus, the symbol duration is 66.7μs.[11] Such a long symbol duration, along with the use of a cyclic prefix in LTE, helps to effectively mitigate ISI challenges. A *cyclic prefix* is essentially a copy of a small trailing piece of a combined OFDM signal, taken at the end of a symbol and inserted before the beginning of that very symbol. Use of a cyclic prefix effectively elongates a symbol's duration, which slightly reduces the effective capacity but counters the effects of ISI.

Another benefit of a long symbol duration is the mitigation of the Doppler effect—a change in frequency occurring when a source or receiver of radio waves moves at substantial speeds. In LTE, a subscriber can move at speeds of up to 350km/h (218 mph) or for some frequency bands even up to 500km/h (310 mph).[12]

The relatively low data rate per single subcarrier resulting from a long symbol duration is compensated for by the large number of subcarriers available in the allocated frequency bands. For example, in the 20MHz band, there are 1200 OFDMA subcarriers that, when combined, can transmit at a rate of 18M symbols per second. When compared to WCDMA, LTE offers a higher symbol rate of 4.5Msps (mega samples per second) over a 5MHz channel. The higher symbol rate translates into higher data speeds for the subscribers.

In order to generate an OFDM modulated signal, a transmitter first converts a stream of bits into symbols using one of the common modulation schemas, such as phase shift keying (PSK) or quadrature amplitude modulation (QAM). Depending on how many constellation points each modulation schema has, these can encode more than 1 bit per symbol. For example, QPSK encodes 2 bits per symbol, while 16QAM and 64QAM encode 4 and 6 bits per symbol, respectively. The stream of symbols is then converted from serial to parallel transmission, with each symbol modulating its individual subcarrier. All subcarriers are mixed after that, forming an OFDM signal. The big advantage of this method is that most of the steps can be done through digital processing. Even modulation of individual subcarriers can be replaced by a mathematical operation called *inverse fast Fourier transform (iFFT)*. The latter can be effectively implemented in OFDM application-specific integrated circuits (ASICs) and does not require complex analog circuits. In a similar way, an OFDM receiver implements the reverse operations.

Use of high-order modulation schemas, such as 16QAM or 64QAM, is dependent on the quality of a signal or on *Signal to Interference and Noise Ratio (SINR)*. These sophisticated modulations require a high SINR ratio, as they need high precision in detecting miniscule amplitude changes to identify symbols accurately. Recently, 3GPP added 256QAM (8 bits per symbol) to the list of supported modulations in LTE downlink in Release 12.[13] Nevertheless, not every subscriber in the cell can enjoy the benefits of higher-order modulations. Typically, the SINR ratios are much better near the cell tower; hence, it is possible to achieve higher data rates by using 256QAM modulation next to the cell tower. As the subscriber moves farther away from the cell tower and closer to the edge of a cell, their mobile device is likely to switch to a lower-order modulation, such as QPSK, thereby reducing the available data rates. Figure 3-7 shows an example of modulation order likely to be used in different parts of a cell.

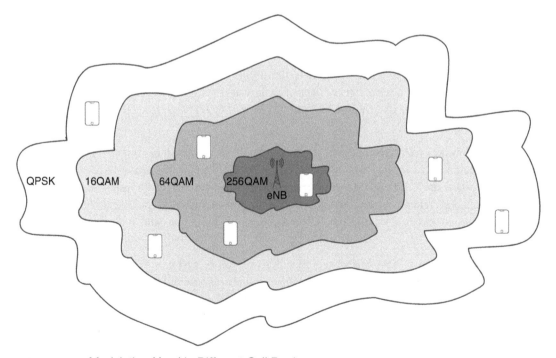

FIGURE 3-7   Modulation Used in Different Cell Regions

In OFDMA media access, each subscriber uses a number of subcarriers to transmit its data. The set of subcarriers can be changed every millisecond to accommodate constantly changing traffic patterns. Dynamic allocation of subcarriers for each subscriber has another benefit: whenever a subscriber experiences a signal quality degradation for a particular set of subcarriers (due to signal fading or other local interference), eNB can assign a different set of subcarriers to this subscriber. Subcarriers previously used by this subscriber may get reassigned to other users, as it is very likely that other users have a different signal propagation path and, therefore, the signal quality on these subcarriers might be acceptable. Figure 3-8 shows an example of subcarrier allocation to different subscribers over time.

Use of multiple subcarriers to transmit different symbols in parallel has implications on power consumption. Composite OFDMA signals have a high degree of power variation and thus require the use of a special power amplifier in transmitters. Unfortunately, these power amplifiers have low energy efficiency and can drain a mobile device's battery very quickly. However, power amplifier inefficiencies are not of a particular concern at the base station. Moreover, this side effect is outweighed by the benefit of independent subcarrier scheduling for different subscribers in the downlink direction. Therefore, OFDMA is used in the downlink direction, while in the uplink direction a more battery-friendly variant of OFDMA called *Single-Carrier Frequency-Division Multiple Access (SC-FDMA)* is used. A more technically accurate term for the SC-FDMA method is discrete Fourier transform spread OFDM (DFT-s-OFDM). A detailed explanation of DFT-s-OFDM concepts is beyond the scope of this book.

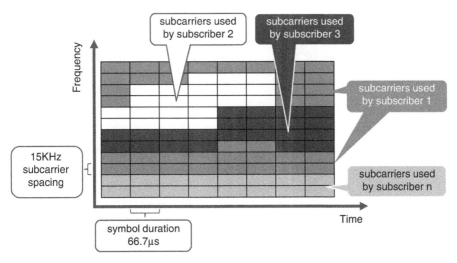

FIGURE 3-8   OFDMA Subcarrier Allocation to Different Subscribers

Carrier Aggregation in OFDMA

3GPP Release 10 officially introduced LTE-Advanced as a true 4G standard. One of the methods to increase achievable data rates in LTE-Advanced is OFDMA carrier aggregation. Each OFDMA channel, comprising multiples of 15KHz subcarriers, can be easily extended by aggregating multiple channels for use by the same transceiver. Each individual channel in the aggregated channels is called a *component carrier*. The wider, concatenated channels fit more subcarriers for parallel data transmission, but for compatibility with previous LTE releases, the width of a component carrier could only be 1.4, 3, 5, 10, 15, or 20MHz. Up to five component carriers are allowed to be aggregated, thus allowing for up to 100MHz aggregated carrier widths.[14]

The most straightforward approach for carrier aggregation is to use contiguous component carriers. This approach does not require guard bands and contributes toward efficient frequency spectrum utilization. If necessary, however, noncontiguous aggregation can also be used, with gaps left for the frequencies that cannot be allocated and used in a particular area. Carrier aggregation also has a utility in inter-cell interference coordination (ICIC) procedures, aimed at reducing interference from the neighboring base stations and mobile devices. More details on ICIC methods are provided in the section "Inter-Cell Interference Coordination (ICIC)" later in the chapter.

Evolved NodeB (eNB)

The radical move to abandon circuit switched voice in EPS allowed the creation of an efficient and flat RAN architecture. A building block of LTE RAN is an evolved successor of UTRAN's NodeB, expected to be called *evolved NodeB(eNodeB)*, or *eNB* for short. eNB is an enhanced and more intelligent node that autonomously executes many functions that were previously controlled by other entities such as RNC.

A noticeable change in E-UTRAN compared to its predecessor is the removal of RNC. Now, eNBs themselves must carry the burden of radio resource management functions, power control, and handover decisions. The departure of RNC resulted in significant simplification of the RAN network. A flat RAN network with fewer elements in the processing chain reduces latency and allows for simpler RAN transport architectures, driving down cost and minimizing the risk of failures.

Like previous generations' base stations, eNB performs radio signal processing, modulation/demodulation, and amplification. On top of these, new functions include radio bearer and admission control, scheduling of uplink and downlink data, execution of paging procedures, broadcasting of emergency messages, termination and processing of IP-based GTP-U tunnels, inter-cell interference coordination (ICIC), and autonomous handover decisions. While radio bearer control and admission control are inherited from RNC, some functions are entirely new. For example, the Earthquake and Tsunami Warning System (ETWS) is a new LTE feature that helps to swiftly deliver information from government agencies about emergencies to all subscribers within the network's reach.

Handover decisions are not a particularly new feature, as these were previously performed by the RNC based on mobile device signal measurement reports. In LTE, handover decisions are implemented autonomously by eNBs themselves. Similar to UMTS, LTE eNB receives periodic reports on signal quality measurements from a mobile device, including its measurements of neighboring eNB signals. By comparing data in these reports, eNB can decide whether handover is the optimal action at the given time. The serving eNB then contacts the neighboring eNB, responsible for the best signal reported by the mobile device. This new eNB is also called the *target-eNB*, and the current serving eNB is called the *source-eNB*. Although entirely possible to complete communication between neighboring eNBs via

MME, it is obviously more effective via direct communication between eNBs. 3GPP specified a new reference interface for inter-eNB communication named the *X2* interface. The X2 interface uses the X2 Application Protocol (X2-AP) over IP for the control plane and GTP-U for the data plane. During the handover procedure, the source and target eNB exchange control information and establish a direct GTP-U tunnel between them. This tunnel is used to forward data packets received from the SGW while the SGW-to-eNB bearer (S1 bearer) is being re-established to the target eNB. While the handover results in changing of radio and S1 bearers, S5/S8 bearer does not need to change, unless the subscriber moves into an area served by a different SGW pool.

In addition to X2, 3GPP defines the S1 reference interface to connect eNB with EPC. S1-MME and S1-U are the control and user planes of the S1 interface, respectively. Although X2, S1-MME, and S1-U serve different purposes and use different protocols, they do not require dedicated physical interfaces and, in most cases, share the same Ethernet interface toward the mobile backhaul.

Figure 3-9 provides a high-level diagram of eNB connectivity to EPC and to each other via X2 interface.

Without a doubt, scheduling packets belonging to very different flows over a single Ethernet interface requires eNB to implement some quality of service (QoS) mechanisms. eNB performs radio scheduling, taking into account QCI values, and to ensure end-to-end QoS, appropriate per-hop behavior must be defined in the transport network for all traffic classes and packets exchanged between the eNB and EPC. The QCI values are mapped to appropriate DSCP/ToS values based on the transport network QoS design.

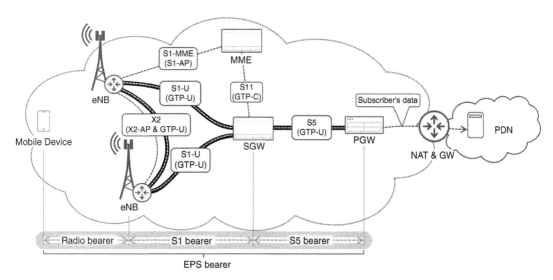

FIGURE 3-9 Interfaces and Protocols Used for eNB Connectivity to EPC

Inter-Cell Interference Coordination (ICIC)

In addition to providing an inter-eNB communication channel during handover procedures, the X2 interface has another critical role. It is used to exchange messages for mechanisms to reduce interference between neighboring cells. The simplest form of interference mitigation is the use of frequency reuse patterns, discussed in Chapter 1. Inter-cell interference coordination (ICIC) offers more sophisticated methods, such as *fractional frequency reuse (FFR)* to optimize frequency use and division across multiple cells. FFR is based on the same idea of using alternating frequency bands in neighboring cells, but it takes this idea even further by distinguishing frequency use in an area closer to the cell tower, versus an area lying at the far edge of the cell. Radio communication in the inner area (that is, the area closer to the cell tower) naturally requires less power from both the mobile device and the base station transmitters; thus, the contribution of such inner areas into inter-cell interference is significantly lower when compared to the edges of the cell.

FFR mechanisms allow the logical option to reuse all available frequency bands, with low-power use in the inner area of all cells, and different frequency bands near the cell boundaries, where higher power requirements could result in more inter-channel interference. Figure 3-10 shows a high-level FFR diagram.

There are different permutations of frequency reuse methods applied in LTE (for example, *Soft Frequency Reuse*), with the main difference being less-restrictive use of the same frequency bands at the edges of the neighboring cells. However, the latter requires more coordination between eNBs over the X2 interface. An example of such coordination is the transmission of an *overload indicator* over X2 by an eNB, when high interference is experienced in the cell. This indicator advises neighboring eNBs to schedule radio traffic using other available subcarriers for the subscribers in the vicinity of the cell experiencing high interference.

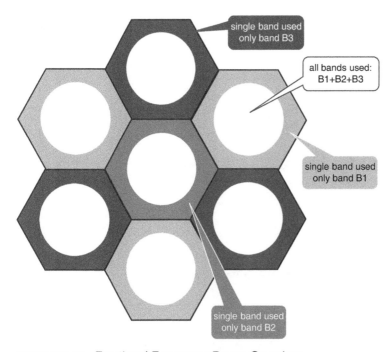

FIGURE 3-10 Fractional Frequency Reuse Overview

Some ICIC methods were developed to control interference in specific scenarios of picocells deployed in the macrocell coverage areas. Picocell deployments within a macrocell coverage area are very popular in places such as shopping malls, sport arenas, and other places with increased subscriber density. Boosting available bandwidth and quality of experience for mobile network users is a desired outcome of deploying these picocells. On the other hand, such picocells can cause and experience interference from the signals of macrocells, covering the same area as well. Restricting which frequency bands can be used by a macrocell and picocell reduces the effective operator's frequency utilization and therefore is not ideal. Coordination of frequency use and radio traffic scheduling between the macrocell and picocell provides a better solution and helps to increase frequency utilization, thereby improving the customer experience. This inter-cell coordination also occurs over the eNB X2 interface. There are more ICIC methods defined in LTE-Advanced and LTE-Advanced Pro (Releases 13 and 14), which are applicable in advanced scenarios involving advanced antenna features. For example, the Coordinated Multi-Point (CoMP) feature requires interaction and coordination between neighboring eNBs to provide multiple transmission streams between a subscriber and the network. Besides serving eNB, neighboring eNBs also transmit data for the subscriber in a controlled manner, increasing the overall bandwidth available for the subscriber and reducing interference. Regardless of the specifics of each ICIC method, almost all of them require interaction between eNBs over the X2 interface.

MIMO

Direct increase of peak data rates in mobile technologies by using wider frequency bands has its limits. Fortunately, there are other innovative ways to improve data throughput without tapping into precious frequency resource. One such way is to use the *multiple-input multiple-output (MIMO)* method to boost the network capacity and bandwidth available for subscribers, both individually and collectively. The idea to employ multiple signal propagation paths to provide independent radio transmission channels while using the same signal frequency is not a new one. The term MIMO is well known to Wi-Fi users, and the same approach was utilized by 3G Evolved High Speed Packet Access (HSPA+) networks. MIMO is an essential part of LTE, allowing it to reach 1Gbps peak data rates and meet formal 4G requirements.

The underlying principle of MIMO is similar to spatial diversity, a method to improve transmission of a single data stream mentioned in Chapter 2, "Anatomy of Mobile Communication Networks." However, in MIMO, both the eNB and the mobile device use multiple antennas to send and receive different data streams on the same carrier frequency. These multiple antennas are mounted at a certain distance from each other such that individual signals are emitted and received in different spatial positions. The surrounding environment always has many features affecting signal propagation, such as buildings, trees, and hills, reflecting and attenuating signal in various directions. Although radio transmissions from all eNB transmit antennas reach every receive antenna on a mobile device (and vice versa), each individual signal has different characteristics, such as phase and amplitude at every receiving antenna. These differences arise from the diverse propagation paths the signals take. Knowing the characteristics of signal propagation between each transmit and receive antenna (phase shift and attenuation), it is possible to use mathematical procedures to distinguish individual data streams at the receiver side.

This technique of transmitting multiple layers of data over spatially diverse paths is called *spatial multiplexing*.

The number of individual data streams or layers a MIMO system can transmit is defined and cannot exceed the number of transmit and receive antennas. In MIMO nomenclature, 2×2 MIMO refers to two transmit and two receive antennas, 4×4 MIMO refers to four transmit and four receive antennas, and so on. LTE-Advanced in 3GPP Release 11 supports up to 8×8 MIMO in the downlink and 4×4 MIMO in the uplink.[15] Figure 3-11 shows a diagram of 2×2 MIMO transmission.

To learn the characteristics of signal propagation between the eNB and a mobile device's individual antennas, special reference signals are periodically transmitted by the eNB. The measurements of these special reference signals at each receiving antenna on the mobile device provide information about propagation paths, which is then reported back to the eNB, thus forming a feedback loop. In the event of insufficient path diversity between the antennas, the eNB reduces the number of individual data streams and may fall back to sending only a single data stream. In this scenario, the MIMO is used to increase the robustness of a single transmission and is no different from the spatial diversity technique.

MIMO transmission methods can be applied to a single user, called *single-user MIMO (SU-MIMO)*, or to multiple users, called *multi-user MIMO (MU-MIMO)*. Further research in MIMO transmission methods resulted in the development of *massive MIMO (mMIMO)* transmissions, which, along with other advanced antenna features, will be discussed in Chapter 5, "5G Fundamentals."

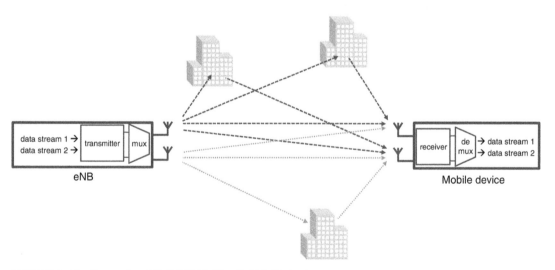

FIGURE 3-11   Example of 2×2 MIMO Spatial Multiplexing

Wi-Fi Offload

An indirect way to improve mobile network capacity is to offload data streams from the mobile network whenever possible. One obvious way is to offload bulky traffic to ubiquitous Wi-Fi networks. Indeed,

Wi-Fi is so popular that it is hard to find a spot where Wi-Fi networks are not detectable. Every time a mobile device connects to a Wi-Fi network or *wireless LAN (WLAN)*, either at home, in the office, or perhaps using a hotspot at the airport, Internet data bypasses the mobile network infrastructure. It is considered a third-party Wi-Fi offload and, in its simplest form, does not require much interaction with the mobile network. As long as the mobile device is configured with the correct WLAN name and credentials for authentication, it is possible to join the WLAN and start using its resources. Nevertheless, public and some private Wi-Fi networks are hard to rely on for quality and security, as they are meant for Internet access only. Access to other PDNs, such as intranets, or calling over Wi-Fi is not possible over third-party Wi-Fi offload, unless secure tunnels are established to the mobile service provider.

> **Note**
>
> Calling over Wi-Fi or Voice over Wi-Fi (VoWiFi) is a separate feature and not to be confused with Wi-Fi offload, although Wi-Fi offload does provide the means for VoWiFi. VoWiFi is a feature similar to VoLTE but uses WLAN instead of LTE to provide access to IMS voice calling features.

3GPP defined an architecture to implement Wi-Fi offload in a more reliable and predictable way. This architecture requires a certain degree of integration between WLANs and mobile networks. Basic Wi-Fi offload was introduced in 3G networks, and since then it has improved significantly, eliminating the need to manually join WLANs and supporting integration with non-operator-owned WLANs.

There are two types of WLANs considered for Wi-Fi offload: trusted and untrusted. Integration with trusted and untrusted Wi-Fi networks requires different gateway types and different procedures to offload data flows. A typical trusted Wi-Fi network is a WLAN infrastructure installed and managed by the mobile operator itself. In such a case, the mobile device connected to the WLAN can expect a sufficient level of security and does not require additional protecting mechanisms. The WLAN is connected to the EPC via *Trusted WLAN Access Gateway (TWAG)*. Offload to the trusted WLAN does not require a subscriber to manually join the WLAN, and this process, including authentication, happens automatically using information from the SIM card.

In the case of untrusted Wi-Fi offload, the gateway to EPC is called the *Evolved Packet Data Gateway (ePDG)*. Both TWAG and ePDG serve the subscriber connected to the WLAN in a similar way as SGW and create a GTP tunnel to the PGW. Additionally, an IPsec tunnel is established between the ePDG and mobile device connected to the untrusted WLAN to provide security and privacy. Figure 3-12 shows an overview of these connectivity models.

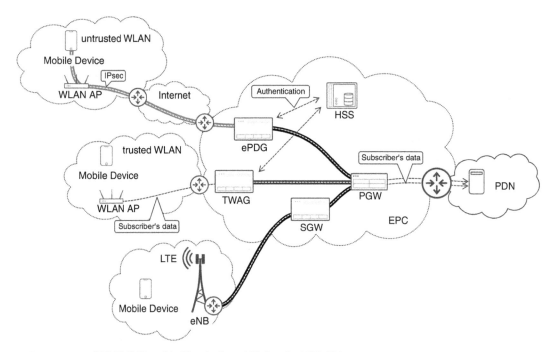

FIGURE 3-12   Wi-Fi Offload in Trusted and Untrusted WLANs

Counterintuitively, trusted Wi-Fi offload allows access to the default APN only. Without additional functionality, the mobile device acts as a native WLAN client. It cannot acquire an additional IP address to access nondefault APNs, such as IMS, and therefore it cannot use calling over Wi-Fi feature, unless special policies are implemented at the PGW to split IMS and non-IMS APN traffic. The downside of this approach is that IMS traffic has to traverse two PGWs and experience higher latency. A few improvements to address this limitation were defined in 3GPP Release 12 and enable TWAG with capability to offer more than one PDN connection.[16] Conversely, an IPsec tunnel over untrusted WLAN can be leveraged to provide connectivity to IMS while offloading default Internet traffic directly via the WLAN provider's Internet gateways.

For better quality of experience, LTE releases defined IP Flow Mobility for Wi-Fi offload scenarios. Without IP Flow Mobility, every time a subscriber moves to and from a Wi-Fi network, the IP address for the APN is reassigned, thus affecting the existing data sessions. IP Flow Mobility allows maintaining the connection and keeping any existing data sessions unaffected during moving to and from Wi-Fi offload.

From Distributed-RAN to Centralized-RAN

The commonly used RAN deployment architectures of today are called *Distributed-RAN (D-RAN)*. The name is derived from the "distributed" nature of macrocell sites across geographical areas, with each macrocell acting as an individual, standalone RAN entity. All the RAN-related equipment to terminate a mobile subscriber's air interface is contained within the NodeB for 3G or eNodeB for 4G/LTE, located at the cell site. As a reminder, the NodeB and eNodeB comprises the antenna, remote radio head (RRH), and the baseband unit (BBU). In a D-RAN architecture, these devices are co-located at the cell site. The architectural approach of D-RAN is contrasted by a relatively small but growing number of *Centralized-RAN (C-RAN)* implementations. In a C-RAN architecture, some of the RAN equipment (more specifically, the BBU) is moved away from the cell site to a centralized location. This approach of spreading out the previously co-located RAN equipment (the antenna, the RRU, and the BBU) across multiple locations is often called *RAN decomposition*.

> **Note**
>
> The acronym C-RAN is also sometimes used for Cloud RAN – a concept introduced later, in Chapter 5. In this chapter, however, C-RAN will be used exclusively to refer to Centralized-RAN.

LTE/4G RAN performance relies heavily on inter-eNodeB coordination, enabled using the X2 connectivity provided through the MBH. However, the MBH may contain multiple devices in the network infrastructure, thus adding latency in the communication between eNodeBs. Pooling several BBUs in a central location helps cut down on the inter-BBU communication latency and enables faster coordination between the eNodeBs, resulting in better RAN performance. The site that houses these multiple BBUs is often referred to as a *BBU hotel* or a *C-RAN hub site*. A BBU hotel is a site with enough real estate, shelter, power, and cooling capabilities to host multiple BBUs. An existing macrosite that fits these criteria could be used as a BBU hotel for C-RAN cell sites.

The BBUs at the C-RAN hub continue to use the Common Public Radio Interface (CPRI) protocol for communication with the RRH at the cell site. The CPRI connectivity between the RRH and BBU is still provided over optical fiber. However, in a C-RAN architecture, this fiber connection may extend over a few kilometers instead of a few feet, as is the case with D-RAN. This extended optical fiber network connecting the C-RAN cell site and BBU hotel is called the *fronthaul*. The backhaul and fronthaul networks are collectively referred to as *xHaul* (sometimes written as *Xhaul* or *XHaul*) networks. Using a generic term like *xHaul* allows for continued evolution of mobile transport by including more transport networks such as the *midhaul*, discussed in Chapter 5. It must be noted that an overwhelming majority of total cell sites deployed (as of this writing) are D-RAN sites and, in many cases, both the C-RAN and D-RAN architectures coexist in a mobile provider's network, as shown in Figure 3-13.

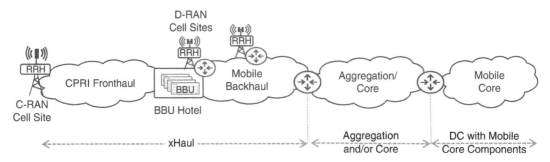

FIGURE 3-13   Fronthaul and Backhaul Networks in an MCN

Open Base Station Architecture Initiative (OBSAI)

Originally proposed in 2002 by ZTE, Hyundai, Samsung, Nokia, and LG Electronics for BBU-RRU communication, *Open Base Station Architecture Initiative (OBSAI)* is a competing standard to CPRI. However, OBSAI failed to gain much traction in the industry. Eventually Nokia joined Ericsson, Huawei, and NEC in backing the CPRI specification as well.

As stated in the previous chapter, growing bandwidth demands and the resulting use of higher frequency spectrum are fueling an increase in small cell deployments. For instance, as of 2019, the city of Dallas, Texas, had approved about 1000 applications for small cell deployments. Many of those sites use smart streetlight utility poles to mount small cell equipment, with no space for a BBU appliance in its proximity.[17] These small cell deployments could benefit from Centralized-RAN architecture and use fronthaul networks to provide RRH-to-BBU connectivity.

While providing significant performance enhancements, C-RAN also enables significant cost savings due to lower real estate and equipment maintenance costs as a result of BBU pooling. Some case studies suggest as much as 30% RAN performance improvements and 50% cost savings over D-RAN architecture.[18] C-RAN architectures also mark the beginning of a tighter integration between RAN and transport networks, where the radio access components move deeper into the transport networks.

Modern Mobile Backhaul Networks

Chapter 2 discussed the physical composition of mobile backhaul networks and the myriad of topology and connectivity choices available to implement it. Irrespective of the physical medium and topology choices, MBH networks require robust connectivity infrastructure to ensure continued MCN operation. This need is also underscored with newer 3GPP releases consolidating more functionality on eNB with the removal of RNC and extending GTP tunnels through to the eNB. Additionally, the introduction of a logical X2 interface between cell sites requires an MBH network that not only provides connectivity from cell site to EPC but also among cell sites.

Enabling Technologies for Backhaul Networks

Early mobile backhaul networks were a combination of legacy transport technology (such as point-to-point T1/E1, ATM, or Frame Relay) and the newer, more scalable Ethernet. Limited by the technology of its time and constrained by capital expense budgets, most *mobile backhaul (MBH)* networks started as Layer 2 access networks, but later transitioned to IP/MPLS-based backhaul.

Multiprotocol Label Switching (MPLS)

Developed in the 1990s, MPLS is a technology that provides differentiated services utilizing Internet Protocol (IP) transport. MPLS operates by assigning a label to an IP prefix and switching traffic between MPLS-enabled nodes using labels instead of IP routes. A label is a 4-byte header placed on the IP datagram and is used by nodes within the MPLS network to forward traffic over a *label switched path (LSP)*.

MPLS provides many advantages over native IP routing, such as the use of *virtual private networks (VPNs)*, *traffic engineering (TE)*, and fast convergence through *Fast Reroute (FRR)*. Because MPLS is an established technology, this book assumes readers have basic familiarity with MPLS principles. However, relevant details about the use of MPLS in the context of MBH will be covered as needed.

Layer 2 Backhaul

At the time of early MBH deployments, Layer 3 transport features were primarily reserved for high-speed core and larger aggregation domains. Layer 3–capable transport devices tended to be costlier than their Layer 2–capable counterparts. With a significantly higher number of devices in access networks than core and aggregation networks, hardware cost plays an important role in the device selection process. Additionally, Layer 2 transport networks were considered simpler to deploy, with almost a plug-and-play functionality that required minimal configuration for inserting a new Ethernet node in an existing network. By contrast, Layer 3 networks require careful IP addressing planning and routing design. The perceived simplicity of deployment, coupled with lower equipment costs, made Layer 2 the technology of choice for access networks. As MBH networks were modeled after existing access networks, Layer 2 transport gained favor as the technology of choice for post T1/E1, Ethernet-based mobile backhaul networks.

While Layer 2 networks might be simpler and cheaper to deploy, they certainly have operational challenges–especially at the scale required of a modern mobile communication network. Chief among these complexities is loop avoidance and traffic duplication. When using Layer 2 switching in a ring-based or dual-homed MBH topology, network architects must take precautions to ensure a loop-free topology and avoid traffic duplication. *Spanning Tree Protocol (STP)* was the de facto loop-avoidance protocol; however, it was intended for much smaller LANs and thus lacked essential features and usability to operate efficiently in large access domains such as mobile backhaul. For instance, STP's lack of suitable troubleshooting tools creates significant headaches for network engineers in case of issues. STP is also inherently slow to convergence. It did, however, go through numerous feature additions and enhancements over several years to try and adapt STP for use outside of LAN. As a result of these enhancements, several variations of STP were brought to market, including Rapid Spanning Tree (RST), Per-VLAN Spanning Tree (PVST), Rapid PVST, and Multiple Spanning Tree (MST), among others. Each of these flavors addressed specific shortcomings of the original Spanning Tree Protocol but also added design complications as well as operational and interoperability challenges between different flavors of STP.

STP's usefulness is also limited to scenarios where a physical and topological loop is detected (that is, closed-ring topologies in MBH networks). However, not all ring-based topologies are closed ring; in such scenarios, STP might not detect a physical loop and thus would not block redundant paths, resulting in duplication of broadcast, unknown unicast, multicast (BUM) traffic at the aggregation nodes. Vendor-specific protocol enhancements tried to address this shortcoming, further complicating the design and operations of Layer 2 access networks.

The design and operational challenges of using a LAN-based protocol in a WAN environment made STP fall out of favor with network operators. To simplify deployments, networking equipment vendors introduced proprietary protocols for loop avoidance in Layer 2 Metro Ethernet networks. Some of these protocols included *Resilient Ethernet Protocol (REP)* by Cisco, *Ethernet Automatic Protection Switching (EAPS)* by Extreme Networks, and *Rapid Ring Protection Protocol (RRPP)* by Hewlett Packard Enterprises (HPE). ITU-T defined *G.8032 Ethernet Ring Protection Switching (ERPS)*, which eventually became the standardized loop-avoidance mechanism for Layer 2 Metro Ethernet networks. In addition to providing a loop-free topology, ERPS (and its proprietary counterparts) also provides fast convergence capabilities in link or node failure scenarios.

Another operational challenge is the use of multiple control planes—one for Layer 2 in MBH and another for Layer 3 in aggregation and core. An operator will have to design and implement two distinct networks (Layer 2 and Layer 3), each with its own protocols, configuration, and design considerations. The network architects, as well as the network support engineers, have to be well versed in both L2 and L3 design and technologies and operational complexities.

Configuring and managing separate L2 and L3 transport domains is cumbersome and introduces additional configuration touchpoints contributing to the overall complexity of the MCN. Most modern MBH deployments shy away from Layer 2 transport and instead rely on Layer 3 IP transport with MPLS technology for value-added features and services.

MPLS/IP Backhaul

Over the years, the cost difference between Layer 2 and Layer 3 devices has become negligible. Simultaneously, the advancements in forwarding processors mean that mobile operators can cheaply deploy the features once reserved for core and aggregation domains, such as MPLS, in MBH networks. The immediate benefit of using an IP- and MPLS-capable *cell site router (CSR)* is the unification of control and data planes between mobile backhaul access and the rest of the transport network. With this unification, mobile service providers do not have to plan and design two different network architectures. Neither do they have to implement additional configuration at Layer 2–Layer 3 boundaries to exchange traffic between the two domains. The result is a single, cohesive, end-to-end architecture, with many of the same features and capabilities in the MBH as that of IP core and aggregation. Some of these features and capabilities include traffic engineering (TE), fast reroute (FRR), and traffic isolation through virtual private networks (VPNs)—each one with a utility in backhauling traffic from cell sites to the packet core or between cell sites for X2 connectivity.

Non-MPLS, IP-Only Mobile Backhaul

When MPLS was introduced in the late 1990s, the debate over whether to use MPLS or keep networks "IP only" had been relentless. Over time, a vast majority of network operators have adopted MPLS due to the countless benefits regarding usability, redundancy, fast convergence, and more. Today, there are no more than a handful of network operators that do not use MPLS and rely on IP-only transport networks for traffic routing. As these operators are few and far between, this book does not cover an IP-only Layer 3 mobile backhaul and instead focuses on IP/MPLS-based MBH and its subsequent evolution.

While the use of MPLS in the MBH brings consistency to end-to-end MCN design, it also presents routing protocol and device scalability challenges. Access networks contain a large number of devices and, as mentioned previously, in the case of mobile backhaul, the number of cell site routers (CSRs) may reach tens or hundreds of thousands of nodes. Each of these CSRs consumes multiple IP addresses that need to be injected into the routing domain that creates a scalability challenge. To exacerbate the scalability challenges, MPLS-based services (such as VPN) require each of these CSR's loopback routes (/32 route) to be advertised without summarization. When injected into the network, these thousands of new prefixes create a scalability challenge for the Interior Gateway Protocols (IGPs). Additionally, due to the introduction of X2 interfaces in LTE, the CSR also needs to be aware of other CSRs' routing information to establish connectivity between their corresponding eNBs. The CSRs tend to be low-cost routers with limited memory and scale capabilities and thus not able to hold tens of thousands of host routes to other CSRs. In other words, the use of MPLS/IP for the MBH network presented a two-prong challenge: the IGP protocol cannot scale to the massive number of nodes, and the low-cost CSR cannot scale its routing table. The solution to these challenges required innovative architecture as well as protocol enhancements, such as BGP Labeled Unicast.

MPLS originated as a niche core network technology that worked in conjunction with IGPs such as *Open Shortest Path First (OSPF)* and *Intermediate System to Intermediate System (ISIS)* and stayed as an IGP-only technology throughout its proliferation into the aggregation and access domain. IGP routing protocols were never designed to handle the scale presented by CSRs in the MBH access and, in an effort to solve the routing protocol scale challenge, network architects turned to a proven protocol that could handle massive routing table scale, for example, Border Gateway Protocol (BGP).

Originally, BGP was considered an inter-AS, peering-only protocol to provide routing information exchange between *autonomous systems (AS)* and it did not have support for assigning MPLS within the AS. Previously introduced proposals from Cisco and Juniper had already enhanced BGP to carry MPLS label information, primarily to facilitate inter-AS VPN deployments by creating an end-to-end label switched path (LSP). These enhancements were standardized in the Internet Engineering Task Force (IETF) as RFC-3107.[19] Using the mechanisms defined in RFC-3107, BGP-enabled devices would establish *Labeled Unicast (BGP-LU)* peering relationships to exchange MPLS-labeled routes through the use of Network Layer Reachability Information (NLRI) messages. Although early use of RFC-3107 was limited to inter-AS implementations, it could also be applicable to intra-AS, as is typically the case with MBH. Implementation of RFC-3107 in intra-AS capacity was a pivotal point in the design and implementation of modern transport networks, specifically the mobile transport networks. It normalized the use of BGP inside autonomous systems for connectivity between various access, aggregation, and core domains.

BGP-LU does not eliminate the need for IGP but rather supplements it. Traditionally, BGP's role in transport networks has been to provide inter-AS peering and connectivity. When BGP is used for intra-AS interdomain connectivity, specific design considerations are needed. The resulting transport architecture from the use of BGP-LU with IGP is defined in IETF's "Seamless MPLS Architecture" draft.[20] This architecture, also called *Unified MPLS* by some network equipment vendors, outlines the architectural framework for a single, unified, end-to-end MPLS domain across multiple IGP domains. Simply put, the Seamless MPLS architecture uses IGP-learned routes to establish connectivity with routers within its domain and BGP-LU to reach the nodes outside the domain. In the context of this architecture, a domain could be a single OSPF or ISIS area or an entirely different IGP process. In a Seamless MPLS architecture, the *control plane* comprises BGP-LU, IGP, and LDP, while the *data plane* uses MPLS labels to switch traffic. The control plane is responsible for exchanging routes and labels, while the data plane is responsible for actual traffic forwarding.

The IGP design in a Seamless MPLS architecture is very similar to commonly used routing designs, where the network is segmented into different areas using ISIS or OSPF. In this case, the MBH is designated as a Level 1 area (for ISIS) or a non-backbone area (for OSPF), while the aggregation nodes act as the area border routers and restrict any inter-area route leaking to avoid scalability challenges. As both the CSR and aggregation nodes are in the same routing area, they don't need any external route leaking or redistribution for connectivity. The same is the case for aggregation and Data Center Interconnect (DCI) nodes that are part of the OSPF backbone or ISIS Level 2 area and can communicate independently. The DCI nodes are the area border routers connecting the IP core with the DC where the packet core is hosted. However, without any route leaking between IGP areas, the CSRs will not be able to communicate with other areas or with the DC. This restriction is by design, as leaking all Level 1 or non-backbone area routes into the core, and vice versa, would create scale challenges for both the Interior Gateway Protocol and the individual CSR nodes. Instead, the end-to-end interdomain reachability is provided by BGP-LU by establishing peering between the CSR and aggregation as well as between the aggregation and core nodes. Figure 3-14 shows the contrast between a legacy IGP-only

MPLS architecture that relies on route leaking between IGP domains and a Seamless MPLS architecture that uses both IGP and BGP-LU to provide the required scale in most modern networks.

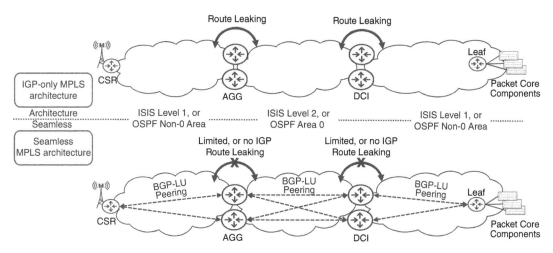

FIGURE 3-14   IGP-Only MPLS and Seamless MPLS Architecture Overview

In the MBH domain, CSRs would typically peer directly with the aggregation nodes, acting as inline route reflectors, connecting to central route reflectors in the core or aggregation domains. This *hierarchical* route reflector approach helps create an optimal, extensible, and scalable routing design. Whereas using the aggregation nodes as inline route reflectors is feasible for MBH domains, for aggregation and core domains, a central route reflector is better suited.

After establishing these BGP-LU peerings, loopbacks can be advertised by the CSRs and DCI nodes, along with their corresponding MPLS labels. These routes reside in the BGP routing table and are not redistributed into IGP, thus ensuring a scaled architecture from a routing protocol standpoint. Even though eBGP might be used, most Seamless MPLS deployments utilize iBGP because the MCN domains are likely to be in the same AS. However, due to the default iBGP behavior, when using iBGP, network architects must explicitly enable the *next-hop-self* feature on inline route reflectors at domain boundaries to ensure the end nodes (such as the CSR) receive the router with a reachable next hop. If the next hop is not explicitly changed, the routes received from the DCI and remote MBH domains are advertised to the local CSR with the remote node's loopback as the next hop, resulting in traffic blackholing because the CSR will not install the BGP-LU route in the routing table while the next hop is unreachable in IGP. Figure 3-15 shows a Seamless MPLS implementation with two MBH access domains and a single collapsed core/aggregation domain with DCI nodes connecting to the packet core. The figure also illustrates inline and centralized route reflector implementations, IGP area boundaries, and a mockup of routing table entries on CSR and DCI nodes.

Routing Table Mockup for CSR1		
Destination	Route Source	Next Hop
CSR2	IGP (ISIS or OSFP)	Outgoing Interface*
AGG1/2	IGP (ISIS or OSPF)	Outgoing Interface*
CSR3/4,	BGP-LU	AGG1 and AGG2
DCI 1/2	BGP-LU	AGG1 and AGG2

Routing Table Mockup for DCI1 and DCI2		
Destination	Route Source	Next Hop
AGG1/2/3/4	IGP (ISIS or OSPF)	Outgoing Interface*
CSR1, CSR2	BGP-LU	AGG1 or AGG2
CSR3, CSR4	BGP-LU	AGG3 or AGG4

* This is the outgoing interface according to the IGP's
Shortest Path First (SPF) algorithm.

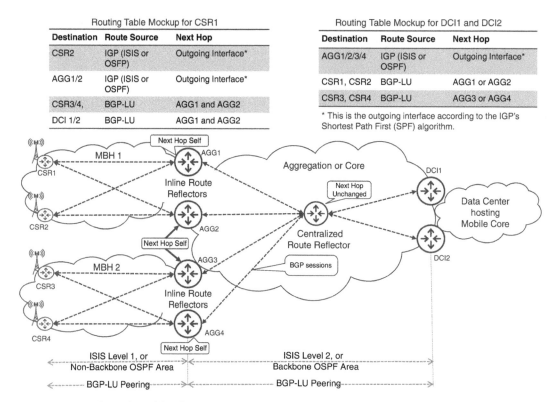

FIGURE 3-15   Seamless MPLS Architecture and Operations

These destinations and their labels are learned through BGP-LU, and the first lookup is to identify the next hop for the final destination. Once the next hop is identified, a second lookup is done in the IGP table to identify the best path to the next hop. Once the two labels are identified, all outgoing traffic is encapsulated within these two labels. The inner label is the final destination of the packet, learned through BGP-LU, while the outer label is the next-hop label, learned through LDP in the local IGP domain. Traffic within the local domain follows the normal MPLS forwarding process. The MPLS Penultimate Hop Popping (PHP) mechanism exposes the packet's inner label on the penultimate hop, which is then sent to the aggregation router. The aggregation node performs a lookup on this label and swaps it with a new two-label stack. Similar to the CSR, this new two-label stack consists of the BGP-LU-learned inner label for the final destination and the next-hop IGP label for its own domain.

The process repeats until the packets reach the gateway routers in the final domain—the DCI, in this case, if considering CSR-to-packet-core communications. The DCI would perform the lookup on the exposed label, realize the destination resides within its domain, and replace it with a single next-hop label for the destination. Figure 3-16 shows this traffic-forwarding process in the Seamless MPLS architecture.

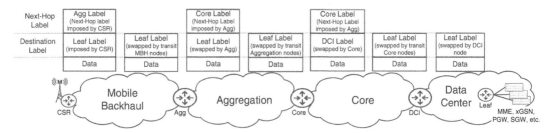

FIGURE 3-16   Data Forwarding in a Seamless MPLS Architecture

It must be noted that these labels are often referred to as *transport labels*, signifying that these are used for traffic forwarding in the transport network infrastructure. There might be additional labels imposed by the Provider Edge (PE) nodes, such as the CSR or leaf router in DC, that can identify the VPN services established between these devices.

What Is a Provider Edge (PE) Router?

The term *Provider Edge (PE)* is a commonly used in the data service provider network and identifies an MPLS-enabled router originating or terminating a VPN service.

In the case discussed so far, the CSR and the DC leaf are both PE routers that implement VPN services between them to ensure RAN and packet core connectivity.

While the use of BGP-LU in a Seamless MPLS architecture successfully solves the IGP routing scale problem, it does little to avoid device-level scalability issues on the CSR itself. Considering the sample topology in Figure 3-15, the CSR routes from MBH1 are advertised and imported into MBH2 using BGP-LU. These routes are then installed into the routing tables of CSRs in MBH2 to enable X2 connectivity between eNBs across the IGP domains. The CSRs, as previously mentioned, are low-cost routers with limited memory. There could be dozens or hundreds of these MBH IGP domains in a given MCN, each with dozens or hundreds of cell sites. If the host routes for every CSR are imported into each of these MBH IGP domains, the CSRs will reach their max routing table capacity long before all CSR routes are installed in the routing table. However, MCN architects need to consider whether eNBs in the MCN require full mesh X2 connectivity. Because X2 interfaces are used primarily for functions that assume close proximity between eNBs (for example, subscriber handoff and ICIC), not all eNBs require X2 connectivity between them. A common tactic is to import BGP-LU routes only from directly adjacent MBH domains, as it is more likely for a user to roam from an eNB from their MBH domain to an eNB in a directly adjacent MBH domain. Figure 3-17 shows this filtering tactic using three mobile backhaul domains, where each one imports routes only from its adjacent domain.

Today, MPLS/IP is the primary MBH transport technology of choice. Almost all current MBH networks utilize various benefits offered by MPLS/IP and implement the Seamless MPLS architecture outlined in the IETF drafts, along with the BGP-LU route-filtering to overcome the routing-protocol limitation as well as the individual CSR routing scale challenges.

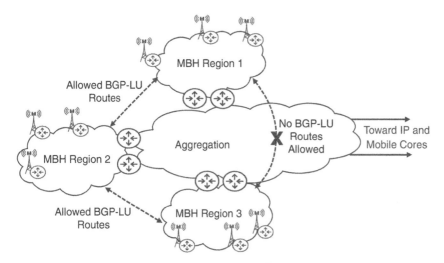

FIGURE 3-17   Route Filtering for X2 Interface Connectivity

Backhaul Transport Services

Regardless of the MBH infrastructure being Layer 2 or IP/MPLS, mobile network operators also implement VPN services between the cell sites and data centers hosting mobile core components.

Similar to the MBH evolution from Layer 2 to MPLS/IP, VPN services also evolved from Layer 2 VPN to Layer 3 VPN. Earlier MCNs would use Layer 2 tunneling technologies such as Ethernet 802.1Q-in-802.1Q (also called Q-in-Q), ATM, or Frame Relay to create Layer 2 tunnels from cell sites to aggregation nodes. These aggregation nodes, connecting to IP/MPLS-enabled aggregation and core networks, would implement Any Transport over MPLS (AToM), as defined in the IETF draft "Transport of Layer 2 Frames over MPLS" and later adopted as RFC-4906.[21, 22]

By the mid-2000s, the implementation of IP/MPLS to cell sites enabled the direct MPLS-based Layer 2 tunnel between cell sites and the data center. By this time, Ethernet was the dominant WAN technology; hence, these Layer 2 tunnels were implemented using Ethernet over MPLS (EoMPLS), as defined in RFC-4448.[23] A direct EoMPLS *pseudowire,* transporting Layer 2 frames over MPLS, eliminated the need for aggregation nodes to provide L2-to-MPLS interworking, thus simplifying the MBH design. However, as the number of cell sites grew, the number of EoMPLS pseudowires started to test the scalability limits on Data Center Interconnect routers. Being the destination for all EoMPLS tunnels originating from cell sites in the region, the DCI router had to potentially terminate thousands of these pseudowires.

What Is a Pseudowire?

A *pseudowire* is a Layer 2 tunnel over an MPLS network that emulates a dedicated back-to-back connection or leased line between two endpoints. This functionality was first defined in RFC-3985.[24]

To counter the growing scale challenges and provide multipoint capabilities, Virtual Private LAN Services (VPLS) and Hierarchical VPLS (H-VPLS) services were implemented.[25, 26] In an H-VPLS implementation for MBH, the cell sites would implement a *spoke* pseudowire to its *hub*—the aggregation node, which aggregates the traffic from all spoke pseudowires and transport over a single pseudowire to the DCI nodes. This significantly reduces the number of pseudowires on the DCI node, creating a more scalable architecture. Chapter 8, "Essential Technologies for 5G Ready Networks: Transport Services," provides more details on Layer 2 tunneling technologies.

The introduction of LTE triggered another architectural shift in VPN services for MBH. This one was driven primarily by the use of the X2 interface for connectivity between eNBs at cell sites. While VPLS and H-VPLS could be used for multipoint connectivity, the inherent shortcomings of a Layer 2 network (that is, flooding for BUM traffic) make VPLS and H-VPLS problematic in large-scale multipoint deployments. These challenges forced mobile network operators to use the more robust and proven MPLS Layer 3 VPN services for MBH transport—a trend that continues to this day. Figure 3-18 shows the gradual transition of Layer 2 point-to-point services to multipoint and Layer 3 VPN services over time, as well as across mobile generations.

From Backhaul to xHaul

Although MBH networks evolved over time to provide packet data transport, they have primarily been limited to D-RAN architectures. In these D-RAN deployments, the latency-sensitive RAN-specific traffic is terminated and packetized into IP by the BBU right at the cell site. As mentioned before, the radio traffic is transported between the RRH and BBU using CPRI, a proprietary transport mechanism implemented over a fiber optic cable. CPRI traffic is particularly latency sensitive, but with co-located RRH and BBU connected using just a few feet of fiber, the propagation delay is negligible in a D-RAN architecture.

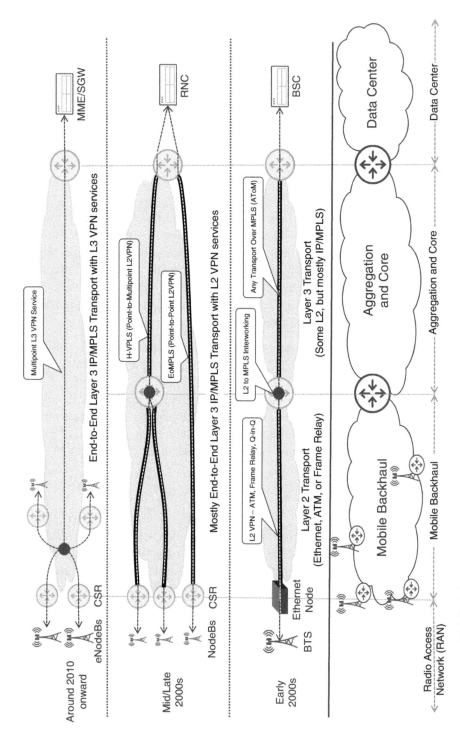

FIGURE 3-18 Mobile Infrastructure and Services Technologies Evolution

Propagation Delay over Fiber

The amount of time it takes for traffic to travel over a medium is called *propagation delay*. The speed of light in the optical fiber translates into a propagation delay of approximately 5 microseconds for every kilometer traveled.

C-RAN deployments, however, are not afforded the same luxury, as the BBU is moved from the cell site to a central location—the BBU hotel. The connectivity requirements for the BBU hotel to the RRH (that is, the fronthaul network) differ significantly from that of the backhaul. Given the real-time and uncompressed nature of CPRI traffic, the latency requirements are much stricter, and bandwidth requirements are much higher. As a comparison, the typical fronthaul latency budget is measured in microseconds, whereas the backhaul can tolerate latency in milliseconds. When designing mobile transport with both the D-RAN and C-RAN deployments, network providers now need to account for two different sets of network requirements—for the backhaul and the fronthaul (that is, the xHaul).

While every C-RAN cell site can connect to the BBU hotel using a dedicated set of optical fiber, such point-to-point fiber deployments are not practical for mass deployments. This section discusses the two other categories for fronthaul transport: Wavelength Division Multiplexing (WDM) and packet-based CPRI transport.

WDM Fronthaul

Almost all current fronthaul deployments for C-RAN use WDM for CPRI transport. WDM is a Layer 1 optical transport technology that uses a multiplexer to combine multiple interfaces operating over different wavelengths into a composite signal for transport over a common fiber. In academia, these wavelengths are represented by the Greek character λ. Hence, different wavelengths are often referred to as different *lambdas*. On the remote end, a demultiplexer separates various lambdas from the common fiber onto each individual interface.

For a CPRI fronthaul, this translates into multiple CPRI interfaces being multiplexed into a common pair of fiber for transport from cell sites to the BBU hotel. A demultiplexer at the BBU hotel would then separate each lambda to its own CPRI interface. The same process applies to traffic from the BBU hotel to cell sites, thus establishing the RRH–BBU fronthaul connectivity through a WDM-based CPRI fronthaul network, as shown in Figure 3-19.

The multiplexers and demultiplexers used in a WDM network could be active or passive, both with their respective benefits and drawbacks. A passive WDM system, where multiplexers and demultiplexers do not use any power, is simple and easier to deploy but lacks any device management capabilities. Each interface on a passive WDM multiplexer can accept only a specific wavelength, and the device connected to the passive multiplexer's interface must use a *colored optic* to transmit the data using the exact same wavelength. The process is repeated on the remote end, where the demultiplexing process decomposes the composite signal and transmits each lambda over its preset port. While easier to deploy, passive WDM requires careful planning and imposes administrative overhead to ensure correct optics are being used on each end of the connection.

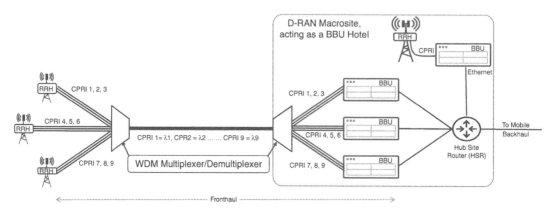

FIGURE 3-19   WDM-Based Fronthaul

Gray, Colored, and Tunable Optics

Optical transceivers can be generally classified into three different categories—gray, colored, and tunable. *Gray optics* are general-purpose, non-WDM optics used in fiber deployments that can be connected only to other gray optics. A *colored optic* is pre-tuned to one of the WDM defined wavelengths. This could be used with active or passive WDM equipment. *Tunable optics* can be colored to any supported wavelength.

Alternatively, an active multiplexer and demultiplexer require power to operate, adding a layer of deployment complexity and cost but also providing higher scalability and flexibility. Active WDM removes some of the administrative complexities of matching colored optics to their pre-set interfaces in a passive solution. If implemented, active WDM multiplexers/demultiplexers can dynamically reconfigure their input and output ports to match the desired wavelength. Additionally, an active WDM device could amplify the outgoing signal natively, whereas a passive WDM solution would require an external amplifier for extended distances. Active WDM devices can be easier to manage, as they provide the capabilities to collect statistics and operational data, as well as allow logging in for troubleshooting. On the other hand, active WDM systems require additional deployment considerations, such as power sources and other environmental factors.

When WDM is used for the fronthaul, passive WDM is more commonly deployed due to its lower cost and complexity. Given the latency sensitivity native to CPRI, the maximum fronthaul distance is limited to approximately under 20 km to avoid longer propagation delay. With such relatively short distances, optical amplification is not required, even with passive WDM solutions. However, some mobile network providers utilize active WDM due to the management capabilities it offers, despite its relatively higher costs.

Packetized Fronthaul

WDM-based fronthaul networks for 4G/LTE C-RAN have been in production for a few years, but they generally lack the flexibility and features readily available in IP-based networks. Additionally, use of WDM in fronthaul networks forces mobile network operators to deploy and maintain two distinct networks—one with MPLS/IP in the backhaul, and another with WDM in the fronthaul. The difference in capabilities of the two networking technologies—WDM being limited to Layer 1 features while IP/MPLS provides a lot more flexibility due to being a Layer 2 transport—also results in added complexity and the lack of a single, unified design.

More recently—driven by the desire for design simplification, advanced capabilities, and cost savings—some mobile network operators have been gravitating toward IP-based fronthaul networks. The primary purpose of these *packetized fronthaul networks* is to circumvent the use of dedicated fiber networks for CPRI transport and instead use an IP network to transport CPRI traffic between the RRH at the cell site and the BBU at the C-RAN hub site.

CPRI, being a proprietary radio communication protocol, needs to be adapted for IP transport. In a C-RAN architecture, when using packetized fronthaul, additional processing is needed at the cell site and BBU hotel to carry CPRI over the IP network. Given the proprietary nature of CPRI communications, the RRH and BBU equipment vendors have a significant advantage to provide this.

A commonly used solution is to map CPRI bitstream traffic into Ethernet, and vice versa, using *Radio over Ethernet (RoE)* technology—an IEEE standard documented in IEEE 1914.3.[27] RoE functions can be implemented on the cell site router (in this case, known as the *fronthaul CSR*) and the *fronthaul hub site router*. Once CPRI is mapped to Ethernet, VPN services can be used to transport Ethernet traffic between the cell site and the BBU hotel, ensuring CPRI connectivity, as illustrated in Figure 3-20. It must be noted that RoE is a bookended solution that must be implemented on both sides—the cell site and the BBU hotel. Chapter 5 covers IEEE 1914.3 RoE specifications in more detail.

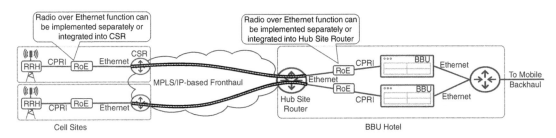

FIGURE 3-20 Packetized Fronthaul with RoE for CPRI-Ethernet Mapping

While the concept of a packetized fronthaul continues to gain momentum, this architecture is still in its infancy, with only a handful of deployments worldwide.[28] Packetized fronthaul is a new market created in the wake of xHaul evolution. RAN equipment manufacturers, with their own network equipment portfolio, have an incumbent advantage in this market, as they can easily incorporate CPRI functionality on their fronthaul CSR offering to provide CPRI transport. Network equipment manufacturers are also trying to tap this market by incorporating CPRI interfaces in their fronthaul cell site routers to provide CPRI transport.

With the growing adoption of packetized fronthaul, IEEE and other industry-led specification organizations have been working on enabling interoperability between RAN and network equipment to further simplify packetized fronthaul architecture and deployments. Chapter 5 discusses the evolution of C-RAN, xHaul, CPRI, and its transport over the packetized fronthaul in more detail.

Summary

This chapter offers a look at the state of mobile communication networks as they are deployed today. Figure 3-21 summarizes the journey to today's mobile networks.

This chapter covered the 3GPP releases leading to Evolved Packet System and its RAN and packet core components (namely, LTE and SAE) as well as current mobile backhaul networks and their ongoing evolution to xHaul.

For SAE, this chapter discussed the following topics:

- Evolved packet core and its building blocks
- Network attach and user registration process for EPC
- Packetized voice as services through IMS

For LTE and RAN, the following concepts were covered:

- New media access methods using OFDMA
- E-UTRAN and its building block, that is the eNB
- Introduction of the X2 interface and its use
- D-RAN to C-RAN architectural shift

For modern mobile backhaul, this chapter went over the following topics:

- Transition from Layer 2 to MPLS-based backhaul networks
- Concepts and use of Seamless MPLS
- Fronthaul and xHaul networks
- WDM-based and packetized fronthaul network implementations

The next chapter will discuss the anticipated changes and market drivers for 5G as well as the services promised to meet those expectations.

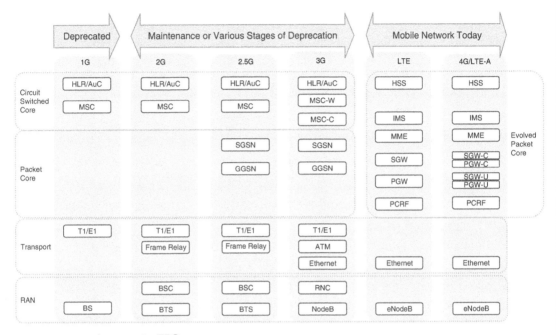

FIGURE 3-21   Journey to EPS

References

1. https://www.forbes.com/sites/simonrockman1/2019/08/01/millions-will-lose-out-when-government-kills-2g/?sh=4ced25bd7cd8 (last visited: Mar 2022)

2. https://www.emnify.com/en/resources/global-2g-phase-out (last visited: Mar 2022)

3. https://www.3gpp.org/ftp/Information/WORK_PLAN/Description_Releases/Rel-08_description_20140924.zip (last visited: Mar 2022)

4. http://www.itu.int/net/pressoffice/press_releases/2010/48.aspx (last visited: Mar 2022)

5. Martin Sauter. *From GSM to LTE-Advanced Pro and 5G: An Introduction to Mobile Networks and Mobile Broadband, Third Edition* (Hoboken, NJ: Wiley, 2017), Section 4.2.4, page 222

6. 3GPP TS 23.401 v12.6.0, Section 4.3.7.2, https://www.etsi.org/deliver/etsi_ts/123400_123499/123401/12.06.00_60/ts_123401v120600p.pdf (last visited: Mar 2022)

7. 3GPP TS 23.401 v12.6.0, Section 4.3.8.2, https://www.etsi.org/deliver/etsi_ts/123400_123499/123401/12.06.00_60/ts_123401v120600p.pdf (last visited: Mar 2022)

8. Sassan Ahmadi. *LTE-Advanced: A Practical Systems Approach to Understanding 3GPP LTE Releases 10 and 11 Radio Access Technologies* (Amsterdam: Elsevier, 2013), Section 5.2.1

9. 3GPP TS 23.203 v12.6.0, Section 6.1.7.2, https://www.etsi.org/deliver/etsi_TS/123200_123299/123203/12.06.00_60/ts_123203v120600p.pdf (last visited: Mar 2022)

10. https://www.3gpp.org/technologies/keywords-acronyms/98-lte (last visited: Mar 2022)

11. 3GPP TS 36.211 v8.9.0, Section 6.12, https://www.etsi.org/deliver/etsi_ts/136200_136299/136211/08.09.00_60/ts_136211v080900p.pdf (last visited: Mar 2022)

12. 3GPP TR 25.913, Section 7.3, https://www.etsi.org/deliver/etsi_tr/125900_125999/125913/08.00.00_60/tr_125913v080000p.pdf (last visited: Mar 2022)

13. 3GPP TS 36.211 v12.6.0, Section 6.3.2, https://www.etsi.org/deliver/etsi_ts/136200_136299/136211/12.06.00_60/ts_136211v120600p.pdf (last visited: Mar 2022)

14. https://www.3gpp.org/technologies/keywords-acronyms/101-carrier-aggregation-explained (last visited: Mar 2022)

15. https://www.3gpp.org/ftp/Information/WORK_PLAN/Description_Releases/Rel-11_description_20140924.zip (last visited: Mar 2022)

16. 3GPP TR 23.861 v1.7.0, Section 7, https://www.3gpp.org/ftp/Specs/archive/23_series/23.861/23861-170.zip (last visited: Mar 2022)

17. https://dallascityhall.com/government/Council%20Meeting%20Documents/msis_3_deployment-update-of-small-cell-network-nodes_combined_051319.pdf (last visited: Mar 2022)

18. https://www.fujitsu.com/us/Imagesgig5/FNC-Fujitsu-C-RAN-Mobile-Architecture-Migration-White-Paper.pdf (last visited: Mar 2022)

19. https://tools.ietf.org/html/rfc3107 (last visited: Mar 2022)

20. https://tools.ietf.org/html/draft-ietf-mpls-seamless-mpls-07 (last visited: Mar 2022)

21. https://tools.ietf.org/html/draft-martini-l2circuit-trans-mpls-00 (last visited: Mar 2022)

22. https://tools.ietf.org/html/rfc4906 (last visited: Mar 2022)

23. https://tools.ietf.org/html/rfc4448 (last visited: Mar 2022)

24. https://tools.ietf.org/html/rfc3985 (last visited: Mar 2022)

25. https://tools.ietf.org/html/rfc4761 (last visited: Mar 2022)

26. https://tools.ietf.org/html/rfc4762 (last visited: Mar 2022)

27. IEEE Standard 1914.3-2018, "IEEE Standard for Radio over Ethernet Encapsulations and Mappings," Oct. 5, 2018, pp. 1–77

28. https://newsroom.cisco.com/press-release-content?type=webcontent&articleId=2058724 (last visited: Mar 2022)

Chapter | 4

The Promise of 5G

Perhaps very few industries have gone through the type of market adoption seen in the mobile communications industry. Today, over 8 billion mobile connections serve more than 5 billion mobile users worldwide.[1, 2] This whopping ten-fold increase from a relatively measly 740 million mobile connections in the year 2000 has been fueled through continued acceleration in service improvements and innovations introduced over multiple mobile generations. Mobile phones and services evolved from being a novelty during the 2G and 2.5G period to becoming relatively mainstream in the 3G era. A key driver for mass adoption of the next generation of mobile services was the introduction of a new breed of *smartphone*, the iPhone, from Apple, Inc., in 2007. Before the iPhone, smartphones were primarily targeted toward enterprise users. Even though the first iPhone supported only 2G speeds, its introduction proved to be a pivotal moment in the telecommunication industry. For the first time, mobile phones and services were geared toward individual consumers, making mobile phones more "personal" and paving the way toward rapid adoption. In the years that followed, more smartphone manufacturers embraced consumer-focused mobile phone designs. Simultaneously, mobile service providers, fueled by the adoption of 4G and LTE, started offering higher data speeds with more coverage and service reliability. The combination of higher data speed coupled with the growing capabilities of smartphones and other mobile devices created a perfect ecosystem, catapulting mobile data services from a nice-to-have category to an absolute necessity.

Over the past several years, the accelerated speed of innovation in the mobile ecosystem has created an *over-anticipation* of what new mobile services in 5G would bring to the market. Simultaneously, the growing reliance on mobile data services has shaped consumer behaviors toward universal connectivity, ever-increasing data speeds, and real-time social experiences. Understanding these emerging trends and consumer expectations is critical to understanding the services offered by 5G networks and the need for underlying infrastructure transformation to support those services.

Emerging Trends and Expectations from Mobile Networks

The modern smartphone has replaced an assortment of single-purpose devices such as a camera, video recorder, personal entertainment systems, GPS navigation systems, and more. The adoption of mobile services has been continuously growing, and the total number of mobile devices is expected to surpass 13 billion by the year 2023.[3] However, services adoption is just one aspect of the impact the mobile industry has had on the market. Equally, if not more, significant are the vast improvements in mobile services over the past generations resulting in personalization and tighter integration of mobile services with a subscriber's personal life. Today's mobile consumers have come to expect a certain level of speed, coverage, and service responsiveness from their mobile service provider, as reflected in Figure 4-1.

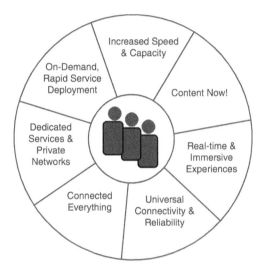

FIGURE 4-1   Subscriber Expectations from Future 5G Networks

This section will briefly look at these emerging trends and expectations to better understand how 5G technology and service offerings align to these market requirements.

Increased Speed and Capacity

Without a doubt, higher data download and upload speeds have been the primary driver in mobile service adoption. This increase in data speeds has been achieved using a combination of factors, including the availability of more frequency spectrum, sophisticated and efficient modulation and encoding techniques, and advanced antenna features such as multiple-input, multiple-output (MIMO). Faster data speeds open up a lot of possibilities in terms of mobile service applications, and chief among them is the use of video.

Be it real-time videoconferencing, over-the-top video-streaming services such as Netflix and Disney+, video-sharing applications such as TikTok and other social media applications, or simply embedded video on websites, video traffic accounted for 63% of the total mobile traffic in 2019 and is expected to grow to 76% by the year 2025.[4] The use of ultra-high-definition, 4K, and 8K video streaming—all of which require higher bandwidth and transmission speeds than ever before—means that the demand for higher speed is expected to continue.

Future 5G networks are expected to deliver data speeds of up to 13 times higher than the current average mobile and offer services reaching peak speeds of 20Gbps.[5, 6]

Content Now

Today, it is no secret that there are more mobile subscribers, and they are consuming more content than ever before. Video remains the primary utilized content category, but the manner in which a typical mobile subscriber utilizes the video content differs from an ordinary broadband user. While streaming video providers such as Netflix, Disney+, Hulu, YouTube, and others make their services available on mobile platforms, only a fraction of streaming video subscribers consume content using mobile devices. Instead, the content generated and consumed by mobile subscribers is mostly peer-to-peer video, in the form of either videoconferencing or video-sharing social media applications. An ever-growing number of mobile subscribers are live-sharing their experiences within their social circles, creating a more evenly distributed bandwidth and capacity demand across a wider subscriber base. For instance, a decade ago, in the year 2010, the top 1% of mobile consumers globally accounted for more than 50% of total mobile traffic. However, in the year 2019, the top 1% of mobile consumers generated less than 5% of today's data traffic.[7]

It's critical to understand and grasp this change in mobile consumer behavior regarding content creation and utilization. Traditionally, the focus of service enhancement for a mobile user's speed enhancements has been in the downlink direction. With users not only consuming but also generating video content anywhere and anytime, however, there has been a steady uptick in upstream traffic growth as well. Higher-resolution video formats, widespread use of high-definition videoconferencing for both leisure and business purposes, along with the rapidly changing future of work to a hybrid "in-person + virtual" employment model, means the need for higher speed in both the uplink and downlink, along with reliable mobile services, will continue not only to grow but also likely evolve from live to more immersive, real-time communications.

Real-Time and Immersive Experiences

It's hard to imagine a more perfect union than that of higher mobile data speed and increased video consumption. More than 80% of all information humans consume is primarily through visual aids such as video. The combination of higher speed and our preference for video acts as a feedback loop that continues to drive demand for even higher speeds and an appetite for more video consumption. More recently, in addition to live-streaming, there has been a growing use of real-time, immersive traffic services, video, and the like. These real-time services require significantly lower end-to-end delay when compared to live or conversational video and voice traffic.

It's easy to mix the concept of *live versus real-time* communications. Live communications can tolerate some measure of delay without much adverse effect. For instance, a sporting event might be broadcasted live but might be received by viewers a few seconds later. Real-time communications are considered to be more instantaneous, where a delay in transmission could render the data obsolete. Examples of real-time traffic include delivery of stock prices in financial markets for high-frequency trading as well as communication between a fleet of autonomous self-driving vehicles in close proximity to avoid collisions and accidents. Both of these are examples where any delay incurred during transmission of data could lead to missed financial opportunities or accidents causing damage and injuries, or even fatalities. In other words, real-time information might become outdated if not delivered and consumed within a very strict, predetermined time frame.

One of the biggest use cases for real-time services is online gaming, where end-to-end latency requirements are much stricter than live video and other commonly used applications. Advancements made in LTE and 4G have already made significant progress in providing near-real-time services and experiences to mobile gamers. Online mobile gaming revenue, a direct result of low-latency mobile services, is expected to grow from US$68 billion in 2019 to US$102 billion by 2023.[8]

5G networks are anticipated to introduce new use cases that continue to push the envelope as it pertains to low-latency service with applications such as industrial robotics, remote medical procedures, haptic feedback for transmitting touch over the Internet, drone communications, and more. These new services go far beyond simple live communication and would be used for both leisure and mission-critical purposes. While today's mobile gaming operates within a 20–30 millisecond latency budget, these new real-time applications and use cases expect much lower network latency—typically in the order of microseconds. The bandwidth requirements can vary depending on the application type, but they all consistently require less than 1 millisecond latency—something that current network architectures would struggle to provide. In order to properly support these applications, 5G networks would not only need to be faster and more reliable but also go through architectural changes to ensure real-time communications.

Universal Connectivity and Reliability

With mobile usage venturing from relative luxury into a necessity and further into mission-critical applicability, service availability and reliability have become a cornerstone of modern mobile networks. Availability of new frequency spectrum and advanced antenna features are enabling faster data speeds, higher capacity, and wider mobile coverage on an unprecedented scale—so much so that, in some cases, future 5G networks could supplement or replace a subscriber's wired Internet access—an implementation called *Fixed Wireless Access (FWA)*. [9]

FWA could be beneficial for residents in remote locations where wired broadband access may not be feasible due to cost and logistical reasons. For these locations, mobile broadband may be an alternative to wired broadband services; in some cases, governments actively subsidize efforts to provide mobile access to its citizens in remote communities. The *5G Rural First* initiative in the United Kingdom and the *5G Fund for Rural America* in the USA are two examples of government projects using eMBB services aimed at extending broadband access to remote or under-served locations.[10,11]

Mobile operators are also starting to position FWA-based mobile-based access as a replacement for wired broadband connectivity. Even though there is some skepticism, and rightly so, as to whether FWA would be able to replace wired services, service providers have already started offering FWA as part of their 5G plans. An example of this is Verizon's 5G Home Internet, that uses its 5G technology to provide residential broadband Internet services[12] – a service that has traditionally been provided by wired technologies such as cable, PON, or DSL.

Connected Everything

By the year 2023, it is expected that there will be three times more IP-connected devices than there are people on earth, translating to about 29 billion devices.[13] A lot of this growth is driven by embedding sensors and mobile transceivers in everyday *things* that can then communicate over the Internet or through private networks, thus creating an *Internet of Things (IoT)*. In essence, IoT is the name given to the network architecture where things, instead of people, communicate and share data between each other. The devices that make up the IoT framework can communicate using a variety of mechanisms, including Bluetooth, Wi-Fi, LoRaWAN, wired connectivity (Ethernet), as well as mobile networks.

IoT applications range from consumer to industrial to public works as well as military-driven use cases, but they are all dependent on ubiquitous connectivity and reliability. Some examples of the IoT ecosystem include connected homes, wearable technology, remote health monitoring, supply chain management, vehicular communications, environmental monitoring, remote surveillance, and many more. For instance, IoT-enabled smart utility meters can automatically upload usage data directly to the billing systems periodically, smart trash cans in public spaces can request a garbage pickup when sensors detect critical levels of trash in the bins, and soil monitors in agricultural fields may communicate with control systems to turn on water in areas where needed. These *machine-to-machine* communications are forecasted to be the fastest growing communication category, on track to account for over 50% of total devices and connections over the coming years.

Most of these connected devices might not use a significant amount of bandwidth and might not even require continuous connectivity. As a lot of IoT devices could be deployed in unmanned locations, they must be low maintenance, and because they are usually battery powered, these devices must conserve power whenever possible. As such, the sensors on these devices might come online periodically, sometimes just once a day or less, and transmit data in small bursts. While not very chatty and bandwidth consuming, the sheer volume of billions of new devices connecting to the mobile network means the future 5G network must take into consideration new services geared toward machine communication.

Dedicated Services and Private Networks

Current mobile networks are mostly geared toward providing bulk data as a service. Live video transmission requires high bandwidth and speed but could tolerate slightly higher network latency. Real-time traffic, on the other hand, demands instant delivery and might or might not require extensive bandwidth. IoT-enabled devices could instead use short-lived, bursty traffic that requires neither high speed nor instant delivery, but the number of connected devices could create a scalability challenge for the network. Another concern across mobile subscribers is data and information security. This becomes especially important for enterprise mobile customers, where compromised communications could have adverse consequences.

Future 5G mobile and transport networks must be able to accommodate these diverse requirements across multiple use cases and provide mobile services customized to individual application. One of the proposed mechanisms in 5G to deal with multiple service types over a common network infrastructure is the use of *network slicing*, which is discussed in the next section.

In addition to the network slicing for dedicated services, 5G is also expected to build upon the concept of private cellular networks introduced in the 4G LTE networks. These private networks allow an enterprise (that is, not a mobile service provider) to build and deploy their own cellular networks on its premises. The adoption of these private networks is fueled by the simplicity of setting up a mobile network offering robust coverage over larger and/or harder-to-reach geographical areas such as factory floors, mines, offshore oil rigs, stadiums, disaster zones, and others. The trend toward a private cellular network is further facilitated by the availability of additional RF spectrum (such as CBRS) in 5G.

On-Demand, Rapid Service Deployment

In today's fast-paced environment, both individual and enterprise mobile subscribers value the speed of execution and agility almost as much as bandwidth and reliability. Subscribers demand quick service activation, instant modifications to their existing service when requested, and up-to-date information on their usage levels. These consumers expect a portal to do all these things, but the tasks performed by residential and enterprise customers using these portals might differ. Residential subscribers might expect a self-service portal to upgrade or downgrade individual services, whereas an enterprise customer might need to integrate new mobile devices with their *software-defined wide area network* (SD-WAN) solution in order to gain connectivity. Either way, providing subscribers with the ability to create their own on-demand service requests with quick fulfillment is a crucial expectation from today's and future mobile subscribers. Automation is fundamental to achieving these self-service, rapid, and on-demand service execution expectations.

However, that's not the only application of automation in the mobile service provider's network. Network operators have been pursuing virtualization of various network elements and functions over the past few years. Based on industry demand and market direction, equipment manufacturers have been introducing virtualized versions of RAN and mobile core components such as Baseband Unit (BBU), Mobility Management Entity (MME), Serving Gateway (SGW), and so on for mobile service providers to deploy. Virtualization's true benefits cannot be unlocked, unless it's coupled with automation to deploy, monitor, manage, and scale. The emerging use of public clouds for hosting virtualized components has compounded the need for automation as the mobile providers now have to integrate their existing tools with the cloud providers' toolset, which typically has been built with an *automation first* mindset. The trend toward virtualization is expected to continue, along with the use of container-based applications better suited to be hosted in a cloud environment. Chapter 5, "5G Fundamentals," covers containers and cloud-native architecture in further detail. Along with virtualization and containerization, the effective use of automation tools in a mobile service provider's infrastructure will be a key component in enabling 5G services.

5G Technology Enablers

5G is expected to deliver unprecedented growth in mobile adoption, bringing a paradigm shift to users' data consumption pattern and rolling out innovative new services. 5G promises to achieve this by building on the foundation already laid out by 4G and LTE; however, the scale of changes expected in 5G is likely to be substantially higher than ever previously experienced. With the already widespread adoption of mobile services among individual subscribers, 5G instead focuses on enhanced service quality, new value-added use cases, extending mobile connectivity to *things*, and bringing more enterprise-focused services into the fold. Given this context, the *International Telecommunication Union* (ITU) published the *International Mobile Telecommunication-2020* (IMT-2020) specification, comparing it with previously published IMT-Advanced or 4G specifications.[14] Figure 4-2 outlines these comparisons between the IMT-2020 specification, widely considered to be 5G specifications, and IMT-Advanced (4G) across multiple key dimensions.

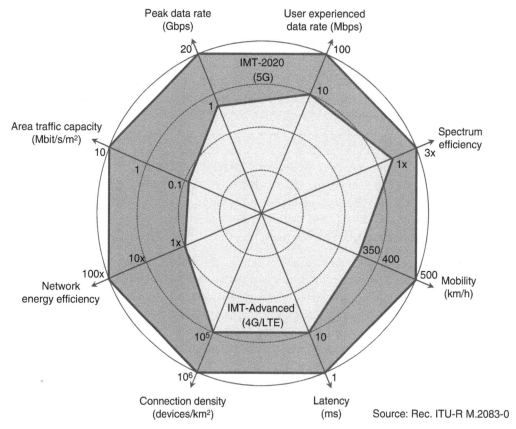

FIGURE 4-2   Comparing IMT-Advanced (4G) and IMT-2020 (5G) Attributes[15]

Next Generation Mobile Network

In addition to ITU and 3GPP, other industry coalitions also exist that have defined 5G-related use cases, requirement documents, and design guidelines as well. One such organization is the *Next Generation Mobile Networks* (NGMN) alliance, which has defined use cases and milestones for 5G services. It must be noted that there are significant overlaps between the ITU/3GPP specification and other coalitions' use cases and guidelines. In most cases, these design guidelines and requirements complement the specification from 3GPP and ITU. Other notable industry groups are the *Open RAN* (O-RAN) Alliance and *Telecom Infra Project* (TIP), which are focused on developing, testing, and deploying mobile solutions.

As Figure 4-2 illustrates, there are significant enhancements being introduced in 5G that will demand tectonic changes in both the mobile and data networks. For instance, achieving 20Gbps peak rate compared to 4G's 1Gbps, reducing latency from 10ms to 1ms, and achieving three times the spectrum efficiency will; all require innovative new technologies to enable IMT-2020 or 5G requirements.

New Spectrum and Advanced Antenna Functions

First and foremost, among these new 5G enabling technologies is the introduction of new spectrum and advanced antenna features. The types of average and peak data rates expected by future 5G networks are not possible without crucial RAN and RF performance enhancements. Unlocking the new sub-1GHz and sub-7GHz spectrum, as well as the use of new mmWave spectrum above 24GHz, provides mobile service providers with a healthy mix of coverage and capacity spectrums, increased data rate, and wider coverage. In addition to the new spectrum ranges, 5G-capable radios called *5G New Radio (5G NR)* have gone through significant upgrades as well. The 5GNR features are aimed at providing a superior customer experience, not only increasing uplink (UL) and downlink (DL) speeds, but also increasing overall cell capacity and reliability. 5G NR extends some of the already existing features, such as MIMO and Coordinated Multipoint, but introduces more, such as beam forming and dynamic spectrum sharing. Chapter 5 covers these advanced antenna functions and their application in more detail.

RAN and Mobile Core Decomposition

With the decomposition of RAN in Centralized-RAN (C-RAN) architectures, the transport and RAN domains started getting intertwined. Pooling the BBUs for multiple cell sites together in the C-RAN hub provides better spectral efficiency as well as cost savings for mobile service providers. RAN architectures for 5G will continue to evolve, creating even more RAN decomposition. This architectural evolution toward RAN decomposition has created an opportunity for open interfaces, instead of the traditionally proprietary ones. Open RAN (O-RAN) Alliance, a consortium of network operators and mobility equipment manufacturers, is working toward defining specifications to support truly open interfaces in the RAN domain.[16]

Simultaneously, and independent of the RAN decomposition, mobile core architecture has undergone a similar process of spreading out 5G Core components across multiple locations. This decomposition is aimed at bringing the components of the mobile core responsible for interacting with user traffic close to the RAN. These user plane (U-Plane) components could be placed in the Centralized-RAN hub sites alongside the BBUs and could thus reduce transit latency, resulting in efficient traffic handling. The control plane (C-Plane) elements of the mobile core could stay in the central DC. This *Control Plane and User Plane Separation (CUPS)* is a fundamental architectural shift in the 5G mobile core and, along with RAN decomposition, is covered in more detail in Chapter 5.

Networking Slicing

Another innovation that 5G is meant to bring is the capability of network slicing. Given the widespread use of mobile services, new use cases that require strict bandwidth or latency requirements, and ongoing security concerns, many enterprises, governments, and other entities are asking for dedicated mobile networks to carry their traffic. Obviously, it is not feasible to create a dedicated network infrastructure for each individual customer; however, network slicing would enable a mobile operator to offer such a service. Network slicing offers a logically partitioned network to provide dedicated services and network characteristics requested by the service and can contain resources across multiple network segments such as transport, data centers, and so on.

In its simplest form, a network slice is akin to a virtual private network (VPN) that provides logical traffic and service separation over a given network infrastructure. However, a network slice instance not only provides traffic segregation but can also offer exclusive use of network resources—interfaces, routers, compute, storage, mobile core components, and RAN resources—based on the characteristics requested by the slice instance. For example, a slice instance created for high bandwidth and capacity would only use higher-bandwidth interfaces, even if it means taking a slightly longer path, whereas a low-latency slice would use the lowest latency path, even if it's different from the IGP shortest path. Similarly, if the slice instance requires high security and confidentiality, it would avoid any unencrypted interface, using only the interfaces that provide traffic encryption, even if the secure path is not the optimal best path. Figure 4-3 show a transport network with multiple slices, each with its own network characteristic.

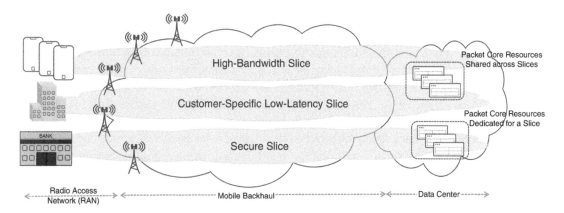

FIGURE 4-3 Network Slicing Concept

Just like any other mobile service, a network slice might not be a permanent entity and go through a full lifecycle of being instantiated, created, managed, and monitored when in use and torn down or deleted when no longer required. Given the intricacies of weaving together a network slice instance across multiple domains, the role of automation is paramount. Network slicing is one of the most anticipated and talked about capabilities made possible with 5G, and use cases such as low latency, high-bandwidth utilization, security, and more are expected to make use of it. Network slicing, more specifically 5G transport network slicing, is further discussed in Chapter 6.

Automation

Automation has already been at the forefront of every service provider's priorities for the past several years. Mobile and Internet service providers have seen exponential growth in the number of devices connecting to the network. These devices and subscribers have been using more data at higher speeds, requiring service providers to upgrade their network infrastructure to meet the demand. In the meantime, the revenues from these subscribers have not grown at a comparable pace, forcing service providers to explore efficient operations through automation for cost savings. With an even higher number of devices connecting to the network, the use of automation for reducing operational cost is expected to not only continue but accelerate when it comes to enabling new technologies and architectures for future 5G networks.

With modern mobile services spanning multiple domains, the scope of automation has grown from single-device or single-purpose automation to cross-domain and business process automation. Today, automation processes and use cases in a modern network can take multiple forms and could be used to provision new cell site equipment with minimal to no human interaction, to instantiate and manage a new network slice, or they could use complex logic to identify and correct commonly encountered issues in the network. Use of automation processes not only expedite deployment times and provide efficiency, but they also contribute to significant OPEX savings by automating repeatable tasks. 5G networks, which are expected to expand mobile service to millions of new users, billions of new devices, and use an intricate integration of RAN, transport, data center, and mobile core domains, will rely on more automation than ever. Chapter 10, "Designing and Implementing 5G Network Architecture," further explores the role of automation in enabling 5G networks and services.

Mapping 5G Enablers to Market Trends

Each of the 5G enabling technologies and innovations mentioned thus far directly correlate with the emerging trends and expectations subscribers have come to expect from mobile networks. For instance, RAN and mobile core decomposition is directly related to providing low-latency traffic, thus enabling an immersive and real-time experience for mobile subscribers. The availability of new spectrum and advanced antenna features collectively increases capacity and data speeds along with better reliability and seamless mobility. On the other hand, automation and network slicing bring dedicated services, agility, and execution speed to 5G networks. Figure 4-4 explores this relationship between various 5G enabling technologies and the market trends and expectations.

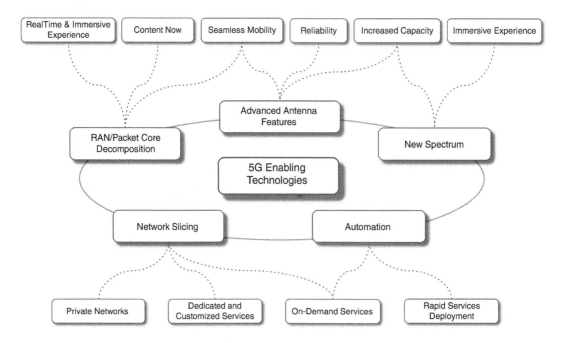

FIGURE 4-4   5G Enabling Technologies

Mobile service providers use catchy buzzwords, loosely connected to their underlying technical characteristics, in their marketing campaigns to differentiate themselves from competitors. Even if a mobile service provider has not implemented a full end-to-end 5G solution, they often boast of their 5G capabilities based on partial implementations. For instance, in the United States, Verizon markets its 5G service offerings as *5G Ultra Wideband* or *5G Nationwide*, which ties back to the frequency spectrum Verizon uses for these service offerings. The ultra-wideband service refers to the high-band mmWave that provides higher speed and capacity but limited coverage. In contrast, 5G Nationwide refers to using a lower, sub-1GHz spectrum, providing greater coverage and reach but at a relatively slower speed.[17] Similarly, T-Mobile labels its 5G service offerings as *5G Ultra Capacity* and *5G Extended Range*, referring to a high- or mid-band frequency spectrum and a sub-1GHz frequency spectrum, respectively, thus providing a mix of speed and coverage.[18] The use of spectrum and the particular service availability are also dependent on what frequency spectrum is available for a mobile service provider in a given geographical region. Chapter 2, "Anatomy of Mobile Communication Networks," covered the details of how a specific frequency spectrum is allocated for use.

5G Service Offerings

In an effort to identify use cases for future market expectations and demands, 3GPP published a technical report titled *Study on New Services and Markets Technology Enablers* (SMARTER), as part of Release 14.[19] The report initially identified five service types for future mobile networks:

- Enhanced Mobile Broadband

- Critical Communications

- Massive Machine-Type Communications

- Network Operations

- Enhancements of Vehicle to Everything

These five services were later consolidated into the following three usage scenarios and adopted by ITU's IMT-2020 recommendation:[20]

- Enhanced Mobile Broadband (eMBB)

- Ultra-Reliable and Low Latency Communications (URLLC)

- Massive Machine-Type Communications (mMTC)

This section takes a closer look at the definition and applications of these services.

Enhanced Mobile Broadband (eMBB)

Enhanced Mobile Broadband (eMBB) is a natural evolution of 4G mobile services and one of the first 5G services to be implemented, primarily focused on providing a better data service experience for mobile subscribers. A better data service naturally includes higher upload and download data speeds, but eMBB also includes provisions for consistent coverage over larger geographical areas as well as better user mobility for scenarios where a subscriber may be moving at high speeds in trains, automobiles, or planes.[21] It must be noted that early 5G service campaigns by mobile service providers focused entirely on eMBB's underlying characteristics—higher speeds (for example, 5G Ultra Wideband or 5G Ultra Capacity) and greater coverage (for example, 5G Nationwide or 5G Extended Range).

In many aspects, eMBB is the first phase of the 5G era that was predominantly implemented using the new (and in some cases repurposed) sub-7GHz and mmWave frequency spectrum and 5G NR advanced antenna functions. The higher data speeds specified by eMBB not only allow faster Internet browsing and live video chats but can eventually rival data speeds typically associated with fixed broadband connections. Another application of eMBB is the use of mobile services as "hotspots" in areas with a high concentration of low-mobility users. In such a case, eMBB would need to provide a larger total area capacity. Figure 4-5 summarizes some of the key aspects of an eMBB service.[22]

FIGURE 4-5   Key IMT-2020 Metrics and Requirements for eMBB

With peak speeds of up to 20Gbps and average user speed in 100s of Mbps, eMBB would be vital to introducing many new services and applications. One such example is immersive experiences like virtual reality (VR) and augmented reality (AR) on mobile platforms. Another could be the use of eMBB to provide FWA-based broadband Internet access, replacing traditional broadband services.

Ultra-Reliable and Low Latency Communications (URLLC)

While eMBB focuses on data speeds and volume, the Ultra-Reliable and Low-Latency Communications (URLLC) service aims at enabling real-time use cases. URLLC use cases have applications in multiple industry verticals such as healthcare, transportation, industrial automation, entertainment, and more. All URLLC applications are rooted in one fundamental requirement: instantaneous delivery of mobile traffic.

However, there are multiple challenges for URLLC implementations originating from existing mobile communications network architectures. First and foremost is that the mobile devices, part of the RAN domain, must communicate with mobile core components such as SGW to send and receive any traffic. The two domains are typically connected by an elaborate mobile backhaul (MBH) network with access, aggregation, and core layers—each with multiple routers. Because the central data center hosting mobile core components could be dozens, if not hundreds, of kilometers from the cell site, propagation delay is also a significant contributor to latency. Besides, the radio interface itself is not optimized for low-latency communications and needs to be improved further. Suffice it to say, the current MCN architectures are not built with URLLC in mind.

RAN and mobile core decomposition and Mobile Edge Compute (MEC) offer an architecture that makes URLLC possible. A lot of the URLLC use cases are geared toward processing the U-Plane traffic as close to the user as possible. Such an arrangement can be achieved through the use of MEC, where applications are placed in data centers closer to the RAN, known as *far edge data centers*. This approach is also aided by mobile core decomposition, where user-plane-specific mobile core components are moved closer to the RAN to reduce the number of devices between the two domains, shortening the propagation delays and lowering the latency for user traffic. Mobile operators may use a low-latency transport network slice to transport traffic between the cell site and far edge DC. Such an architecture may meet the 5G latency requirements of *1ms or less* for URLLC services. An example of this architecture could be industrial automation, where robotics applications could be placed in the on-prem data center right next to the mobile core's user plane components and can communicate with automated machinery on the factory floor without delay.

Massive Machine-Type Communications (mMTC)

The last of the three services defined by 3GPP is *Massive Machine-Type Communications (mMTC)*, which is characterized by connection density rather than data speed, capacity, or latency. mMTC is geared toward accommodating a large number of Internet of Things (IoT) devices that require reliability, coverage area, low cost, and longevity. Even before 5G, there have been multiple standards, platforms, technologies, and network types defined for machine-type communications. Collectively called *low-power wide area network (LPWAN)*, these networks aim to provide long-range, energy-efficient connectivity for IoT devices. *Narrowband IoT (NB-IoT)* and *LTE Machine-Type Communications (LTE-MTC or LTE-M)* are two examples of LPWAN specifications first defined in 3GPP Releases 13 and 14. There are other network types and specifications for IoT connectivity defined outside of 3GPP, including Long Range (LoRa), which is a proprietary IoT protocol, DASH-7, which is an open protocol developed as an alternative to LoRa, IEEE's 802.11ah (Wi-Fi HaLow), and several others.

mMTC is an evolution of NB-IoT and LTE-M aimed at enabling massive connection density of up to a million devices per km^2. The mMTC service type is not latency sensitive and can tolerate service latencies in the order of seconds, as opposed to typical latencies of microseconds or milliseconds, as is the case with URLLC and eMBB. Low-band sub-1GHz frequencies are typically used to implement mMTC service, as devices utilizing these services are often spread over larger coverage areas and do not require high data speeds. However, it must be noted that these devices might still require registration and communication with the mobile core and can cause scale challenges on the mobile network's control plane. mMTC service definition aims at minimizing these interactions in order to allow ultra-high scale of IoT devices to connect to mobile networks without straining the control plane. 3GPP has defined multiple features such as power saving mode (PSM), extended discontinuous reception (eDRX), and others that allow IoT devices to optimize their power consumption while maintaining minimal interaction with the mobile network.

Private Mobility

Although not defined exclusively as a service, use of *Private 5G* networks is increasing among large enterprises—especially in the industrial and manufacturing sectors. Simply put, Private 5G refers to a non–mobile service provider setting up their own 5G mobile network. For enterprises, using a private cellular network provides them with consistent and reliable coverage as well as an opportunity to implement URLLC and mMTC services, which may not yet be available from mobile service providers. While private mobility is not just limited to 5G and could be deployed with 4G as well, but the technological innovations and enhancements in 5G have made private mobility feasible.

Over the years, the unlocking of the frequency spectrum means enterprises can buy their own spectrum or lease it from a local mobile service provider.[23] Another option would be the use of the Citizens Broadband Radio Service (CBRS) spectrum, which allows enterprises to use publicly available frequencies without the cost associated with spectrum purchase. Virtualization, cloud hosting, and a move toward open interfaces in the RAN and mobile core are also key enabling factors facilitating the adoption of Private 5G. The RAN and mobile core decomposition and the move toward virtualization have allowed enterprises to use a hybrid model with on-prem and cloud-based deployment. In this case, only the components of the RAN and mobile core that require proximity to the mobile device would be deployed on-premises. The remaining components, including the majority of the mobile core, would be deployed offsite, usually in a cloud environment. Using a hybrid cloud and on-premises deployment model reduces the CAPEX required to set up a private mobility network and uses a much smaller footprint, which may not have been possible in the pre-cloud era.

Using private mobility networks and MEC, enterprises could easily deploy URLLC and mMTC services on their premises—something that major mobile service providers are currently lacking. For manufacturing and distribution warehouses, this could mean massive improvements in operational efficiency with automated assembly lines, robotic process control, autonomous forklifts, guided vehicles, and location tracking—all using local, private mobile networks. Private 5G is still evolving, and new use cases are being identified for industrial IoT, oil and gas exploration, cargo handling at seaports, and more. Private 5G, officially called *NPN*, was originally defined by 3GPP in Release 16, followed by enhancements in Release 17.[24] GSMA also published technical guidelines for 5G campus network deployment in November 2020.[25] Private 5G networking holds great potential for replacing large-scale Wi-Fi deployments, and some cloud providers are already tapping into this market by offering streamlined ordering and deployment of Private 5G networks with just a few clicks.

Summary

This chapter offers a glance at the trends and expectations that have emerged in the wake of successful 4G and LTE services, which in turn have been creating an over-anticipation of what future 5G networks would offer. It also explores key technical and architectural innovations driving the capabilities enhancement in 5G over its 4G and LTE counterparts. A summary of 3GPP-defined 5G services—Enhanced Mobile Broadband (eMBB), Ultra-Reliable and Low-Latency Communications (URLLC), and Massive Machine-Type Communications (mMTC)—and their applications was also provided in this chapter, along with private mobility drivers and use cases. Figure 4-6 maps the relevance of various key capabilities for each of the three 5G services.[26]

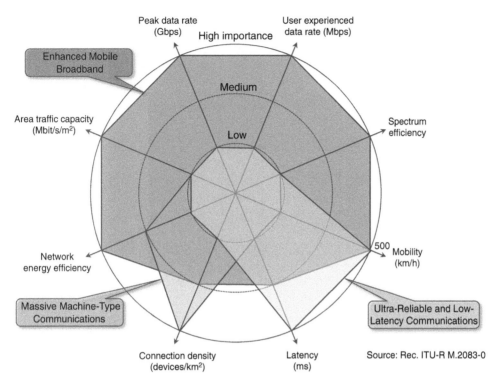

FIGURE 4-6   5G Services-to-Capabilities Mapping

Chapter 5 will dive into the details of technology and architecture changes that are crucial to realizing the promise of 5G.

References

1. https://www.statista.com/statistics/262950/global-mobile-subscriptions-since-1993/ (last visited: Feb 2022)

2. Cisco Annual Internet Report, https://www.cisco.com/c/en/us/solutions/collateral/executive-perspectives/annual-internet-report/white-paper-c11-741490.html (last visited: Feb 2022)

3. Ibid.

4. Ericsson Mobility Report 2020, https://www.ericsson.com/49da93/assets/local/mobility-report/documents/2020/june2020-ericsson-mobility-report.pdf (last visited: Feb 2022)

5. Cisco Annual Internet Report, op. cit.

6. https://spectrum.ieee.org/telecom/wireless/3gpp-release-15-overview (last visited: Feb 2022)

7. Cisco Annual Internet Report, op. cit.

8. "Global mobile gaming app revenues worldwide from 2019 to 2024," https://www.statista.com/statistics/536433/mobile-games-revenue-worldwide/ (last visited: Feb 2022)

9. https://www.lightreading.com/5g/is-5g-fixed-wireless-getting-ready-for-its-comeback/d/d-id/763866 (last visited: Feb 2022)

10. https://www.5gruralfirst.org/ (last visited: Feb 2022)

11. https://www.fcc.gov/5g-fund (last visited: Feb 2022)

12. https://www.verizon.com/5g/home (last visited: Feb 2022)

13. Cisco Annual Internet Report, op. cit.

14. https://www.itu.int/dms_pubrec/itu-r/rec/m/R-REC-M.2083-0-201509-I!!PDF-E.pdf (last visited: Feb 2022)

15. Ibid.

16. Open RAN (O-RAN) Alliance, https://www.o-ran.org/ (last visited: Feb 2022)

17. https://www.verizon.com/coverage-map/ (last visited: Feb 2022)

18. https://www.t-mobile.com/news/network/fastest-largest-5g-network (last visited: Feb 2022)

19. 3GPP TR 22.891, "Study on New Services and Markets Technology Enablers," http://www.3gpp.org/ (last visited: Feb 2022)

20. https://www.itu.int/dms_pubrec/itu-r/rec/m/R-REC-M.2083-0-201509-I!!PDF-E.pdf (last visited: Feb 2022)

21. 3GPP TR 21.915, 3GPP Release 15 description, http://www.3gpp.org/ (last visited: Feb 2022)

22. https://www.itu.int/dms_pubrec/itu-r/rec/m/R-REC-M.2083-0-201509-I!!PDF-E.pdf (last visited: Feb 2022)

23. https://www.networkworld.com/article/3609841/john-deere-invests-500k-in-private-5g-licenses-to-support-more-flexible-factory-networks.html (last visited: Feb 2022)

24. "Study on Enhanced Support of Non-Public Networks (NPN)," https://portal.3gpp.org/desktopmodules/Specifications/SpecificationDetails.aspx?specificationId=3655 (last visited: Feb 2022)

25. https://www.gsma.com/newsroom/wp-content/uploads//NG.123-v1.0.pdf (last visited: Feb 2022)

26. https://www.itu.int/dms_pubrec/itu-r/rec/m/R-REC-M.2083-0-201509-I!!PDF-E.pdf (last visited: Feb 2022)

Chapter | **5**

5G Fundamentals

Perhaps very few market segments have gone through the type of market adoption seen in the mobile industry. 5G does not start the mobility revolution from scratch but rather builds on the concepts and innovations of previous generations. For instance, near-real-time services have already been available in 4G, enabling real-time gaming and augmented reality applications for leisure. 5G is expected to push this further with enhanced reliability and low-latency capabilities for applications such as industrial automation, self-driving vehicles, remote medical care, and other mission-critical applications.

Similarly, mobile bandwidth has already been steadily growing to allow live video or video-on-demand over LTE, as well as multipoint videoconferencing. 5G aims to enable enhanced mobile broadband for everyone.

The fundamentals covered thus far in the previous chapters lay the foundation for the generational leap to 5G. This chapter brings those fundamentals together and dives deeper into the innovations that shape 5G. This chapter continues to focus on three domains of the mobile communication network—RAN, mobile core, and transport—and explores how each of these evolves to create a complete 5G experience.

5G Radio Access Network

Among the many parts comprising a fifth-generation mobile network, not many are entirely novel. Undeniably, significant innovations distinguish 5G radio technology from its predecessors, but all of these essential innovations are deeply rooted in technologies developed for previous generations of networks. After all, LTE proved its ambitious name by giving a solid foundation for mobile radio network evolution in the long term. Proper understanding of these innovations is fundamental for 5G mobile core network (MCN) capacity planning, architectural definitions, as well as technology selection.

Air Interface Enhancement

The radio access technology of 5G networks is called *5G New Radio (5G NR),* or *NR* for short. Although it is based on the same Orthogonal Frequency-Division Multiple Access (OFDMA) technology, a few important innovations distinguish it from LTE radio access. Unlike LTE with its fixed subcarrier spacing in Orthogonal Frequency Division Multiplexing (OFDM), NR supports multiple spacings with wider subcarriers. In addition to 15 KHz, NR also supports OFDM subcarrier widths of 30, 60, 120, and 240 KHz.[1] The radio frame of NR has the same duration of 10ms as in LTE and is divided into 10 subframes. However, the similarities in the frame structure between LTE and NR end here, and further subdivision of an NR subframe differs significantly from that of LTE. There are two slots per subframe in LTE, with each normally carrying seven OFDM symbols (or six in some cases). In contrast to that, 5G NR slots carry 14 OFDM symbols.

Subcarrier width and OFDM symbol duration are inversely proportional; therefore, the use of wider subcarriers effectively reduces the duration of an OFDM symbol. With a fixed number of OFDM symbols per slot, a 1ms NR subframe can have anything from one slot (with 15 KHz subcarrier spacing) to 16 slots (with 240 KHz spacing).[2] The use of wider subcarrier spacing and shorter slots decreases radio interface latency, thereby benefiting URLLC scenarios. Figure 5-1 illustrates the difference in NR framing structure depending on subcarrier spacing.

In both LTE and NR, slots are used to schedule data over the radio interface, but NR can schedule data in a more efficient way. Besides using more diverse slot durations, 5G NR offers flexible use of individual symbols within a slot. Contrary to LTE, the use of slots and OFDM symbols within each slot is not rigidly prescribed by the 5G specification. The control information, data, and receipt acknowledgment can be sent within a single slot, significantly reducing latency in the network and allowing faster retransmissions of lost data.

Just like in previous generations, both FDD and TDD duplexing methods can be used in NR. When FDD duplexing is used, all the slots in the frame are used for either downlink or uplink communication in their respective bands. On the other hand, a frame in TDD duplexing may contain slots for both downlink and uplink communications. The TDD concept is taken even further in NR, with each individual OFDM symbol being used for downlink or uplink communication within a single slot. There are a number of different formats for uplink, downlink, and flexible (either down or uplink) symbols in a slot defined in the 3GPP *5G; NR; Physical layer procedures for control* specification.[3] As a result, the receiver does not have to wait for the beginning of a new slot to start receiving data after control information, and then for another slot to send an acknowledgment back. Everything can be done within a single slot, provided the chunk of data is short enough. Such a slot is said to be *self-contained*, as it has all necessary information to decode and use the data it delivers. This helps not only TDD but FDD as well, as all necessary information is delivered in a self-contained slot.

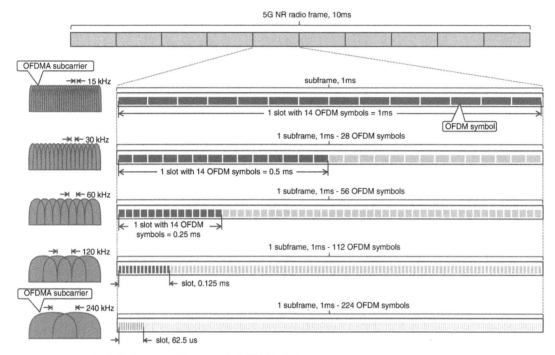

FIGURE 5-1   5G NR Frames, Slots, and OFDMA Subcarriers

To improve latency characteristics of NR for ultra- and very-low-latency scenarios even further, 3GPP's *Study on new radio access technology* proposes the use of a mini-slot with a smaller number of OFDM symbols.[4] A mini-slot can have as few as only one OFDM symbol and can be scheduled immediately, without waiting for the beginning of a new regular slot. In some cases, mini-slots can preempt data already scheduled for transmission via a process called *puncturing*, reducing latency for URLLC use cases even further.

5G NR Channel Widths and Carrier Aggregation

To boost the peak rates and overall cell capacity, 3GPP defined wider channels for 5G NR, ranging from 5 MHz to as wide as 400 MHz, depending on the frequency range used. For sub-7 GHz bands, also known as Frequency Range 1 (FR1), channel widths can be between 5 MHz and 100 MHz.[5] Channel widths of 50 MHz through 400 MHz are specified for the bands above 24 GHz, known as Frequency Range 2 (FR2).[6]

Not every combination of subcarrier spacing and channel width is supported by 3GPP specifications. For example, 15 KHz subcarrier spacing can be used in channels 5–50 MHz wide but is not supported with wider channels. Moreover, subcarrier spacings of 15 KHz and 30 KHz are not supported in FR2 at all, due to significantly different propagation characteristics of mmWave, as was mentioned in

Chapter 2, "Anatomy of Mobile Communication Networks." Subcarrier spacings of 15 KHz and 30 KHz, with their longer OFDM symbol duration, are effective in combating inter-symbol interference in macrocells covering large areas but would make transceivers unnecessarily complex and expensive in mmWave bands. A comprehensive list of supported subcarrier spacings and channel widths is defined in 3GPP's "*5G; NR; User Equipment radio transmission and reception.*"[7, 8]

Besides the wider channels definition in NR, the width of the guard bands is also optimized, providing a slight increase in the number of usable subcarriers in each channel compared to LTE. For example, a 20 MHz channel with 15 KHz spacing in NR can have 1272 subcarriers, versus 1200 subcarriers in the same 20 MHz LTE channel.[9] Each of these subcarriers is organized in sets of 12, forming a *resource block*. Resource blocks were briefly introduced in Chapter 3, "Mobile Networks Today," but unlike LTE, resource blocks in NR are not defined as a number of subcarriers per subframe. Instead, 5G NR defines a resource block as just 12 OFDMA subcarriers, without relation to time. This allows more flexible use of resource blocks within a slot, as was described in the previous section. Figure 5-2 shows a high-level view of 12 OFDMA subcarriers to a resource block mapping and multiples of resource blocks in a single NR channel. For example, there are 106 resource blocks in a 20 MHz NR channel.[10]

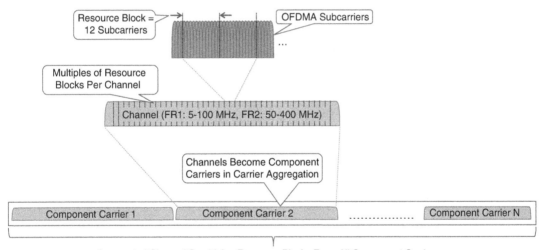

Aggregated Channel Combining Resource Blocks From All Component Carriers

FIGURE 5-2   Carrier Aggregation in 5G NR

When a bandwidth of an individual channel is not sufficient, up to 16 channels can be aggregated using the *carrier aggregation (CA)* technique, just like in LTE. Individual channels become *component carriers* in a larger, aggregated channel, also shown in Figure 5-2. To be part of an aggregated channel, component carriers do not need to be consecutive and could belong to different frequency bands. Resulting aggregated channels in CA provide significantly more resource blocks to schedule transmissions, thereby allowing higher data rates for individual mobile devices. The total amount of resulting aggregated bandwidth is dependent on frequency range and subcarrier spacing, as well as the mobile device class.[11, 12] In a best possible scenario, an LTE-Advanced subscriber can achieve almost 4 Gbps peak data rate using eight MIMO layers and five aggregated channels.[13] NR, in turn, can offer almost 600 Mbps over a single 100 MHz channel with a single MIMO layer. With 400 MHz channels from the bands above 7 GHz, a single MIMO layer transmission can offer more than 2 Gbps peak data rates.[14] Peak data rates for an individual subscriber can greatly exceed IMT-2020's requirement of 20 Gbps with 4×4 or 8×8 MIMO and CA.

Beyond Orthogonal Frequency-Division Multiple Access

The work to enhance radio transmission efficiency does not stop with OFDMA. Multiple vendors and academia continue their research on *Non-Orthogonal Multiple Access (NOMA)* techniques in hopes of adopting it in fifth- or sixth-generation mobile networks. NOMA was introduced under different names in a number of different studies, including LTE releases.[15] As the name implies, NOMA does not rely on orthogonal subcarriers; instead, it leverages interference cancellation techniques at the receiver. In simple terms, a receiver detects one, typically stronger, transmission, constituting a single layer from a composite signal. Once the stronger signal is retrieved, its original form is reconstructed and subtracted or cancelled out from the composite transmission, thereby revealing a weaker signal.[16] Implementing NOMA is challenging but could provide some increase in spectral efficiency. Although the gain in efficiency is moderate, amplified by a high number of layers in multi-user MIMO transmissions, it can provide significant benefits for future air interface implementations.

5G NR Advanced Antenna Functions

The air interface enhancements in 5G NR are not limited to wider channels and new frequency bands, but also bring advanced features such as *beamforming, Coordinated Multi-Point (CoMP)*, and *multi-radio connectivity*, offering better reliability and data rates for subscribers. 5G base stations use advanced antenna systems to simplify installation and provide even more layers for multi-user MIMO transmissions, achieving unprecedented cell capacities and targeted communication with mobile devices.

Active Antennas

Strictly speaking, an antenna is passive hardware designed to emit and receive radio waves. In its simplest form, it is just a piece of wire forming a *dipole antenna*. Since the early days of mobile communication networks, antennas have undergone phenomenal transformations, and today's advanced antennas look very different from those simple pieces of wire used a century ago. The ever-increasing demands for efficiency, speed, and reliability of radio communications led to many innovations and ingenious solutions in those recognizable elements of modern life—antennas.

Antennas today are extremely sophisticated pieces of hardware. Virtually all installations today have antennas and radio heads (a.k.a. RRUs) mounted in close proximity on the radio towers, avoiding long spans of RF cables and associated energy losses. Nevertheless, RRUs and antennas are still connected with multiple RF jumper cables. These external cables are susceptible to environmental degradation, introduce losses, and are cumbersome to maintain, especially with a higher number of MIMO layers used in today's systems. Eliminating these jumpers and putting RRUs inside the antenna enclosure created what is known today as an *active antenna*. Use of active antennas dramatically reduces the number of cables needed, making installation simpler, cleaner, and less prone to wear and tear. Figure 5-3 depicts a comparison between a passive and active antenna.

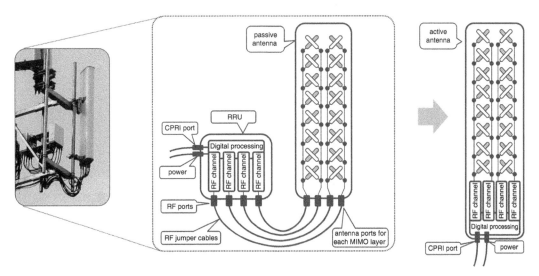

FIGURE 5-3   Passive and Active Antennas

Beamforming

Early attempts to adjust antenna radiation patterns without the use of bulky reflector hardware have led to *beamforming* and *null-forming* techniques, which facilitate dynamically adjusting the antenna radiation patterns and reusing the frequency spectrum with high efficiency. Coordinated use of beam-forming and null-forming by neighboring base stations significantly reduces interference, thereby allowing many individual subscribers to enjoy high data rates. Beamforming is one of the fundamental features empowering 5G NR radio access technology.

Antennas used in today's radio access are collections of fancy-shaped elements, intricately arranged into patterns inside the antenna's radio-transparent enclosure called a *radome*. Nevertheless, the foundational principles of today's advanced antennas operation are not overly complicated—everything starts with a dipole. The radiation pattern of a simple vertically installed dipole antenna has a donut shape with radio waves propagating in all directions except vertical (although, in the real world, radio waves may scatter in the vertical direction, albeit greatly attenuated). A typical mobile antenna used in previous generation networks had a number of dipole elements, all connected in parallel to a single antenna port. An RF signal from a BBU's radio transceiver would be radiated by the dipoles, each forming a donut-shaped electromagnetic field around them. The composite signal of multiple dipoles and the steel plate behind them shape the signal, redirecting it perpendicular to this plate and the column of dipoles, effectively forming a horizontal beam. It is said that an antenna has *gain* in a particular direction. This simple process helps divert otherwise wasted energy in the desired direction, while shielding the space behind the antenna from the unwanted interference. More technically, this beam is called the *main lobe* of an antenna radiation pattern, and its width is determined by the number, shape, and relative positioning of individual antenna elements. An antenna with many elements can form quite a narrow beam, but unfortunately the narrower the main lobe is, the more complex-shaped side lobes are created at the same time. Radio engineers and antenna designers seek for an optimal balance in antenna radiation patterns, creating a variety of antennas for different implementation scenarios. Figure 5-4 shows an example of a sector antenna with a column of short dipoles, with side and top views of a combined radiation pattern.

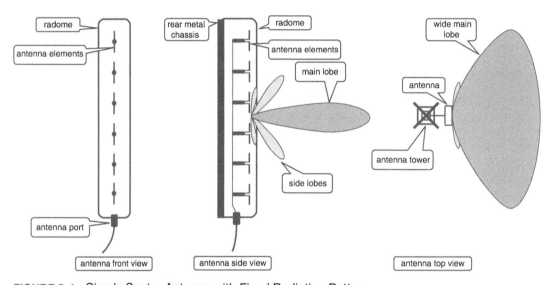

FIGURE 5-4   Simple Sector Antenna with Fixed Radiation Pattern

Popular antenna design features a vertical column of dipoles, redirecting otherwise wasted energy into a vertically focused beam, while covering a whole sector horizontally. These antennas with narrowly focused beams have to be tilted downward to ensure strong signal reception throughout the cell. Instead of mechanical tilting, the antennas once again rely upon the effect of constructive and destructive interference of radio waves emitted by closely placed antenna elements. Each of these antenna elements is connected to an individual analog phase-shifting device that *delays* the RF signal by a carefully selected, miniscule amount of time to influence the resulting radio waves' interference peaks and troughs position in space. In simple terms, the effect of shifting phases for individual antenna elements is the tilt of the radiation pattern in the vertical direction and is displayed in Figure 5-5.

The amount of a phase shift for each antenna element can be adjusted, allowing for a change in the vertical direction, and is commonly referred to as an *electric tilt*. It is important to note that the whole column of antenna elements is fed by a single RF circuit, which is sometimes also called *RF chain*. Although the RF chain shown in Figure 5-5 primarily refers to a transmitter, a typical RF chain is composed of both the transmitter and receiver.

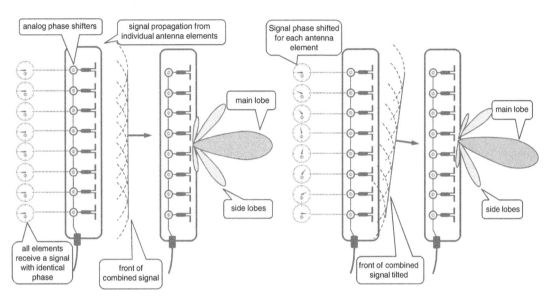

FIGURE 5-5   Radiation Pattern of an Antenna with Electric Tilt

The electric tilt is just a way to adjust the vertical angle of an antenna radiation pattern or, more technically, to control the antenna's gain in the vertical direction. It is also sometimes called *analog beamforming*, as it steers the beam in a downward direction with the use of analog phase shifters. The use of analog phase shifters, instead of mechanical tilting, might sound like a complex solution for a simple task, but in reality, the phase shifters are rather simple inexpensive devices, usually controlled by a stepped DC motor inside the antenna enclosure.[17] The amount of tilt is typically controlled through the BBU, via a special tilt control circuit on the antenna. Analog beamforming allows for tilting the antenna radiation pattern with great precision post-installation, without touching the antenna physically.

Analog beamforming was instrumental in improving overall energy efficiency of the radio interface, but it provided little utility to segregate different users or user groups. Indeed, the beams formed by most legacy LTE antennas are vertically narrow, but they still have horizontally wide radiation patterns, thereby illuminating the whole sector. As a result, all mobile devices within the sector have to share the limited number of resource blocks assigned to the base station, thus limiting the transmission data rates. In order to achieve a higher reuse of frequency, or rather resource blocks within a sector, 5G NR technology uses more advanced *three-dimensional beamforming (3D beamforming)* technology.

3D beamforming relies on the same principle of using multiple elements to form the beam, but this time the beams are formed by two-dimensional arrays, or *planar arrays*, of antenna elements. With the right spacing between antenna elements, it is possible to create a beam narrow in both the vertical and horizontal dimensions. By applying different phase shifts to the antenna elements in such a planar array, the resulting beam can be steered both vertically and horizontally, while illuminating only a small part of the sector occupied by one or more target mobile devices. By controlling the antenna gain and allowing steering in both the vertical and horizontal directions, 3D beamforming allows more independent transmissions using the same frequency, thus providing higher cell capacity and higher data rates. Figure 5-6 provides a simplified view of 3D beamforming.

Antennas supporting beamforming sometimes are also referred to as *beamformers*. A typical beam-former is a planar antenna with many elements organized in columns and rows. In an ideal scenario, 3D beamforming can be implemented with all individual antenna elements connected to independent RF chains. These RF chains allow each element to act as an independent antenna transmitting the same signal with different phase shifts. The amount of a phase shift for each antenna element is controlled digitally and applied in their respective RF chains. This is in contrast to analog beamforming, where a single RF chain is used to feed multiple antenna elements while the phase shifts are applied by analog circuits. This beamforming technique is called *digital beamforming*, which offers great precision in beam width and direction and allow beams to follow individual subscribers.

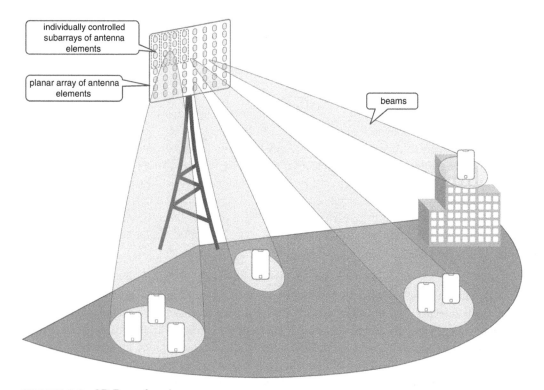

FIGURE 5-6   3D Beamforming

Unfortunately, controlling dozens or hundreds of antenna elements with individual radio chains is often not feasible and might also be cost prohibitive in the case of mmWave bands. Therefore, for a more practical approach, *hybrid beamforming* is more commonly used. Hybrid beamforming combines analog beamforming to steer beams in vertical direction, while horizontal steering is achieved via digitally controlled phase shifts applied by individual RF chains. In this scenario, an antenna is divided into a number of different vertical subarrays of antenna elements, which might have different, preset vertical tilts. Each subarray, in turn, is controlled by an independent RF chain. A few subarrays with the same vertical tilt are used to create a beam, which can be dynamically steered in a horizontal direction, illuminating a particular spot in the sector, covering a single or a cluster of mobile devices. When the beams are narrow enough and the side lobes of a particular beam do not interfere with other mobile devices, it is possible to reuse OFDMA subcarriers within a single sector for multiple transmissions at once. Figure 5-7 shows different beamformers.

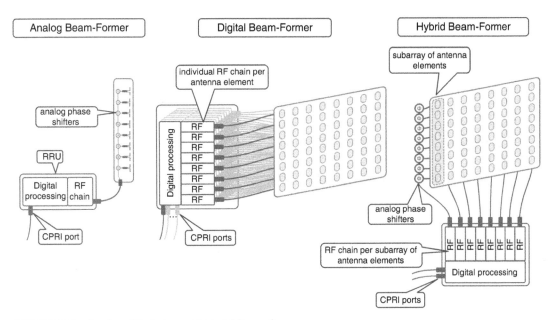

FIGURE 5-7   Analog, Digital, and Hybrid Beamformers

Hybrid beamforming is a cost-effective yet flexible solution for 3D beamforming. Individual mobile devices as well as base stations use special reference signals for *sounding* purposes, thus probing which beams within the sector are most optimal for a transmission. Sounding signals are transmitted every few dozens of milliseconds over each beam, and based on the feedback from the sounding signal, a mobile device can be switched to another beam, if appropriate.

Massive Multiple Input Multiple Output (mMIMO)

Fundamental for 5G radio technology is the principle of multiple simultaneous data transmissions using the same carrier frequency, known as *multiple input multiple output (MIMO)*, the basics of which were covered in Chapter 3. MIMO technology has been instrumental in increasing spectral efficiency and boosting peak data rates for individual subscribers as well as the entire cell capacity in previous generation mobile networks. 4×4 and 8×8 MIMO systems are commonly used in LTE systems, yet increasing the order of MIMO beyond these numbers is not straightforward. The path to densification of spatial multiplexing collides with the size limitations imposed on the handheld mobile devices. Specifically, the limiting factor is how many antennas can be packed into a single mobile device. Antennas cannot be miniaturized infinitely, and the distance between multiple antennas is determined by the carrier frequency and, therefore, cannot be arbitrary. This limits the number of parallel transmissions in the case of single-user MIMO. Nevertheless, when many mobile devices are served by a cell, it is possible to apply the principles of MIMO and multiplex data streams belonging to different subscribers using the same frequency. This approach is called *multi-user MIMO (MU-MIMO)*, and it helps to significantly increase cell capacity as well as improve data rates for multiple subscribers simultaneously.

MU-MIMO is not limited by the size of an individual mobile device; hence, more antennas can be used at the base station to further increase the order of spatial multiplexing of data streams for different subscribers. When a MU-MIMO system uses a large number of antennas at the base station and more than one antenna is used to communicate with a single antenna at the mobile device, such a system is called *massive MIMO (mMIMO)*.[18] However, there are many other definitions of mMIMO systems used by industry engineers. These definitions might focus on various aspects of technology but, as a rule of thumb, a system with 16 or more independent antennas, each one connected to a respective individual RF chain, is considered a mMIMO system.

Strictly speaking, a mMIMO system can be constructed in many ways (for example, a line of antennas distributed over the roof of a building or even stretched over multiple building roofs). As long as all these antennas illuminate a single sector and are part of the same base station, this would be a mMIMO system. In reality, however, the most common mMIMO implementation is based on planar beamformers with many antenna elements. Use of beamformers in mMIMO systems is so popular that sometimes beamforming is used as a synonym for mMIMO, which, of course, is not technically accurate. Beamforming is just one of the applications of a mMIMO system.

Interestingly enough, modern beamformers (both analog and hybrid) use a clever technique to conserve precious space on the cell tower by reducing antenna size. This technique leverages the electromagnetic phenomenon of *polarization*, where electric and magnetic fields oscillate in a specific direction. Two polarized radio waves are said to be *cross-polarized* and do not interfere when their respective electric and magnetic fields oscillate in orthogonal directions. When two antenna elements are cross-polarized, they emit radio waves with little to no interference. Thus, these antenna elements can be placed one behind the other, effectively squeezing two antennas into one.

One important consideration of MIMO transmissions using hybrid and digital beamforming techniques should be noted here. As was explained in Chapter 3, the concept of MIMO transmission is the use of different spatially diverse paths to transmit multiple data streams, with each distinct data stream representing a separate *MIMO layer*. In digital and hybrid beamforming techniques, however, multiple RF chains are used to form a single beam, and all these RF chains transmit, in fact, the same data. Therefore, the number of independent MIMO layers offered by hybrid and digital beamformers is not equal to the number of RF chains. This can be further exemplified by the antennas shown in Figure 5-8, which shows 4×4 MIMO (often called 4T4R to signify the transmit and receive RF chains respectively) and 16×16 (also called 16T16R) mMIMO antennas.

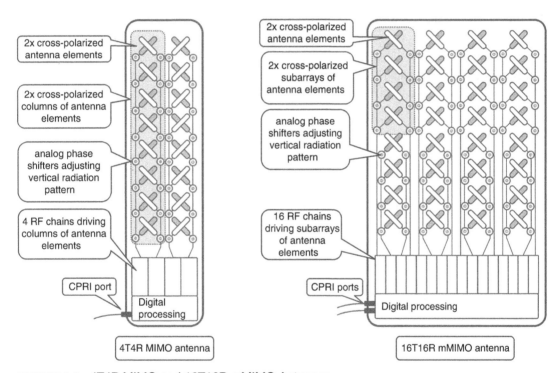

FIGURE 5-8 4T4R MIMO and 16T16R mMIMO Antennas

The legacy 4T4R MIMO antenna shown in Figure 5-8 is used as a four-layer MIMO system—2× columns, 2× different polarizations, creating a total of four independent antennas. Each of these four antennas is connected to an individual RF chain and may transmit or receive *distinct* data streams. On the other hand, the 16T16R mMIMO antenna shown in the same figure is a hybrid beamformer. In this particular example, the antenna is organized into vertical subarrays of four antenna elements each. There are eight subarrays of each polarization, with a total of 16 independent subarrays. Each subarray relies on analog phase shifters to achieve downward tilt and is connected to an individual RF chain.

The total number of RF chains required to drive this antenna is 16, defining its 16T16R mode of operation. However, to implement horizontal beam steering using this antenna, a few individual RF chains, connected to subarrays of the same polarization in a single row, have to transmit the *same* data, applying various phase shifts digitally. Hence, in the case of four subarrays used in horizontal beam steering, this particular organization of the 16T16R beamformer can offer four independent MIMO layers.

It is possible to use the same beamformer with wider horizontal beams and less precision in horizontal steering by reducing the number of RF chains for each beam to only two. This way, the same antenna can provide up to eight independent MIMO layers. The number of RF chains and MIMO layers is critical for proper radio access network dimensioning. Chapter 10, "Designing and Implementing 5G Network Architecture," covers the topic of xHaul dimensioning in greater detail.

Some obvious benefits of mMIMO application in 5G networks include improved spectral efficiency, faster and more robust transmission, and energy efficiency among others. On the flip side, it can be challenging to implement with FDD, due to the lack of channel reciprocity, as explained in Chapter 2. Also, it might be expensive and hard to build mMIMO systems in mmWave bands.

Multi-Radio Connectivity

Strictly speaking, the transmission of subscriber data over multiple radios is not a new 5G feature. Ever since the introduction of MIMO, multiple radios are being used to transmit data over spatially diverse paths, but such transmissions normally utilize radios residing on the same cell site/tower and connected to the same BBU. Similarly, the carrier aggregation technique relies on multiple radios, and although it is possible to leverage remote radio units (RRUs) placed on different towers, these have to belong to the same eNodeB or, its 5G equivalent, *gNodeB*. In other words, there is only one RF scheduler, controlling the allocation of resource blocks over the air interface for a given mobile device.

Another example of multi-radio connectivity introduced in LTE Release 11 is *Coordinated Multi-Point (CoMP)* transmission.[19] Substantial interference from the neighboring cells near the cell borders is always a serious challenge for mobile radio engineers and is traditionally addressed by using appropriate frequency reuse patterns. Restrictive frequency reuse patterns help to mitigate interference problems but dramatically reduce spectral efficiency. As explained in Chapter 3, LTE networks allowed moving away from strict allocations of frequencies in the whole cell by dividing cells into inner and outer parts. The same frequency channels can be used in the inner parts of the neighboring cells, yet the outer parts still have to follow stringent rules of frequency reuse patterns. One of the goals of the CoMP transmission technique is to solve this challenge. CoMP defines various scenarios ranging from coordination only within a single site, mainly between multiple sectors of the same eNB, to coordination between neighboring cells, which could be a combination of either macro-macro or macro-pico cells.

The basis of CoMP technology is the coordinated scheduling of radio resources used by neighboring radios or, in 3GPP terminology, *transmission points (TPs)*. Multiple TPs can be represented by a collection of RRUs, which can be controlled by the same or different eNBs. In the latter case, the scheduling information must be exchanged over the X2 interface to achieve the desired cooperation across eNBs. Nevertheless, all coordinated transmissions are considered by the mobile device as if they are controlled by a single RF scheduler.

Transmission Point (TP)

3GPP defines a transmission point as a set of co-located transmit antennas; however, it must be noted that multiple sectors of the same site are considered separate TPs.

A few different approaches to implement radio resource scheduling by multiple TPs are defined under the CoMP umbrella:

- **Joint transmission:** Multiple TPs can send the same symbols on the same frequency, for the same subscriber, and if coordinated properly, can greatly improve signal quality received by a mobile device. However, such coherent joint transmission requires very accurate coordination and, thus, is very sensitive to the latency between participating TPs and/or eNBs.

- **Coordinated scheduling/coordinated beamforming:** Neighboring TPs coordinate scheduling of transmissions using certain beams, where respective low-gain radiation pattern (null) points in the direction of subscriber, attached to a neighboring cell, participating in coordination. The benefit of using this approach is increased spectral efficiency, and it can also be combined with the joint transmission method.

- **Dynamic point selection:** A transmission point sending the data to the subscriber can change every subframe, with one TP used at a time. Dynamic point selection enables reacting to quickly changing transmission conditions by changing the transmission point, thus improving overall reliability.

Figure 5-9 illustrates these CoMP approaches.

CoMP transmission is an effective way to improve signal quality, reliability, and data rates at the edges of cells and in picocells within macrocells. CoMP techniques can be instrumental in improving signal robustness in 5G URLLC scenarios, preventing potential signal dropouts in complex industrial environments involving mission-critical applications of M2M communications. On the other hand, CoMP techniques impose tight latency and reliability requirements on backhaul for inter-eNBs/gNBs coordination. It is considered that CoMP relies on an *ideal backhaul* and hence can greatly benefit from C-RAN architectures, where BBUs are co-located and have virtually no latency between them. Application of CoMP in 5G networks is an area of active research among 3GPP members.[20]

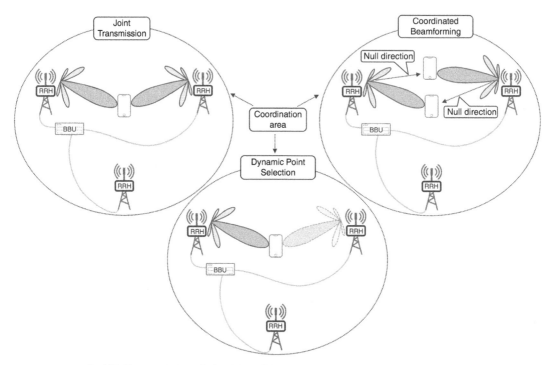

FIGURE 5-9   CoMP Transmission Scheduling Methods

Dual connectivity is another form of multi-radio connectivity that was introduced for LTE in 3GPP Release 12. This approach was further generalized and expanded in Releases 15 and 16 and called *Multi-Radio Dual Connectivity (MR-DC)*.[21] Unlike CoMP, where coordination and scheduling happen using a single RF scheduler, MR-DC involves higher layers of 5G protocol stack (more details on 5G protocol stack are covered in the upcoming sections), allowing RF schedulers to operate independently in two participating RAN nodes, such as eNB or gNB, which allows operation in non-ideal backhaul environments. However, this connectivity model requires mobile devices to support simultaneous communications with two separate eNBs/gNBs.

It is anticipated that current large mobile network deployments will coexist with 5G networks for quite some time and will require well-defined procedures to transition from previous generation to 5G network. Some of these deployment challenges can be addressed through the use of standalone (SA) and non-standalone (NSA) 5G deployments, where 5G NR can communicate with the previous generation packet core—Evolved Packet Core (EPC).

MR-DC can operate in such heterogeneous environments and use:

- **en-gNB:** A 5G NR RAN node, which is capable of establishing user-plane communication with EPC and works as a secondary node with the control plane established over the X2 interface via the main eNB.

- **ng-eNB:** An LTE RAN node, which can establish control- and user-plane communication with 5G Core. These nodes also establish communication with gNB nodes over 5G's Xn interface.

MR-DC defines two roles for RAN nodes: *master node (MN)* and *secondary node (SN)*. MN is responsible for all regular tasks of a typical eNB or gNB in a single connectivity deployment; that is, it establishes both control- and data-plane connections with the mobile core, controls data transfers, and schedules radio resources. Additionally, MN establishes a control-plane connection with the SN over the X2 interface in the case of eNB—or its equivalent, *Xn* interface, in the case of gNB. The secondary node also establishes a user-plane connection with the mobile core, allowing both the MN and SN to schedule their own radio resources separately, through the use of respective radio bearers. However, 3GPP defines another way of delivering user data, through the use of a *split bearer*. This mechanism allows the bearer to be terminated at the MN, while pooling the radio resources of both the MN and SN. The user data stream is then split between the MN and SN and is transported over the X2/Xn interface between these two RAN nodes. The use of split bearers can result in a significant amount of user-plane data exchanged over X2/Xn interfaces.

> **Note**
>
> Use of the term *master* is only in association with the official terminology used in industry specifications and standards, and in no way diminishes Pearson's commitment to promoting diversity, equity, and inclusion and challenging, countering, and/or combating bias and stereotyping in the global population of the learners we serve.

A number of different permutations for dual connectivity are specified by 3GPP, such as whether RAN nodes connect to 5G Core or to legacy EPC, if a gNB or an eNB is a master node, and what is being used as a secondary node. Figure 5-10 shows a few options of using MR-DC with EPC and 5G Core (5GC) network.

It is important to note that carrier aggregation can be used along with MR-DC connectivity options; however, the number of component carriers aggregated over two cells or cell groups cannot exceed 32, which is defined as the maximum number of component carriers in 5G NR.[22]

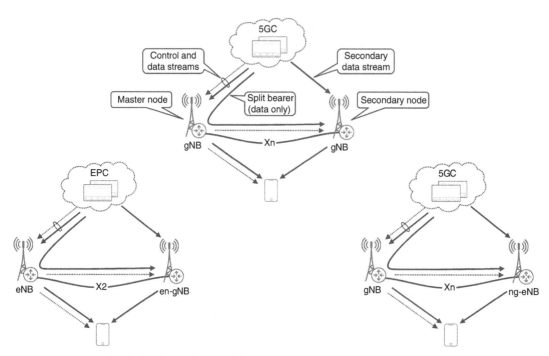

FIGURE 5-10   Multi-Radio Dual Connectivity Options

Dynamic Spectrum Sharing

Transition to a newer radio access technology is always a challenging and complex endeavor. Thanks to 5G NR capabilities to communicate with EPC, it is possible to implement gradual deployment of 5G NR technology. Yet, this provides little relief to the spectrum repurposing aspect of this transition.

Spectrum repurposing, or reallocation of bands and frequencies from older to newer radio access technology, can be complicated, especially in the areas of high traffic. In a simple and direct approach, the newer radio access technology uses a separate set of frequencies, when coexisting with the older technology. Although it might be a feasible approach to deploy 5G NR using high bands, as these are not used by LTE, it requires much more planning when low and mid bands have to be reused. The low- and mid-band frequencies are typically a very scarce resource, as these provide the sweet spot between capacity and optimal propagation. Providing 5G radios with their own set of mid- and low-band channels typically requires carving those channels out of current LTE allocations. This task requires careful resource planning by radio engineers, as it is not easy to find an optimal balance between 5G and 4G resources. Repurposing spectrum statically could result in an imbalance, where the previous generation users might not get enough RF resources, while resources assigned to another radio access technology are wasted in the absence of a substantial number of subscribers.

Dynamic spectrum sharing (DSS) helps to avoid such suboptimal scenarios and offers flexible distribution of radio resources, adjusting to the fluid ratio between 5G and 4G subscribers in a cell.

DSS leverages the fact that both LTE and NR use OFDM and can be deployed with the same subcarrier frequency spacing and symbol duration. In fact, NR was designed with such interoperability in mind. In DSS setup, LTE and NR radio nodes, serving the same cell, rely on coordination between their radio resource schedulers, such that resource blocks belonging to the same channel can be used by one of these radios, as needed. This allows the use of the same channel on both radios, without subdividing for hard allocations to a particular radio: NR or LTE.

DSS is an area of active research in 3GPP.[23] Most current deployments rely on a proprietary interface between the eNB and gNB for scheduler coordination, thus limiting the choice of RAN node vendors to match those already deployed.[24]

Vehicle-to-Everything Communication

Originally introduced as an LTE study item, *Cellular Vehicle-to-Everything*, or *C-V2X*, became a standard in Release 14 and was adopted for 5G NR implementations in Release 16.[25, 26] C-V2X communication is aimed at providing additional communication channels between vehicles, and between vehicles and other road users as well as parts of road infrastructure.

C-V2X uses a concept of a *sidelink*, effectively turning a vehicle into a RAN node by extending connection from nearby eNB/gNB to other mobile devices. It is also possible for a single vehicle to coordinate direct communications between a group of vehicles, thus creating a mesh of direct interconnections, enabling robust communication between multiple vehicles and a network.

The Vehicle-to-Everything communication approach encompasses a number of different use cases: Vehicle-to-Network (V2N), Vehicle-to-Vehicle (V2V), Vehicle-to-Infrastructure (V2I), and Vehicle-to-Pedestrian (V2P). Vehicles communicating with each other and with the road infrastructure may coordinate different parameters, such as speed, lane selection, and even path, based on dynamic conditions on the road. Such communication and coordination make transportation much more effective and safer, especially in the case of self-driving cars. New safety features, such as "Do not pass warning," can be a result of V2V communication, warning a driver or a self-driving car about the upcoming traffic on non-divided highways.[27] All these features require strict coordination and impose new and stringent requirements on the underlying transport network, addressed by the implementation of URLLC-type services. C-V2X communications can also improve safety of pedestrians by warning nearby cars about their presence, complementing obstacle-detection systems currently adopted by some vehicles.

C-V2X communications standards and implementations are still in their infancy, but this is an area of active research and growth. It is anticipated that vehicular communications become a widely adopted phenomenon and enable future innovations in transportation.

RAN Virtualization and Decomposition

Centralized RAN (C-RAN) architecture was proposed around 2010 by China Mobile Research Institute, in collaboration with hardware vendors such as Intel, ZTE, Nokia, Huawei, among others.[28] It was originally geared toward offering a sustainable *green* solution for RAN, while offering cost savings through BBU pooling at a centralized location. It had been shown that cell sites are responsible for more than 70% of overall power consumption in a mobile service provider's network, with over 50% of each cell site's power consumption going toward air conditioning.[29] The C-RAN cost reductions come from a leaner cell site footprint, significantly lower cooling and power costs, and lower maintenance costs due to reduced truck rolls to every cell site in case of BBU issues. Although C-RAN started primarily as a green initiative, the BBU pooling offered other advantages such as improvement in RAN utilization through increased spectral efficiency, reduced interchannel interference, and simplified use of CoMP transmission.

Despite these benefits of real estate and power savings as well as RAN efficiency that mobile operators could realize by using C-RAN architectures, they still had to deploy the same number of these chassis-based BBUs and would not be able to optimize BBU usage across cell sites. This was because the BBU was still a purpose-built, vendor-specific, physical hardware and was allocated to its specific cell site. Based on the subscriber load, some BBUs might be underutilized while others might be oversubscribed, depending on factors such as the cell site location they are serving and time of the day. The net result was the pooling of physical BBUs in a central location, but not the sharing of *baseband-processing* resources across cell sites. The transition toward the virtualization of RAN components offered a solution to this inefficiency.

Centralized, Cloud, and Virtualized RAN

Network Functions Virtualization (NFV) was initially proposed in 2012 (around the same time as 3GPP Release 11) by a consortium of service providers as a solution for cost and complexities associated with vendor-locked hardware.[30] The solution proposed through NFV was to decouple the hardware and software layers and, by using virtualization techniques, remove the vendor lock-in for devices performing network functions. Dynamic scalability, deployment velocity, and easy upgradability through use of orchestration and automation tools were also among the goals of NFV.

General-purpose compute functions were first to be virtualized and decoupled with hardware. Soon after, new networking startups started offering *virtual networking functions (VNFs)* for various networking roles such as firewall, NAT, and route reflectors. These initial VNF implementations were predominantly focused on functions that relied heavily on software processes; however, the functions that had more dependency on the hardware took longer to be virtualized. BBU functions were also considered for virtualization and dubbed *virtual BBU (vBBU)*.

New RAN equipment vendors such as Altiostar, COTS hardware vendors such as Dell, and silicon providers such as Intel partnered to offer vBBU solutions. Though it was demonstrated that vBBU would offer many benefits over specialized hardware, it was not commonly deployed as a single VNF but rather split into two RAN components—the *distributed unit (DU)* and the *centralized unit (CU)*, which are discussed in detail in the next section.

The effort to drive RAN architecture toward the use of software-based, virtualized RAN components was given the name *Virtual RAN (vRAN)*. The vRAN architectures gained industry momentum around the time when virtualization of applications was often equated with a transition to cloud-based environment. This perception led to the terms Virtual RAN and *Cloud RAN* being used interchangeably. Some vendors preferred the term Cloud RAN, whereas others opted to use vRAN terminology. More recently, however, a clear distinction has started to emerge between the two terminologies and the underlying architecture they represent. Virtual RAN (vRAN) now refers to the generic drive towards the use of software-based RAN components instead of physical hardware such as the BBU. On the other hand, Cloud RAN is now considered a subset of vRAN where the software-based RAN components are designed to be *cloud-native*. Later sections of this chapter will expand on the characteristics of cloud-native applications.

Note that the term Cloud RAN can also be abbreviated as C-RAN, which can easily be confused with Centralized RAN. Due to the similar abbreviations, and a lack of clear definitions, casual industry observers sometimes use the terms Centralized RAN and Cloud RAN interchangeably, which is not accurate. Centralized RAN refers to an architecture where the BBU or its decomposed RAN components (that is, the CU and DU) are moved away from the cell site and placed in one or more central locations. Cloud RAN, as mentioned above, is a subset of vRAN, and refers to an implementation where the RAN components are virtualized to be cloud-native. The virtualized RAN components (whether for vRAN or Cloud RAN) are referred to as *virtualized CU (vCU)* and *virtualized DU (vDU),* and could be placed at the cell site (that is, a D-RAN architecture) or in one or more DCs (that is, a Centralized RAN architecture).

RU, DU, and CU Naming Conventions

The book will refer to the centralized unit as CU and distributed unit as DU, irrespective of virtualization. If the virtualization aspect has to be specifically pointed out, the terms vCU and vDU will be used. Similarly, in a decomposed RAN architecture, the abbreviation RRU is often shortened to radio unit (RU)—keeping in line with the two-letter CU and DU acronyms. Despite omitting the word *remote* from the abbreviated format, this RU continues to be remote to the DU, installed alongside the antenna panels at the top of the cell tower. This book will use the terms RU and RRU interchangeably from this point onward.

It is helpful to think of Distributed/Centralized and Virtual/Cloud RAN architectures as orthogonal dimensions. Distributed or centralized RAN deployments could use physical RAN components (for example, a BBU or CU and DU appliance) or software-based RAN components (that is, a vRAN or Cloud RAN deployment). As mentioned previously, the software-based RAN components are usually decomposed into a vCU and vDU. Similarly, a vRAN deployment (including Cloud RAN deployment) could use a Distributed RAN model (where RAN components are distributed across Cell Sites) or a Centralized RAN model (where RAN components, that is, the CU and/or DU are placed in one or more Data Centers).

This book will use the term vRAN when referring to the architecture pertaining to software-based RAN components, which implicitly covers Cloud-RAN as well. The terms Centralized RAN and Cloud RAN will not be abbreviated from this point on to avoid any confusion. The term decomposed RAN will be used to refer to splitting of BBU into a CU and DU, which may or may not be virtualized and may be placed at the cell site, remotely at a data center, or a combination of the two. The placement of decomposed RAN components is discussed in the next section.

Virtualized RAN (vRAN) Architecture

A BBU performs a lot of specialized digital signal processing, converting radio traffic from RU into IP, and vice versa. The functions performed by BBU could be classified into two broad categories— *real-time* and *non-real-time*. Real-time functions would include scheduling, interference coordination, precoding MIMO and beamforming, modulation, and error correction, while non-real-time functions include bearer configuration, connection management, subscriber handovers, data encryption, header compression, and various operations, administration, and maintenance (OAM) tasks. In short, BBU tasks associated with direct traffic processing and forwarding are considered real-time functions, whereas management and control-related functions would classify as non-real-time.

Redesigning a BBU with functions *split* across two separate entities based on task classification made it easier for BBU to be virtualized. This was further supported by the performance improvements of available COTS hardware. The real-time functions are grouped in the DU, whereas the non-real-time functions were grouped in the CU. The decomposed vRAN architecture, that is, the virtualized CU and DU, is quickly becoming the go-to solution for new RAN deployments.

Given that the DU would be required to perform most real-time functions, it needs to be placed close to the cell sites to ensure low-latency communications with the RRU. Hence, the DUs should be hosted at the *far edges* of a mobile communication network, closer to the cell sites. The data center hosting the DU functions, depending on the number of cell sites it services, could be composed of just a few servers connected to the aggregation routers or a few racks of equipment. In a vRAN architecture, this DC is referred to as a *far-edge data center*. The transport network connecting the cell sites and the far-edge DC is still called the fronthaul, with CPRI-based RU to DU communications that could use either packet-based or WDM-based transport, as previously described in Chapter 3. Newer RAN components may use an enhanced version of CPRI, called eCPRI, which is discussed later in this chapter. As such, a fronthaul network might need to carry both CPRI and eCPRI traffic.

Naming Convention for Data Centers in a 5G Mobile Network

In earlier mobile generations, there were two main categories of data centers hosting various mobile core functions. The *regional data centers* would host the devices implementing the packet core, while a very small number of these regional data centers typically host the database servers as well. The latter can be further categorized as *national data centers* and were also referred to as *central DCs, core DCs, telco DCs,* or *main DCs.*

With 5G's transition to decomposed RAN architectures, new data center categories were introduced—namely, *edge DC* and *far-edge DC* to host virtualized RAN components. The edge DCs, sometimes referred to as *metro DCs*, are significantly smaller than the national and regional DCs. The size of far-edge DCs, often called *micro DCs*, depends on the number of DUs hosted and may range from just a few servers to multiple racks of equipment.

CU, on the other hand, is responsible for non-real-time functions and could tolerate higher latency compared to the RU-DU connectivity. So even though CU is part of the RAN infrastructure, it can be placed further from the RU compared to the DU. The CUs could be pooled in *edge data centers* that are placed farther away from the cell sites in comparison with a far-edge DC, but still much closer than a traditional centralized DC. The network that connects the CUs to DUs is called the *midhaul.* The umbrella term *xHaul*, which was previously used for a combination of backhaul and fronthaul networks in Centralized RAN, is also used to refer to midhaul. Figure 5-11 shows the traditional D-RAN, present-day Centralized RAN, and the next generation vRAN architectures and their corresponding xHaul domains.

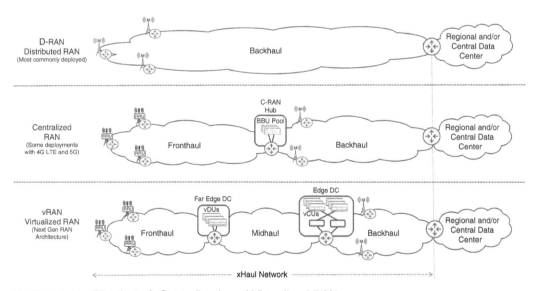

FIGURE 5-11 Distributed, Centralized, and Virtualized RAN

Table 5-1 outlines the latency requirements and typical distance allowed for fronthaul, midhaul, and backhaul networks.[31, 32]

Table 5-1   xHaul Networks and Their Characteristics

xHaul Domain	Purpose	Max One-Way Latency*	Max/Typical Distance
Fronthaul	RU–DU(5G)/BBU(4G) connectivity	~100 usec (4G/LTE)* ~150 usec (5G)*	20/10 km
Midhaul	DU–CU connectivity	~ few milliseconds	200/40–100 km
Backhaul	BBU(4G)/CU (5G)–5GC connectivity	~ few milliseconds	200/40–100 km

* These numbers are guidelines by various standard bodies. Exact latency tolerance between RAN components should be provided by the equipment vendor and must be validated in test labs before deployment.

An xHaul implementation in vRAN can use any combination of fronthaul, midhaul, and backhaul networks, depending on the placement of the CU and DU relative to the RU. For instance, the DU and CU can both be co-located, but away from the cell site, in which case only a fronthaul network exists between the RU and the data center hosting the DU and CU. In other instances, the DU might be placed at the cell site with the RU. In this case, the fronthaul is *collapsed* within the cell site, while a midhaul network connects the cell site to the CU hosted in the edge DC. Another example of a co-located RU and DU is the Active Antenna System for mmWave bands, where the DU is integrated into the RU and antenna panel. This allows all real-time functions to be performed at the cell site, thus eliminating the need for a fronthaul network. Lastly, deploying the physical or virtual BBU, or its decomposed components (DU and CU), at the cell sites results in a traditional D-RAN-like architecture with a backhaul network connecting the cell site containing both the DU and CU to the 5G Core network. Figure 5-12 illustrates these various deployment models.

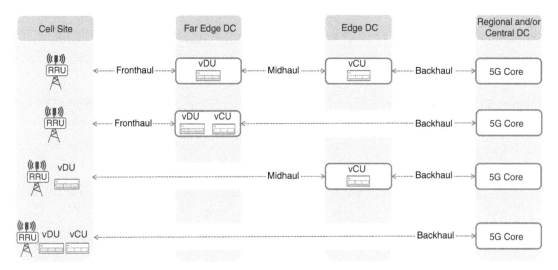

FIGURE 5-12   DU and CU Placement in Various vRAN Deployment Models

IEEE 1914.1: Standards for Packet-based Fronthaul Transport Networks

In an effort to standardize next-generation mobile network architectures, IEEE defined the *"Standards for Packet-based Fronthaul Transport Networks" (1914.1)*. The standard outlines various xHaul deployment scenarios, similar to those shown in Figure 5-12, and defines the *Next Generation Fronthaul Interface (NGFI)* reference architecture consisting of *NGFI-I* (equivalent of fronthaul) and *NGFI-II* (equivalent of midhaul) networks. It also outlines various network functions and design elements such as packet-based transport, quality of service, scalability, availability, timing and synchronization, as well as operation, administration, and maintenance (OAM) requirements for the xHaul network.[33]

When a transformation to vRAN is being planned, there might be instances where a C-RAN hub could be rebranded as either an edge or far-edge DC, depending on its location and distance from existing or newly installed cell sites. In other cases, as cellular networks and cell sites continue to grow, there may be a need for new data centers. In a vRAN environment, edge DCs are typically fewer in number than far-edge DCs and, thus, CUs located in these edge DCs may provide services to cell sites over a larger geographical area. The edge DCs also tend to be larger than far-edge DCs, resembling a traditional data center spine-leaf architecture, and could be used to house additional components, not just the CU. There typically is a one-to-many relationship between the CUs and DUs, and both these functions are part of the 5G base station, known as *gNodeB (gNB)*.

gNodeB

NodeB in 3G and evolved NodeB (eNodeB or eNB) in 4G LTE have been responsible for terminating the subscriber's air interface and performing baseband traffic processing. In 5G networks, this functionality is performed by a *gNodeB (gNB)*, short for *next-generation NodeB,* where *n* is simply omitted for better readability. There are fundamental architectural differences between the gNB and its predecessors, most notable being the decomposition of BBU functions. *Next Generation RAN (NG-RAN)* architecture, originally introduced in 3GPP Release 14 and refined in subsequent releases, conceptualizes the gNB architecture where the functions of BBU are split into the centralized unit (CU) and distributed unit (DU). 3GPP Release 15 officially named these functions the *gNB-CU* and the *gNB-DU*.

As per 3GPP specifications, a gNB can contain one gNB-CU and one or more gNB-DUs. 3GPP does not limit the number of DUs in a gNB but rather leaves it up to individual deployments. The number of gNB-DUs in a gNB is typically a derivative of processing capabilities and resources available on the gNB-CU.

The DUs connect to the CU using an F1 interface, while the CU connects to the 5G Core using *NG interfaces*, which is a collective name given to interfaces from 5G RAN to 5G Core. Various *NG interfaces* are discussed in the "5G Core Network" section.

An *Xn-C* interface, equivalent of an X2 interface in 4G LTE, is used for connectivity between gNBs and terminates on the gNB-CU. It must be reiterated that all these interfaces, like other 3GPP-defined interfaces, are logical in nature and use the underlying network infrastructure to establish connectivity.

For better scale and more granular separation of functions, the gNB-CU can be further decomposed into *gNB-CU-CP (control plane)* and *gNB-CU-UP (user plane)*. The gNB-CU-CP is primarily responsible for control and management tasks of the gNB-CU's functions, such as selecting the appropriate gNB-CU-UP for user data and establishing an F1 interface connection between the gNB-CU-UP and gNB-DU. On the other hand, gNB-CU-UP transports user data between the gNB-DU and gNB-CU and provides functions aimed at improving data speed, efficiency, and reliability through data retransmission in case of radio link outage, status reporting, and redundant data discarding.

A gNB-CU can consist of a single gNB-CU-CP instance and one or more gNB-CU-UP instance(s), thus allowing both the control and user planes to scale and operate independently of each other. The gNB-CU-CP and its corresponding gNB-CU-UPs communicate through the *E1* interface. The F1 interface between the DU and CU is subdivided into *F1-Control Plane (F1-CP)* and *F1-User Plane (F1-UP)* to provide connection from gNB-DU to gNB-CU-CP and gNB-CU-UP, respectively. A gNB-DU could connect to a single gNB-CU-CP and one or multiple gNB-CU-UPs, as long as all those gNB-CU-UPs are managed by the same gNB-CU-CP. Figure 5-13 provides an overview of these various gNB components and interfaces.[34]

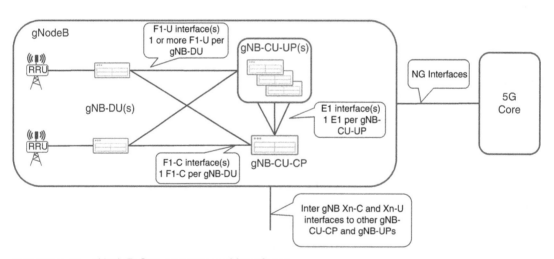

FIGURE 5-13   gNodeB Components and Interfaces

Together, the gNB-DU and the gNB-CU (along with the RRU) make up the gNB in the Next Generation RAN (NG-RAN) architecture. However, exactly how the BBU functions are split between the CU and DU has been a topic of intense discussion in various standardization bodies and organizations. As these splits have significant implications on the overall network architecture, the next section will discuss the various BBU functional split options across the RU, DU, and CU.

Understanding the RAN Functional Splits

The relocation of the baseband unit (BBU) from the cell site to a centralized location was the beginning of RAN decomposition in mobile networks that was further accelerated with the introduction of BBU functional splits. The CU and DU, or rather their more commonly used virtualized versions, are an integral part of current and future vRAN deployments. The capabilities of CU and DU depend on the *functional split option* implemented. The functional split option, more commonly called the *split option*, refers to precisely how the 5G protocol stack gets divided between the CU and the DU, and whether or not some of the baseband processing is offloaded to the RU. To understand the split options, it's useful to first understand the functions performed by the BBU at various layers of the 5G protocol stack.

5G Protocol Stack Overview

The 5G protocol stack consists of three layers, which can be loosely correlated, though not directly mapped, with the bottom three layers of the OSI model.[35, 36] Layers in the 5G protocol stack are mostly similar to those in 4G, but the tasks performed at each layer have been enhanced and new functions added to support 5G services. As shown in Figure 5-14, the lowest layer of the 5G protocol stack is called the *physical layer (PHY)*. Layer 2 is further subdivided into the *Media Access Control (MAC), Radio Link Control (RLC), Packet Data Convergence Protocol (PDCP),* and *Service Data Adaptation Protocol (SDAP)* layers. *The Radio Resource Control (RRC)* and IP encapsulated PDCP frames make up Layer 3 of the 5G protocol stack.

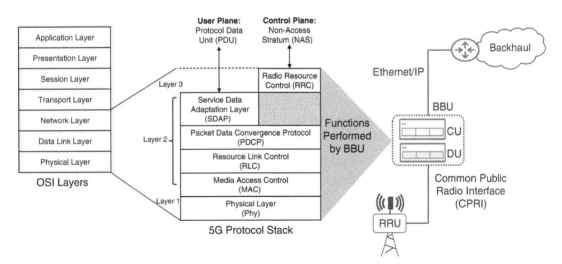

FIGURE 5-14   5G Protocol Stack and Functions Performed by BBU

Non-Access Stratum

3GPP defines the concept of Non-Access Stratum (NAS), which is a collection of protocols used for control plane connectivity between mobile devices and the mobile core in both 4G LTE and 5G.

The physical layer (PHY) performs functions such as upstream and downstream link adaptation, modulation and encoding, signal power adjustment, and assisting user equipment in initial cell search and signal acquisition. The physical layer defines the frame format based on the FDD or TDD duplexing schema and the use of appropriate encoding—OFDMA in the downlink and SC-FDMA for the uplink—which have previously been discussed in detail. The physical layer is responsible for assisting in advanced antenna functions such as MIMO layer processing, beamforming, and transmission diversity management.[37]

The MAC layer, which is a sub-layer of Layer 2, is responsible for scheduling, prioritizing, multiplexing, and demultiplexing data to and from the mobile devices. 5G's MAC layer has also been enhanced to support additional physical layer features such as beamforming and transmission diversity. Data integrity verification and error correction through retransmissions or Forward Error Correction (FEC) are also done at the MAC layer.

The RLC layer, also part of Layer 2, is primarily responsible for segmentation, reassembly, and buffering of protocol data units (PDUs). In certain modes of operation, the RLC sub-layer might require acknowledgment of receipt from the remote device, thereby adding transmission overhead but providing additional capabilities such as duplicate traffic detection and protocol-level error correction.[38]

The third sub-layer within Layer 2, the PDCP layer, is responsible for the actual data transmission for both the control-plane and user-plane traffic over the radio bearers. This sub-layer also provides data security and integrity through encryption as well as header compression and duplicate traffic detection. The PDCP sub-layer may customize processing for various 5G service types (for example, header compression and decompression may not be implemented for URLLC services to reduce latency).

In 4G LTE implementation, traffic from the PDCP sub-layer is passed on as IP data to the packet core. 5G specifications, however, add another sub-layer called SDAP in the protocol stack. SDAP's sole purpose is to build upon the existing QoS capabilities. It provides QoS for user-plane traffic by mapping a traffic flow to a radio bearer based on its requirements.[39] Layer 3 of the 5G protocol stack is the RRC layer, which is primarily focused on management function and does not explicitly participate in traffic forwarding. RRC is responsible for establishing, maintaining, and releasing radio bearers (both signaling and data bearers). Mobility functions such as mobile device handover and cell-selection functions are managed by the RRC layer as well. RRC also closes the feedback loop with the PHY layer by analyzing measurements of radio signals and ensuring appropriate resources are allocated on the air interface.

Based on the tasks and functions performed by each individual layer, it is easy to infer that lower layers such as physical, MAC, and RLC are responsible for more *real-time* functions, such as encoding, scheduling, segmentation, and reassembly, that require near constant communication with the RRU. On the other hand, the higher layers—PDCP, SDAP, and RRC—are involved with *non-real-time* tasks such as data compression, encryption, and configuration management.

This clear distinction forms the basis of the CU-DU functional splits, where the real-time functions (performed by lower layers, that is, PHY, MAC, and RLC) are delegated to the DU, whereas the non-real-time functions of the PDCP and upper layers are assigned to the CU. Given the complexities of the tasks performed by the BBU and the closed nature of the RAN ecosystem, more variations in functional splits were introduced for both the high and low layer split, as explored in the next section.

Split Options

RAN has historically been a closed, proprietary system where RAN equipment vendors would engineer their products as they see fit. There is widespread agreement among standard bodies, equipment vendors, and mobile network operators regarding the benefits of a decomposed vRAN architecture and the need for CU and DU functional split, but there are also different opinions on how to split the BBU functionality between the two. Given the complexities of the tasks performed by the BBU and the closed nature of the RAN ecosystem, 3GPP defined multiple split options in Release 14. This allowed the RAN equipment vendors the flexibility to implement the BBU functional split based on their individual product architecture, while still adhering to the 3GPP specifications. These split options, aptly named Options 1 through 8, provide a possibility to split the BBU functionality into CU and DU at every individual layer in the 5G protocol stack and, in some cases, within the layer itself, as shown in Figure 5-15. It's worth noting that some split options, such as Options 2, 3, and 7, have multiple sub-split options; however, Figure 5-15 shows only the sub-splits for Option 7, which is more commonly used in the industry.[40]

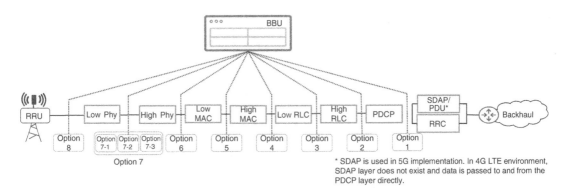

FIGURE 5-15   3GPP-Defined BBU Functional Split Options

The BBU functionality is split between the CU and DU based on the split option chosen by the RAN equipment manufacturer. Each of the split options represents a deliberate decision on how processing will be distributed between the CU and DU. If more processing is done on the DU, less processing is needed on the CU, and vice versa. The distribution of functions between the two (that is, the choice of split option) also determines the bandwidth required between the CU and DU. A brief description and typical uses of each split option are mentioned in the list that follows:[41]

- **Split Option 8: PHY–RF Layer Split:** This is not a new split option but rather a formalization of the traditional deployment where the RF processing is done on the RU, while 5G protocol stack processing is performed at a centralized location in the BBU. Option 8 continues to use *CPRI* transport between the RRU and BBU and is already used in Centralized RAN deployments. This option requires very high amounts of bandwidth across the fronthaul network and has strict latency requirements between the RRU and BBU, limiting the maximum distance to 20 km or less.

- **Split Option 7: Intra-PHY Layer Split:** This option splits the PHY layer functionality between the DU and CU. Option 7 defines even more granular split choices within the PHY layer called Options 7-1, 7-2, and 7-3. Each of these split options defines a list of PHY layer tasks, such as encoding, modulation, MIMO, and beamforming processing, to be divided between the DU and CU. 3GPP allows the use of different sub-options in uplink and downlink directions for added efficiency. For instance, Option 7-1 or 7-2 could be used for uplink, and at the same time Option 7-3 could be used for downlink. Using any of these split options greatly reduces the bandwidth between the DU and CU, but does not relax latency restrictions between the two. Option 7, along with Option 6, is one of the favored split options by 3GPP.

- **Split Option 6: MAC–PHY Layer Split:** This is where all MAC and higher layer functions reside in the CU, while PHY layer functions are delegated to the DU. Option 6 further reduces the bandwidth requirements between the CU and DU but does not offer much in terms of relaxing latency requirements.

- **Split Option 5: Intra-MAC Layer Split:** This option splits the functions performed by the MAC layer into High MAC and Low MAC. CU performs the High MAC functions, such as centralized scheduling and intercell interference coordination, along with RLC and PDCP functions, whereas DU performs the Low MAC, PHY, and RF functions. Option 5 relaxes the latency requirements between the CU and DU, thus allowing longer distances, but is more complex to implement and thus not favored over Split Options 6 and 7.

- **Split Option 4: RLC–MAC Layer Split:** This option delegates the functions of the RLC, PDCP, and RRC layers to the CU, whereas the DU performs the MAC and lower-layer functions. Option 4 is not used, as it does not offer any discernible advantages over other split options.

- **Split Option 3: Intra-RLC Layer Split:** This option further divides the RLC layer functions of segmentation, reassembling, buffering, and error correction into High RLC and Low RLC. In this split option, the High RLC, PDCP, and RRC functions reside in the CU, whereas the Low RLC, MAC, PHY, and RF functions reside in the DU.

- **Split Option 2: PDCP–RLC Layer Split:** This option has been recommended by 3GPP for standardizing the CU–DU split. Using Option 2, the PDCP and RRC layers reside in the CU, whereas the DU performs the functions of the RLC and lower layers. The functionality offered by this split option has previously been finalized in 4G LTE, and, thus, it makes Option 2 much more feasible for standardization with marginal incremental efforts. Option 2 offers much lower bandwidth as compared to its lower-layer counterparts as well as much better latency tolerance between the CU and DU. Option 2 has become the industry standard for implementing the so-called *Higher Layer Split (HLS)* between the CU and DU. More details on HLS and its counterpart, the *Lower Layer Split (LLS)*, is covered in the next section.

- **Split Option 1: RRC–PDCP Layer Split:** This option is also allowed by 3GPP. In this split option, only the RRC functions are implemented in the CU while the rest of the functions of the 5G protocol stack are performed by the DU. If implemented, this option results in a complex and bulky DU and thus is typically not used.

Single vs. Dual Split Architecture

The split options can be grouped into two categories: Options 1 and 2 map to the non-real-time functions and are classified as *Higher Layer Splits (HLS)*, while Options 3 through 8, which map to real-time functions, are called *Lower Layer Splits (LLS)*.

In a typical 5G MCN deployment, both the HLS and LLS options are utilized simultaneously, resulting in disaggregating the BBU into the DU and CU, as well as offloading some of the functionality to the RU—all working together to implement a decomposed, virtualized RAN architecture. HLS is used to implement the CU functions, whereas one of the LLS options is used to further disaggregate the functions of lower layers between the DU and RU. For instance, if the RAN equipment vendor chooses to implement HLS Option 2 for CU and LLS Option 6 for DU, then:

- The CU must implement the PDCP and RRC layer functions.

- The DU must implement the MAC and RLC layer functions.

- The RU must implement the PHY layer functions.

Consequently, if Option 7 is used for the DU, which is an intra-PHY split, then the RU must implement some of the PHY functionality, while the DU implements the rest of PHY layer functions, along with the MAC and RLC functions. In other words, depending on the LLS option used, the RU now needs to perform additional processing of the RF signal before sending it over to the DU. The same is true in the reverse direction. The use of dual split options is also documented in the IEEE 1914.1 standards. Figure 5-16 shows various single split and dual split architecture scenarios.

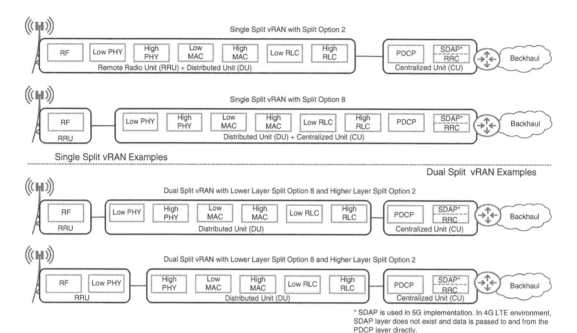

FIGURE 5-16   Single vs. Dual Split vRAN Architectures

Allowing the DU to offload some of its functionality to the RU through an LLS option serves a few purposes. First, it provides the RAN equipment vendor with the flexibility to distribute the real-time functions of the BBU between the RU and DU as they see fit. Second, offloading some of the DU functions to the RU reduces the bandwidth required in the fronthaul network. Lastly, certain LLS options may be better suited for the latency-sensitive nature of communication between the RU and DU. On the flip side, moving too much processing on the RU may make it bulkier, power-hungry, and more susceptible to overheating. The RUs are typically external, pole-mounted devices, where such changes in the hardware form factor could be undesirable. The key is therefore to choose an LLS option that is best suited to provide an optimal balance between too much or too little processing on the RU. To that end, Options 8 and 7 have emerged as the frontrunners of industry adoption and have also been the focus of standardization by various industry bodies.

Choosing a Suitable Split Option

While 3GPP has standardized the use of Option 2 for HLS, it did not definitively recommend a specific LLS option.[42] Over the past few years, Option 7 has emerged as the frontrunner of various standardization efforts. To a lesser degree, Option 6 is also discussed, but rarely, if ever, considered for implementation. To better appreciate the feasibility of Option 7, one must recall that Option 8 still uses CPRI traffic, which requires massive amounts of bandwidth in the fronthaul network.

What Is CPRI Traffic?

CPRI uses serialized communication for user data, control, management, and synchronization between the RU and BBU/DU. CPRI transports the RF signals in the form of *in-phase* and *quadrature* components, called *IQ data*, sampled at a constant rate. A single CPRI interface may carry multiple RF streams, thus reducing the amount of fiber required but increasing the overall CPRI line rate.

CPRI is uncompressed, digitized RF data and uses constant bitrate (CBR) traffic; that is, the signal is continually transmitted at a predetermined bitrate regardless of whether there is user data present. The amount of traffic carried over a single CPRI interface depends upon the *CPRI rate option* used to meet RF design. Over the years, as more spectrum is unlocked and wider channels allowed more bandwidth and capacity, higher bitrate CPRI options have been introduced. Both the RU and BBU/DU must agree on one of these CPRI rate options to establish connectivity between the two. These rate options are a measure of the line bitrate supported by CPRI implementation and must not be confused with the BBU functional split options that define how the BBU functionality is split between the CU and DU. The CPRI rate options, as defined in the CPRI specifications, are as follows:[43]

- **CPRI Rate Option 1:** 614.4Mbps
- **CPRI Rate Option 2:** 1228.8Mbps (1.22 Gbps)
- **CPRI Rate Option 3:** 2457.6Mbps (2.45 Gbps)
- **CPRI Rate Option 4:** 3072.0Mbps (3.07 Gbps)
- **CPRI Rate Option 5:** 4915.2Mbps (4.91 Gbps)
- **CPRI Rate Option 6:** 6144.0Mbps (6.14 Gbps)
- **CPRI Rate Option 7:** 9830.4Mbps (9.83 Gbps)
- **CPRI Rate Option 7a:** 8110.08Mbps (8.11 Gbps)
- **CPRI Rate Option 8:** 10137.6Mbps (10.13 Gbps)
- **CPRI Rate Option 9:** 12165.12Mbps (12.16 Gbps)
- **CPRI Rate Option 10:** 24330.24Mbps (24.33 Gbps)

CPRI bandwidth has not been an issue in traditional D-RAN deployments, where the RRU and the BBU both reside at the cell site and are connected through dedicated fiber optic cables. However, with each individual CPRI interface in excess of 10 or 20 Gbps of CBR traffic, as is the case with CPRI rate

8 and higher, transporting raw CPRI traffic over the fronthaul access network presents a significant challenge. This challenge is compounded in cases where multiple sectors are used on the cell site or if multiple frequency bands are used, each of which might require a dedicated CPRI interface. In these cases, the cumulative bandwidth requirement from a single cell site location may exceed tens or sometimes hundreds of gigabits per second. Additionally, with the availability of mmWave frequencies in 5G and advanced antenna features such as mMIMO, the sheer amount of bandwidth required to transport CPRI traffic over fronthaul makes Option 8 bandwidth-prohibitive. However, Split Option 8 will continue to be useful for both 4G and some 5G deployments. It is expected to coexist alongside Option 7-*x* for vRAN deployments.

eCPRI

To deal with the challenges presented by traditional CPRI transport in the fronthaul network, the coalition of Huawei, Nokia, Ericsson, and NEC proposed the evolution of CPRI standards called *eCPRI* in 2017.[44] The drivers for creating a new eCPRI standard were multifold; chief among them was the need for significant reduction in CPRI bandwidth overall, use of flexible bandwidth scale based on user data instead of CBR, and the adoption of packet-based transport using Ethernet and IP technologies with advanced networking and OAM features.

> **Note**
>
> The term *eCPRI* was never spelled out in the original specification and was thus sometimes (incorrectly) called Ethernet CPRI due to current implementations of eCPRI using Ethernet (Layer 2) as the transport. However, eCPRI was intended to be an *evolution* or *enhancement* to traditional CPRI, and, as such, both *evolved CPRI* and *enhanced CPRI* are typically acceptable definitions. Besides, as eCPRI allows both Ethernet (Layer 2) and IP (Layer 3) encapsulation, calling it Ethernet CPRI would be neither technically accurate nor future-proof should vendors choose IP-based eCPRI implementations.

A critical distinction between CPRI and eCPRI is the lack of control, management, and synchronization traffic in the latter. Control and management of the RU (for example, initialization and configuration) make up a small portion of the overall traffic and could be implemented independently of user data transport. As defined the by CPRI forum, eCPRI carries only the user data, or the U-plane traffic, and some real-time traffic control information, whereas the control and management traffic, referred to as the *C-plane* and *M-plane*, is implemented independently over Ethernet (VLANs or L2 VPNs) or IP (L3 VPNs). Additionally, eCPRI does not carry embedded synchronization information between the RU and DU. Synchronization between the two is achieved by implementing the *S-plane* using an external clock source and propagating timing information through the fronthaul network. The concepts of *timing* and *synchronization* are discussed in Chapter 9, "Essential Technologies for 5G-Ready Networks: Timing and Synchronization."

Just like CPRI, the eCPRI implementations continued to lack cross-vendor interoperability and stayed a closed, proprietary system. In alignment with 3GPP, eCPRI encourages the use of the popular intra-PHY Option 7 due to its advantages in implementing antenna functions such as MIMO, multipoint connectivity, and carrier aggregation, but does not explicitly restrict the vendors from implementing other split options. The following split options are supported in the eCPRI specifications:[45]

- **eCPRI Split Option A:** The equivalent of 3GPP Split Option 1

- **eCPRI Split Option B:** The equivalent of 3GPP Split Option 2

- **eCPRI Split Option C:** The equivalent of 3GPP Split Option 4

- **eCPRI Split Option D:** The equivalent of 3GPP Split Option 6

- **eCPRI Split Option ID:** The equivalent of 3GPP Split Option 7-3

- **eCPRI Split Options IID and IIU:** The equivalent of 3GPP Split Option 7-2

- **eCPRI Split Option E:** The equivalent of 3GPP Split Option 8

The choice of split option has an impact on the overall fronthaul bandwidth requirements. When more processing is done on the RU, signifying a higher split option, the bandwidth requirements for the fronthaul network go down proportionally. While the actual fronthaul bandwidth requirements will vary based on the individual deployment scenario, Figure 5-17 highlights the significant bandwidth savings based on the choice of split option implemented. The use case shown in the picture assumes an aggregated RF bandwidth of 500 MHz, with 64T64R mMIMO, but 4×4 MIMO layers and 64 QAM modulation. This implementation would require more than 1Tbps (terabits per second) for Split Option 8, 600 Gbps with Split Option 7-1, and 38 Gbps for Split Option 7-2. If Split Option 2 or 3 is used, the bandwidth requirement falls below 10 Gbps, similar to traditional backhaul.[46]

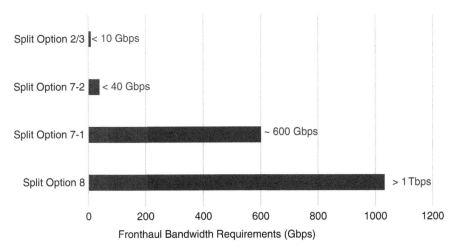

FIGURE 5-17   Example of Required Fronthaul Bandwidth Across Split Options

The introduction of eCPRI helped modernize legacy CPRI transport by utilizing Ethernet and IP for transport as well as lowered the bandwidth requirements between the RU and DU. However, it did nothing to provide open interfaces and interoperability across vendors. While new entrants in the vRAN space were looking to take advantage of virtualization and revolutionize the RAN networks, mobile networks were still subject to vendor lock-in with limited to no interop between RU and DU provided by different RAN vendors. Mobile network operators, wanting to drive interoperability in vRAN, created the *Open RAN (O-RAN) Alliance* in an effort to collectively influence the industry and speed up the pace of their 5G deployment.

Open RAN

The RAN industry has been dominated by a small number of incumbents, which has shrunk even further through various mergers and acquisitions, resulting in a select few (Huawei, Ericsson, and Nokia) exerting a near-total monopoly on all RAN deployments.[47] The evolution to vRAN has created a lot of ambiguity in the industry in choosing the best-suited split options.

Mobile network operators—already vendor-locked with existing RAN architectures and weary of the same restrictions in 5G and vRAN—demanded a multivendor, open, and interoperable RAN ecosystem where they could deploy RU, DU, and CU from any combination of new or incumbent vendors. Incumbents in any industry, especially the ones with large market share, are not only slow to adapt to disruptive changes, they often also resist the calls for openness and interoperability that might lead to loss in their market share. The leading mobile operators, AT&T, SK Telecom, and Deutsche Telekom, along with members of academia from Stanford University, created the *xRAN Forum* in 2016 with the objective to standardize the components of a software-focused, extensible radio access network. The forum was quickly joined by other industry stalwarts like Telstra, NTT Docomo, Verizon, and vendors such as Samsung, Fujitsu, Intel, Cisco, NEC, Nokia, Radisys, Altiostar, Mavenir, and others. In 2018, the xRAN Forum joined forces with the *C-RAN Alliance*—which was an effort led by China Mobile and focused on adoption of Centralized RAN architectures. As part of this merger, AT&T, China Telecom, DT, Orange, and NTT Docomo became the founding members of the *Open RAN (O-RAN) Alliance*, intending to create an intelligent, open, programmable, and virtualized RAN network. The key tenets of the O-RAN Alliance are as follows:[48]

- Use of open and interoperable interfaces, fully virtualized components, and an artificial intelligence–assisted smart RAN network

- Minimize proprietary hardware and promote the use of commercial off-the-shelf (COTS) hardware and merchant silicon

- Define and drive standardization and subsequent adoption of application programming interfaces (APIs), along with the use of open source software for vRAN deployments

The O-RAN Alliance has quickly grown to include some of the largest mobile operators in the world (Verizon, Jio, Vodafone, Telefonica, and KDDI, to name a few) and over 200 contributors consisting of various equipment vendors and members of the academia. In a very short amount of time, the O-RAN Alliance has had a sizable impact on fostering and nurturing an Open RAN ecosystem through its various *workgroups (WGs)*. A total of 10 workgroups, dubbed WG1 through WG10, have been defined so far, focusing on defining various specifications that collectively make up the O-RAN reference network architecture.[49] The O-RAN Alliance uses the baselines defined in the vRAN architecture, and the resulting reference design is often referred to as O-RAN. These specifications defined by the O-RAN design consist of the overall reference architecture as well as components such as the Open Fronthaul interface, RAN controller, orchestration, cloudification, and xHaul transport design—all of which are discussed in this section.

Open RAN, O-RAN Alliance, and OpenRAN

There is a lot of confusion regarding various different terminologies used when discussing Open RAN architectures and solutions. The term *Open RAN* refers to an ecosystem dedicated to promoting open interfaces resulting in vendor interoperability for RAN components (that is, the RU, DU, and CU). The O-RAN alliance is the leading industry body that defines various specifications to accelerate adoption of the Open RAN ecosystem.

OpenRAN (notice the absence of space between Open and RAN) is a sub-project of *Telecom Infra Project (TIP)*—another industry organization working towards driving infrastructure solutions to enable global connectivity. TIP and the O-RAN Alliance have signed a liaison agreement to ensure interoperability and compatibility between O-RAN and TIP solutions.

O-RAN Architecture and Use Cases

The O-RAN Alliance was founded on the basic principles of creating an intelligent, smart RAN network by virtue of automation, analytics, machine learning (ML), and artificial intelligence (AI), along with the use of standardized, open interfaces across the various virtualized RAN network components. As such, the overall O-RAN reference architecture uses a multifaceted approach in addition to Open Fronthaul nodes and interfaces. Figure 5-18 provides an overview of the building blocks of the overall O-RAN architecture, and the interfaces between them, as specified by *ORAN WG1: Use Cases and Overall Architecture Workgroup*.[50]

As Figure 5-18 illustrates, Open Fronthaul (and its components) is just one part of the overall O-RAN reference architecture, while automation, orchestration, Network Function Virtualization Infrastructure (NFVI) framework, and RAN controller make up the rest of this architectural framework. Different WGs within the O-RAN Alliance define specifications for each of these individual components.

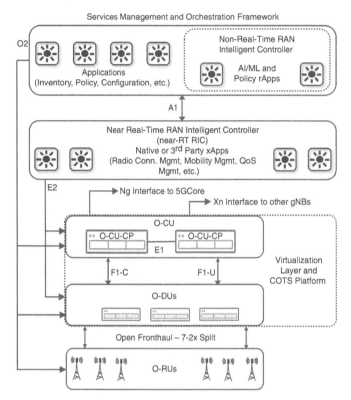

FIGURE 5-18   O-RAN Architectural Framework

Open Fronthaul Nodes and Interfaces

One of O-RAN Alliance's primary goals is to standardize the LLS option and accelerate the use of open, interoperable fronthaul RAN nodes. With input from both vendors and operators, WG4 (the Open Fronthaul Interfaces Group) defined the use of *Split Option 7-2x* between the RU and DU for what is known as Open Fronthaul.[51] Option 7-2x is another PHY layer split, which should not be confused with 3GPP Option 7-2. It is logically placed between 3GPP Split Options 7-1 and 7-2, and assigns pre-coding, modulation, RF resource element mapping, and other higher-layer functions to the DU and allocates lower-layer functions like analog-to-digital conversion, inverse fast Fourier transform (iFFT), and certain beamforming management functions to the RU. Split Option 7-2x is focused on making it easier to implement the DU functions to run in a virtualized environment using generic COTS hardware. The RUs and DUs that support Open Fronthaul (that is, the O-RAN-compliant implementation of fronthaul through the use of Split Option 7-2x) are called *Open RU (O-RU)* and *Open DU (O-DU)*, respectively.[52]

> **Note**
>
> The terminologies *O-RU*, *O-DU*, and *O-CU* signify the use of open, interoperable RAN nodes, where Split Option 7-2x is used between O-RU and O-DU, while Split Option 2 is used between O-DU and O-CU. The O-CU functions can still be further subdivided into O-CU-CP and O-CU-UP, signifying the separation of the control and user planes.

The interface used between the O-RU and O-DU is still called eCPRI, which uses Ethernet or IP encapsulations. However, this 7-2x O-RAN-compliant eCPRI must be distinguished from the eCPRI interface defined by the CPRI forum. The two specifications do share the same naming convention (that is, Evolved or Enhanced CPRI, or eCPRI) and the use of Ethernet for transport, but they differ on the split options used. As mentioned in the previous section, the CPRI forum's eCPRI implementation allows 3GPP-defined LLS Options 6, 7-1, 7-2, and 8, but mapped to eCPRI's naming conventions of Option D, ID, IID/IIU, and E. In comparison, O-RAN-compliant eCPRI uses Split Option 7-2x and mandates open interfaces and interoperability between the O-RU and O-DU. Figure 5-19, included in the next section, provides a pictorial mapping of various split options defined by 3GPP, CPRI Forum, and O-RAN Alliance.

Open versus Vendor-Specific eCPRI

The use of eCPRI, O-RAN compliant or otherwise, is still in the very early stages of adoption. Depending on how the industry progresses, it is possible that over the coming years the term eCPRI will become synonymous with the O-RAN-compliant, Split 7-2x-based implementation.

In addition to the Open Fronthaul specification through WG4, the O-RAN Alliance also defines open specifications for various other RAN interfaces through WG5 (Open F1/W1/E1/X2/Xn Workgroup), as well as the use of a Fronthaul Gateway (FHGW) through WG7 (Whitebox Working Group). The use of various RAN interfaces was showcased previously in Figure 5-18. More details on Fronthaul Gateway and its applications in the fronthaul transport network are discussed later in the "Transporting Radio Traffic over Packet-Based Fronthaul" section.

RAN Intelligent Controller (RIC)

The past several years have seen a significant increase in the use of software-defined, analytics-driven networks, and the mobile communication networks (MCNs) are no exception. *RAN Intelligent Controller (RIC)* is the software platform that can be considered the brain of the RAN domain. Using advanced analytics, artificial intelligence (AI), and machine learning (ML), a RIC utilizes the usage data generated in the RAN to provide performance visualization, perform predictive analysis, and create actionable intelligence. These capabilities can then be used to enforce or modify RAN policies to improve resource management, increase RAN efficiency, and optimize overall performance with little to no human interaction. Two different flavors of RIC are defined in an O-RAN architecture: *near real-time (near-RT) RIC* and *non-real-time (non-RT) RIC*.

A near-RT RIC interacts with the O-RAN nodes (O-DU and O-CU) and performs near-real-time monitoring and optimization of the radio access network resources. While a near-RT RIC controls the O-DU and O-CU behavior, in reality it acts as an *enforcer* for the policies defined by the non-RT RIC.

As shown in Figure 5-18 earlier, a non-RT RIC is part of the overall *Services Management and Orchestration (SMO)* framework, which uses ML/AI and analytics to provide policy guidelines to the near-RT RIC using the A1 interface. A non-RT RIC uses complex algorithms on the usage data and directs near-RT RIC to enforce policies, thus creating an intelligent and smart RAN network.

RIC is not just a single piece of software; it is rather a platform that allows extensibility through hosting third-party apps. Apps hosted on near-RT RIC are called *xApps*, whereas non-RT RIC apps are referred to as *rApps*. The use of third-party apps fosters an innovation-based ecosystem using RAN algorithms from various sources instead of being tied only to the software provided by the RIC vendor. Suggested use cases for xApps and rApps include QoS-based resource optimization, mMIMO and beamforming optimization, DSS, dynamic resource allocation for unmanned aerial vehicle, and handover in Vehicle-to-Everything (V2X) scenarios, among others.

RIC is an active area of research and development in the industry and is one of the critical foundations of the O-RAN reference architecture with two working groups (WG2 and WG3) defining non-RT and near-RT RIC specifications. At the time of this writing, there have not been any large-scale production deployments of RIC, but multiple mobile network operators such as AT&T, Deutsche Telekom, KDDI, and China Mobile have publicly commented on production trials for RIC.[53, 54]

Cloud and Orchestration

Radio access networks have been moving toward a cloud-based architecture for some time. Centralized RAN architecture pioneered the concept of BBU pooling in a central *cloud*, even though, in most cases, this cloud was an offsite data center hosting specialized BBU hardware. vRAN changes this concept with virtualized RAN nodes (that is, the CU and DU). To ensure that future RAN networks take full advantage of the virtualization, the O-RAN WG6 (the Cloudification and Orchestration Workgroup) provides design guidelines to leverage and drive adoption of generic COTS hardware for virtualized RAN nodes.

Virtualization and cloudification typically go hand in hand, with some virtual functions being moved offsite to an *application-hosting facility* (that is, *a cloud*). O-RAN introduces the concept of an *O-Cloud*, a cloud platform composed of hardware and software components capable of providing RAN functions. An O-RAN-compliant MCN might contain multiple *O-Cloud instances*, where each instance is a collection of *resource pools*. These resource pools are essentially servers that contain CPU, memory, storage, network interface cards (NICs), and so on, which can host various individual O-Cloud network functions such as O-DU and O-CU. Given that these O-RAN nodes are typically distributed in multiple locales, a comprehensive automation, orchestration, and management framework is required to ensure consistent and efficient deployment. The Service Management and Orchestration Framework (SMO) defined by WG6 provides a general structure to accomplish just that.[55]

Use of Public Cloud for RAN Functions

As O-CU and O-DU components are virtualized and considered "cloud ready," there is a strong inclination among mobile network operators to host these RAN *functions* in a public cloud. This allows the mobile network operators to expedite RAN deployments while providing CAPEX savings.

While hosting certain RAN functions (such as the O-CU) in the public cloud is possible, a similar solution might not fit the latency budget for applications such as the O-DU. Later parts of this chapter, as well as Chapter 10, will discuss various design considerations for the use of a public cloud for hosting RAN components.

In order to efficiently operate this distributed, diverse network spread across a vast geography, the use of a robust orchestration and automation framework, such as the one defined by WG6, is vital. While the detailed automation framework is out of scope for this book, the use of automation for 5G transport network deployment and continued operation will be discussed as needed.

O-RAN xHaul Network Architecture

O-RAN WG9 (the Open X-haul Transport Workgroup) has been focused on defining a baseline transport network architecture that encompasses the fronthaul, midhaul, and backhaul domains. As part of this objective, WG9 provides guidance on best practices and design strategies for the xHaul network using two primary transport mechanisms: WDM-based transport for fronthaul and the packet switched transport architectures for fronthaul, midhaul, and backhaul.[56, 57] WDM-based fronthaul transport was briefly covered in Chapter 3; however, more details on WDM are out of scope for this book.

The WG9's *xHaul Packet Switched Architecture and Solution Specification* outlines various 5G xHaul deployment scenarios, transport network technologies, VPN services implementations, quality of service guidelines, timing and synchronization architectures, as well as other details critical to the transport domain of an MCN. The specification and guidelines put forth by WG9, and the newly formed WG10 (the OAM Workgroup), are useful for data network engineers and architects tasked with designing and deploying a 5G mobile transport network. Later parts of this chapter, and the rest of this book, will exclusively focus on the technologies required to architect these smart, open, scalable, and programmable 5G transport networks.

Summarizing vRAN Split Options and Architecture

While an overwhelming majority of mobile deployments are still D-RAN based, major mobile network operators and vendors are coalescing around the vRAN architecture as the path forward for the mobile industry, given the benefits it provides with respect to resource pooling, efficient RF coordination, cost-effectiveness, and deployment agility. Based on a recent service provider survey, it is estimated that over 70% of the total service providers are planning to switch to vRAN architectures, with just under 50% of them planning to deploy fronthaul networks as well. The rest will use a midhaul-based vRAN architecture where the RRU and DU are collocated at the cell site.[58]

With the vRAN architecture still in its (relative) infancy, it is understandable that there are multiple standard bodies and organizations defining various BBU split options and deployment choices. Figure 5-19 summarizes the most commonly referenced split option choices.

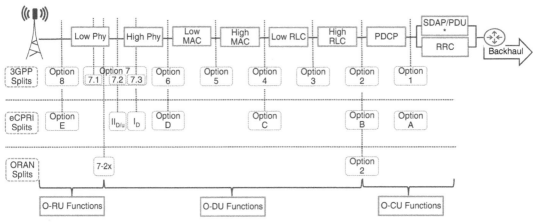

FIGURE 5-19   Comparing Split Options Across Various Standards

Of all the split options shown, the following are the most commonly used:

- **3GPP**: Option 8 for LTE, Options 7.2 and 2 for dual-split architecture

- **Vendor-specific eCPRI**: Similar to 3GPP with eCPRI names

- **O-RAN**: Options 7-2x and 2 for dual-split architecture, Option 8 for LTE co-existence with 5G

Although O-RAN is relatively new, it has gained significant industry momentum and its reference architecture is expected to become the dominant choice for vRAN deployments. Nonetheless, the dual-split vRAN architecture is quickly becoming the gold standard of mobile network deployment and has widespread implications on the underlying transport design. The underlying xHaul transport not only has to accommodate the transformative dual-split vRAN architectures but may also have to simultaneously support vRAN, Centralized RAN, and D-RAN coexistence in a multigeneration MCN. These implications and their impact on mobile transport network evolution are discussed later in this chapter.

5G Core Network

Similar to previous generations of mobile networks, in the fifth generation of mobile networks, the changes in RAN are accompanied by changes to the mobile core architecture. Although enhancements and incremental changes to the packet core introduced through 3GPP Releases 8 through 13 were generally viewed as extensions to 4G EPC, it's the concept of *Control and User Plane Separation (CUPS)*, introduced in Release 14, that is widely considered as the first step toward the new mobile core architecture that is now labeled as the 5G Core (5GC) network. Subsequent 3GPP releases further perfected this idea, making it an integral part of 5GC.

Aside from the changes brought through 3GPP specifications, a parallel yet independent transformation of the packet core was taking place in the context of NFV. While NFV and its framework (driven by ETSI) was completely independent of 3GPP's work, mobile networks (particularly vRAN) were among the initial use cases considered for NFV. As this idea of virtualizing network functions gained popularity among the network service providers, extending these principles to the mobile packet core became a more compelling and promising use case.[59] As a consequence, many packet core vendors started to offer NFV-based EPC, dubbed as *virtual EPC (vEPC)*. This virtualization trend continued and accelerated in the transition toward 5GC.

Two key concepts redefined vEPC to become 5GC—namely, Control and User Plane Separation (CUPS), and Service-Based Architecture (SBA), leading to a cloud-native packet core.

Control and User Plane Separation (CUPS)

System Architecture Evolution–related changes in 4G EPC had resulted in separation of the devices that implement the user-plane functionalities (for example, data forwarding) and control-plane responsibilities (for example, session establishment and device registration). Though this separation allowed both user- and control-plane devices to independently scale based on their respective requirements, they were still deployed in the same centralized data centers across the mobile network's coverage areas. As these data centers were naturally some distance away from the cell sites, the voice and data traffic would incur a small delay while traversing the xHaul networks. While voice traffic is generally handed off to IMS within the same data center, the data traffic experiences additional latency introduced by the PDN/Internet network providing connectivity to the remote servers. The overall latency has been fairly tolerable for the services and applications in the 4G era; it did not, however, meet the requirements and expectations set by URLLC applications that 5G promises to enable.

Aside from latency, the deployments based on the EPC/LTE architecture were also challenged by the soaring bandwidth demands for traffic consumed by and originating from mobile devices. Although the EPC, with its independently scalable control and data planes, could cope with this challenge, this traffic does significantly strain the xHaul networks that had to transport it between the EPC and the cell site. This problem is exacerbated in a backhaul network, with traffic being aggregated from multiple midhauls and fronthauls. As this traffic is expected to increase significantly with 5G, especially with eMBB-type services, the challenge increases multifold. A different approach was therefore needed to remove both these barriers to allow 5G to offer its promised capabilities.

Control and User Plane Separation (CUPS) addresses these challenges and provides a solution by re-architecting the packet core. CUPS finds its roots in the separation of the two planes, which was conceived in SAE/4G and helped with scalability and cost. The proposed solution recognizes that the bulk of the traffic in the mobile networks is user data, which is predominantly sent between the mobile devices and endpoints reachable through the Public Data Network (PDN) interface of the packet core. These endpoints could include content delivery servers, gaming servers, peer-to-peer applications, and so on. Hence, if this PDN connectivity is provided closer to the cell sites, the mobile transport network wouldn't need to carry the burden of transporting this massive amount of data between the mobile user and the centralized packet core locations. CUPS, therefore, takes the plane separation idea one step further and advocates that instead of co-locating the devices implementing user-plane and control-plane functions, these should be deployed independently—with the user-plane devices deployed much closer to the cell site. PDN connectivity or local servers are also typically implemented along with the user plane, consequently enabling the data communication between the mobile device and remote endpoints without being transported over the entire xHaul network. This architecture, therefore, provides a solution to the transport network's bandwidth challenge. The latency challenge is addressed by *Multi-Access Edge Compute (MEC)*.

Because control-plane traffic does not require high bandwidth and is relatively less sensitive to latency, the control plane continues to stay at the main data center with CUPS.

Multi-Access Edge Compute (MEC)

CUPS architecture can address the latency challenge by using special-purpose compute resources deployed at the same data centers where the mobile core's user plane is implemented. These compute resources, called *Multi-Access Edge Compute (MEC)*, can be used to process and locally terminate the time-sensitive traffic. Termination of traffic flows closer to the edge significantly reduces latency compared to transporting this traffic over data networks to remote servers. Therefore, the use of MEC in the CUPS architecture makes it possible to fulfill the goal of 5G URLLC applications.

As data is consumed at the edge locations instead of being sent toward the data network, MEC also offers an additional benefit of fog computing by consuming and analyzing data at a location close to the source. This also benefits mMTC-type applications where IoT-generated traffic is best suited to be processed, analyzed, and reacted upon locally and closer to the data sources.

Although the term coined for the compute resources placed close to the (mobile) network edge was *Mobile Edge Compute*, in 2017, ETSI decided to give it a more generic name and rebrand it to *Multi-Access Edge Compute*.[60] Even though MEC has gained popularity as a 5G capability, its architecture is defined to be independent of 5G and can be implemented in 4G-based networks as well.[61] The placement of MEC is further discussed in the "What's Hosted at the Data Centers" section.

Placement of the 5GC User Plane

The vRAN architecture benefits by placing the disaggregated RAN components deeper into the mobile network, closer to the 5GC—as much as latency and other constraints allow. Similarly, deploying the 5GC user plane close to the cell sites offers the benefits of reduced latency, especially in the case of MEC and local content delivery network (CDN) servers, and lower bandwidth requirement for the backhaul network. Therefore, a mobile network architect would want to place the 5GC user-plane devices and functions as close to the cell site as possible. That makes the far-edge data center, with a typical distance of 10–20 km from the cell site and boasting a one-way latency of under 150 usec, ideally suited for the 5GC user plane, MEC and CDN server, and PDN connectivity. However, more commonly it's the edge data center that is the optimal choice instead.

There are two main constraints that limit how close to the mobile network's periphery the user plane can be deployed:

- The packet core functions can't be placed before the disaggregated RAN components, or more specifically the CU. Placement of the CU will be influenced by the RAN design (with the aim to move it as far away from the edge as possible). Hence, an optimal choice has to be made between the RAN and packet core design to place the O-CU and user-plane 5GC functions; this criterion favors the edge data center as the best choice.

- The location that hosts these 5GC devices should also be able to host services or compute, such as MEC, CDN, or peering routers connecting to an Internet service provider or corporate intranet (in the case of Private 5G). Providing these services may not be practical at each far-edge data center due to their smaller serving area, high deployment density, and typically miniature design. Therefore, the edge data centers are once again the preferred choice. In certain cases, it may not be feasible for even edge data centers to meet these requirements, and in such cases traffic is routed to the user-plane functions in the main data center instead.

What's Hosted at the Data Centers

With the decomposition of RAN and implementation of CUPS for the packet core, the building blocks of mobile networks are now sprinkled across a larger number of data centers spread across the entire MCN. Figure 5-20 represents the composition of these various data centers and the parts of RAN and 5GC that are hosted there.

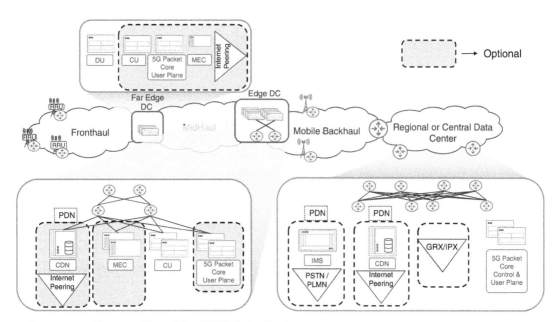

FIGURE 5-20   Composition of the MCN Data Centers

As the figure shows, the devices and functions hosted at the main data center are not much different from EPC—that is, devices implementing the control plane of the mobile network, PDN connectivity to IMS servers (which then connect to PSTN and PLMN), PDN connectivity to reach the Internet (with CDN servers often hosted on the same premises), and connectivity to GRX/IPX exchanges for handling roaming scenarios. Note that even though the data plane is also deployed separately as a result of CUPS, the main DC continues to host data-plane functions. This is meant to handle data traffic that wasn't offloaded at the edge of the network—either because it wasn't feasible to do so, the content is latency tolerant, the content is available through the mobile provider's own servers, or any combination of these. Such data traffic is expected to be only a fraction of the total user traffic and, hence, may not strain the entire xHaul network.

The edge data center, in addition to hosting the CU functionality from the decomposed RAN, will likely also host the 5GC data plane. To send or source this data from the Internet, these edge DCs will also require Internet peering. Additionally, CDN servers can be deployed to reduce the amount of traffic exchanged over this peered network through content caching. Even if Internet peering is not available at an edge DC, CDN servers could still be beneficial. Though MEC is more likely to be hosted at the far-edge data center or even at the cell sites where lower latency can be achieved, it can also be deployed at the edge DC.

The far-edge DC typically hosts only the DU; however, there might be circumstances where it's required to process or offload the user data even closer than what the edge DC can offer. In that case, the far-edge DC will also host the CU as well as the 5GC user plane and MEC. Examples of such deployment are scenarios where far-edge and edge DCs are collapsed into one location.

CUPS Influence on 5GC Layout

CUPS is considered one of the key influencers in the transformation from EPC to 5GC. As a consequence, instead of a monolithic mobile core, the 5GC is a distributed mobile core with PDN peering points quite close to the user, and away from the relatively less-distributed control-plane functions of the packet core.

Towards a Cloud-Native 5G Core

The application of virtualization techniques and principles of NFV had a major impact on the transformation from EPC to vEPC and subsequently to 5GC. It is therefore meaningful to understand these technologies that facilitate the transition toward a fully virtualized, cloud-native 5G core network.

Virtualization, Containerization, and Docker

In the initial days of server virtualization—to achieve isolation, application security, and resource sharing—hardware-assisted virtualization through a hypervisor was the commonly used implementation. Hypervisor functionality running in a host operating system allows for instantiation of a *virtual machine (VM)*, where a guest operating system (OS) and virtualized applications can independently run. Hence, initial implementations of NFV followed the same model, and the VNFs included an operating system ready to be instantiated as a VM. vEPC followed the same path.

Even though this technique provided great isolation and security, there was a cost to it in the form of slight wastage of hardware resources and longer instantiation time. For deployments where the balance is more toward agility and resource optimization than a high level of isolation, the alternate approach of OS-level virtualization became attractive. This type of virtualization, also referred to as *containerization*, leverages the capabilities built into the OS to provide some degree of separation, resource sharing, and independence. This segregated environment is referred to as a *container*.

Compared to VMs, containers have a smaller footprint and make better utilization of the host's resources while providing a relatively less amount of security and isolation. For example, containers do not require a guest OS, thus making them light on system resource requirements. However, because they share the host's OS with other containers, they aren't fully isolated from each other. Most importantly, because containers use built-in OS capabilities, they are free of additional software overhead and resource emulation that would have been required for VMs. This makes containers the preferred choice for dynamic and agile environments.

However, additional capabilities are needed for packaging, porting, maintaining, and managing the containerized applications. *Docker* is a definite frontrunner among the tools that offer these capabilities and has been the most popular choice. Today, the words *Docker* and *container* are used interchangeably, almost completely overlooking the fact that a container is a virtualized application while Docker is an application to package, build, manage, instantiate, version-control, and ship a containerized application.

Microservices Architecture

Virtual machines have their benefits, but they are better suited to a monolithic virtual environment that contains the entire ecosystem of the application. However, the low overhead of containers brings a high level of modularity when virtualizing a set of intertwined applications. The individual applications, or even the individual functions within them, can be containerized. With carefully defined interactions between these applications or functions as well as facilitating these communications through APIs, the containers can easily interact with each other and work cohesively as intended, without knowledge of each other's inner structure. Thus, each one of these can be independently developed, maintained, spun-up, scaled, upgraded, and patched.

Such an implementation of the software function by breaking it down into individual services-oriented, self-contained, independent, and isolated virtualized building blocks is called a *microservices*-based implementation. This architecture offers all the benefits of virtualization for each building block (typically a container) that implements a part (service) of the entire application, and through its modularity brings additional benefits such as independent scalability, upgradability, and resiliency of each of these services.

Orchestration and Kubernetes

Managing, orchestrating, instantiating, monitoring, and ensuring the availability of the virtualized functions are best suited for applications designed for these tasks—commonly known as *orchestrators*.

Management and orchestration (MANO) has always been a critical part of the NFV-based implementation.[62] With a microservices-based approach resulting in a high number of individual containers, along with the networking connecting them together, the need for sophisticated orchestrators becomes even more significant. Various orchestrator choices (many of which are open source) have been available for this purpose, but the most popular and predominantly preferred and used choice at the time of this writing is *Kubernetes*.

Kubernetes Background

Kubernetes originated from a Google internal tool for managing a cluster container deployment called *Borg* (named after the alien group in the sci-fi series *Star Trek*), and its successor project called *Omega*. The internal Google project was hence named *Seven of Nine*, after one of the Borg characters. This name led to the seven-sided Kubernetes logo.[63]

Developed originally by Google engineers, Kubernetes is now an open source container orchestration tool. Often abbreviated as *Kube* or *K8s*, Kubernetes offers everything that's expected of an orchestrator. Some of the popular Kubernetes distributions include RedHat's OpenShift, VMware's Tanzu, Amazon's Elastic Kubernetes Service (EKS), Google Kubernetes Engine (GKE), and so on. It's worth noting that in addition to container orchestration, additional tools and functions may be required to orchestrate and/or automate services and networking. These functions are performed by tools such as Cisco's Network Services Orchestrator (NSO), RedHat's Ansible Automation Platform, Juniper Network's Contrail, and Nokia's Nuage, among others.

Cloud-Native Applications

A cloud environment, in its simplest form, is any data center that is designed to host applications, provide storage, enable interconnectivity, and offer tools and means to orchestrate, deploy, monitor, and manage these services. This could be a commercially available *public cloud* (such as AWS, GCP, Azure, and many others), a *private cloud* (owned and managed on-premises by a corporation), or a combination of the two (called a *hybrid cloud*). The choice of the cloud environment typically comes down to the cost factor, security considerations, and latency limitations. The capital cost of using a public cloud are very low; however, the operating costs of that might be significantly higher than a privately hosted cloud infrastructure. Cloud platforms have made significant strides in meeting security requirements through the use of sophisticated encryption techniques for storing and transferring data, to an extent that governments are starting to feel comfortable moving their data to the cloud.[64, 65] Latency limitations create a requirement of deploying the applications within a certain distance from the users. Deployment of DU is an example of such a restriction, where it has to be within 20 km of the RU. To solve this challenge, most major public cloud providers also offer on-premises versions of their cloud environment, thus extending their cloud to on-premises privately owned locations, while still offering the same orchestration tools and experience as their regular public cloud environment. Some examples of this are AWS Outpost, Azure Stack, and GCP Anthos.

Irrespective of the type of cloud environment, and whether it's on-premises or publicly hosted, the concept of this ecosystem stays the same. Such an ecosystem with virtualized and containerized applications implemented as a microservices architecture, along with orchestration capabilities, is colloquially referred to as a *cloud-native* implementation.

Automation capabilities are implied for any cloud-native orchestrator. It's generally assumed that the containers and their networking in a cloud-native environment have predefined instantiation and deployment templates, lifecycle rules, availability and scalability criteria, and are being actively monitored for failure detection and recovery. The orchestrator is expected to use these and seamlessly run the entire environment with high availability and performance.

Cloud-Native 5G Core

5GC is conceived as a microservices-based architecture ready for cloud-native implementation. The use of Service-Based Architecture (SBA), discussed next, is an essential part to realize this goal. The use of virtualization had already started to remove the dependency on specific vendor hardware, and now the cloud-native nature of 5GC implies that it doesn't need to be hosted at a data center owned and operated by the mobile provider. Rather, such a cloud-native core could be deployed and run on any type of cloud infrastructure. Of course, the developer of the application or service containers claiming cloud-native capability will need to ensure flawless integration into any cloud environments they are being deployed in and can be managed by the orchestrator and tools being used in that environment.

The 5GC adoption of the industry trend toward open and standards-based APIs means that the individual containers implementing 5GC functions can be from any vendor that the mobile operator finds to be most suitable for that particular service. Hence, 5G Core is ripe to be a multi-vendor, cloud-hosted, highly scalable, and resilient mobile core.

Service-Based Architecture: Decomposition of Packet Core

Mobile core architectures of all the previous generations were designed with a device-centric approach, and, in most cases, multiple functions were implemented on specialized hardware. Even with an NFV-driven transformation of EPC to vEPC, the VNFs, developed to disaggregate from the custom hardware, did not focus on reorganizing the roles and functions implemented by those devices. This was because the device roles were not originally designed for a virtualized environment; hence, vEPC missed out on the full potential of virtualization.

A new approach was therefore needed to reimagine the roles and functions of the packet core, conceived with a virtualization mindset. This new architecture would accomplish the following:

- Continue the decoupling effort, by breaking down the functions contained within the virtualized application into separate entities. Reorganize these functions using a cloud-native and microservices approach.

- Offer CUPS to separately and dynamically deploy both user and control planes.

- Scale and update the relevant functions independently.

- Accommodate the needs of 5G-promised services such as low-latency applications.[66]

Additionally, this approach was expected to facilitate the implementation of new and emerging concepts such as *network slicing*,[67] which was briefly discussed in the previous chapter.

Starting with Release 15, 3GPP developed a new mobile core architecture dubbed *Service-Based Architecture (SBA)*, which draws its inspiration from a combination of microservices architecture and a decades-old software design concept called *Service-Oriented Architecture (SOA)*. While the microservices architecture influenced the repackaging of the VNFs, making them independent, modular, and scalable, its SOA defines how these functions should communicate with each other. SOA defines nodes that offer a service, called *service provider* or *service producer*, by registering the services at a *service registry*. The *service consumer* nodes then seek and use those services. The beauty of SOA is that each entity, called a *function*, can be reached by any other through a common communication bus.

Devices, Nodes, and Functions

The previous chapters have been using the terms *nodes*, *devices*, and *functions* interchangeably. The functions are, of course, implemented on "devices," and because they take a specific place in the architecture as well as physical deployment, the term *node* can also be used. However, now with the roles being implemented as virtualized functions, the terms *devices* and *nodes* are not applicable—3GPP uses the term *Network Functions* (NFs) exclusively, and hence going forward this book will use the same terminology to refer to the entities implementing the user- and control-plane functions in the 5GC.

SBA defines the 5GC as a collection of loosely coupled, independent, scalable, and microservices-based entities that it calls *Network Functions (NFs)*. The NFs of SBA can be either service consumers, service producers (*providers*), service registrars, or a combination of these three. Each NF performs a certain role and is able to interface with other functions, while acting as a black box itself (that is, the internal implementation of each function is independent of the others and the interaction between them is only through the exposed interfaces and APIs). 3GPP defined a number of NFs for a very granular implementation of the 5GC, which are discussed next.[68]

5GC User Plane Network Function

The *User Plane Network Function (UPF)* is the cornerstone of CUPS and is responsible for the routing and forwarding of mobile user's traffic to an external network. To achieve low latency, UPF may be placed in the edge or far-edge data centers, in addition to the main DC, as previously discussed in the placement considerations for the 5GC user plane. Additionally, to provide ultra-reliability, either redundant UPF or redundant traffic paths to the same UPF may be used.[69]

Just like 4G, the 5G packet core also makes use of GTP-U protocol over IP to encapsulate data traffic between the RAN and gateway to the external network, simply referred to as *Data Network (DN)* in 5G terminology. This GTP-U tunnel is established between the gNB and UPF over the *N3 reference interface* (thus sometimes referred to as *N3 GTP-U*). The UPF terminates this GTP-U tunnel and forwards the user traffic to the DN. The UPF (like other cloud-native implementations) is meant to be scalable to meet traffic demands, and multiple UPFs can be spun up when needed.

The mobile device and the UPF use a construct called a *protocol data unit session (PDU session)* for traffic forwarding. This is similar in concept to the EPS bearer that was defined in 4G networks, but it has some subtle differences—the most important being the granularity of the QoS mechanism. Unlike the EPS bearer, where a single QoS treatment is applied to all traffic, a PDU session can apply different QoS behaviors to individual traffic flows.[70]

In contrast to the EPS bearer, the PDU session doesn't carry any signaling information and is composed of a *data radio bearer (DRB)* between the UE and gNB, coupled with a GTP-U tunnel between the gNB and UPF. The UPF inherits the SGW functionality of anchoring the GTP-U tunnel, and hence when a user moves across the gNB (but within the service area of the UPF), the GTP-U tunnel destination stays unchanged and traffic continues to flow to the same UPF. If the mobile user moves outside of the UPF's service area, the control-plane functions trigger the procedure to select a new suitable UPF.

5GC Control Plane Network Functions

As of 3GPP Release 17, around 30 control-plane NFs have been currently defined, and this might continue to evolve as 5GC matures further. Some of these functions are optional and are not required in all 5GC implementations. Diving into the detailed description of each of these control plane NFs is beyond the scope of this book; instead, the NFs will be described by logically grouping them together based on their roles. Some studies[71] have classified these roles into the nine groups depicted in Figure 5-21.

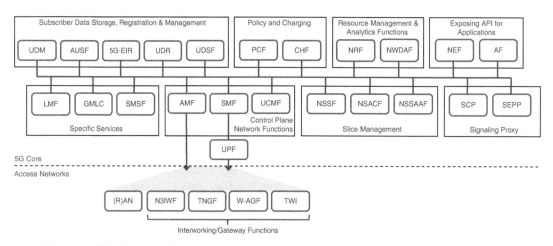

FIGURE 5-21 5GC Network Functions

This section will describe each of these groups, with more emphasis on the groups with higher significance, while only briefly describing the rest.

Primary Control Plane Network Functions

The NFs that form the backbone of the control plane are categorized in this group. As a recap, in an EPC core, the MME and PGW performed most of the control plane functions. The MME would communicate with the eNB and mobile device and would facilitate user registration, mobile device connection management, temporary identity allocation, roaming, SGW/PGW selection, and bearer management. The most important of PGW's control-plane roles included IP address allocation and policy implementation.

Access and Mobility Management Function (AMF) inherits some of these roles and is meant to terminate all the signaling from the mobile device. The AMF communicates directly with the mobile device, or *user equipment (UE)* as 3GPP prefers to call it, using an interface called *N1*, and is responsible for control-plane roles related to the user device (that is, managing the registration process, connectivity, mobility, authentication, authorization, and so on). AMF also has a point-to-point connectivity, referred to as the *N2 interface*, with the gNB—more specifically with the CU component of the gNB. The N2 interface is used for control plane communications such as PDU session establishment.

Session Management Function (SMF) implements the portion of the control plane that relates to the user's session. Hence, the bearer management role of the MME is delegated to the SMF. This includes selecting the appropriate User Plane Functions (UPF) for the mobile traffic and then establishing, maintaining, and updating the bearer path between the mobile device and those UPFs. The SMF uses a parameter called *Data Network Name (DNN)* to select the UPF. The DNN is the 5G equivalent of APN used in previous generation packet cores. Additionally, the PGW's session management functions also get implemented by the SMF—namely, DHCP and IP address allocation, authorizing a user to access a specific PDN, and providing charging information to the relevant function for billing purposes.

UE radio Capability Management Function (UCMF) is another NF that could be part of this group. The UCMF is meant to store the capability information of the mobile devices, such as vendor information and configuration.

Network Functions for Subscriber Information, Registration, and Management

The registration of a user in EPC relied heavily on Home Subscriber Server (HSS), which consolidated the Home Local Register (HLR) and Authentication Center (AuC) roles. The SBA for 5GC defines two network functions called *Authentication Server Function (AUSF)* and *Unified Data Management (UDM)*, which implement similar functions.

The AUSF acts as an authentication server, relying on the UDM for subscribers' identity information (analogous to IMSI). As AMF terminates the mobile device registration request, it uses an interface called *N12* to communicate with AUSF for authentication, which in turn uses an *N13* interface to communicate with the UDM. SMF also references the UDM for retrieving subscribers' profiles for the purpose of data session management. The two database network functions, called *Unified Data Repository (UDR)* and *Unstructured Data Storage Function (UDSF)*, are used by other network functions to store structured data (that is, defined in 3GPP specifications such as subscriber information, policies, and other application data) and unstructured data (that is, not defined in 3GPP specifications), respectively. The UDR and UDSF databases are used by other 5GC network functions, such as the UDM, to access subscriber and policy information as appropriate. Similar to the previous generations, a *5G Equipment Identity Register (5G-EIR)* database is optionally maintained to store the device IMEI information to detect devices that are fraudulent, illegal, or not allowed to register for other reasons.

Network Functions for Policy and Charging

EPC's Policy and Charging Rule Function (PCRF) responsibilities are now delegated to a newly defined Network Function, called the *Policy Control Function (PCF)*. The PCF works with UDM to learn the services a user is allowed to use and then facilitates control-plane functions (such as SMF) to enforce the appropriate policies. Among other things, the policy includes quality of service (QoS) parameters for the user's traffic streams. Another related function, called the *Charging Function (CHF)*, can be included in this group. The CHF provides an interface to the charging and billing systems.

Network Functions for Exposing 5GC APIs

Two NFs—namely, the *Network Exposure Function (NEF)* and *Application Function (AF)*—can be grouped in this category. AF is a generic name for any system inside or outside of the operator network that securely interacts with the PCF or NEF. The NEF provides the actual mechanism and APIs that allow these applications to interact with the other NFs in 5GC.

Resource Management and Analytics Functions

The *Network Data Analytics Function (NWDAF)* is defined to collect data from various NFs for the purpose of analytics and applying machine learning for optimized resource management. The *Network Repository Function (NRF)*, as the name implies, acts as the service registry and hence a central block of the SBA. Other NFs register with the NRF and advertise the services they provide. When a Network Function requires any of these services (hence acting as a service client), it seeks information about its availability by reaching out to the NRF.

Network Functions for Slicing Management

Three NFs are defined in the 5GC SBA that relate to management, provisioning, and maintaining of network slices—namely, *Network Slice Admission Control Function (NSACF)*, *Network Slice Specific Authentication and Authorization Function (NSSAAF)*, and *Network Slice Selection Function (NSSF)*. NSSF helps select the appropriate slice and resources based on the parameters provided by the mobile user, while NSSAAF helps with authentication and authorization specific to network slicing. NSACF provides slice management, such as limiting the maximum number of devices that may be allowed for a particular network slice.

Network Functions for Signaling

The *Service Communication Proxy (SCP)* and *Secure Edge Protection Proxy (SEPP)* are NFs that act as signaling proxies and are defined to help make the SBA implementation distributed and secure. SCP can act as a proxy to other NFs that are registered with NRF and deployed as a single group. SEPP's proxy role is primarily to make intra-PLMN signaling secure. By using their respective SEPPs to communicate, the mobile providers can ensure authentication, integrity, and security for their signaling message exchanges.

Specific Functions

3GPP defines a category of Specific Functions, which includes functions such as SMS, Location Services, and others. The Network Function responsible for SMS is called *Short Message Service Function (SMSF)*. Two functions are defined to deal with the location and position of the mobile user. The *Location Management Function (LMF)* gathers this information about the mobile device as well as additional parameters to predict location change, and it exposes this information for the AMF. The *Gateway Mobile Location Center (GLMC)* provides an interface for external applications and clients to request this information from the 5GC. One example of such applications is law enforcement and emergency services, which may want to know the precise location of a mobile user.

5GC Network Functions' Interaction with Access Networks

5G doesn't restrict access to just the RAN. It allows a variety of other access methods, both from trusted and untrusted networks, including Wi-Fi and broadband access. The access network abstraction, referred to as *(R)AN* by 3GPP, represents the 5G RAN as a single functional piece of the SBA. The use of parentheses in (R)AN indicates that the access network can be a radio network or another type of network, such as a wireline access network. 3GPP also defines interworking and gateway functions, which are meant to adapt the access technology protocols to the 5G control plane. A few mentionable NFs in this category are *Non-3GPP InterWorking Function (N3IWF)*, which offers a user's mobile device to register with the 5GC using an untrusted Wi-Fi network, and *Trusted Non-3GPP Gateway Function (TNGF)*, which offers gateway functionality when a mobile device connects using a trusted Wi-Fi network. The *Wireline Access Gateway Function (W-AGF)* is similar in concept to TNGF but defined for wireline access such as broadband cable networks. For mobile devices that don't support 5GC control-plane signaling protocols and connect using a trusted Wi-Fi network, an interworking function called *Trusted WLAN Interworking Function (TWI)* has been defined.

Communication Interfaces Between 5GC Network Functions

3GPP defines two different nomenclatures to represent the interfaces between the Network Functions. The first nomenclature, called *service-based representation*, is defined only for the Control Plane NF. The service-based representation calls out an exposed interface for every NF (for example, *Namf* for AMF and *Nsmf* for SMF). These are general-purpose exposed interfaces open for any Control Plane NF to communicate with any other Control Plane NF using the common SBA connectivity bus. The other nomenclature is defined for point-to-point communication between two NFs, similar to the concept of interfaces in previous generations. The point-to-point interfaces were previously called "S" interfaces in the case of EPS, "G" interfaces for GPRS, "I" interfaces for UMTS, and now in 5GC they are defined as "N" interfaces to signify the next generation nature of 5G. For example, the interface between AMF and SMF is called N11; however, it uses the common Namf and Nsmf interfaces of AMF and SMF, respectively, and is often not shown explicitly. Figure 5-22 shows a graphical representation of common 5GC interfaces using both nomenclatures.[72]

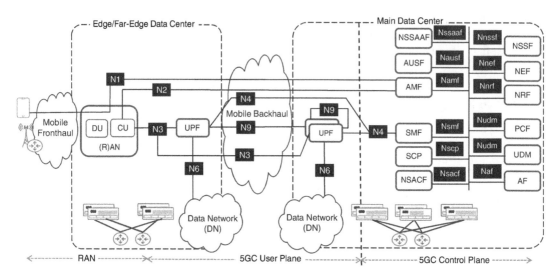

FIGURE 5-22   5GC Communication Interfaces

For the control functions, SBA chose Representational State Transfer API (REST-API)–based messaging for communication between these function, with JavaScript Object Notion (JSON) as the encoding format.[73] The reference interfaces related to user plane functions, RAN, and the mobile device use other IP-based protocols such as GTP-U.

User Authentication and Registration

Compared to its predecessors, 5G's user registration and authentication process is much more secure. The procedure for the initial registration and authentication of the mobile user is similar to that of predecessors, but some well-known vulnerabilities are now addressed. Recall that in 4G, or even before 4G, the mobile device would send the IMSI, which was safely stored in the USIM, to the packet core. Subsequently, the MME would allocate a locally significant temporary identifier, TMSI. However, the initial IMSI value is susceptible to interception by a malicious entity—a vulnerability called *IMSI catching*.

Instead of IMSI, 5G uses a newly defined identifier called *Subscriber Permanent Identifier (SUPI)*. SUPI is the same as IMSI for the 3GPP-based radio access technologies. For non-3GPP access technologies, where USIM is not being used, the SUPI uses Network Access Identifier (NAI), which is a standards-based method to identify an Internet user.[74]

Instead of sending the SUPI as cleartext in the initial registration message, the 5G mobile device encrypts a part of the SUPI (the MSIN, to be specific) using the public key of the mobile provider, which is stored on the USIM. The MCC and MNC portions of the SUPI, as well as information about the SUPI type and the encryption method used, are still sent as cleartext since this is already publicly known information. The encrypted identifier, called the *Subscriber Concealed Identifier (SUCI)*, is received by the AMF and decrypted using the mobile service provider's private key. The AMF works with the AUSF and UDM to authenticate using the decrypted MSIN and set up the relevant services.

Establishing a PDU Session

Once a mobile device is authenticated with the 5GC, it initiates the request (either on its own or triggered by the AMF) to initiate a PDU session. This request, sent to the AMF, includes information such as the location parameters and desired DNN by the mobile device. AMF selects the appropriate SMF, which is then asked to set up the user's data session. After consulting with the PCF and authorizing the user's request, the SMF selects an appropriate UPF and, using the *N4 interface*, programs it with packet-handling information using a protocol called *Packet Forwarding Control Protocol (PFCP)*. In parallel, to establish the end-to-end PDU session, the SMF sends instructions to the CU and mobile device (via the AMF, which then uses its N4 interface to the CU and its N1 interface toward the mobile device). This process also establishes a *data radio bearer (DRB)* as part of the PDU session.[75]

Packet Forwarding Control Protocol (PFCP)

Packet Forwarding Control Protocol (PFCP) is a specially designed protocol used between the control and data planes in 5GC. Its function is to control communication between the SMF and UPF.

PFCP is used to program the UPF with rules for packet handling. These rules include the Packet Detection Rule (PDR) for the match criteria, the Forwarding Action Rule (FAR) to program the forwarding behavior for the matched flow, the QoS Enforcement Rule (QER) for QoS enforcement, the Buffering Action Rules (BAR) for determining the processing and buffering behavior, and the Usage Reporting Rule (URR) for measuring and reporting traffic statistics.[76]

QoS in 5G

5G allows QoS parameters to be separately defined for each data flow between the mobile user's device and the UPF. The QoS parameters are defined as a *5G QoS Identifier (5QI)*, which is analogous in concept to the QCI used in 4G. The 5QI uses *QoS Flow Identifier (QFI)* to identify the desired QoS behavior of individual traffic flow and to apply the QoS profile. To draw an analogy with the data networking concepts, this is similar to using DSCP to classify a traffic flow and then using QoS policies to implement the desired traffic treatment. In this example, the QFI is akin to the DSCP marking, whereas 5QI is equivalent to holistic QoS profile that defines the desired behavior of packet delay, error rate, priority, and congestion management.

The initially established PDU session has a default QoS treatment associated with it. Because there can be multiple flows within a single PDU session, these flows, referred to as *Service Data Flow (SDF)*, might not necessarily require separate QoS treatments, and hence the same QFI could be used for all of them—a process called *SDF binding*. However, if a different QoS behavior is needed for any of the traffic flows, or SDF, then the requirements are requested from the SMF. The SMF authorizes this request by consulting the PCF and allocates a new QFI for the flow, instructs the mobile device to use this QFI for the respective flow, and programs the UPF and RAN to implement the appropriate QoS treatment for this new QFI.

3GPP has defined QoS profiles for the standardized 5QI values, mapping them to specific services. On the transport network, the IP packets are marked with the appropriate value of QoS parameters such as Differentiated Services Code Point (DSCP), experimental bits of MPLS (MPLS-EXP), and so on, based on the 5QI profile for those flows. The transport network QoS policy will then provide the QoS treatment to these packets in accordance with the 5QI profiles defined by 3GPP. Chapter 10 covers this mapping between 5QI and transport network QoS in further detail.

Transition to 5G Core Network

Figure 5-23 summarizes the journey from 3G Mobile Core to 4G Evolved Packet Core and finally the transition to the 5G Core network. The figure shows the correlation between various components of the mobile core across generations, and how these roles have evolved, regrouped, or split into the functions that build the 5GC.

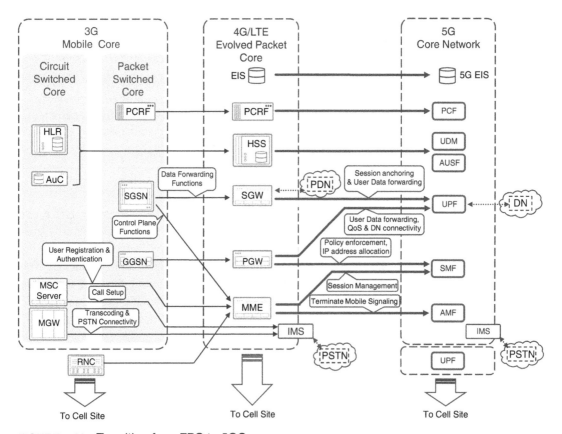

FIGURE 5-23 Transition from EPC to 5GC

5G Transport Network

Irrespective of the mobile generations, transport networks have historically been planned, designed, and deployed with a single purpose—to provide Layer 2 or Layer 3 connectivity from cell sites to the mobile core. However, with the introduction of Centralized RAN and vRAN, previously siloed and distinctly separate RAN and mobile transport domains have become so closely intertwined that it's unrealistic to draw a clear boundary between the two. The mobile transport has to adapt to provide transport of radio traffic across the fronthaul network as well as support connectivity between RAN nodes and 5GC NFs sprinkled all across the service coverage area in far-edge, edge, and regional DCs. It also has to ensure adequate Internet peering throughout the xHaul to realize the benefits promised by CUPS.

Keeping in mind the overlap between the RAN and transport domains, I implicitly covered many of the aspects of the transport evolution earlier when we discussed topics such as the placement of RAN nodes across the fronthaul, midhaul, and backhaul as well as various DC categories. This section will dig deeper into the evolving role of the underlying packetized xHaul transport network supporting 5G services.

Transporting Radio Traffic over Packet-Based Fronthaul

In a traditional D-RAN architecture, radio traffic is confined to the cell site by virtue of RU and BBU co-location. In this case, the BBU receives radio traffic over the CPRI interface from the RU, performs baseband processing, packetizes the radio traffic, and hands it over to the cell site router (CSR) to be transported over mobile backhaul. The evolution to Centralized-RAN, as well as to RAN decomposition, presented a challenge in terms of transporting CPRI traffic over the fronthaul network. The RAN discussion from earlier in this chapter touched on the introduction of vendor-specific eCPRI and O-RAN-compliant 7-2x-based eCPRI, both of which use Ethernet framing, thus making it possible for a CSR to transport them over a packet-based fronthaul. As eCPRI is a relatively new development, some early 5G RUs and virtually all existing 4G LTE deployments still employ RUs that use CPRI. Radio traffic from these RUs needs to be *adapted* for transport over the packetized fronthaul using techniques such as *Radio over Ethernet* or *Fronthaul Gateway*.

Radio over Ethernet (RoE)

As the name implies, the *Radio over Ethernet (RoE)* standard, defined by the IEEE 1914.3 specification, describes CPRI transport over a packetized fronthaul using Ethernet. To encapsulate CPRI within Ethernet frames, IEEE RoE standard defines a new Ethertype (0xFC3D), frame format, and introduces the concept of an *RoE Mapper* and *deMapper*. Network equipment vendors can implement this RoE Mapper and deMapper functionality on their fronthaul CSR (FH CSR) and the far-edge DC routers to create a bookended solution across a packet-based fronthaul. In this case, the FH-CSR mapper function receives the constant bitrate CPRI traffic, converts it into a packet stream using RoE, and transports over the fronthaul network to the far-edge DC, where the router connected to the DU or BBU re-creates the CPRI stream using the RoE deMapper function, thus enabling RU-to-DU/BBU communication. Traffic from the DU/BBU to the RU follows a similar process.

The IEEE 1914.3 RoE standard defines multiple mapper types for implementation flexibility. Different modes of RoE operations with commonly used mapper types in a packet-based fronthaul are as follows:

- **RoE Mapper Type 0:** This is the *structure-agnostic tunneling mode*, where CPRI traffic is simply encapsulated within Ethernet frames without any further processing. In this mode of operation, Ethernet traffic rates in the fronthaul mimic those of CPRI rate options. For instance, CPRI Rate Option 7 (9.83 Gbps) would require slightly more than 9.83 Gbps Ethernet bandwidth to accommodate additional bits added by the Ethernet header. Similarly, transportation of CPRI Rate Option 10 over a packet-based fronthaul would require more than 24.4 Gbps of Ethernet bandwidth. Various CPRI rate options are covered earlier in this chapter.

- **RoE Mapper Type 1:** This is the *structure-agnostic line-code-aware mode*. In this mode of operation, the RoE mapper function removes the line-coding from CPRI traffic. CPRI Rate Options 1 through 7 use *8b/10b line-coding*, which puts 10 bits on the wire for every 8 bits of data for redundancy. Stripping 8b/10b line-coding ensures the transport of 8 bits of CPRI over Ethernet instead of encoded 10 bits, saving up to 20% fronthaul bandwidth. CPRI Rate Options 8 through 10, however, use 64b/66b line-coding and hence save only 3% of the bandwidth in the fronthaul (2 bits of Ethernet savings for every 64 bits of CPRI traffic).

  RoE Mapper Type 1 is often preferred over Type 0 by network operators due to substantial fronthaul bandwidth savings, especially with CPRI Rate Options 7 and below, but it requires some level of interoperability between network equipment and RRU vendors as the fronthaul transport network element would need to remove and then add back the 8b/10b line-coding on either side of the CPRI connection. This often represents a challenge because RAN equipment vendors may use special characters and messaging between the RU and DU/BBU in their CPRI implementation, thus making RoE Type 1 harder to implement. Both RoE Types 0 and 1 are still CBR in nature.

- **RoE Mapper Type 2:** This is the *structure-aware mode* where the router implementing this function deconstructs and reconstructs the CPRI stream. Structure-aware mode requires the network equipment vendor to acquire significant knowledge of radio implementation by the RAN equipment vendor, including any proprietary information.

  When implemented, however, RoE Type 2 could take advantage of statistical multiplexing of CPRI traffic, allowing the network element (that is, a fronthaul CSR) to receive a constant bitrate CPRI stream, identify useful data (that is, the actual data being sent by the radio or DU/BBU), and convert only this data into Ethernet frames. In essence, this process converts the constant bitrate CPRI stream into variable bitrate Ethernet traffic. This data is converted back into a CBR CPRI stream using a deMapper on the remote end. While highly desired by mobile network operators due to massive amounts of bandwidth savings, the real-life implementation of structure-aware RoE mappers remains scarce because it requires the RAN equipment vendors to open their CPRI stack for the networking equipment vendors to be able to deconstruct and reconstruct the CPRI stream.

RoE represents a significant step toward the adoption of a packet-based fronthaul. However, its usefulness is limited to scenarios where both the RU and DU/BBU use legacy CPRI interfaces. As mentioned earlier, newer radios have started using eCPRI, where the RU and DU both transmit/receive CPRI traffic using Ethernet framing. It must be mentioned that in both these cases—that is, CPRI over RoE and vendor-specific eCPRI—the RU and BBU/DU have to be provided by the same RAN vendor. Interoperability between RAN nodes from different vendors is only possible if O-RU and O-DU are used that adhere to the O-RAN Alliance's defined Split 7-2x-based eCPRI.

Fronthaul Gateway (FHGW)

With virtualization taking root in mobile network deployments through vRAN, it's likely to have scenarios where the traditional BBU could be replaced by a CU+DU pairs, where the DU supports eCPRI only, while legacy RUs continue to be used. In those cases, a *Fronthaul Gateway (FHGW)* could be used to provide conversion between legacy CPRI and eCPRI. FHGW provides an inter-working function (IWF) between a traditional RU (which uses CPRI) and a newer DU or vDU that uses eCPRI. This is done through a RAN logic function embedded in the FHGW device, likely to be a cell site router. In essence, the CPRI traffic received from the RU is converted to eCPRI through this RAN processing function and sent to the DU through the uplink interfaces. Similarly, the eCPRI traffic received on the uplink Ethernet interfaces from the DU is converted into CPRI before being sent to the RU. Figure 5-24 shows the FHGW concept as define by the O-RAN Alliance.[77]

As one can infer, the radio signal processor is an indispensable component of an FHGW, without which the device concept shown in Figure 5-24 is effectively an Ethernet router. Any network equipment vendor looking to implement FHGW functionality on its CSRs must implement this radio signal processor to convert traditional CPRI into eCPRI. It has been previously mentioned that CPRI implementation is proprietary; as such, RAN equipment vendors with a networking equipment port-folio have an inherent advantage in embedding this functionality into their current CSR offerings. Examples of such vendors include Ericsson and Nokia, both of which have an extensive RAN and networking equipment portfolio and have FHGW functionality available on their networking products geared toward 5G xHaul.[78, 79] It must be noted that many of these FHGW products provide conversion between traditional CPRI and vendor-specific eCPRI and thus require both the RU and DU from the very same vendor.

This poses a challenge for networking equipment manufacturers such as Juniper and Cisco that have a limited RAN portfolio and are thus dependent on the RAN equipment manufacturers to implement the radio signal processing functions needed to create an FHGW product offering. As one can expect, incumbent RAN equipment manufacturers, which in many cases are direct or indirect competitors of networking equipment manufacturers, might be reluctant to share their intellectual property (that is, their proprietary CPRI/eCPRI structure) to protect and expand their market share. Networking equipment manufacturers realize this challenge and are working on a two-pronged strategy to carve out a place for their products (such as CSR or aggregation nodes) and protect their market share in this transforming landscape. First, they are working with the O-RAN Alliance to define not only the Open Fronthaul Interfaces (that is, Option 7-2x eCPRI) but also the hardware specifications for an

Open Fronthaul Gateway.[80] Additionally, the network equipment manufacturers are forging partnerships with new entrants in the RAN market, such as Altiostar (now acquired by Rakuten), to create joint go-to-market strategies and products for 5G networking.[81]

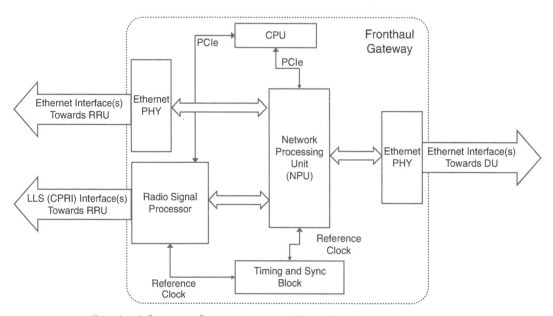

FIGURE 5-24   Fronthaul Gateway Components and Block Diagram

All of these CPRI adaptation mechanisms are expected to be deployed in mobile networks for CPRI transport over a packetized fronthaul. Figure 5-25 summarizes various scenarios for transporting radio traffic across a packet-based fronthaul network.

At the time of this writing, virtually all packet-based fronthaul products use either CPRI over RoE or vendor-specific eCPRI, both of which requires all RAN nodes (RU, DU, CU) to be provided by the same RAN vendor. A handful of new entrants also have O-RU and O-DU available but with limited real-life deployments so far. This is expected to change as mobile network operators demand more openness from RAN vendors and new entrants trying to capture RAN market share from incumbents. FHGW is also a relatively new concept, with the first O-RAN specification defining FHGW being made available in 2021 as part of Working Group 7's "Hardware Reference Design Specification for Fronthaul Gateway."[82] FHGWs, however, is likely be an interim solution, geared toward the reuse of legacy RUs with newer DUs. Over time, as traditional RUs gradually get upgraded and replaced, the FHGWs will be phased out.

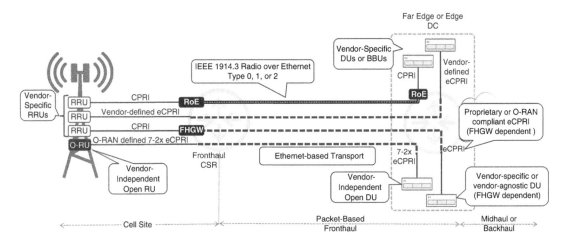

FIGURE 5-25   Transporting Radio Traffic over Packet-based Fronthaul

5G xHaul Transport Choices

Chapter 2 previously discussed various transport mechanisms and connectivity models for mobile transport networks such as fiber, cable, DSL, microwave, and satellite. While all of these options can be used in 5G xHaul, additional considerations apply to ensure their feasibility. With midhaul's bandwidth requirements being substantially lower than fronthaul and somewhat closer to that of a traditional backhaul, all the transport mechanisms discussed earlier could easily be used for both midhaul and backhaul domains. The real challenge lies in the fronthaul, where bandwidth requirements are typically multifold higher than midhaul or backhaul due to the CBR nature of the CPRI transport. Therefore, the bandwidth-restrictive transport mechanisms such as cable, DSL, and satellite, while still viable for midhaul and backhaul, are unfit for a fronthaul environment.[83] Fiber optic and microwave are two of the transport mechanisms that can be used for the entire xHaul.

Optical Fiber-Based xHaul Transport

Fiber-based transport networks have long been considered the gold standard of network connectivity due to their flexibility regarding bandwidth capacity, speed, and distances they could cover. While the cost of deployment continues to be a concern, fiber-based transport technologies like WDM, passive optical network (PON), and Ethernet continue to be the leading choices for all xHaul domains, including fronthaul networks.

As mentioned earlier, WDM has already been in use for fronthaul in 4G Centralized RAN deployments and provides ample capacity to meet bandwidth-intensive FH deployment scenarios. Although it's expected that it will continue to be useful in 5G xHaul, WDM lacks the flexibility offered by packet switched transport networks.

PON is another fiber-based transport technology that has and will continue to provide xHaul connectivity. Lower-bandwidth PON solutions like GPON, NG-PON, and XGPON may be suitable for midhaul and backhaul but may not satisfy the bandwidth requirements for fronthaul. Innovations like NG-PON2 using WDM technology to provide speeds as high as 40 Gbps are needed to fulfill the high-bandwidth requirements of transporting radio traffic over fronthaul. In fact, some network operators already have 5G transport deployed using PON-based technologies.[84] The PON ONTs and OLTs are typically equipped with Ethernet Interfaces, which can be used to connect to RU and DU/BBU, respectively, provided the RU and DU/BBU use eCPRI. If the RU and DU/BBU use CPRI, then additional processing will be required to adapt the CPRI traffic to Ethernet for transport over PON based Fronthaul.

Ethernet-based packetized fronthaul, however, is where most of the innovation has been taking place with respect to the 5G transport. The introduction of RoE and eCPRI has made it possible to transport radio traffic using Ethernet, allowing the fronthaul network to benefit from the same features and functionalities as midhaul and backhaul (for example, MPLS VPN, traffic engineering, and rapid restoration). The packet-based xHaul concept, while new and thus limited in adoption at the time of this writing, is expected to grow in the coming years.

The O-RAN "*xHaul Packet Switched Architectures and Solutions*" specification focuses on the use of packet-based fronthaul, midhaul, and backhaul and documents the use of innovations such as *Segment Routing (SR)* and *Segment Routing v6 (SRv6)*, both of which are discussed in the next chapter.

Wireless xHaul

As mentioned in Chapter 2, the microwave-based backhaul constitutes a majority of all backhaul links, courtesy of large-scale deployments in developing countries. The unlocking of new and higher frequency bands has opened new possibilities for wireless xHaul. For instance, in addition to microwave allocations in the traditional 6–42 GHz range, more spectrum, particularly in E-Bands (71–86 GHz), W-Bands (75–110 GHz), and D-Bands (110–170 GHz), has been allocated for use for wireless xHaul. Higher frequency band translates into higher capacity, which can provide needed bandwidth for the fronthaul. However, as mentioned in Chapter 2, higher frequencies are best suited for shorter distances.

3GPP has also standardized the use of wireless technology for xHaul transport through the use of the *Integrated Access Backhaul (IAB)* architecture. In short, IAB allows a RAN node (such as gNB) to act as a donor cell that provides services to mobile users in its coverage area, simultaneously connecting other cell sites to the rest of the network. These IAB-connected cell sites can, in turn, provide services to mobile subscribers in their own coverage zone or act as a donor site for other sites, thus creating a cascading mesh of wirelessly connected cell sites.[85] The combination of microwave and IAB technologies allows a mobile operator to mix wired and wireless technologies to create an xHaul deployment suited to its requirements. Figure 5-26 illustrates a sample xHaul deployment using MW, IAB, and wired connectivity.

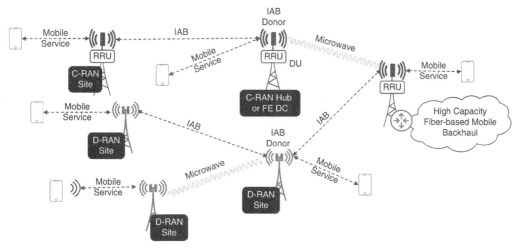

FIGURE 5-26   Wireless xHaul Connectivity Example with Microwave and IAB

Incorporating Data Centers into xHaul

The introduction of new, highly distributed data centers to accommodate the decomposed virtualized RAN and 5GC nodes, and their placement all across the xHaul domain, represent a fundamental paradigm shift in the design and composition of mobile transport networks. Where previously the mobile transport was merely a bridge between the RAN and mobile core domains, now it needs to incorporate DC connectivity in its baseline design—a task that is easier said than done.

Historically, data center and mobile transport networks in large service providers have been designed and maintained by entirely different engineering teams. The technologies used in the both domains are also different, with transport networks using IP and MPLS due to their feature-rich capabilities, whereas a lot of DCs use L2 for fast switching using low-cost hardware. Nonetheless, hundreds of new far-edge DCs as well as dozens of edge DCs need to be incorporated into the xHaul transport, as shown in Figure 5-27.

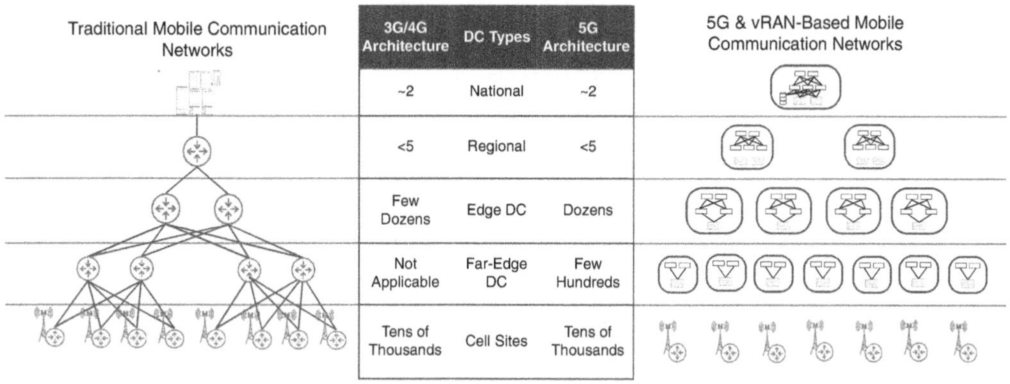

Traditional Mobile Communication Networks	3G/4G Architecture	DC Types	5G Architecture	5G & vRAN-Based Mobile Communication Networks
	~2	National	~2	
	<5	Regional	<5	
	Few Dozens	Edge DC	Dozens	
	Not Applicable	Far-Edge DC	Few Hundreds	
	Tens of Thousands	Cell Sites	Tens of Thousands	

FIGURE 5-27   Data Centers Across the xHaul Transport

Chapter 10 provides details on designing xHaul networks with services spanning multiple layers of DC as well as for RAN nodes and 5GC scattered across multiple DCs.

Distributed Peering Across xHaul

Separation of the control and user planes is one of the defining aspects of the 5G Core, where CUPS allows the placement of additional UPFs closer to the mobile user, typically co-located with the CU in the edge DC. As previously discussed, this reduces bandwidth consumption in the xHaul network and enables low-latency applications.

However, CUPS benefits can only be fully realized if user traffic is also offloaded to the DN as close to the edge as possible. The decomposition of RAN and the placement of RAN nodes, specifically the CU, in edge data centers, where UPF could also be deployed, presents an opportunity to offload user traffic. But in order to do so, Internet peering points that were once limited to a few locations in regional or centralized DCs now need to be made available at many edge DCs, and possibly at far-edge DCs if the CU and UPF are placed there as well. This distributed peering architecture helps xHaul save bandwidth by not having to *backhaul* user data all the way to the central DC. Figure 5-28 shows a sample deployment of an xHaul network where the mobile network operator offloads its Internet traffic at edge DCs in addition to the central or regional DC.

Distributed peering is another aspect of new 5G transport networks that has an impact on the xHaul design. The underlying technologies must be able to seamlessly integrate packet transport, data center integration, and data handoff to external peers.

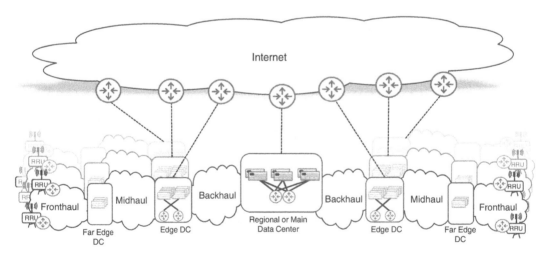

FIGURE 5-28   Distributed Peering for CUPS

Summary

This chapter covered the technical fundamentals of the three domains of the 5G network: 5G RAN, 5G Core network, and 5G transport. The chapter also shows how the 5G transformations shaping these three domains are going to help the promises of 5G be realized.

For 5G RAN, this chapter discussed the following topics:

- Air interface enhancements leading to improved spectrum utilization, communication robustness, and higher speeds

- Advanced antenna function for 5G New Radio such as beamforming, massive MIMO, multi-radio connectivity, and dynamic spectrum sharing

- RAN decomposition and virtualization of RAN decomposition and virtualization of it components

- BBU functional splits, how each split option maps to the 5G protocol stack, and its impact on the transport network

- The Open-RAN Alliance and the O-RAN reference architecture

For 5G Core network, the following concepts were covered:

- Control Plane and User Plane Separation (CUPS) and its benefits

- Placement of the 5G Core user plane

- Cloud-native and microservices architectures

- Service-Based Architecture and the Network Functions that build the 5G Core

- User authentication, session establishment, and QoS

For 5G transport, this chapter went over the following topics:

- Overview of Radio over Ethernet (RoE) and Fronthaul Gateway (FHGW) to transport CPRI over packet-based xHaul networks

- Transport technology choices for xHaul networks

- Integration of the growing number of data centers in the xHaul network

Figure 5-29 captures the full essence of the 5G mobile communication network as explained in this chapter. This figure presents a bird's-eye view of what the 5G network looks like with CUPS, decomposed RAN, distributed peering, and xHaul transport integrated with data centers.

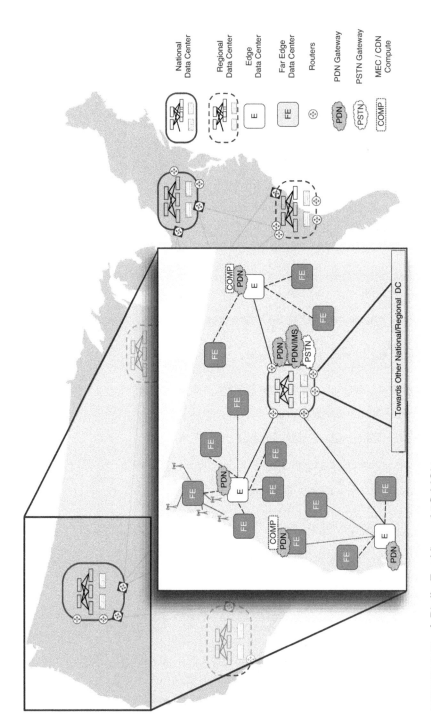

FIGURE 5-29   A Bird's-Eye View of 5G MCN

The upcoming chapters will exclusively focus on the new capabilities and enhancements for the transport network to enable end-to-end 5G services. These chapters will cover topics such as Segment Routing to build a resilient, programmable transport infrastructure, data center architecture for integration with the transport network, VPN technologies to provide connectivity and services between RAN and 5GCore, the critical concepts of timing and synchronization, and finally a detailed discussion of the considerations and the methodologies to architect transport for 5G MCN.

References

1. 3GPP TS 38.211, "5G; NR; Physical channels and modulation," Table 4.2-1

2. Op. cit., Table 4.3-1

3. 3GPP TS 38.213, "5G; NR; Physical layer procedures for control"

4. 3GPP TR 38.912-8.1, "5G; Study on New Radio (NR) access technology"

5. 3GPP TS 38.101-1, "5G; NR; User Equipment (UE) radio transmission and reception; Part 1: Range 1 Standalone"

6. 3GPP TS 38.101-2, "5G; NR; User Equipment (UE) radio transmission and reception; Part 2: Range 2 Standalone"

7. 3GPP TS 38.101-1, Loc. cit.

8. 3GPP TS 38.101-2. Loc. cit.

9. 3GPP TS 38.101-1, Loc. cit.

10. Ibid.

11. Ibid.

12. 3GPP TS 38.101-2. Loc. cit.

13. 3GPP TS 36.306, "LTE; Evolved Universal Terrestrial Radio Access (E-UTRA); User Equipment (UE) radio access capabilities, Release 12," Table 4.1-1

14. Calculated using equation in Section 4.1.2 of 3GPP TS 38.306, "5G; NR; User Equipment (UE) radio access capabilities"

15. 3GPP TR 36.866, "Study on Network-Assisted Interference Cancellation and Suppression (NAIC) for LTE, Release 12"

16. Yuya Saito et al., "Non-Orthogonal Multiple Access (NOMA) for Cellular Future Radio Access," https://doi.org/10.1109/VTCSpring.2013.6692652

17. Dr. Mohamed Nadder Hamdy, "Beamformers Explained," https://www.commscope.com/globalassets/digizuite/542044-Beamformer-Explained-WP-114491-EN.pdf (last visited: April 2022)

18. Emil Bjornson, Jakob Hoydis, and Luca Sanguinetti, *Massive MIMO Networks: Spectral, Energy, and Hardware Efficiency* (New Foundations and Trends, 2017)

19. 3GPP TR 36.819, "Coordinated multi-point operation for LTE physical layer aspects"

20. Siva Muruganathan et al., "On the System-level Performance of Coordinated Multi-point Transmission Schemes in 5G NR Deployment Scenarios," https://arxiv.org/ftp/arxiv/papers/1906/1906.07252.pdf (last visited: April 2022)

21. 3GPP TS 37.340, "LTE; 5G; NR Multi-connectivity; Overall description; Stage-2"

22. Ibid.

23. 3GPP, "DSS – Dynamic spectrum sharing," https://www.3gpp.org/dss (last visited: April 2022)

24. "Nokia dynamic spectrum sharing for rapid 5G coverage rollout" (whitepaper), https://onestore.nokia.com/asset/207265 (last visited: March 2022)

25. 3GPP TR 36.786, "Vehicle-to-Everything (V2X) services based on LTE; User Equipment (UE) radio transmission and reception"

26. 3GPP TS 24.587, "5G; Vehicle-to-Everything (V2X) services in 5G System (5GS); Stage 3"

27. "Cellular-V2X Technology Overview," https://www.qualcomm.com/media/documents/files/c-v2x-technology-overview.pdf (last visited: April 2022)

28. J. Wu, S. Rangan, and H. Zhang Green, *Green Communications: Theoretical Fundamentals, Algorithms, and Applications* (Boca Raton, FL: CRC Press, 2013), Chapter 11

29. Ibid.

30. R. Chayapathi, S. Hassan, and P. Shah, *Network Functions Virtualization (NFV) with a Touch of SDN* (Boston: Addison-Wesley, 2017)

31. Gabriel Brown, "New Transport Network Architectures for 5G RAN: A Heavy Reading White Paper for Fujitsu," https://www.fujitsu.com/us/Images/New-Transport-Network-Architectures-for-5G-RAN.pdf (last visited: March 2022)

32. IEEE 1914.1, "Standard for Packet-based Fronthaul Transport Networks," https://sagroups.ieee.org/1914/p1914-1/ (last visited: March 2022)

33. Ibid.

34. 3GPP TS 38.401, "NG-RAN (Next Generation RAN) Architecture description, Release 16"

35. Jyrki T. J. Penttinen, *5G Explained*. (Hoboken, NJ: Wiley, 2019), Section 6.6.2

36. Sassan Ahmadi, *LTE-Advanced: A Practical Systems Approach to Understanding 3GPP LTE Releases 10 and 11 Radio Access Technologies*. (Amsterdam: Elsevier, 2014), Chapter 3

37. 3GPP TS 38.300, "5G; NR; Overall description; Stage-2"

38. Ibid.

39. Ibid.

40. 3GPP TR 38.801, "Study on new radio access technology: Radio access architecture and interfaces"

41. Ibid.

42. Ibid.

43. CPRI v 7.0 specification, http://www.cpri.info/downloads/CPRI_v_7_0_2015-10-09.pdf (last visited: March 2022)

44. eCPRI v1.0 specification, http://www.cpri.info/downloads/eCPRI_v_1_0_2017_08_22.pdf (Last visited: March 2022)

45. Ibid.

46. Patrick Marsch et al., *5G System Design: Architectural and functional considerations and long term research* (Hoboken, NJ: John Wiley & Sons, 2018)

47. "The RAN market will continue to be controlled by the current three companies, including with OpenRAN," https://on5g.es/en/the-ran-market-will-continue-to-be-controlled-by-the-current-three-companies-including-with-openran/ (last visited: March 2022)

48. O-RAN Use Cases and Deployment Scenarios, O-RAN Whitepaper, February 2020, https://www.o-ran.org/resources (last visited: March 2022)

49. About O-RAN, https://www.o-ran.org/about (last visited: March 2022)

50. O-RAN Use Cases and Deployment Scenarios, O-RAN Whitepaper, Loc. Cit.

51. O-RAN Fronthaul Control, User and Synchronization Plane Specification, O-RAN WG4, https://www.o-ran.org

52. Ibid.

53. Gabriel Brown, "The Role of the RAN Intelligent Controller in Open RAN Systems," https://www.stl.tech/white-papers/pdf/STL%20-%20Role%20of%20the%20RAN%20Intelligent%20Controller%20in%20Open%20RAN%20Systems_Final%20WP.pdf (last visited: March 2022)

54. "AT&T and Nokia Accelerate the Deployment of RAN Open Source," https://about.att.com/story/2019/open_source.html (last visited: April 2022)

55. O-RAN Cloud Architecture and Deployment Scenarios for O-RAN Virtualized RAN, O-RAN WG6, https://www.o-ran.org

56. O-RAN WDM-based Fronthaul Transport, O-RAN WG9, https://www.o-ran.org

57. O-RAN Xhaul Packet Switched Architectures and Solutions, O-RAN WG9, https://www.o-ran.org

58. Sterling Perrin, "Operator Strategies for 5G Transport: 2020 Heavy Reading Survey," https://www.infinera.com/wp-content/uploads/HR-Operator-Strategies-for-5G-Transport-July-2020_WP.pdf (last visited: March 2022)

59. Craig Matsumoto, "Packet Core Looks 'Ripe' for Virtualization," https://www.lightreading.com/mobile/packet-core/packet-core-looks-ripe-for-virtualization/d/d-id/701518 (last visited: March 2022)

60. The Standard, ETSI Newsletter, Issue 2, 2017, https://www.etsi.org/images/files/ETSInewsletter/etsinewsletter-issue2-2017.pdf (last visited: March 2022)

61. F. Giust et al., "MEC Deployments in 4G and Evolution Towards 5G," ETSI White Paper, No. 24, February 2018

62. R. Chayapathi, S. Hassan, and P. Shah, Loc. Cit.

63. Craig McLuckie, "From Google to the world: The Kubernetes origin story," https://cloud.google.com/blog/products/containers-kubernetes/from-google-to-the-world-the-kubernetes-origin-story (last visited: March 2022)

64. Stevan Vidich et al., "Azure Government security," https://docs.microsoft.com/en-us/azure/azure-government/documentation-government-plan-security (last visited: March 2022)

65. Mark Haranas, "Microsoft Azure Creates Top Secret Government Cloud as JEDI Battle Rages On," https://www.crn.com/news/cloud/microsoft-azure-creates-top-secret-government-cloud-as-jedi-battle-rages-on (last visited: March 2022)

66. 3GPP TR 23.799, "Study on Architecture for Next Generation System," Section 4.1

67. Op. cit., Annex B

68. Georg Mayer, "3GPP 5G Core Network Status," https://www.3gpp.org/ftp/information/presentations/Presentations_2017/webinar-ct-status-11-2017.pdf (last visited: March 2022)

69. Shunsuke Homma et al., "User Plane Protocol and Architectural Analysis on 3GPP 5G System," https://datatracker.ietf.org/meeting/105/materials/slides-105-dmm-user-plane-protocol-and-architectural-analysis-on-3gpp-5g-system-00 (last visited: March 2022)

70. Andrea Detti, " Functional Architecture," https://www.5gitaly.eu/2018/wp-content/uploads/2019/01/5G-Italy-White-eBook-Functional-architecture.pdf (last visited: March 2022)

71. Marvin Ivezic, "Introduction to 5G Core Service-Based Architecture (SBA) Components," https://5g.security/5g-technology/5g-core-sba-components-architecture/ (last visited: March 2022)

72. 3GPP TS 23.501, "5G; System architecture for the 5G, Release 17," Sections 4.2.1 and 4.2.3

73. Georg Mayer, Loc. cit. (last visited: March 2022)

74. https://datatracker.ietf.org/doc/html/rfc4282 (last visited: March 2022)

75. 3GPP TS 23.502, "5G; Procedures for the 5G System," Section 4.3.2

76. 3GPP TS 29.244, "LTE; Interface between the Control Plane and the User Plane nodes"

77. O-RAN Deployment Scenarios and Base Station Classes for White Box Hardware, O-RAN WG7, https://www.o-ran.org

78. https://www.ericsson.com/en/mobile-transport/fronthaul-gateway (last visited: March 2022)

79. https://www.nokia.com/networks/products/airframe-fronthaul-gateway/ (last visited: March 2022)

80. https://blogs.cisco.com/sp/cisco-strengthens-o-ran-market-position-with-open-fronthaul-gateway-public-demo (last visited: March 2022)

81. https://global.rakuten.com/corp/news/press/2021/1026_02.html (last visited: March 2022)

82. O-RAN Deployment Scenarios and Base Station Classes for White Box Hardware, O-RAN WG7, https://www.o-ran.org83. O-RAN Xhaul Packet Switched Architectures and Solutions, Op. cit., Section 10.2.3.2

84. GSMA Association, "Innovative Fronthaul Network Economics: SKT case study," November 2018, https://www.gsma.com/futurenetworks/wp-content/uploads/2018/11/SKT_GSMA_Case_Study-v2.1-FINAL-Website.pdf (Last visited: March 2022)

85. 3GPP TS 38.174, "5G; NR; Integrated Access and Backhaul (IAB) radio transmission and reception"

Chapter | 6

Emerging Technologies for 5G-Ready Networks: Segment Routing

As discussed thus far, mobile communication networks have evolved significantly since their introduction in the 1970s. In the same timeframe, transport networks have gone through technological advances of their own and have brought the latest transport technology into mobile communication networks (MCNs) to provide reliable and effective connectivity between cell sites and the mobile core. These mobile transport networks have evolved from T1/E1 in the early days of MCNs, to ATM and Frame Relay in the second generation, and finally to an all-IP transport in the third and fourth generations of mobile networks. With more recent enhancements in the radio access network (RAN) and mobile core, the traditional mobile backhaul (MBH) has also seen a move toward a more sophisticated xHaul network. In parallel to all these changes, and given the shift toward software-defined transport, there is also a desire to incorporate network programmability into mobile transport.

Today, IP- and MPLS-based transport networks make up the bulk of all MBH deployments. Being more than two decades old, Multiprotocol Label Switching (MPLS) has become a versatile protocol with a multitude of features and custom knobs. The enhanced functionality comes at the expense of added complexity, however, primarily through augmentation of multiple features and functions in existing network architectures.

Mobile network operators demand simplicity with a higher degree of programmability and control over traffic in the transport network. *Segment Routing* is one of the emerging transport technologies that promises to remove a lot of complexity, while at the same time offering network programmability and integration with higher-layer application, which have become critical in the next generation of transport networks.

Complexity in Today's Network

Since its inception in the late 1990s, MPLS has been widely adopted as the transport technology of choice, becoming the bedrock of virtually all large-scale networks, including transport for MCN. It borrows the old ATM and Frame Relay concepts of traffic switching, quality of service (QoS), and path-based traffic forwarding, while adapting them for IP transport. MPLS works by encapsulating IP data within a 4-byte label, which is pushed on the IP packet at the source router. This label is used to make forwarding decisions by routers along the *label switched path (LSP)*, where every transit router examines the label information, compares it with its own *forwarding information base (FIB)*, swaps the label with the new forwarding information (that is, the new label), and forwards it toward the destination. It can also impose (push) or remove (pop) labels according to the local FIB. An IP and routing table lookup is not performed during the forwarding process, making MPLS a Layer 2.5 technology according to the Open Systems Interconnect (OSI) model.

MPLS was originally designed for fast packet switching in core networks, and later offered additional value through traffic engineering, fast reroute, and virtual private network (MPLS-VPN) capabilities. MPLS technology makes use of purpose-built protocols to provide extensibility and flexibility, which has allowed it to keep up with the growing traffic patterns and network evolution for over two decades. For instance, in addition to the IGP for route and topology distribution, *Label Distribution Protocol (LDP)* is used to propagate label information through the network, and *Resource Reservation Protocol (RSVP)* is needed to provide traffic engineering capabilities. The trade-off, however, is that the use of each additional protocol adds a layer of complexity as well as contributes to scalability limitations on the routers running these protocols. In order to exchange labels, every router establishes and maintains an LDP adjacency with each one of its neighboring routers. This TCP-based adjacency is in addition to any Interior Gateway Protocol (IGP) and Border Gateway Protocol (BGP) adjacencies that the router might already have, using memory and CPU resources as well as contributing to network traffic in the form of periodic hellos. RSVP, used to provide traffic engineering and bandwidth reservation for services throughout the network and thus called RSVP-TE, is even more taxing on routers' resources than LDP. For RSVP-TE to work, every router along the path (called *midpoints*) must be aware of how to forward the traffic based on the traffic engineering or bandwidth requirements established at the source—also called the *headend*. Over the last several years as networks grew larger and traffic engineering was deployed to ensure guaranteed bandwidth or assured path, midpoint scaling has emerged as a major resource strain and scalability roadblock. Although MPLS has enabled a number of value-added services for the transport network over the past quarter century, what was once a revolutionary and exciting innovation now seems cumbersome and too complicated to operate and manage with all the add-ons.

The biggest challenge for MPLS as the transport protocol of choice emerged when it gained a foothold in access networks such as MBH. As explained earlier in Chapter 3, "Mobile Networks Today," MPLS-based services are established using a router's host route without summarization—relatively easy to accomplish within a smaller domain (such as the IP Core) comprising a relatively small number of routers. However, when implemented in access networks such as MBH, where device numbers can range in the hundreds of thousands of nodes that require connectivity across multiple access, aggregation and core domains, scalability challenges start to emerge. The introduction of Seamless MPLS architectures, using a combination of IGP, careful route filtering, and enhancements in BGP to carry label information, as defined in RFC 3107, enabled mobile network operators to circumvent the scalability challenges and deploy MPLS in some of the world's largest mobile communication networks with 200K cell sites.[1]

Despite being more than a decade old and one of the most deployed backhaul architectures, however, Seamless MPLS concepts remain too complex for some. The layers of reachability defined in the Seamless MPLS architecture—IGP within each domain, BGP across domains through next-hop self-manipulation—present a complicated solution, which was discussed earlier in Chapter 3. It requires a deep and thorough understanding of the interworking of multiple communication protocols for any network architect designing an MPLS-enabled backhaul or any operations engineer troubleshooting connectivity issues to navigate through the multiple layers of reachability. Simply put, the Seamless MPLS architectural framework provides scalability and uniformity across domains but is high maintenance and complex to design, manage, and operate.

Introducing Segment Routing

In everyday life, a path to a destination can be described in different ways. for example, "walk to the intersection of streets A and B and walk east for one block," or "hop on a bus number X, get off at the railway station, and take a train to city Y." Each of these path examples can be dissected into individual *segments*; for example, "walk to the intersection of streets A and B" is the first segment and "walk east for one block" is another one. These are examples of predetermined routing decisions made at the source. *Segment Routing (SR)* relies on a similar concept—it uses a collection of segments, or rather *instructions*, that make up the entire path to reach the destinations. This information is added to the traffic at the source, before it's passed on to a data network that is capable of understanding and acting upon these instructions.

SR addresses the complexities and challenges that were faced in Seamless MPLS-based networks and offers a simplified, SDN-friendly, scalable solution that could help scale services offered by the data network. Its simplicity and ease of implementation have made it gain popularity and become a favored choice for service-oriented data networks, such as an xHaul transport network in an MCN. Figure 6-1 shows a simple, end-to-end overview of the use of SR in a mobile transport network providing connectivity between cell sites and the 5G Core.

Concept of Source Routing and Segments

Source routing has always been desirable, as the data source is often the most informed entity about the preferred or required treatment for the data it generates; however, implementing source routing in an IP network would have meant using IP options in the header. This could support only a limited number of hops as well as make the IP header bulky and inefficient to parse. It also requires a holistic view of the network topology and link states, whereas typical IP routing protocols provide only the next-hop information. Hence, source routing is neither efficient nor easy to achieve because, without the appropriate knowledge of the data network that has to transport this traffic or the ability to influence those data paths, very little could be done at the source to control the destiny of data. Mechanisms such as QoS marking, traffic engineering, and policy-based routing (PBR) have been used to exert some amount of control, but all of these have their own drawbacks and limitations. QoS markings allow the source to request a specific traffic treatment; however, this requires a hop-by-hop QoS definition across the entire network to classify and honor those markings. PBR can be used to match against a specific source attribute, overriding the global routing table, but it, too, has to be defined on every transit router and hence is not practical for influencing the end-to-end traffic path. Traffic engineering, commonly implemented using MPLS, also faces many challenges discussed in previous sections.

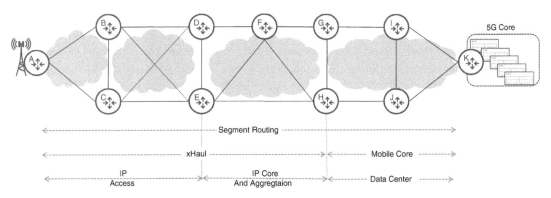

FIGURE 6-1 Segment Routing in Mobile Communication Networks

So, it's no surprise that all dynamic routing protocols implemented today use traffic destination information to make forwarding decisions. These protocols depend on best path calculations using various metrics and forward traffic toward the next hop, with the expectation that the subsequent hop knows what to do next. The applications sourcing the traffic have no visibility of the topology and no control or influence over the decision-making process for the path used. It's technically possible to define a source-routed path on the application itself, which in case of an MCN could be the subscriber's mobile devices. This, however, poses a security threat, as these applications and data sources reside outside the service provider's trust boundary. As such, any decision to influence the traffic path within an SP network must be delegated to the equipment within the trusted network and with appropriate topology information, such as the CSR or IP routers in the 5GC domain.

Segment Routing (SR) includes the path instructions in the packet itself at the source and, hence, in essence uses the concept of source routing.[2] It offers a much simplified and scalable mechanism to achieve this while still leveraging the dynamic destination-based routing of the network, and at the same time instructing the transit routers of the desired behavior. These instructions, called *segments*, are defined in the RFC as follows: "A segment can represent any instruction, topological or service based."[3] The segments can therefore represent a link, a networking node (router), a portion of the traffic path, a specific forwarding instruction, a particular traffic treatment, or a combination of these. Segments can vary in the level of detail and can be very precise, defining the exact routers and links that the traffic should take, or they can be loosely defined to ensure that specific routers or links are in the path used to reach the destination. Connecting back to the analogy of directions used by humans to reach a destination, each part of an instruction can be considered a segment, and the specific details of how to reach the end of a segment may be omitted and left for the person to pick any available option. Similarly, in SR, the segments might require that a certain router (which might not be the preferred next hop based on dynamic routing) be reached, while not necessarily enforcing the exact link or intermediate node to reach that router.

Segment IDs (SIDs) and Their Types

To distinguish between segment instructions, an SR-capable device relies on special identifiers, called *segment identifiers (segment IDs, or SIDs* for short). Although the term *SID* pertains to the identifier of a segment rather than the segment itself, the industry uses the term to describe both segments and their respective identifiers. The term *SID* will be used in both senses throughout this book, unless the difference is highlighted.

When we take a closer look at the path analogy from the previous section, it is possible to observe that some segment instructions can be recognized and executed at any starting point ("walk to the intersection of streets A and B"); thus, these have global significance. Others are relative, or locally significant, and can only be executed from a very specific position (for example, "walk east for one block"). While the latter can potentially be executed anywhere, it will hardly result in the desired outcome, if not done at the specific location. SR uses the same concept and distinguishes globally significant, or *global SIDs*, and locally significant, or *local SIDs*.

For the SR-capable routers to act according to the instruction encoded in the SID, it has to be expressed in the transmitted packet. At the time of publication, two main approaches exist:

- **SR-MPLS**: Uses MPLS labels to express SIDs.

- **SRv6**: Uses the IPv6 destination address field and additional IPv6 routing headers to express SIDs.[4, 5]

Figure 6-2 shows the SID expression in SR-MPLS and SRv6 packets. The SRv6 concepts will be introduced later in this chapter, while this section's focus is on SR-MPLS.

FIGURE 6-2   Segment ID (SID) Representation in SR-MPLS and SRv6

A number of different segment types and SIDs are defined by the Segment Routing Architecture IETF standard; some are global, while others have local significance:[6]

- **Prefix-SID**: This is one of the most common SIDs used in SR and serves as an identifier for the *IGP-Prefix segment*, an instruction to reach a specific IGP prefix. How this IGP prefix is reached is not explicitly specified, and if multiple equal-cost paths to this prefix exist, all of them can be used simultaneously; that is, Equal Cost Multi Path (ECMP) is used. The Prefix-SID is a global SID and can be recognized by any SR-capable router in an IGP domain. It is akin to an instruction such as "walk to the intersection of streets A and B."

- **Node-SID**: This is a type of the Prefix-SID and therefore is also globally significant. It represents an IGP prefix uniquely identifying a node, which is usually the router's loopback interface.

- **Anycast-SID**: This is another type of the Prefix-SID and is tied to an IGP prefix announced by multiple nodes in the same IGP domain. Anycast-SID is a global SID and is used to instruct an SR-capable router to forward a packet to the closest originator of the *Anycast IP prefix*. In everyday life, this instruction type is similar to "drive to *any* of the closest gas stations."

- **Adjacency-SID (or Adj-SID for short)**: This is an example of a local SID. This SID identifies a router's particular IGP adjacency, persuading the router to forward a packet over this adjacency, regardless of a best path installed in the routing table. Applying SR jargon to the original "walking" analogy, the Adj-SID would be the "walk east for one block" segment.

- **Binding-SID**: This identifies an instruction to forward a packet over a *Segment Routing Traffic Engineered (SR-TE)* path or, using SR jargon, an *SR policy*. The SR traffic engineering concepts and constructs will be covered in the upcoming sections of this chapter. Binding-SID is equivalent to taking a predetermined bus route from a bus station. Although Binding-SID can be implemented either as a local SID or a global SID, at press time, most of the Binding-SID implementations are locally significant.

- **BGP Prefix-SID**: This can be used in scenarios where BGP is used to distribute routing information. BGP Prefix-SID is very similar to the Prefix-SID but is bound to a BGP prefix and has global significance.[7]

The next few SID types belong to segments used in *BGP Egress Peering Engineering (BGP EPE)*, an approach defined in the Segment Routing EPE BGP-LS Extensions IETF draft.[8] In simple terms, BGP EPE applies concepts of SR to BGP peering in order to forward packets toward a specific BGP peer, or a set of peers. Expanding the original human analogy to this case, the use of BGP EPE segments can be viewed as an instruction to change transportation authority and hop off the bus to take a train to the final destination. A few different types of BGP EPE SIDs are defined the Segment Routing Architecture IETF standard:[9]

- **BGP PeerNode-SID**: This instructs a router to forward a packet to a specific BGP peer, regardless of the BGP best path. By using this SID type, a packet source can define the *autonomous system (AS)* exit point. However, being a local SID, the BGP PeerNode-SID allows the use of any adjacency toward the BGP peer.

- **BGP PeerAdj-SID**: In contrast, this is used to specifically define which adjacency or link has to be used to forward a packet to the BGP peer.

- **BGP PeerSet-SID**: This is another form of BGP EPE SID and is used to designate a set of BGP peers, eligible for packet forwarding. Because the BGP PeerSet-SID can identify more than one BGP peer, a load-balancing mechanism can be used to forward packets toward these BGP peers.

With the growing list of SR adopters, new use cases for Segment Routing may emerge requiring new SID types. The list of SIDs presented in this section is not exhaustive and will likely expand. Figure 6-3 provides an example of different SID types in SR-MPLS networks.

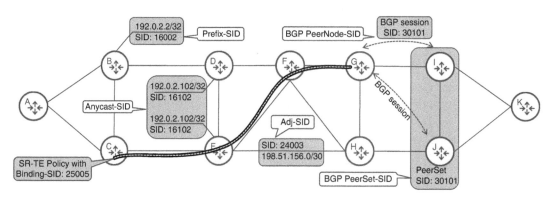

FIGURE 6-3 Segment ID Examples

Another characteristic feature of Segment Routing is its elegant approach to the distribution of instructions or SIDs throughout the network. In an effort to simplify network design and implementation, SR does not rely on additional protocols but rather leverages the existing IGP or BGP protocols instead. Figure 6-4 highlights the simplification brought in by SR, as compared to existing Seamless MPLS architectures, and shows how SR simplifies the protocol stack by leveraging existing routing protocols to perform functions other than basic reachability and connectivity. The SR implementation of these functions is discussed in subsequent sections.

	Seamless MPLS	Segment Routing
Network Programmability	N/A	PCEP
Services (e.g., L2 and L3 VPN)	LDP and/or BGP	BGP
Interdomain Connectivity	BGP Labeled Unicast (BGP-LU)	IGP with Segment Routing Extensions
Redundancy & Traffic Engineering	Resource Reservation Protocol (RSVP)	
Label Distribution	Label Distribution Protocol (LDP)	
Connectivity & Reachability	IGP (IS-IS or OSFP)	

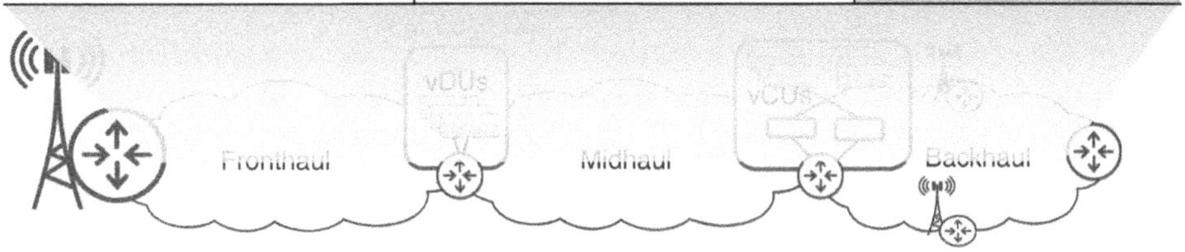

FIGURE 6-4   Protocol Stack Simplification with Segment Routing

Defining and Distributing Segment Information

In a typical network, information such as router's capabilities, prefixes, adjacencies between the routers, and link attributes are distributed by an Interior Gateway Protocol (IGP). The popular IGPs used by service providers are designed to be friendly for functionality expansion and use *type-length-value (TLV)* tuples to carry chunks of information within IGP data units. Allowing an IGP to carry additional information about routers or their links is only a matter of adding new TLVs or sub-TLVs to the protocols' specification. A few IETF RFCs propose adding SR extensions to the three popular IGPs: namely, RFC 8667 for ISIS, RFC 8665 for OSPF, and RFC 8666 for OSPFv3.[10, 11, 12] In essence, all these RFCs propose additional TLVs and sub-TLVs to propagate SR Prefix-SIDs along with the prefix information, Adjacency-SIDs with information describing adjacencies, as well as some non-SID information required for SR operation.

Unlike traditional MPLS implementations, where labels are always locally significant (with the exception for some special use labels), SR heavily relies on the use of global SIDs, which require special precautions in the case of SR-MPLS. Indeed, a global SID should have the same meaning on all the nodes in a particular domain; therefore, if the SID value is expressed as an MPLS label, either this label must be available on every node or another form of unambiguous mapping of this SID to the label that's understood by the downstream devices should exist.

Suppose a prefix of 10.0.0.1/32 is propagated throughout the domain and has a corresponding Prefix-SID, represented by an MPLS label 16001. It is not always reasonable to assume that this MPLS label is available on all the nodes in the domain. This MPLS label may already be in use by some other protocol, or outside the label range supported by the device, and thus cannot be used by SR-MPLS. The problem is easily solved if the Prefix-SID or any other global SID is propagated as a value relative to some *base*, instead of the actual label. This relative value is called an *index*, and the base with the range allocated for SR global SIDs becomes a *Segment Routing Global Block (SRGB)*. Each node can then advertise its own SRGB, allowing neighbors to correctly construct MPLS labels mapped to the global SIDs by this node. Put simply, if the Prefix-SID of 10.0.0.1/32 is propagated as an index of 1, it is translated to an MPLS label of 16001, provided that the downstream neighbor's SRGB starts at 16000. Standards allow SID distribution as both an index or actual value; however, current implementation uses an index for Prefix-SIDs and the actual value for Adjacency-SIDs.

The distribution of Adjacency-SIDs as values is particularly interesting, as the standard also defines a *Segment Routing Local Block (SRLB)* to be used for some types of local SIDs. Although Adj-SID is a local SID, the adjacency itself is always unique and thus does not require any coordinated use of a particular value across multiple nodes. A node can simply allocate a label from its dynamic label space and propagate it as a value because no other node is required to have this local label installed in the FIB. The proposed use of SRLB is rather for locally significant but non-unique intent, such as "forward a packet to a locally attached scrubber" or something similar.

Another important type of non-SID information propagated by IGP and worth mentioning is the *SR algorithms* supported by a node. Any SR-capable node supports at least one algorithm—*Shortest Path First (SPF)*, which is the same algorithm used by IGPs without SR extensions. SPF is the default algorithm used in SR, but other algorithms may be supported as well. For example, the *Strict SPF* algorithm may be supported by default, based on vendor's implementation. Simply put, Strict SPF is the same as regular SPF, with one exception: it does not allow any transit node to redirect the packet from SPF path. By using Strict SPF, the source can be sure that a packet does not deviate from the intended path due to a local policy on a transit node. Other types of SR algorithms can also be defined and are generally known as *flexible algorithms*. SR flexible algorithms are discussed later in this chapter.

Another example of non-SID information required by SR is the *Maximum SID Depth (MSD)* supported by a node. The MSD is valuable in SR-TE scenarios, where a list of SIDs expressed in an MPLS label stack might exceed the capabilities of some platforms. If every node's MSD is known, the end-to-end path can be calculated using the allowed number of SIDs.

In ISIS, most non-SID information is carried in sub-TLVs under *Router Capability TLV*. Prefix-SIDs are propagated as sub-TLVs under *Extended IP Reachability TLV*, along with multiple flags and algorithm field tying the Prefix-SID to a particular algorithm (SPF, Strict SPF, or flexible algorithms). Finally, Adj-SIDs are propagated under the Extended IS reachability TLV using sub-TLVs defined for this purpose. Figure 6-5 illustrates an example of an ISIS packet capture with SR extensions.

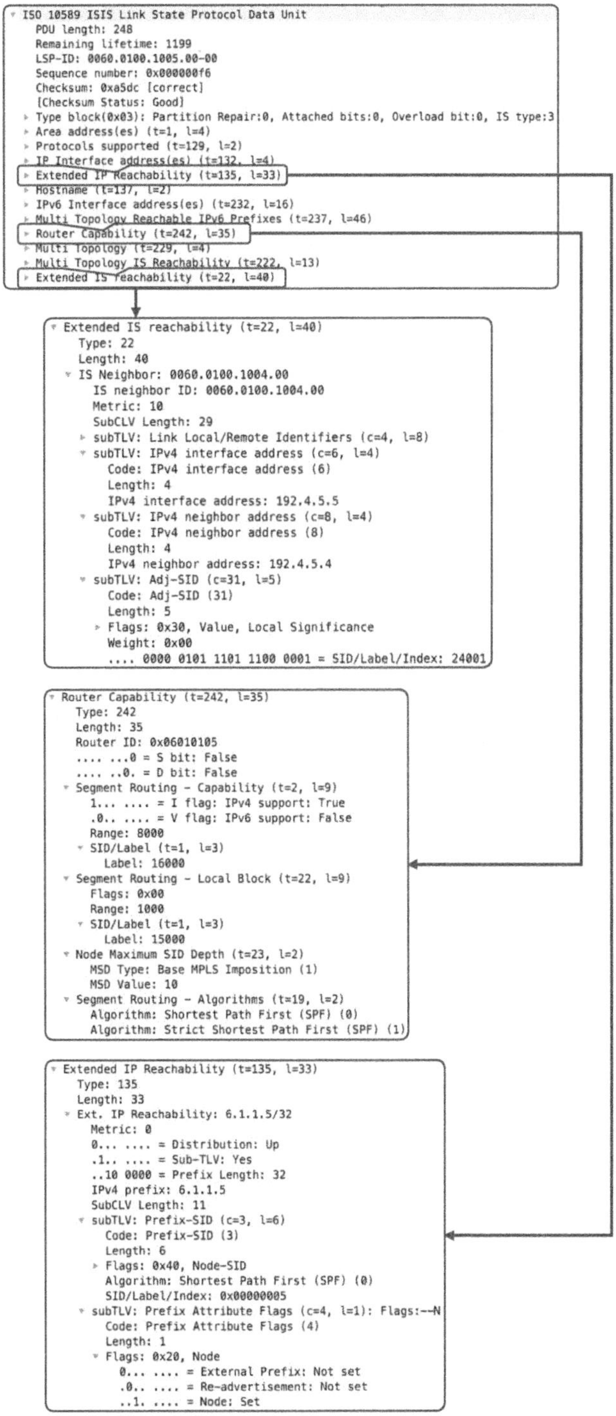

```
▼ ISO 10589 ISIS Link State Protocol Data Unit
    PDU length: 248
    Remaining lifetime: 1199
    LSP-ID: 0060.0100.1005.00-00
    Sequence number: 0x000000f6
    Checksum: 0xa5dc [correct]
    [Checksum Status: Good]
  ▶ Type block(0x03): Partition Repair:0, Attached bits:0, Overload bit:0, IS type:3
  ▶ Area address(es) (t=1, l=4)
  ▶ Protocols supported (t=129, l=2)
  ▶ IP Interface address(es) (t=132, l=4)
  ▶ Extended IP Reachability (t=135, l=33)
  ▶ Hostname (t=137, l=2)
  ▶ IPv6 Interface address(es) (t=232, l=16)
  ▶ Multi Topology Reachable IPv6 Prefixes (t=237, l=46)
  ▶ Router Capability (t=242, l=35)
  ▶ Multi Topology (t=229, l=4)
  ▶ Multi Topology IS Reachability (t=222, l=13)
  ▶ Extended IS reachability (t=22, l=40)
```

```
▼ Extended IS reachability (t=22, l=40)
    Type: 22
    Length: 40
  ▼ IS Neighbor: 0060.0100.1004.00
      IS neighbor ID: 0060.0100.1004.00
      Metric: 10
      SubCLV Length: 29
    ▶ subTLV: Link Local/Remote Identifiers (c=4, l=8)
    ▼ subTLV: IPv4 interface address (c=6, l=4)
        Code: IPv4 interface address (6)
        Length: 4
        IPv4 interface address: 192.4.5.5
    ▼ subTLV: IPv4 neighbor address (c=8, l=4)
        Code: IPv4 neighbor address (8)
        Length: 4
        IPv4 neighbor address: 192.4.5.4
    ▼ subTLV: Adj-SID (c=31, l=5)
        Code: Adj-SID (31)
        Length: 5
      ▶ Flags: 0x30, Value, Local Significance
        Weight: 0x00
        .... 0000 0101 1101 1100 0001 = SID/Label/Index: 24001
```

```
▼ Router Capability (t=242, l=35)
    Type: 242
    Length: 35
    Router ID: 0x06010105
    .... ...0 = S bit: False
    .... ..0. = D bit: False
  ▼ Segment Routing - Capability (t=2, l=9)
      1... .... = I flag: IPv4 support: True
      .0.. .... = V flag: IPv6 support: False
      Range: 8000
    ▼ SID/Label (t=1, l=3)
        Label: 16000
  ▼ Segment Routing - Local Block (t=22, l=9)
      Flags: 0x00
      Range: 1000
    ▼ SID/Label (t=1, l=3)
        Label: 15000
  ▼ Node Maximum SID Depth (t=23, l=2)
      MSD Type: Base MPLS Imposition (1)
      MSD Value: 10
  ▼ Segment Routing - Algorithms (t=19, l=2)
      Algorithm: Shortest Path First (SPF) (0)
      Algorithm: Strict Shortest Path First (SPF) (1)
```

```
▼ Extended IP Reachability (t=135, l=33)
    Type: 135
    Length: 33
  ▼ Ext. IP Reachability: 6.1.1.5/32
      Metric: 0
      0... .... = Distribution: Up
      .1.. .... = Sub-TLV: Yes
      ..10 0000 = Prefix Length: 32
      IPv4 prefix: 6.1.1.5
      SubCLV Length: 11
    ▼ subTLV: Prefix-SID (c=3, l=6)
        Code: Prefix-SID (3)
        Length: 6
      ▶ Flags: 0x40, Node-SID
        Algorithm: Shortest Path First (SPF) (0)
        SID/Label/Index: 0x00000005
    ▼ subTLV: Prefix Attribute Flags (c=4, l=1): Flags:--N
        Code: Prefix Attribute Flags (4)
        Length: 1
      ▼ Flags: 0x20, Node
          0... .... = External Prefix: Not set
          .0.. .... = Re-advertisement: Not set
          ..1. .... = Node: Set
```

FIGURE 6-5   ISIS Extensions for Segment Routing Example

OSPF carries similar sub-TLVs in various *Type 10 Opaque LSAs*. Non-SID SR information is flooded in the *Router Information Opaque LSA*, while the Prefix-SID and Adj-SIDs are transported as sub-TLVs in the *Extended Prefix Opaque LSA* and *Extended Link Opaque LSA*, respectively.

Although IGP has the most comprehensive set of SR extensions, it is possible to propagate SR information using Border Gateway Protocol (BGP) as well. BGP is a highly flexible protocol and a popular choice to convey routing information not only between autonomous systems but within many data centers as well. The RFC 8669 defines a new optional transitive path attribute to transport both the Prefix-SID label index and originator's SRGB range. This *BGP Prefix-SID* path attribute can be attached to BGP labeled Unicast prefixes and used to distribute SR information across the network.[13]

Segment Routing Traffic Engineering (SR-TE)

Growing network complexities, exploding traffic volumes, and diverse traffic types have rendered networks using only the SPF algorithm to calculate optimal paths inadequate. Because network links are expensive assets, service providers wish to utilize them as much as possible; however, in many cases, they remain idle and not generating revenue. An attempt to reclaim these idle or underutilized links and transport appropriate traffic types over them has created a new field of networking—traffic engineering (TE). TE brings innovative approaches to steer traffic over a vast number of potential paths through the network, improving the overall efficiency of network resources utilization, reducing the cost of transportation for critical and sensitive traffic, and offering a customized forwarding path for certain traffic types.

Current Approach to Traffic Engineering

In a way, rudimentary TE capabilities were offered by routing protocols via link metric manipulation. Due to its nature, however, metric manipulation affects all traffic types; hence, instead of distributing, it shifts all traffic flows without adding much improvement in network resources utilization efficiency. However, when mixed with strategically provisioned logical tunnels, acting as pseudo-links between a few network nodes, static routing or PBR enables achieving some degree of traffic distribution over multiple paths. Unfortunately, when IP-based logical tunnels are used, such as *Generic Routing Encapsulation (GRE)*, this poses a risk of routing instabilities and potential routing loops, as IP-based tunnels can be easily affected by interaction with static routing and metric changes in routing protocols. Although this method still remains in a network architect's tool inventory, more sophisticated and powerful methods were invented to comply with demanding service level agreements (SLAs) and provide granular control over different traffic types as well as optimal link utilization in complex and large topologies.

The MPLS forwarding plane created an opportunity to take the tunnel-based approach to a whole new level. A labeled switch path (LSP), an equivalent of a tunnel, can be established in the MPLS forwarding plane by programming an appropriate state on each node along the desired path. Every node along this path would need to allocate a special label associated with that LSP, and the packet received with this label at the top will be forwarded down the LSP.

Normally, traffic is steered into an LSP at the *headend* node by various methods. Some of these methods include preferential use of labeled paths over regular *Routing Information Base (RIB)* entries to reach BGP next hop(s), special IGP tweaks, and static routing. Once the decision to steer the packet into an LSP is made, an MPLS label is pushed on top of this packet, and it is forwarded along the LSP.

Forwarding a packet along the LSP means sending a packet to the immediate downstream neighbor over a specific adjacency. Before the packet hits the link toward the next downstream node, the ingress label is typically swapped with a label assigned to the same LSP by a downstream node. The process repeats until the penultimate hop, where a label can be swapped with label zero or removed completely, depending on the configuration. Using this process, a packet can be forwarded along any pre-negotiated path toward the destination, regardless of the result of SPF algorithm calculations for a particular destination, as shown in Figure 6-6. This method is called MPLS-TE, and it proved to be effective in achieving the goals of sending traffic over an engineered path. MPLS-TE is currently a widely deployed technique in many service provider and enterprise networks.

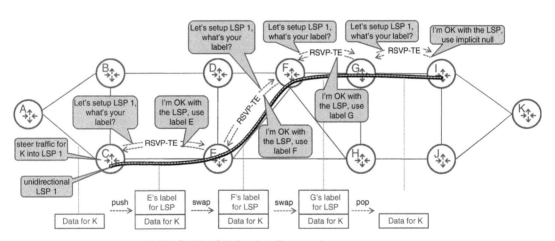

FIGURE 6-6   Example of MPLS-TE LSP Packet Forwarding

The desired path of an LSP can be calculated at the headend node by executing a special version of the SPF algorithm, called *Constrained Shortest-Path First (CSPF)*, on the known network topology. As the name implies, CSPF is based on SPF but uses additional constraints for the calculations, such as "exclude certain links from the topology" or "use special metric for calculations." While the number of LSPs originating at a particular headend can be significant, with powerful CPUs and ample memory resources, today's routers can easily cope with all those path calculations. The impact on midpoint nodes, however, can be much more pronounced. Because every node in the path of any LSP has to program and maintain the forwarding state, in large networks a typical midpoint node might be in the path of hundreds of thousands of LSPs, which creates a significant scalability challenge.

Negotiating the use of MPLS labels for each LSP across the network relies on extensions to Resource Reservation Protocol (RSVP), referred to as RSVP-TE.[14] The RSVP-TE protocol signals the desired path and secures MPLS labels for LSP hop-by-hop, such that every node down the path is aware and ready to forward traffic down the LSP. If an LSP has special demands, such as a certain level of available bandwidth along the path, RSVP-TE takes care of the bandwidth requests and provides arbitration for the situation when multiple LSPs request more bandwidth than is available at a particular node. These mechanisms come with a price, as the appropriate state has to be created and periodically refreshed on all these nodes, which exacerbates scalability challenges faced by MPLS-TE midpoint nodes. Additionally, these negotiations may impose a delay in establishing an LSP.

Besides scalability challenges, the use of an additional protocol for MPLS-TE operation can bring more network vulnerabilities and requires attention when securing the network perimeter. All of these challenges, combined with increased complexity of deployment, operation, and troubleshooting, create significant backpressure, slowing down the MPLS-TE adoption rate. TE with SR takes a different approach and provides a way around these serious challenges.

Traffic Path Engineering with Segment Routing

TE was an integral part of SR since its very inception. In fact, enabling SR on a network immediately makes it TE-ready—no additional protocols, labels, negotiations, or tunnel maintenance on transit nodes required. Instead, *Segment Routing Traffic Engineering (SR-TE)* uses SIDs as *waypoints*. The collection of these waypoints (that is, various types of SIDs) forms a *navigation map* helping all nodes to send packets along desired paths. A headend, in turn, can craft the path instructions by listing the IDs of all segments a packet has to traverse. The resulting *SID-list* becomes the path instruction, which can be expressed as an MPLS label stack and pushed on top of a packet. The packet is then forwarded according to the top label, until it reaches the end of the current segment, where the label is popped and the next label becomes active. This process continues, taking the packet through all segments over the desired path, as shown on Figure 6-7, where Router C implements an SR policy toward Router I, which uses the Prefix-SID of Router G as a first waypoint, relying on intermediate routers to implement ECMP wherever possible. Router G forwards traffic to the next waypoint over adjacency to Router I, as prescribed by Router C.

Having the complete set of instructions attached to the packet itself removes the need for label negotiations along the LSP. Because there are no negotiations, no additional protocols are needed and, more importantly, no additional state is created on mid- and endpoints. As far as the midpoint is concerned, all necessary actions are already programmed in its FIB for every MPLS label used by SR, thanks to the routing protocol's SR extensions. Hence, the midpoint can simply forward packets, sent over SR-TE path, as yet another MPLS packet with no additional per-LSP state created. The same is true for endpoints; however, endpoints typically receive either unlabeled packets or packets with the service label exposed, due to the penultimate hop popping (PHP) behavior.

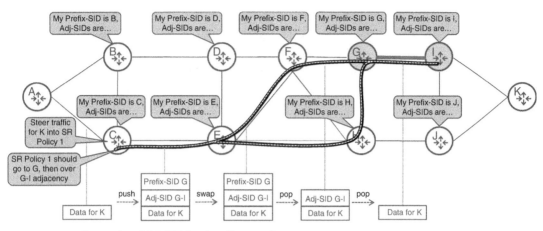

FIGURE 6-7   Example of SR-TE Packet Forwarding

Without the need to maintain extra state on mid- and endpoints, the SR approach to TE is ultra-scalable. All the necessary state for each SR-TE path is created and maintained on headend nodes, with a major component being the SR-TE path's SID-list. The SID-list can either be defined statically via configuration, dynamically calculated on the headend itself, or programmed by an external application through APIs (if supported by the headend's software). The CSPF algorithm is used to calculate the path, applying the desired constraints and optimization criteria on the SR-TE topology database. In SR terminology, the resulting SID-list, combined with some additional parameters, creates an *SR policy*—the equivalent of an MPLS-TE tunnel.[15]

Segment Routing TE Policies

Justifiably, there are no references to tunnels in SR-TE jargon, as there is no extra state created at the end of or along the LSP; therefore, no actual tunnels are created. In SR, a packet is forwarded along the desired LSP using instructions attached to the packet itself, typically in the form of MPLS labels. These instructions rather define a policy on how a packet should be forwarded across the network, thus the name *SR policy*.

SR policy is a construct used to create and attach traffic-forwarding instructions to the packets. This policy defines the *intent* on how traffic should be treated and forwarded across the network. In a simple scenario, an SR policy is associated with a single SID-list, providing instructions on how to forward packets across the network. When such a SID-list is programmed in the FIB, SR policy is considered to have been *instantiated* on the headend.

Even the most stable networks are prone to link and node failures thus programmed SID-lists might become obsolete and cause traffic blackholing. This scenario is quite likely in the case of statically defined SID-lists. Yet, even with dynamically calculated SID-lists, it is still plausible that CSPF would not be able to find another path, due to the constraints defined in the SR policy after the failure in the network. To provide more flexibility, SR policies can have more than one *candidate path*. Each candidate path is paired with a preference value and can prescribe to use a different path for SR policy, if a more preferred candidate path is unavailable. Moreover, each candidate path can have more than one SID-list, each with its own *weight*. When a candidate path with multiple SID-lists is active, the traffic is load-balanced across these SID-lists based on the ratio of their weights, as shown on Figure 6-8.[16] Only one candidate path can be active at a time for a given SR policy, and if none of the candidate paths are valid, the whole SR policy becomes invalid and is removed from the forwarding table.

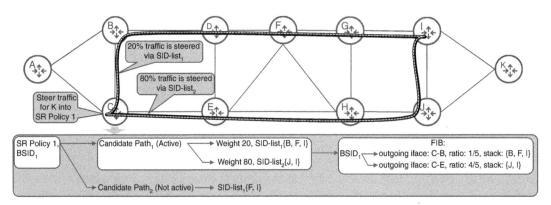

FIGURE 6-8 SR Policy Construct

Depending on communication flows, a significant number of SR policies can be programmed on each individual headend node, let alone in the whole network. It is entirely possible to have multiple SR policies with different paths, or otherwise different traffic treatment, between a given headend and endpoint pair. Thus, every SR policy cannot be differentiated based only on the headend–endpoint pair but requires an additional parameter for proper identification. This parameter is *color*—an arbitrary 32-bit number used to form the tuple (*headend, color, endpoint*) that uniquely identifies the SR policy in the network.[17] Oftentimes, color is also used to identify the intent (that is, it can represent how traffic will be treated by the network) and can further be connected to specific SLAs such as Gold, Silver, and Bronze traffic types.

When instantiated, each SR policy is assigned its own *binding SID (BSID)*, which is one of the primary mechanisms to steer traffic into the SR policy. Typically, the BSID is locally significant and is swapped with a stack of labels representing the SR policy's active SID-list, effectively steering a packet labeled with BSID into its respective SR policy. The use of BSID is not the only available mechanism for traffic steering, however, as seen in the next section.

Traffic-Steering Mechanisms

The most straightforward approach to steer traffic into an SR policy is to use a BSID, but it requires an upstream node to impose the BSID on top of the packet. When a packet with the BSID arrives on the node with the SR policy instantiated, the BSID is expanded into the SR policy's actual SID-list. In addition to the BSID, a few other mechanisms exist to steer traffic in the SR policy locally.

Although it depends on the vendor's implementation, one obvious way to steer traffic locally into the SR policy is to use static routing (altering routing table pointers); however, such direct use of static routing doesn't scale very well.

A modified version of static routing, or rather routing table tweaking, is used to steer traffic flows into SR policies. In many cases, it might be desirable that traffic flows for destinations beyond the endpoint of an SR policy be steered into that SR policy. To accomplish this, a node instantiating the SR policy tweaks its routing table to point to this SR policy as its outgoing interface for any prefixes that are advertised by nodes beyond the SR policy's endpoint. In some implementations, it is even possible to identify a set of prefixes that are eligible for this behavior, thus limiting the traffic flows automatically steered into the SR policy. Cisco routers implement this behavior under the name of *autoroute*.

Another, even more scalable and flexible approach is to use the color of the SR policy for *automated steering*. Automated steering is the go-to solution in environments with services connected via BGP L2 and L3 VPNs. These VPN services rely on a potentially large number of service prefixes advertised by provider edge (PE) routers. This approach normally results in the color being attached to a prefix as a special BGP *Color Extended Community* defined in the IETF draft *Advertising Segment Routing Policies in BGP*.[18] The 32-bit color value in the Color Extended Community is used to form a tuple (headend, color, prefix's BGP next hop). This tuple is then compared with the active SR policies' identifying tuples on this headend. The active SR policy with the matching color and endpoint (the headend value always matches for obvious reasons) is then used to forward traffic destined to this BGP prefix. This automated steering solution works for both service (VPN) and transport routes.[19] Figure 6-9 shows both automated steering and autoroute mechanisms.

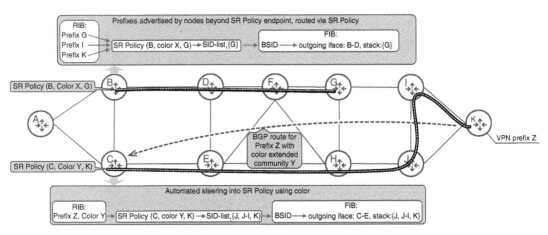

FIGURE 6-9   Steering Traffic Flows into SR Policy

This automated steering approach can be combined with an automated SR policy instantiation mechanism in a feature known as *On-Demand Next Hop (ODN)*. In addition to automated traffic steering into matching active SR policies, ODN can create and instantiate SR policies if a matching SR policy does not exist. ODN uses BGP next-hop as an endpoint and the value from Color Extended Community as the SR policy's color. Depending on the vendor's implementation, some form of color authorization may be present on the headend, as well as some form of SR policy templates defining optimization criteria and constraints for each color. Put simply, an ODN template removes the need for configuring a separate SRTE policy for destinations that share the same policy constraints. With color authorized through the ODN policy template, any BGP prefix with matching Color Extended Community attribute will result in an automatic SR policy instantiation toward its next hop.

ODN offers a highly scalable solution, removing the need to provision and instantiate a mesh of SR policies between PE routers in advance. Use of this feature can greatly reduce management overhead and operational complexity in a typical MCN with its numerous cell sites-given that there is a need to establish connectivity between cell sites (for Xn communications) as well as between cell sites and the Mobile Core. CSRs can now be configured with only a handful of SR policy templates, allowing ODN to instantiate SR policies to the remote nodes that are advertising service routes with appropriate colors. Figure 6-10 illustrates an overview of ODN operation.

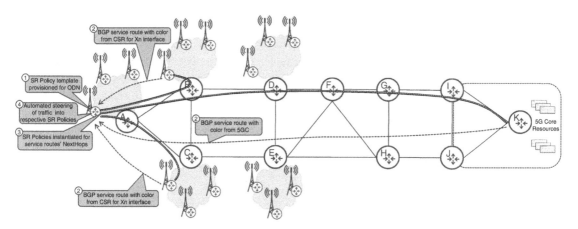

FIGURE 6-10   ODN Operation Overview

Software-Defined Transport with Segment Routing

In everyday life, a commuter might rely on map applications (Google Maps, Apple Maps, and so on) to learn the most optimal route to a destination. Even though the shortest route to the destination may already be known, the state of traffic, congestion, and road closures might result in a different route being faster or better. The cloud-based map application, with better overall visibility of these variables, can therefore provide a better path at that instant. Similarly, in a data network, even though the routing protocols would have already calculated the shortest path, these protocols are not designed to dynamically optimize the path based on network utilization and constraints other than IGP metric. If an external controller has full view of the network's topology, applicable constraints, current state of links, and possibly their utilization, it can then make a more informed and better decision about the traffic path compared to the dynamic routing protocols. The network utilization and efficiency can be significantly improved, provided this controller can influence the traffic's path in the transport network, rerouting it through its computed path. It is this idea that led to *software-defined networking (SDN)*, which has gained a lot traction in the last few years and has now become an important part of any network architecture, especially in service provider networks.

Hybrid SDN Approach

SDN doesn't necessarily require the presence of IGP. In fact, the classic SDN definition expects that the network is composed of forwarding devices that are not playing any part in the routing decisions, and all routing instructions are being dictated through the external SDN application using protocols such as OpenFlow. When the forwarding devices have a routing protocol of their own and the SDN controller's instructions override some of those routing decisions, it's considered a *hybrid SDN* implementation. This is the more commonly deployed SDN scenario in today's networks, in contrast to the idealistic SDN definition of intelligence only in the external controller.

At the time SDN started to gain popularity, almost a decade ago, MPLS-TE was already being used to override IGP-computed routing paths in transport networks. Although it could be adapted and used in software-defined transport, MPLS-TE was not invented with SDN in mind. Its scalability limitations, in addition to the slow reaction time to establish a TE tunnel, didn't make it a very convincing choice for transport SDN. In contrast, SR-TE, a new entrant, presented itself as a viable alternative to MPLS-TE for implementing software-defined transport.

Building Blocks for Software-Defined Transport

The controller performing the brain functions of the software-defined transport, generally called an *SDN controller*, would need to learn sufficient information about the network. At a bare minimum, it would need to be aware of the full network topology as well as any changes occurring in it, such as link or node failures. Additionally, its path computation can be more accurate if it has real-time information, such as link utilization, latency of the links, allocated bandwidth over a link, constraints and affinity associated with the links, type of links (encrypted vs. unencrypted), and so on. The controller will also need to be able to communicate the path decisions to the network devices.

None of the existing protocols could fulfill these requirements. Hence, implementation of SDN for transport networks gave birth to the following new protocols and functions that could facilitate the implementation of its concepts and methods:

- Path Computation Element (PCE)
- BGP Link State (BGP-LS)
- Path Computation Element Communication Protocol (PCEP)

These protocols and functions will be discussed next.

Path Computation Element (PCE)

The SDN controller used by SR-TE is called the *path computation element (PCE)*.[20] Although the PCE was not defined exclusively for SR-TE, it has become the de facto transport SDN controller used across the networking vendors. The PCE relies on a hybrid SDN model rather than completely removing intelligence from the forwarding devices. In fact, by definition, the PCE functionality can be implemented on the forwarding device directly, instead of being deployed externally. Irrespective of the deployment model used, the following are the three key functions a PCE is meant to perform:

- **Topology collection**: As highlighted earlier, topology awareness is a primary requirement for the SDN controller to be able to compute the desired path. Hence, the PCE should be able to learn this information from the network. One protocol of choice for topology collection is BGP-LS, discussed in the section that follows.

- **Path computation algorithms**: In MPLS-TE networks, the headend was responsible for path computation using its limited topological awareness. In SDN-based transport, this function of Constraint-based Shortest Path First (CSPF) computation is delegated to the PCE.

- **Communication with the headend**: The PCE should be able to receive a path computation request from the headend router, which now acts as a client to the PCE and is referred to as the *path computation client (PCC)*. Consequently, the PCE should be able to communicate the computed path to the PCC. Since none of the existing protocols provided the capability for such message exchange, a new protocol called *PCE Communication Protocol (PCEP)* was defined to fill the void.[21] PCEP will be discussed in detail in the next section.

BGP Link State (BGP-LS)

Both of the protocols that are predominantly used in transport networks (OSPF and ISIS) are link-state protocols, and hence the routing database for these contains complete information about the links, nodes, and prefixes that build the network. Additionally, through the use of SR extensions, these protocols also communicate SR-related information such as SID values, SRGB, and SRLB ranges, as well as SPF algorithms being used by a router. In MPLS-TE, the link-state information from the IGPs was used to populate a *traffic engineering database (TED)* utilized by the headend nodes to compute the TE path.

One apparently simple way for the PCE to learn the TED information is by making it part of the IGP domain. This would enable the PCE to learn the IGP link-state information directly and generate the TED. A challenge with this approach, however, is that a typical large-scale transport network is composed of multiple IGP domains. The link-state information, including the SR-related extensions, is not meant to be propagated across IGP domain boundaries—this would have defied the purpose of creating these domains. Hence, by only participating in IGP, the PCE's visibility will be limited to only one domain. Even if the PCE resides in IGP's backbone (Area-0 in OSPF or level-2 ISIS), it can only learn the prefixes (and not the link states and SR details) from other areas due to the nature of IGP.

Therefore, for gathering and sharing the TED with the PCE, a new method was required. BGP, being a scalable and efficient protocol for bulk updates, was chosen for this, and a new BGP Network Layer Reachability Information (BGP NLRI) was defined to carry TED information.[22] Known as BGP Link State (BGP-LS), this address family uses BGP peering between the PCE and the IGP network to gather and provide the full picture of the network to the PCE.

The area border routers are typically used as the BGP peering points and source of link-state information, thus reducing the number of BGP-LS sessions. Furthermore, BGP-LS can leverage the existing BGP route reflector hierarchy for scalability and high availability.

Path Computation Element Communication Protocol (PCEP)

As hinted earlier, the PCE and the PCC need to communicate for exchanging path computation requests and responses. PCE Communication Protocol (PCEP) provides the capability for this communication between PCC and PCE.[23] Just like PCE, the definition of PCEP pre-dates SRTE, and hence PCEP can be also used for SDN-type implementation for MPLS-TE. However, the widespread use and deployment of this protocol has been for SR-TE. In addition to the basic functions mentioned, PCEP is also used for the PCC to discover the PCE, carry periodic keepalive messages between them to ensure connectivity, event notification exchange, and error messages related to path computation. The PCE may also use PCEP to initiate a policy that hasn't been requested by the PCC but rather initiated by an external application.

Using BGP for PCE-PCC Communication

Aside from PCEP, another option that has been suggested for communication between PCC and PCE is via BGP.[24] A new sub-address family in BGP has been proposed for Segment Routing Policy information. However, this has limited uses—primarily focused on PCE initiated policies— and still in its infancy. PCEP remains the predominant protocol for PCE–PCC communication at this time.

Application Integration with Transport Network

The need for traffic engineering has always been driven by applications, as it's the applications that require a certain SLA. However, while leveraging an SDN framework, instead of applications directly interacting with the network elements, the PCE acts as an abstraction of the underlying network, providing a communication medium between the application and the transport network. To work coherently with external applications, the PCE is expected to provide a northbound API interface. Figure 6-11 illustrates the transport SDN building blocks and their operation in a Segment Routing network.

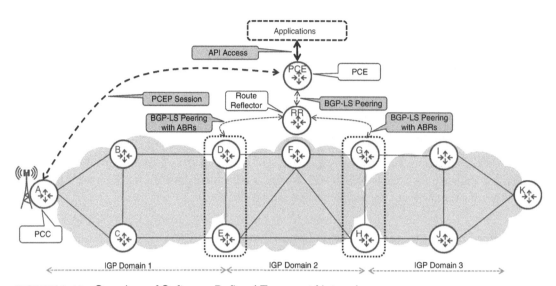

FIGURE 6-11   Overview of Software-Defined Transport Network

While it's the application that dictates the traffic policy, it uses this API interface to communicate those requirements and constraints to the PCE. The PCE is then responsible for computing the path based on those constraints, communicating that path information to the PCC, and maintaining the path. In some cases, the applications may even override the PCE's computation function and instead provide a pre-computed path for the PCE to implement on the network.

Some networking vendors might choose to integrate the PCE functions and applications together as a single product offering. For example, Juniper Network's *Northstar Controller* boasts of capabilities such as topology visualization, analytics, and real-time monitoring—thus reducing the need for an additional external application.[25] Similarly, Cisco's *Crosswork Optimization Engine* adds visualization to the PCE functions, while delegating detailed analytics to closely knit external applications that are part of the *Cisco Crosswork Cluster*.[26]

5G Transport Network Slicing

Perhaps one of the most promising new concepts introduced in 5G is that of network slicing, which allows a mobile service provider to offer differentiated services to a particular traffic type or an enterprise customer. Traditionally, providing special treatment to traffic types has been synonymous with quality of service (QoS), and although QoS is one of the tools within the slicing *toolkit*, a network slice is defined end-to-end rather than a per-hop behavior like QoS. This end-to-end *network slice,* spanning across the MCN domains, is identified using a *network slice instance (NSI)*. Each of the MCN domains uses its respective technology toolkit to implement a corresponding *subnetwork slice* identified by a *network slice subnet instance (NSSI).*[27] These subnetwork slice instances within various domains combine together to form an end-to-end NSI, as shown in Figure 6-12.

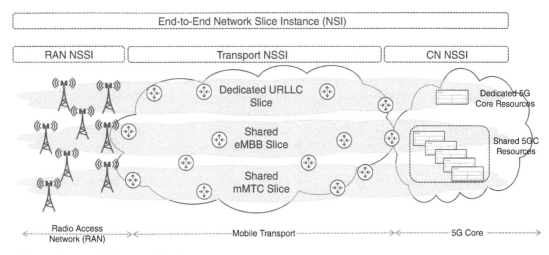

FIGURE 6-12   A Network Slice Instance

The set of technical tools in the RAN and 5GC networks may allow an NSI to use its own dedicated UPF and antennas as well provide its own QoS classification. However, it is the transport network that offers a rich and diverse set of capabilities to *complete* an end-to-end slice by implementing network functions to comply with the slicing requirement imposed by the NSI. One such capability is the use of an SDN controller, as mentioned in the previous section, to administer end-to-end transport slices by using SR-TE policies. Transport network slices might not have a 1:1 correlation with RAN or 5GC slices, and in most cases might not even be aware of the slices in those two domains. However, the transport domain's role is instrumental in ensuring the end-to-end slicing requirements are met while transporting slice traffic between the RAN and 5GC domains. For an end-to-end NSI to be established using the NSSIs in every domain, a *slice manager* is needed to not only stitch together subnetwork slices across domains but also to provide a workflow for creating, operationalizing, managing, and tearing down a slice instance.

Network slicing remains an area of active research and development with many vendors offering a slew of products or solutions working together to realize an end-to-end network slice. While 3GPP has defined various slicing requirements and functions for the RAN and 5GC domain, it has relied on other standard bodies such as IETF, and now O-RAN alliance, to define transport slicing mechanisms. This section will exclusively focus on the technology toolkit available within the mobile transport domain to implement network slicing function based on the type of network slice implemented.

Network Slicing Options

Using the previous example of roads and directions, a network slice can be considered a choice between toll roads, High-Occupancy Vehicle (HOV) lanes, and bus lanes. Toll roads are exclusive to the group of travelers willing to pay extra in exchange for a faster, less-congested route. On the other hand, both HOV and bus lanes are *shared resources* to enable mass transport. The HOV lanes cater to commuters who meet certain criteria and provide them with a less-congested route, thus reducing commute times. On the other hand, bus lanes move a lot of people but might not use the best route for everyone, thus getting everyone to their destinations, but with added delays.

Similarly, network slicing can be classified into two broad categories: *hard slicing* and *soft slicing*. When using hard slicing, network resources are dedicated for an NSI and are off limits to other types of traffic, much like an exclusive toll road. These might be newer, high-capacity, lower-latency networks that might implement state-of-the-art features and functions for premium, high-paying customers. Soft slicing is similar in concept to the shared traffic lanes, where the network resources can be shared between different subscribers and types of traffic. Although the network resources (that is, routers and links) can be shared between multiple slices, they could still provide differential treatment to various traffic classes. For instance, similar to HOV lanes, traffic for network slices that meet specific criteria could be prioritized and sent over an optimal path, whereas bulk data traffic could use under-utilized, high-capacity links that might not always be best in terms of latency.

How Many Network Slices?

Inevitably, the most frequently asked question by network architects is, how many network slices should be configured?

The real answer is that nobody knows. Depending on the requirements, mobile service providers may implement a slice per enterprise customer or per service type (for example, eMBB, URLLC, mMTC, or a combination thereof).

The O-RAN Alliance's xHaul Packet Switched Architectures and Solutions Specification defines transport network slicing for various types of traffic, such as management (M-Plane), control (C-Plane), and user (U-Plane).[28] Subsequent specifications, under development at the time of this writing, will also define service or customer-specific transport network slices.

The network slicing options should not be considered binary choices but rather a spectrum that can be mixed and matched to provide the desired treatment to the traffic based on the individual slice objective. Basic transport network slicing, for instance, can be implemented by a simple MPLS-based VPN providing traffic isolation between different customers or types of traffic. Various QoS mechanisms, such as prioritization, queuing, and bandwidth allocation, can also be used to define the treatment that a particular traffic type or a slice must receive through the transport network. In fact, the early O-RAN xHaul Packet Switched Network Architecture Specifications define transport network slices using a combination of just MPLS VPN and QoS mechanisms.[29] More advanced slicing implementations—for instance, dedicating network resources exclusively to a network slice or using a custom algorithm to calculate the best path instead of the IGP metric—require additional features and capabilities. One such feature is the use of *Segment Routing Flexible Algorithm* to implement both soft and hard network slices.

Segment Routing Flexible Algorithm

Routing protocols and their respective forwarding algorithms have always been a fundamental component of IP networks, continuously calculating the *best path* for routers to send traffic over. These routing protocols have gone through a variety of upgrades and enhancements to ensure the calculation of the best possible path, ranging from simply counting the number of hops to using the networks links' bandwidth to calculate the shortest path to the destination. This use of link-speed-based metrics leaves room for suboptimal routing. For instance, if the mobile network has a few low-bandwidth links in its topology and new higher-bandwidth links are added, there will be scenarios where the multi-hop, high-bandwidth link combo is preferred over a low-bandwidth direct link. The resulting network utilization is skewed in favor of high-bandwidth links, while lower-bandwidth links remain underutilized. In fact, the more *mesh* of links a service provider uses across their network, the more suboptimal link usage may become. Any changes to the IGP's default algorithm to accommodate the low-capacity link would result in the path changing for *all* traffic, resulting in the oversubscription of the shorter but low-capacity link. The optimal solution would be to allow low-bandwidth traffic to continue using the low-capacity link while bandwidth-intensive services use high-capacity links.

Is Link Bandwidth the Only Metric Used?

Some routing protocols use a composite metric to calculate the cost of a link, taking into account components such as traffic load, latency, reliability, and others. However, the use of those protocols in service provider networks is virtually nonexistent, and the most commonly used metric is the cost of the interface, derived from its link speed.

Segment Routing introduces the concept of Flexible Algorithm, called *Flex-Algo* for short, which makes it easier for network operators to customize the IGP to calculate a constraints-based best path to a destination, in addition to simultaneously calculating a default metric-based best path. In other words, Flex-Algo allows a network operator to use custom metrics in parallel to the IGP's default link-bandwidth based metric. The routers participating in the SR Flex-Algo use the *Flexible Algorithm Definition (FAD)*, composed of calculation type, metric type, and the set of constraints, all of which are flooded through the network by IGP through Segment Routing Extensions TLVs. Using these TLVs, the routers also learn about other routers participating in the same Flex-Algo and thus form a *per-algo virtual topology*. The IGP SPF calculations for the said Flex-Algo are performed over this virtual topology using the metric and constraints specified in FAD. The net result is a best path, calculated using customized constraints and a metric defined by the service provider, utilizing a subset or a *logical slice* of the network composed of routers participating in that Flex-Algo instead of the whole network. In addition to the default IGP algorithm, called Algo 0, up to 128 Flex-Algos, represented numerically from 128 through 255, can be defined.[30] Figure 6-13 illustrates the concept of logical topologies based on default algos and Flex-Algos.

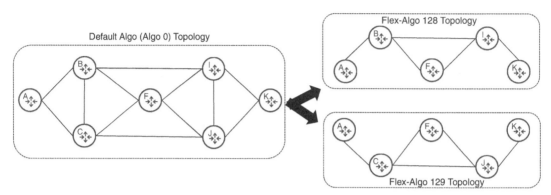

FIGURE 6-13   Creating Network Subtopologies with Segment Routing Flex-Algo

One of the commonly used constraints in a Flex-Algo implementation is the inclusion or exclusion of certain links or nodes based on their capabilities (for example, whether they support link encryption), speed (for example, low-capacity links that could be used for mMTC and high-capacity links preferred for eMBB services), geographical placement (for example, government affairs traffic never leaving an approved geographical region), or the monetary cost of traversing that link. Three different metrics have thus far been defined for Flex-Algo: namely, IGP metric (the link cost), unidirectional delay, and traffic engineering (TE) metric. Today, delay is one of the commonly used metrics for value-added services over Flex-Algo—which can be used in lieu of, or in addition to, the IGP- or TE-based metric.

The strict delay-based metric can be used for URLLC services such as remote medicine and self-driving cars, whereas a combination of predefined *delay range* and bandwidth-based metrics can be used for services such as live video, which is bandwidth intensive but more tolerant of the delay. To use delay as a metric, the network must support latency measurement across the network and advertise it to the devices computing the end-to-end path. There are multiple existing standards to advertise delay-related metrics into IGP and BGP, such as RFC 8570 and RFC 7471 to advertise TE extensions in IS-IS and OSPF, as well as an IETF draft to allow BGP Link State to carry such information. [31, 32, 33] Delay measurements are typically network-vendor-specific implementations but loosely based on repurposing or enhancing existing performance monitoring protocols and specifications such as *Two-Way Active Measurement Protocol (TWAMP)* and *Packet Loss and Delay Measurement for MPLS Networks*. [34, 35]

SR Flex-Algo provides the capability for implementing soft and hard transport slices for 5G. Figure 6-14 shows a few such examples of mobile transport networks using Flex-Algo to create network slices and offer differentiated services. The first example showcases a scenario where the mobile service provider has put together a new, faster transport network connecting the CSRs and the 5GC using more direct, freshly laid-out connections through Router L. This network allows traffic to bypass existing IP aggregation and core, thus cutting down on transit latency and avoiding any congestion. In doing so, the newly deployed network connections also become the best path for all traffic types originating from the cell site. However, just like the case of a toll road, the mobile service provider might want to restrict access to this part of the network and allow only premium services over this network. The mobile service provider might therefore implement Flex-Algo on Routers A, B, I, L, and K, thus creating a *network slice*, and steer traffic into this transport network slice using an SR policy. In this case, Router L and its interfaces are dedicated for exclusive use of premium services, emulating a hard network slice, while the rest of the routers share their network resources across other services, as shown in Figure 6-14. The network operator can also implement separate slices for each of these services to influence traffic behavior. For instance, mMTC services can be configured to use any available path, whereas eMBB traffic might be instructed to avoid low-capacity links, even if it results in traffic taking a longer path, as shown in Figure 6-14 as well.

While Flex-Algo plays a critical role in implementing transport network slicing, its ability to optimize the number of SIDs for a given constrained path makes Flex-Algo an effective network-scaling mechanism. As mentioned earlier, a constrained path might require multiple SIDs to be stacked on top of the packet, thereby increasing the packet size as well as introducing the risk that some devices might not have the hardware capability to impose or parse the excessively large SID list. While a mechanism such as MSD propagation is used as a preventive measure, it does not offer a solution to lower the numbers of SIDs in the packet. Flex-Algo, on the other hand, not only provides a slicing mechanism, but it can also reduce the number of SIDs required to forward traffic along a constrained path.

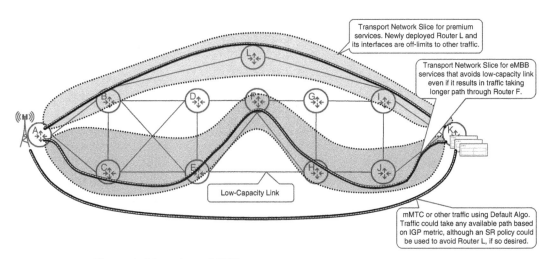

FIGURE 6-14   Network Slices in an MCN

Because Flex-Algo fundamentally alters the metric used to calculate a path, the next hop (or rather the SID associated with the next hop within the Flex-Algo domain) becomes an *instruction* to reach that *waypoint* using the metric associated with the FAD. For instance, if a Flex-Algo uses delay as the metric, then the SID for the destination would represent the best path using the lowest delay, instead of the lowest link cost. This is in contrast to the default algo, where if the lowest delay path were to be used, the headend would need to impose multiple SIDs, representative of the lowest latency path, should that path be different from the cost-based path. In essence, Flex-Algo not only makes it easier and efficient to implement transport network slicing, it inherently optimizes and reduces the number of SIDs a headend may need to impose on the packet, as shown in Figure 6-15. Due to its rich feature set and effectiveness, Flex-Algo is also listed as both a transport-slicing and network-scaling mechanism in O-RAN's xHaul Packet Switched Architecture Specification.

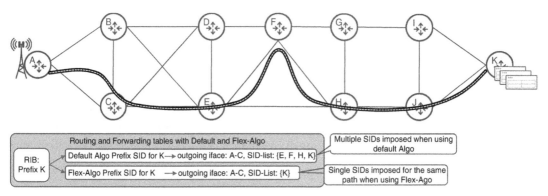

FIGURE 6-15   Lowering SID List with Flex-Algo

Redundancy and High Availability with Segment Routing

Besides achieving the primary objectives of efficient network utilization and custom forwarding paths for certain traffic types, MPLS-TE was instrumental in another aspect of network operation—rapid restoration of traffic forwarding. Thanks to its fast reroute (FRR) capabilities, MPLS-TE offered various types of path protection, typically restoring traffic forwarding within 50ms upon failure detection.[36] In fact, MPLS-TE FRR became so popular that many networks deployed MPLS-TE for the sole intention of using its FRR feature.

MPLS-TE FRR features were followed by *IP Fast Reroute (IP-FRR)*, also known as *Loop-Free Alternates (LFA)*.[37] Being an IP-only feature, LFA offered a path-protection mechanism that does not require an MPLS forwarding plane for detours. LFA leverages the IGP's SPF algorithm to pre-calculate backup paths toward destinations, while considering a failure in the directly connected links or nodes that are used as the primary path to those destinations. For all destinations, the FIB is programmed with a pre-computed backup path, which takes over immediately upon detection of a failure on the primary link, thus reducing convergence times.

While LFA is a very effective and simple-to-use mechanism for path protection in IP-only networks, it has a major drawback. LFA is topology dependent and, in some networks, it cannot offer any backup paths to protect traffic. If paired with LDP, it can further be extended to such topologies and is called *Remote LFA* or *rLFA*. Using rLFA, a backup path in the form of MPLS LSP is established to remote nodes, thus providing FRR capabilities to scenarios where IP-only LFA is not possible.

Segment Routing offers a new *Topology-Independent Loop-Free Alternate (TI-LFA)* path-protection mechanism by extending LFA and rLFA principles to use Prefix- and Adjacency-SIDs for effective and topology-independent restoration of a traffic path after link or node failures.[38]

Segment Routing Topology Independent Loop-Free Alternate

The TI-LFA mechanism is based on the same theory as LFA and rLFA, but applied to an SR-enabled network. Similar to its predecessors, the feature is local to the node and can provide rapid traffic path restoration for local adjacency failure scenarios. No additional information, besides what is already known in the SR-enabled network, is needed for TI-LFA operation. The core of the TI-LFA algorithm is the analysis of *what-if* scenarios, where a primary adjacency, used as an outgoing link for a given destination, fails. The analysis results in a pre-calculated backup path being installed for each destination into the FIB. This backup path must use a different outgoing interface, compared to the primary path, and may involve a few SIDs added on top of the packet to enforce the desired backup path.

Depending on the configuration, TI-LFA can treat the failure of an adjacency as a link or a node failure. In the latter case, the backup path is calculated to avoid the whole node rather than just the link. If no suitable backup paths are found for node protection, the routers may fall back to link-protection calculations.

Although TI-LFA is called "topology independent," strictly speaking it still depends on the topology because at least one alternate path should exist. Moreover, the SID-list, calculated by TI-LFA for a destination prefix, also depends on the topology. This SID-list may be composed of multiple SIDs to force traffic over certain links in the network regardless of their metric, or may be empty. As shown in Figure 6-16, node B's primary path toward K goes via nodes C, E, H, and J. If the adjacency with C fails, node B simply switches the outgoing interface to the adjacency with node D. No additional SIDs are required to enforce a loop-free backup path toward K. Conversely, besides switching the outgoing interface, the backup path from node C toward prefix K requires pushing two SIDs: the Prefix-SID of node B and the Adjacency-SID of B's adjacency to node D. This is due to the high metric on the link between nodes B and D. Without this SID-list, node B will try to forward packets with Prefix-SID K back to node C, causing a loop.

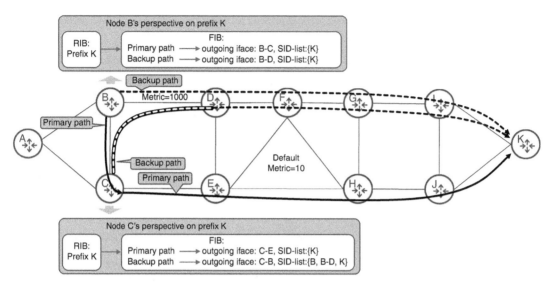

FIGURE 6-16   TI-LFA Backup Paths Example

When enabled, the TI-LFA algorithm is executed by the IGP for each destination as soon as that destination is learned. If a loop-free alternate is found for the destination, the appropriate SID-list and outgoing interface is installed in the FIB as a backup path for the destination. With the pre-computed backup path installed, the decision to switch over is made by the FIB without waiting for IGP to reconverge. Upon detection of an adjacency failure, all destinations using this adjacency as a primary outgoing interface immediately switch over to their respective backup paths, which remain active until the network reconverges.

TI-LFA and ECMP Paths

Packet forwarding based on Prefix-SIDs inherently uses all available ECMP paths. When there are multiple paths toward a particular destination, TI-LFA does not install additional backup paths, but rather multiple ECMP paths are used as a natural backup for each other.

As in the case of MPLS-TE FRR or IP-LFA, the failure detection is critical to any rapid restoration mechanism. Just enabling TI-LFA may not achieve the goal of recovering from a failure within 50ms without suitable failure detection. Normally, link failures are detected by the loss of signal on the receive side of the interface transceiver. In this ideal failure-detection scenario, the detection is instantaneous and restoration of traffic forwarding, by switching to a backup path in the FIB, is almost immediate and can easily meet the 50ms target. However, if the link to another node is transported by some other device (for example, WDM transport), the fiber cut might not necessarily result in the loss of signal on the router's interface. In the absence of other detection mechanisms, the router would need to wait until IGP declares the link as down, which may take a few dozen seconds with default IGP timers.

To avoid such scenarios, many network architects prefer to use the *Bidirectional Forwarding Detection (BFD)* mechanism, ensuring detection of link failures within just a few milliseconds.

Segment Routing Loop Avoidance Mechanism

TI-LFA rapid restoration acts quickly to repair a broken path, but in doing so it may use a non-optimal path toward the destination. After IGP converges over the new topology, the router updates primary paths toward impacted destination prefixes, recalculates backup paths, and, if SR-TE is used, re-optimizes the SR policy path.

TI-LFA is effective in reacting to local adjacency failures and, if enabled on all nodes in the network, delivers a reliable rapid restoration method. Nevertheless, link failures or sometimes even link-up events might cause short-lived or *transient loops* in the network. As shown in Figure 6-17, a new link between nodes F and H comes up with a metric of 5 and node B's IGP receives and processes the topology change information before node D does. Due to the high metric between nodes G and I, node D might still consider B as a best next hop to reach K. Yet, node B already knows that the best path to K is via D, F, H, and J. This results in a microloop between B and D for a short period of time.

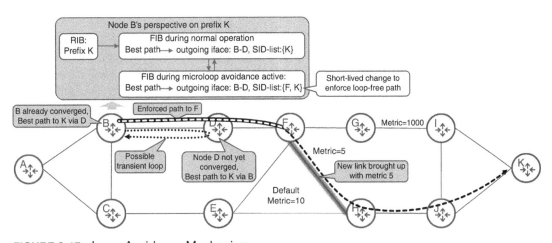

FIGURE 6-17 Loop-Avoidance Mechanism

The mechanism to avoid transient loops is proposed in the IETF draft *Loop Avoidance Using Segment Routing* and is already implemented as the SR *microloop avoidance* feature by multiple vendors.[39] Using the example from Figure 6-17, the loop-avoidance mechanism alters node B's behavior. In order to avoid packets from looping between B and D, node B enforces traffic to be safely delivered to node F, by pushing Prefix-SID of F on top of the packet, justifiably assuming F's IGP has already converged. This enforced path remains in effect for a preconfigurable duration and then removed from the FIB, reverting back to normal forwarding.

The loop-avoidance mechanism is triggered by IGP upon receiving remote or direct link-down or -up events and uses a timer-based approach to keep loop-mitigating path enforcement in place. This mechanism is not intended to replace TI-LFA but rather complement it.

Segment Routing for IPv6 (SRv6)

Although current deployments of Segment Routing are predominantly SR-MPLS, where labels are used as a representation of SIDs, an alternate approach is starting to emerge for IPv6-enabled networks. Instead of relying on the MPLS forwarding plane, Segment Routing can use the IPv6 forwarding plane almost natively, thanks to IPv6's enormous address space and extensible headers. Technically speaking, source routing capabilities were part of the IPv6 standard a long time before Segment Routing was introduced. Extension headers could include the routing header, which lists a set of IPv6 addresses for a packet to visit. What is different in *Segment Routing v6 (SRv6)*, however, is how IPv6 addresses are used both in the destination address of an SRv6 packet and in the routing extension header. This section expands on the SRv6 implementation in an IPv6 network.

IPv6 Adoption and Challenges

SRv6 requires an IPv6 forwarding plane, be it dual-stack (IPv4 and IPv6) or native IPv6 network. Although the promise of transitioning the networking world from IPv4 toward a future-proof IPv6 address space remains unfulfilled after more than two decades, the strides to get broader IPv6 adoption have resulted in more than 35% of users accessing the Internet using IPv6 natively today.[40] Significant challenges, such as a lack of capable customer premises equipment (CPE) to support IPv6, complex migration paths, massive software and hardware upgrades, and outright inertia, to name a few, have slowed down this trend over the preceding years. In the wake of these challenges, innovative mechanisms, such as *Carrier-Grade Network Address Translation (CGNAT)*, allowed many service providers to stay in the IPv4 comfort zone. Some say that IPv6 lacks a *killer application* to push for a fast transition and, although debatable, there is a possibility that by selecting SRv6 as one of the 5G technology enablers, the O-RAN Alliance might have just made SRv6 a killer app for the industry's transition to IPv6.

Segment Information as IPv6 Address

The fundamentals of Segment Routing implementation for the IPv6 network (SRv6) do not differ from SR-MPLS (that is, the concept of segments, the use of SIDs, and the use of IGP by the control plane to propagate SID information across the network). Instead of using MPLS labels as SIDs, as was done for IPv4 networks, SRv6 repurposes the 128-bit *Destination Address (DA)* field in the IPv6 header.

Just like in SR-MPLS, the SRv6 SID identifies an instruction on a particular node. For SRv6, this instruction is advertised as a single 128-bit value that can be logically split into two parts. The first group of bits, called *Locator,* uniquely identifies the node, while the remaining bits, called *Function,* are used to define special traffic treatment upon reaching the node. Depending on the *Function*, the SID can represent a Node-SID, Adjacency-SID, or other types of SIDs. Thus, the *Functions* here are analogous to SID types in SR-MPLS. A node may define multiple such SID values, each with a different Function. Figure 6-18 shows the use of the DA field in an IPv6 header for an SRv6 SID.

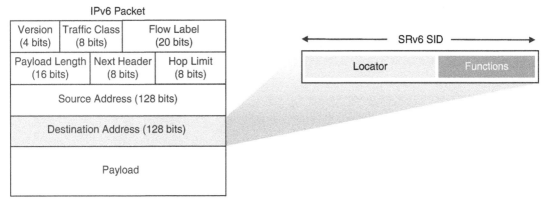

FIGURE 6-18   Repurposing IPv6 Header's DA for SRv6 SID

These SIDs can then be advertised to the IPv6 network using newly defined IGP TLVs for SRv6.[41] The SRv6-capable routers in the network will interpret the TLVs and build their information table for advertised SIDs, while installing the appropriate entries in their forwarding table. Additionally, the Locator portion of the SIDs is advertised as an IPv6 prefix. It allows for any non-SRv6-capable router in the network to learn the Locator like any other IPv6 prefix, while ignoring the SRv6 TLVs. The SRv6-capable routers can now send traffic toward any of these SIDs by simply using that SID as a destination address in the IPv6 packet, letting the packet take the best IGP path. This simple idea of using IPv6 predefined fields was further extended for SR-TE capability in SRv6. The SID list is computed using the constraint-based SPF calculations (just like in case of SR-MPLS), either locally at the headend router or by the PCE. This SID-list is then embedded into the IPv6 Header. If this list comprises more than one SID, then a newly defined IPv6 routing extension header called *Segment Routing Header (SRH)* is used to embed this list into the IPv6 header.[42] The SRH uses a predefined option in IPv6 to add a header field called *routing header*. The type field of the routing header is set to type 4, indicating the header will be used for SIDs. SRH then stores the SID-list in the type-specific data field of the routing header.

IPv6 Extension Headers

The IPv6 standard allows the use of optional extension headers, and the Next-Header field in the IPv6 header can identify the presence and type of the extension header included. One of these extension headers is the Routing-Header (RH), identified by Next-Header Type 43. The Routing-Header itself can include routing information in its data field and uses the Routing-Type field to classify it. SRv6 specifications have defined Routing-Header Route-Type-4 to carry SID information in the RH.

The first SID from the list is also copied to the DA field of the IPv6 header, and standard IPv6 routing and forwarding take care of the rest. That destination router recognizes the presence of SRH, copies over the next SID from the SRH as a new destination address, and decrements the Segments-Left field in the SRH. It then proceeds to forward the packet to the new destination. The process will be repeated, until the Segments-Left counts down to 0, at which point the SRH is removed and the last SID is copied over to the DA. This process is called *Penultimate Segment Pop (PSP)*. The packet then gets routed toward the DA, which was effectively the last SID in the list. This results in the flow of data through the exact engineered path that was determined at the headend node. Figure 6-19 shows this process as the packet traverses the network.

Despite its simplicity, the use of SRH for SR-TE experienced some headwinds for real-world implementations. The SRH with the list of 128-bit SIDs bloats up the IPv6 header, thus adding significant overhead. Additionally, the imposition of this stack at the headend and the processing of it at the intermediate nodes are resource heavy for the forwarding CPU. More recently, to overcome and avoid these potential inefficiencies, a few new approaches have been proposed. These ideas revolve around recognizing that using the entire 128-bit space is overkill for a single SID value and instead suggest using shorter SID values. This offers more efficient use of the IPv6 header space, and either significantly reduces the need for SRH or makes SRH compact. With these implementations, the SRv6 routers will now need to use special manipulation on the DA field, instead of replacing it with a new SID from the list. There are multiple competing IETF drafts that are currently under discussion and making their way through the standardization process. Two current front-runners that suggest shorter SRv6 SIDs are *SRv6 micro-segment (uSID)* and *Segment Routing Mapped to IPv6 (SRm6)*.[43,44]

Segment Instructions in SRv6

As mentioned earlier, an SRv6 SID consists of a locator and a function. Each of these functions defines a certain instruction to be executed upon reaching the Locator node. These instructions are called *behaviors* in SRv6 specification, and an SRv6-capable node should support some, if not all, of these. This section details some of the primary *behaviors* performed by the SRv6 forwarding plane.

Headend Encapsulation (*H.Encaps*) is a behavior implemented by SRv6 headend when it steers a packet into SRv6 policy. This behavior can be compared to an MPLS label push operation, when a stack of labels expressing a SID-list is added on top of the packet. Instead of a label stack, SRv6 pushes another IPv6 header and installs SRv6 SID into the Destination Address (DA) field of the packet. In its current implementation, when the SRv6 SID-list contains more than one SID, an SRH is added to the packet. H.Encaps can be optimized by one of the emerging SRv6 drafts discussed earlier.

The same behavior can be applied to L2 frames, for example, while using L2VPN service, in which case it is called *H.Encaps.L2*. The entire frame can be encapsulated into an IPv6 packet following the same logic, by putting the SRv6 SID into the DA field and the possible addition of SRH.

H.Encaps.Red and *H.Encaps.L2.Red* are flavors of H.Encaps and H.Encaps.L2, respectively, with a simple difference: these behaviors do not include the first SRv6 SID, already installed in the DA field, in their SRH. This reduces the SRH size and hence the name of the behavior.

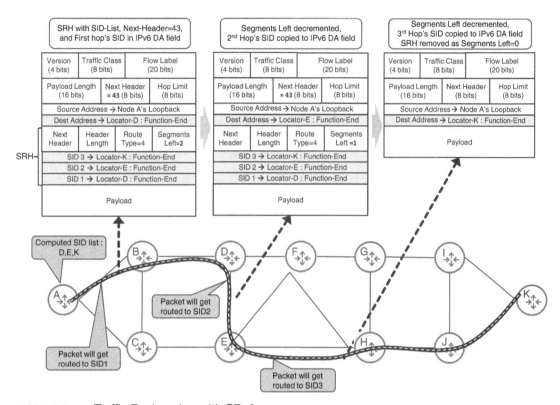

FIGURE 6-19   Traffic Engineering with SRv6

The MPLS label-swap operation equivalent is not specifically called out in the standard. For any *non-end-of-segment* node, it is simply usual forwarding operation based on the DA field. Interestingly enough, this means that any IPv6-enabled router can forward SRv6 packets, even if it does not explicitly support SRv6. Of course, such a router cannot be an SRv6 headend or endpoint or otherwise act as an end-of-segment node.

The *End* behavior in SRv6 can be mapped to the MPLS label pop operation, whereupon reaching the end of the segment, the active SID should be removed from the packet. The SRv6 endpoint implements this operation by replacing the SRv6 in the DA field by the next SID from the SRH. When there is no SRH or no active segment in the SRH, the endpoint should pop the current IPv6 header and start processing the next header. The basic End behavior in SRv6 can be seen as an equivalent of a Prefix-SID. Besides this basic End behavior, there are many other, more specialized flavors of the End behavior defined in the standard to implement a rich set of instructions supported by SRv6, a few of which are covered in this section.

End.X behavior is a flavor of End SRv6 behavior. The X in its name stands for the L3 Cross-Connect action, and this behavior is an equivalent of an Adjacency-SID in SR-MPLS. Besides replacing the

DA field in the SRv6 packet, or removing the header and SRH altogether, the SRv6 node forwards the packet over a specific L3 adjacency, without any further processing or lookups.

End.DX4 and *End.DX6* behaviors instruct a router to decapsulate a packet and cross-connect it with IPv4 or IPv6 adjacency, respectively. It pops the IPv6 header and exposes the underlying IPv4 or IPv6 packet, which is then forwarded over a specific IPv4 or IPv6 adjacency without additional lookup. These behaviors can be considered as an equivalent of a *per-CE L3VPN* label paired with a transport label for the advertising PE. Indeed, the locator part of the SRv6 SID helps to bring the packet to the correct PE, while the function part of the SRv6 SID identifies which VRF to use.

End.DT4 and *End.DT6* behaviors are very similar to the previously described End.DX4 and End.DX6, with one significant difference. These behaviors instruct the router to execute a lookup on the exposed packet in the appropriate table. The direct equivalent of using these behaviors would be L3VPN with *per-VRF* label allocation.

End.DX2 is another flavor of an End behavior, applicable to L2 Ethernet frames. The End.DX2 behavior is typically associated with L2VPN or EVPN services, but otherwise works similarly to the End.DX4 and End.DX6 behaviors.

> **Note**
>
> End behaviors, like other SRv6 components, may evolve with the development of existing and new SRv6 specifications.

Many other types of End behaviors are already defined in the IETF "Segment Routing over IPv6 (SRv6) Network Programming" standard; however, this list is likely to grow over time.[45]

Implementing Services with SRv6

A few characteristic features of SRv6 make it an attractive option for network architects. First off, it is ultra-scalable. With 128 bits available for SRv6 locators and functions, it is hard to imagine a network exhausting this enormous space. SRv6 can easily support a typical MCN deployment with its vast number of cell site routers and numerous domains, without the need of a Seamless-MPLS-type workaround.

Secondly, SRv6 runs natively on the IPv6 forwarding plane and can even leverage non-SRv6 routers running vanilla IPv6 along the path of an SRv6 policy. For an IPv6-enabled network, the use of SRv6 may eliminate the need to keep special MPLS tables, freeing up NPU's precious on-die memory resources. The ability to incorporate information about the VPN itself and reachability to the PE in a single SRv6 SID provides an efficient way to deploy services with SRv6. The same functionality requires multiple labels in an SR-MPLS environment.

While SRv6 is starting to gain popularity, it should not be a surprise that at the time of this writing, SR-MPLS is the technology of choice for Segment Routing deployments. The transition from MPLS-LDP to SR-MPLS is greatly facilitated by the ability of SR-MPLS to run in parallel with existing label distribution protocols. SRv6, on the other hand, requires end-to-end IPv6, yet the level of IPv6 adoption in today's networks falls behind the ubiquitous MPLS in the SP and enterprise world. Nevertheless, SRv6 is considered a pathway forward in mobile communication networks, whereas SR-MPLS is here today.

Summary

This chapter took a deep dive into the fundamentals of Segment Routing, an emerging transport network technology that is fast becoming a de facto standard for any 5G-ready mobile transport network.

This chapter discussed the following topics:

- Evolution of the MPLS-based networks through the use of purpose-built protocols and resulting operational complexities

- Fundamentals of Segment Routing and various types of segment IDs

- Segment Routing Traffic Engineering and its role in programming a traffic path through the network using Constraint-based Shortest Path First algorithms

- Mechanisms of traffic steering into SR policies

- Building blocks of a software-defined transport

- Use of PCE as a transport SDN controller and its interaction with the network and higher-layer applications

- 5G transport network slicing with SR Flexible Algorithms

- Rapid restoration and loop-avoidance mechanisms used by Segment Routing

- An introduction to Segment Routing on the IPv6 network (SRv6)

Chapter 7, "Essential Technologies for 5G-Ready Networks: DC Architecture and Edge Computing," will focus on data centers, which is another critical technology to build 5G networks. The chapter will discuss design principles of these DCs and their integration with SR-enabled xHaul networks.

References

1. "World's Largest LTE Deployment—Reliance JIO India," https://www.ciscolive.com/c/dam/r/ciscolive/us/docs/2017/pdf/CCSSPM-1004.pdf, slide 20 (last visited: July 2021)

2. IETF RFC 8402, "Segment Routing Architecture"

3. Ibid.

4. Ibid.

5. IETF RFC 8986. "Segment Routing over IPv6 (SRv6) Network Programming"

6. IETF RFC 8402, op. cit.

7. IETF RFC 8669, "Segment Routing Prefix Segment Identifier Extensions for BGP"

8. "BGP-LS Extensions for Segment Routing BGP Egress Peer Engineering" (IETF draft), https://datatracker.ietf.org/doc/html/draft-ietf-idr-bgpls-segment-routing-epe-19 (last visited: July 2021)

9. IETF RFC 8402, op. cit.

10. IETF RFC 8667, "IS-IS Extensions for Segment Routing"

11. IETF RFC 8665, "OSPF Extensions for Segment Routing"

12. IETF RFC 8666, "OSPFv3 Extensions for Segment Routing"

13. IETF RFC 8669, op. cit.

14. IETF RFC 3209, "RSVP-TE: Extensions to RSVP for LSP Tunnels"

15. "Segment Routing Policy Architecture" (IETF draft), https://datatracker.ietf.org/doc/html/draft-ietf-spring-segment-routing-policy (last visited: Mar 2022)

16. Ibid.

17. Ibid.

18. "Advertising Segment Routing Policies in BGP" (IETF draft), https://datatracker.ietf.org/doc/html/draft-ietf-idr-segment-routing-te-policy/

19. Ibid.

20. IETF RFC 4655, "A Path Computation Element (PCE)-Based Architecture"

21. RFC 5440, "Path Computation Element (PCE) Communication Protocol (PCEP)"

22. IETF RFC 7752, "North-Bound Distribution of Link-State and Traffic Engineering (TE) Information Using BGP"

23. RFC 5440, op. cit.

24. "Advertising Segment Routing Policies in BGP," op. cit.

25. "Northstar Controller," https://www.juniper.net/content/dam/www/assets/datasheets/us/en/network-automation/northstar-controller.pdf

26. https://www.cisco.com/c/en/us/td/docs/cloud-systems-management/crosswork-infrastructure/4-0/InstallGuide/b_cisco_crosswork_platform_40_and_applications_install_guide/m_overview.html (last visited: Feb 2022)

27. 3GPP TS 28.530 version 15.0.0, Release 15, "5G; Management and orchestration; Concepts, use cases and requirements," https://www.3gpp.org/

28. O-RAN xHaul Packet Switched Architectures and Solutions, https://www.o-ran.org/specifications

29. Ibid.

30. "IGP Flexible Algorithm" (IETF draft), https://datatracker.ietf.org/doc/html/draft-ietf-lsr-flex-algo (last visited: Feb 2022)

31. IETF RFC 8570, "IS-IS Traffic Engineering (TE) Metric Extensions"

32. IETF RFC 7471, "OSPF Traffic Engineering (TE) Metric Extensions"

33. "BGP-LS Advertisement of IGP Traffic Engineering Performance Metric Extensions" (IETF draft), https://datatracker.ietf.org/doc/html/draft-ietf-idr-te-pm-bgp (last visited: Feb 2022)

34. IETF RFC 5357, "A Two-Way Active Measurement Protocol (TWAMP)"

35. IETF RFC 6374, "Packet Loss and Delay Measurement for MPLS Networks"

36. IETF RFC 4090, "Fast Reroute Extensions to RSVP-TE for LSP Tunnels"

37. IETF RFC 5286, "Basic Specification for IP Fast Reroute: Loop-Free Alternates"

38. "Topology Independent Fast Reroute Using Segment Routing" (IETF draft), https://datatracker.ietf.org/doc/html/draft-ietf-rtgwg-segment-routing-ti-lfa (last visited: Feb 2022)

39. "Loop Avoidance Using Segment Routing" (IEFT draft), https://datatracker.ietf.org/doc/html/draft-bashandy-rtgwg-segment-routing-uloop/ (last visited: Feb 2022)

40. IPv6 usage statistics, https://www.google.com/intl/en/ipv6/statistics.html

41. "IS-IS Extensions to Support Segment Routing over IPv6 Dataplane," (IEFT draft), https://datatracker.ietf.org/doc/html/draft-ietf-lsr-isis-srv6-extensions (last visited: Feb 2022)

42. REF2: IETF RFC8754, "IPv6 Segment Routing Header (SRH)"

43. "Network Programming extension: SRv6 uSID instruction" (IETF draft), https://datatracker.ietf.org/doc/draft-filsfils-spring-net-pgm-extension-srv6-usid (last visited: Feb 2022)

44. "Segment Routing Mapped to IPv6 (SRm6)" (IETF draft), https://datatracker.ietf.org/doc/html/draft-bonica-spring-sr-mapped-six (last visited: Feb 2022)

45. Ibid.

Chapter | **7**

Essential Technologies for 5G-Ready Networks: DC Architecture and Edge Computing

As alluded to throughout the book thus far, data centers (DCs) play an important role in hosting critical applications and components that enable full-stack services for mobile subscribers. Historically, DCs have included packet core components, management functions, authentication, and authorization tools, as well as security apparatus such as firewalls. Until recently, network architectures were developed to administer these functions from a few central locations, dubbed the *main DC* or *central DC*. However, the evolving service requirements as well as the mobile core and radio access network (RAN) decomposition have led to distribution of these data centers throughout the network. In this distributed DC model, the transport becomes more intertwined with the DC infrastructure, and thus any transport network design must consider DC placement and integration. The technologies discussed in this chapter will cover DC architectural evolution as well as provide foundational knowledge for implementing and integrating DCs in a 5G-ready mobile communication network (MCN).

Data Center Basics

Modern-day DCs find their roots in mainframe or server rooms, where the equipment necessary for continued system operation would be located. In hindsight, earlier mobile telephone exchanges that housed the equipment and databases required to register mobile subscribers and process mobile calls could be considered a DC for mobile networks of that time. Oftentimes, data was not a primary resource in these locations but rather a peripheral asset used by the equipment placed there. As the networks and systems grew, these specialized locations sometimes spanned the whole floor or even multiple building floors. These locations also required special considerations such as rows of racks to mount various equipment, raised floors, ceiling-mounted cable runners, and ample cooling capabilities. While present in virtually every service provider network, it was not until the late 1990s and early 2000s when the need for storing enormous amounts of user data was realized by the large DCs as we know them today.

Rise of Large-Scale Data Centers

DCs are a mainstay of any service provider network, acting as a data and application repository. Originally starting off as locations to store giant mainframes, big computer systems, and relevant data storage devices such as tape drives, the data centers of today have gone beyond the confines of a single floor or a building and instead cover hundreds of thousands of square feet of land.[1] A large-scale DC might house hundreds of thousands of devices, providing not only data storage but also computation power for applications, data processing, management, and analysis. Across all of its DC locations, a large service provider's network may easily contain north of a million devices, and these numbers continue to grow.[2]

The growth in the size and relevance of DCs was driven by the introduction and mass adoption of the Internet. Collectively, these DCs have to store unfathomable amounts of World Wide Web data as well as provide services to billions of Internet subscribers around the globe. Digitizing of everyday tasks, such as Internet banking, e-commerce, and navigation, as well as over-the-top (OTT) services like music and video streaming, created a need for larger, more extensible data centers, which was further fueled by the growing mobile communications industry. In the early 2000s, prompted by the continual growth of DCs, the *Telecommunications Industry Association (TIA)*, in collaboration with the *American National Standards Institute (ANSI)*, published the ANSI/TIA-942 specification to identify guidelines for DC planning and classification. ANSI/TIA-942 defines four different tiers of DCs, starting from Tier 1, which is a simple, basic DC with no redundancy, all the way to Tier 4, which includes super-scaled large DCs with layers of built-in redundancy and high availability, including geo-redundancy. ANSI/TIA-942 also defines guidelines for physical layout, site space specifications, cabling infrastructure, rack sizes, physical entry/exit locations, as well as environmental consideration within the DC.[3]

The growing need for DCs also spurred different business models, such as on-premises (on-prem) DCs, co-location DCs or co-location racks, managed hosting services, and, more recently, public cloud. As the name suggests, an on-prem DC is located on the premises of, and wholly owned and operated by, the business entity requiring services from it. For larger DCs, this model may represent a steep upfront cost, deep DC technology expertise, as well as ongoing maintenance and upgrade expenses. The use of on-prem DCs for services offers the highest level of flexibility and customization, albeit at a higher cost compared to the other models. This is by far the most deployed model today and accounts for approximately 55% of all application workloads across all DC deployment models.[4]

Public cloud is the other end of the spectrum, where a *cloud service provider* offers general-purpose data center infrastructure for businesses to deploy their application workloads. Cloud-based DCs offer significantly lower startup costs, with the flexibility to scale up or scale down resource usage, as required. Although public clouds are geared toward generic applications meant to be run on commercially available servers, specialized applications requiring custom hardware (such as some Mobile Core and RAN components) are increasingly being rearchitected to make them "cloud friendly." Today, public cloud–based DCs account for just under a quarter of all application workloads but are expected to grow significantly, mostly at the expense of on-prem DCs.

Co-location and managed hosting make up the rest of the data center deployment models. When using a co-location DC or co-location rack model, a company could rent the whole data center or a few racks from the co-location service provider. In this case, multiple companies may have DC equipment co-located in a single location, hence the name. Co-location allows smaller enterprises to reduce their real estate CAPEX by renting the required space instead of building their own DC. However, only the facility (location, power, peering points) is provided by the co-location provider, while the equipment, its installation, and maintenance remain the responsibility of the company planning to use the DC, resulting in higher startup costs when compared to a managed hosting or public cloud model.

In a managed hosting option, an enterprise customer rents not only the DC space but also the equipment, such as servers and storage. These servers are installed and maintained by the managed hosting provider but are dedicated to the customer whose applications are being hosted on them. In some cases, service providers use their own on-prem DCs to provide managed hosting services.[5] In some ways, managed hosting is similar to public cloud, but it acts like an *off-prem* DC in the sense that the data center requirements are more customized than in a public cloud. This allows a lot more specialized applications to run in a managed hosting environment; however, the capability gap between the public cloud and managed hosting models is quickly narrowing. At the time of this writing, managed hosting and co-location collectively account for less than a quarter of all application workloads and are expected to lose market share to more flexible and cheaper public cloud–based options.[6]

Regardless of the size or deployment model used, the building blocks of an effective, efficient, and extensible DC have remained the same and are discussed in the next section.

Building Blocks of a Data Center Fabric

The term *data center fabric* is commonly used today to collectively refer to compute and storage equipment, as well as the transport network that efficiently interconnects them. The networking between these devices is expected to provide full connectivity with high bandwidth while minimizing the number of connections and maximizing availability in case of any link or network device failure. The simplest way to achieve such inter-device connectivity would be to use full-mesh connectivity, with every device talking to every other device. Such a mesh network, however, is challenging to implement due to the high number of interfaces needed. Also, it would not be efficient in maximizing link utilization and would potentially result in a large number of idle or under-utilized links.

Instead, large-scale DCs today use a design conceived many decades ago called the *Clos architecture* to implement their networks. The design is named after its inventor, Charles Clos, who published a design in 1953 comparing different hierarchical switching stages and their advantage over fully meshed connectivity.[7] Even though this was initially proposed as a solution for telephone exchanges, the idea is very much applicable and used for designing networks in a modern DC. This simple idea describes a hierarchy (called *stages*) of switching devices, with the devices in the first or last stage representing the input or output into the Clos-based network, whereas the devices in each intermediate stage connect only to the devices in the next or preceding stage.

This DC architecture is also called a *fat-tree* design, because the number of subsequent stages typically has fewer switching devices, with a fatter yet lower number of downlinks. Consequently, the switching devices at the periphery of this network are commonly called *leaf* nodes, while the subsequent layers are commonly referred to as *spine* and *super-spine* nodes. As this design can be visualized through the analogy of threaded fabric being stretched, the resulting network of these spines and leaves is commonly referred to as a *Clos fabric*. Figure 7-1 illustrates how these spine and leaf nodes collectively form the fabric. As shown in the figure, the number of stages can vary depending on the data center requirements. Network architects can easily spot the similarities between this architecture and the traditional access-aggregation-core architecture that is commonly used in IP transport networks. Leaf nodes can be compared to the access routers, the spines are the equivalent of the aggregation layer, whereas super-spines are comparable to high-speed core routers.

Spines are typically deployed in multiples of two for a collection of leaf nodes. Depending on the design choices, the spines may or may not have a link between them. The Clos fabric requires only as many uplinks from the leaf nodes as the number of spine nodes to which they are connecting, which due to the fat-tree design, is typically fewer than the number of leaf nodes. These connections are then used as equal-cost links with traffic load-balancing techniques used at higher layers. The path between any two leaf nodes can therefore use all of these equal-cost links, thus equally utilizing them for the inter-device traffic (also called *east-west traffic* in the DC world). The use of multiple spines, and corresponding spine-leaf links, automatically offers protection against link or device failures. The beauty of this design is not limited to its efficient network utilization and failure resilience, but can also be found in its simplicity and extensibility by replicating for scale. Additionally, Clos fabric provides predictable latency between all pairs of connected hosts, making it a highly suitable and reliable choice for the DC fabric.

Although the east-west traffic, which essentially is the traffic within the DC fabric, is expected to be the dominant traffic, the DC devices do need to communicate with the outside world as well. The devices or routers implementing this external connectivity are called *Data Center Interconnect (DCI)*, and the traffic through them is colloquially referred to as *north-south traffic*. DCI is further discussed later in this chapter.

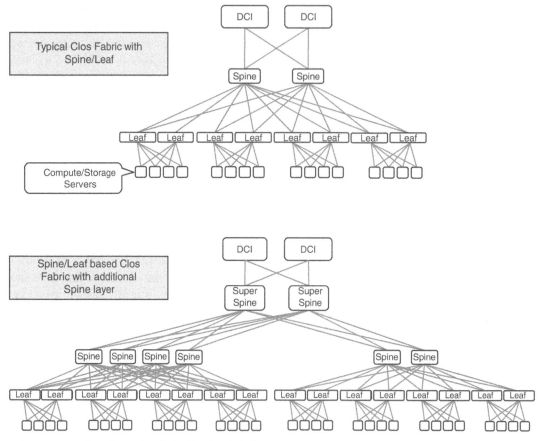

FIGURE 7-1   Overview of a Data Center Fabric

The DCs of today use the spine-leaf architecture irrespective of their physical scale and size. In a typical large DC, a pair of leaf nodes is connected to servers within each rack—thus giving rise to the term *top of rack (ToR) devices* for referring to the leaf nodes. Rows of these racks can be served by a pair of spine nodes. These spine nodes, in turn, can connect to the DCI for facilitating the outside world connectivity, as Figure 7-2 illustrates.

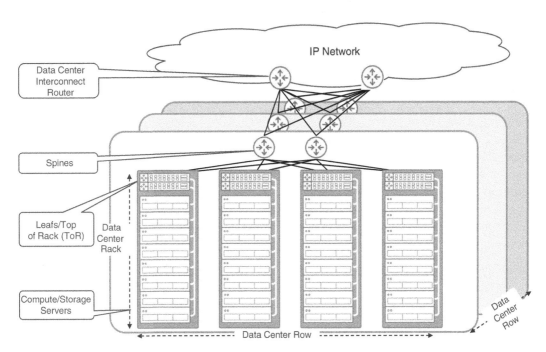

FIGURE 7-2 Typical Data Center Layout

Considerations for Space, Power, and Cooling

Typically, network architects focus on technical aspects of a design, such as feature capability, scalability, redundancy, extensibility, and so on, whereas nontechnical considerations like space, physical layout, power, and cooling often take a backseat and are left for the consideration of the deployment teams. Given the increase in the size of DCs and with the tens of thousands of devices deployed in each one of them, these considerations have moved to the forefront of deployment and operational concerns. From a business standpoint, while the DC *must* be able to fulfill all the service requirements, it must also perform these functions while minimizing the overall costs—both capital and operational.

Real estate availability at a reasonable cost is one of the key factors for any operator in deciding where to place its large DCs. Driven by the number of racks and devices required to fulfill service requirements, the provider must ensure ample physical space is available to house current and forecasted devices. Selecting a suitable facility, which can sometimes span hundreds of acres for large cloud DCs such as the ones built by Microsoft, Google, and Amazon, is the first step toward building a viable DC infrastructure. There might not always be vast open spaces, however, at least not in the desired location. In those cases, DCs use alternate approaches such as vertical expansion (across multiple floors in a building) instead of horizontal buildouts. This is especially true when DCs need to be placed in proximity to their users or essential utilities in densely populated cities such as New York, Tokyo, Hong Kong, and other similar places. In these cases, consideration of additional structural and cabling requirements across different floors comes into play. The placement of DCs in more urban locations becomes especially important with the growth in mobile services and multi-access edge computing, where mobile functions must be hosted closer to the end subscriber. Both the horizontally and vertically scaled DCs are an essential part of today's networking infrastructure, which deliver services essential for running an end-to-end network.

Whether it is a large or small DC, power consumption is another key consideration when planning a data center. The total power requirements for any DC is a combination of the power consumed by equipment contained in the DC and the power required to maintain the cooling and other auxiliary systems to ensure a viable operating environment across the facility. Over the past several years, telecom and networking equipment manufacturers have focused on reducing power consumption by their devices while increasing features and functionality. In fact, environment friendly products using reduced power while providing equal or highest functionality are routinely featured as a value-added differentiation by major networking equipment providers.

Aside from the power required to run the devices in the DC, additional power is required to provide cooling in the facility itself. DC owners use a metric called *Power Usage Effectiveness (PUE)* to measure the effectiveness of power used in a given DC. PUE is defined as a ratio between the energy required to turn on all devices in the data center and the total power used in said data center. The goal is to use as much power as possible toward the IT equipment and lower the cooling system's power consumption, thus providing a better PUE value. In order to achieve the best PUE and to lower the cooling and heating costs, DC owners are experimenting with new and innovative approaches. Some of these techniques include using reusable and geothermal power sources wherever feasible and even placing DC modules underwater.[8] Placing technical equipment in a fully submersible environment presents its own set of challenges, but with the help of new, cutting-edge technology, innovators and early adopters are continually pushing the envelope to create more energy-efficient data centers. In addition to power consumption, the availability of uninterrupted power brings another aspect of considerations. Besides relying on multiple feeds from the power grid for redundancy, additional backup power sources such as generator and battery backup are also used in all DCs.

For optimal DC planning, more logistical considerations need to be taken into account, such as terrain, risk of natural disasters, temperate weather conditions, and so on. Even though these are important considerations, going into a detailed analysis of these factors digresses from the technical focus of this book. Entire books are dedicated to the cost modeling of DCs and could be used to learn more about the nontechnical aspects of a DC, such as site selection, layout planning, and buildout.[9] This section aims to introduce network architects to the challenges of a DC site selection that otherwise might not be apparent when using a technical-only point of view. With the growing number of DCs in 5G networks, courtesy of packet core and RAN decomposition, site selection as well as heating and cooling of these DCs have become important operational considerations. At the same time, given the rise of cloud-based services, mobile service providers are increasingly opting to minimize the startup cost and are outsourcing the complexities of maintaining and managing DCs to cloud service providers wherever possible, as discussed in the next section.

From Centralized to Distributed to Cloud Data Centers

Like other technologies, the type and nature of DCs in MCNs have evolved significantly over the generations. Even though these DCs have continued to be based on Clos architecture, their scale, capacity, size, and network positioning have evolved. The bulk of that evolution has taken place in the post-3G era, with the advent of *Network Functions Virtualization (NFV)* technologies in 4G as well as the use of Control and User Plane Separation (CUPS) and decomposed RAN in 5G. As explained in the earlier chapters, 5G's transport network is expected to include multiple DCs of varying size across the entire xHaul and IP core. This section will go over the transition of data center implementations across mobile generations.

Centralized DC in Mobile Networks

The DCs in earlier mobile networks were typically co-located with, or even replaced, the equipment located in the switching centers. These were, therefore, owned and operated by the mobile service provider. It was also no surprise that these DCs, which were few in count, were concentrated into a handful of quasi-centralized locations. The centralized locations, called *telco data centers*, had the inherent disadvantage of impacting a significant number of subscribers in cases of natural disasters or the malfunctioning of the hosted devices.

As previously explained, the user's voice and data traffic as well as the mobile network's signaling traffic had to travel to one of these central DC locations before it could be switched or routed to its destination. Not only did the use of centralized DCs burden the entire transport network with this traffic volume but also added undesirable latency to it. Continued growth in mobile traffic makes this situation worse, forcing the mobile provider to upgrade the transport bandwidth. These DCs were also constrained by the space, power, and cooling capacity available in the centralized locations. On the other hand, a smaller number of locations meant that maintenance and truck-roll activities were easier to perform.

At the time of initial 4G MCN implementations, the centralized telco DCs were the only locations where mobile functions such as mobile core devices, Internet peering points, and voice gateway connectivity were hosted. Initially the mobile devices in these DCs were the purpose-built vendor equipment; however, with the popular use of NFV resulting in vEPC, these telco DCs provided connectivity and hosting of VNF running over COTS servers. This helped with the cost and real estate utilization but created the additional burden of orchestrating the virtual functions through use of tools such as OpenStack. Also, the use of NFV didn't resolve the challenge of the consumer traffic needlessly traversing the entire mobile transport in the centralized data center model.

Distributed DC in Mobile Networks

The move toward Centralized RAN, during the 4G timeframe, was the first step toward the use of smaller, distributed data centers in a mobile network, which were used to host the physical or virtual BBUs. 5G's implementation of CUPS, as well as a decomposed RAN architecture with BBU split into DU and CU, led to the use of additional data centers in the mobile transport. These distributed DCs, already introduced in an earlier chapter as *edge* and *far-edge DCs*, are much higher in number and significantly smaller in size compared to the main telco DC. A far-edge DC, in some cases, might be very lean and just be composed of servers directly connected to the transport network nodes.

The mobile providers transitioning from 4G to 5G are looking to implement distributed data centers in their existing mobile transport network. In a lot of cases, they address the issue of overloading the transport network with mobile traffic by offloading or processing it closer to the subscriber locations when possible, helping realize 5G's goal of Enhanced Mobile Broadband (eMBB) and Ultra-Reliable Low-Latency Communications (uRLLC) services. The equipment hosted within these distributed DCs is still expected to be COTS servers running VNFs performing the needed mobile core, edge compute, and RAN functions. Thus, the VNF management and orchestration functions now need to take into account the distributed nature of the DCs.

These distributed DCs are still expected to be designed and implemented by the mobile service provider; hence, the architectural complexity of interconnecting and integrating them into the transport network lies squarely with that provider. Further, because the distributed DCs are owned, operated, and managed by the mobile provider, their distributed nature makes them a few notches harder than managing a centralized DC. Repurposing an existing macrocell site as a far-edge or edge DC in a decomposed RAN deployment is an example of distributed DCs in an MCN. These cell sites are often leased from a cell tower provider, however, making these far-edge or edge DCs the equivalent of a co-location DC. Distributed DCs are not meant to eliminate the centralized or regional DC locations but rather offload functions and roles away from them.

Cloud DC for Mobile Networks

The concept of large-scale DCs providing cloud-based service offerings has become mainstream within the last decade. Although they were not initially considered an alternative to centralized and distributed DCs, the benefits of such hosting environments were too tempting to overlook. Public cloud environments offer a high level of availability by spreading out physical deployments across geographies, as well as availability zones within each geographical location. For the mobile service provider, the upfront cost to procure, deploy, and manage the infrastructure is extremely low. The orchestration, management, monitoring, and maintenance are either greatly simplified or mostly offloaded to the public cloud provider.

More recently, some new entrants into the mobile service provider market have started to explore the possibility of using the public cloud infrastructure to host the functions that previously resided across various data centers owned by the providers themselves. The 5GC functions that would normally be hosted in the main DC could now be placed in a few different regions of the cloud provider's network.

A cloud-based DC can also be used for hosting the functions that would normally be hosted on an edge DC, such as User Plane Function (UPF), Open Central Unit (O-CU), or Multi-access Edge Compute (MEC). This could be achieved by establishing a direct peering between the mobile transport network and the cloud provider, or by extending the cloud provider's infrastructure into the mobile provider's data centers. This makes it possible to meet the distance and latency requirements of the edge DC–hosted functions while still offering the benefits of public cloud. In both cases, the mobile provider doesn't need to separately implement Internet peering points (typically done at edge DC locations), as this, too, will be taken care of by the cloud service provider. An example of such as a service is *Amazon Web Services (AWS) Wavelength* offering.[10]

The RAN components hosted at the far-edge DC (that is, the DUs) are the most latency-demanding and distance-limited, which makes it harder to implement them in a public cloud. The anticipated large number of such far-edge DCs in a 5G network, their small size, and their need for proximity to cell sites, makes it less feasible for the cloud provider to extend its hosting services to the far-edge sites. However, cloud providers offer services where their management and orchestration framework can be extended to such far-edge locations, while the physical infrastructure deployed is owned by the mobile provider. This creates a hybrid cloud environment, and the use of common orchestration and management across different types of DCs (far edge, edge, main) makes this an attractive option to mobile service providers. *AWS Outposts, Google Anthos,* and Microsoft's *Azure Stack* are examples of such an offering by cloud providers.[11, 12]

One of the advantages of using cloud hosting for mobile services is the offloading of the DC network planning and design as well as the hosting environment to the cloud service provider. Cloud hosting of mobile functions is still in its early stages. One would assume that most industry incumbents would gravitate toward a fully owned distributed DC approach (that is, private cloud) as they can leverage their existing transport infrastructure; however, the public-cloud-based approach, with its simplicity and low initial investment, makes it an attractive alternative for new and existing mobile service providers. A combination of both of these approaches is likely to be deployed, where some of the DCs are moved to a public cloud infrastructure while other DCs continue to be privately owned and managed by the mobile provider.

Figure 7-3 provides a comparison view of the three approaches described in this section. Note that while the figure shows only fronthaul for the cloud DC implementation, it's also possible that the DU and RRH are co-located (as would likely be the case with mmWave-based cell sites), resulting in midhaul network peering with the cloud provider network. Similarly, in the case of D-RAN deployment, this could be a backhaul network instead. Chapter 10, "Designing and Implementing 5G Network Architecture," covers these approaches in more detail.

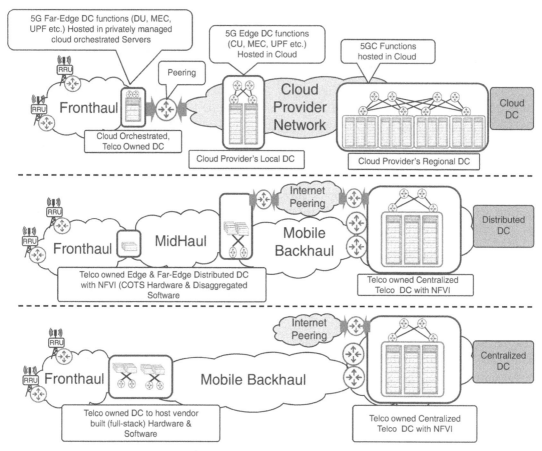

FIGURE 7-3   Centralized, Distributed, and Cloud DC Models

Deploying Data Centers

In its simplest form, a DC is just another network domain that allows hosts and devices contained within it to communicate among themselves as well as with devices and hosts in other domains. Just like transport networks, DC network architecture also grapples with design choices, such as whether to use a Layer 2 or Layer 3 infrastructure and how to accommodate various different traffic flows, among other design considerations. This section provides insight into various connectivity mechanisms inside a DC.

To Route or Not to Route? That Is the Question

Whether to switch Layer 2 (L2) frames or route Layer 3 (L3) packets across a network is a debate as old as the Internet itself. Both approaches have their own benefits and drawbacks; L2 switching is considered to be simpler and faster, while L3 routing provides scalability and feature richness. Ever since the early days of IP networks, L2 switching has been used in access domains and in local area networks (LANs), whereas L3 routing was used extensively in aggregation and core networks. This choice was dictated by many factors, chief among them the cost and technology available at the time. L2 switches tended to be cheaper and were usually a smaller form factor when compared to their L3 routing counterparts. Considering the characteristics of a typical access domain, where the number of devices is many times higher than the rest of the network, both low cost and small form factor are highly regarded characteristics.

A typical DC, however, eclipses the device density of any other network domain, and, as such, cost and overall design simplicity are of paramount importance. Real estate considerations are also a concern in DCs; therefore, the physical dimensions of devices are also taken into account when finalizing what products go into a DC. Given all these factors, early DC implementations used L2 switching to provide networking functions within the DC. This approach led to a lot of benefits, such as simpler setup, a more familiar LAN-like environment, as well as cheaper and cost-effective devices.

As previously discussed in Chapter 3, "Mobile Networks Today," Layer 2 switching is not without its challenges. As the network grows in size, continued operations in a L2 environment become a challenge due to its broadcast nature. Broadcast, unknown unicast, and multicast traffic (collectively called *BUM traffic*) presents a significant concern in larger L2 environments. Even small and medium-sizedDCs, with just a few thousand devices, might start suffering from performance degradation due to potential duplication of such traffic. From a topological standpoint, loops are inevitable in a highly redundant L2 environment such as a Clos-based fabric. Protocols such as Spanning Tree Protocol (STP) and its derivatives are required to combat L2 loops and ensure a loop-free topology. Apart from blocking some links entirely, thus contributing to an overall inefficient network usage, these loop-prevention protocols present their own set of complications—a topic also briefly covered in Chapter 3.

In terms of traffic forwarding in a L2 network, MAC learning also poses a scalability challenge. Because all traffic forwarding decisions are made based on MAC address, every device in the network must learn as many MAC addresses in the network as possible for effective traffic forwarding. Given that a DC can house tens of thousands of servers and possibly multiple hundreds of thousands of hosts, each with one or more MAC addresses, the MAC address–related memory usage on DC networking devices must also be taken into consideration. In a way, this problem is similar to IP routing table scale for routers in large Layer 3 networks, but there is a fundamental difference between how the IP routing table scale is handled. L3 IP routing allows for techniques such as route summarization and dividing the network into multiple areas, thus limiting route exchange between areas; however, these mechanisms are not available in L2 networks where every single MAC address must be learned on all switches. New protocols and technologies such as *provider backbone bridges (PBB)* were developed and later standardized as 802.1ah to handle MAC address scaling in Layer 2 networks. PBB uses the concept of *backbone bridges*, which are L2 devices that aggregate traffic from hosts in the local L2 domain and encapsulates it within another Ethernet header. In PBB, the source and destination MAC addresses of the *outer* header, called the *Backbone Source Address (B-SA)* and *Backbone Destination Address (B-DA)*, respectively, are the only MAC addresses exposed to the rest of the L2 network, instead of MAC addresses of all the hosts connected to the backbone bridge. The original host's MAC addresses are referred to as *Customer Source Address (C-SA)* and *Customer Destination Address (C-DA)* and are only visible in the remote L2 domain, when the traffic is received on the remote backbone bridge, and the outer MAC header is removed. The original L2 traffic with the host's MAC addresses is then sent to its destination. This methodology, often referred to as *MAC-in-MAC*, hides the host MAC addresses from all the intermediary devices and exposes only a handful of backbone MAC addresses on the network, thus allowing MAC address scaling in a large L2 environment. PBB was a novel idea, fashioned after a similar approach called *Q-in-Q* (Q referring to 802.1Q VLAN) used to encapsulate a *customer VLAN (C-VLAN)* within a *service provider VLAN (S-VLAN)* in Metro Ethernet networks. However, while Q-in-Q continued to be a relative success in Carrier Ethernet networks, PBB, while effective in scaling the number of MAC addresses in a given network, proved to be too complicated and was not very successful.

Given the various challenges of operating a large-scale Layer 2 network, particularly with loop avoidance and link utilization, the industry tried to find innovative solutions to retain the simplicity of L2 forwarding but reduce the complexities and nuances presented by the L2 control plane protocols such as STP. One of the proposed solutions was *Transparent Interconnection of Lots of Links (TRILL)*, specified in RFC 6326, which allowed flat Layer 2 networks to be created using IS-IS.[13] Vendors such as Cisco and Brocade implemented their own versions of TRILL to provide efficient L2 forwarding in the DC environment. Cisco's implementation was called *Fabricpath*, which uses IS-IS to propagate Fabricpath-related information, while Brocade's TRILL implementation was called *Virtual Cluster Switching (VCS)*, which also enabled the use of multiple links within a Clos fabric. Yet other networking equipment vendors implemented their own proprietary L2 forwarding mechanisms, such as Juniper Network's *Q-Fabric*, which also uses IS-IS, and Arista's *Spline* architecture. However, as the DCs started to grow larger in size, the networking industry started to realize that L2 forwarding might be more hassle than it's worth. Most DC network designs started gravitating toward Layer 3, and as a result, nearly all modern DCs use the L3 routing infrastructure to provide connectivity within and across the DC networks.

Routing in a Data Center

Without a doubt, L3 routing within a DC offers several benefits when compared to L2 switching. By virtue of route summarization, L3 infrastructure scales better than its L2 counterpart, which is based on MAC address forwarding. Routed infrastructure typically also offers better link utilization through *Equal Cost Multi-Path (ECMP)*, as opposed to an L2 environment, where, at any given time, some links might be blocked to avoid L2 loops. The large number of *Bridge Protocol Data Units (BPDUs)* required for some of the L2 loop-avoidance protocols may be taxing on the CPU and memory resource as well. Additionally, L3 also offers a degree of fault isolation by reducing the *fault-domain* (or *blast radius*, as it's sometimes called) and thus lowers the chances of a network-wide outage. Due to the typically flat and broadcast nature of Layer 2 networks, they create a larger blast radius, where a misconfiguration or malfunction on a single L2 device can impact (or rather "blow up," metaphorically speaking) the whole L2 network. Given the device density in a DC, this blast radius of thousands of devices is simply not acceptable. All things considered, it's not a surprise that most DCs today use L3 routing to provide infrastructure connectivity; however, the choice of Layer 3 routing protocol used in the DC may vary.

To a casual observer, a DC might seem like a large LAN, in the sense that it has hosts and networking equipment stuffed together in a single facility. But DCs are much different from LANs, or in fact from other network domains, in the sense that they have a vast number of devices within a small geographical location. Interconnecting that many devices across the L3 fabric would generate a large number of routes, much higher than what a typical IGP can handle. Hence, when choosing a routing protocol for large-scale DCs, IGPs may not be the best option.

Border Gateway Protocol (BGP) is typically not at the forefront of any design choices when considering a routing protocol for use within a facility. After all, BGP has long been reserved for inter–autonomous system (inter-AS) connectivity between different service providers and, sometimes, across larger network domains within a service provider. BGP has earned its reputation as a stable, scalable, and extensible protocol over the past several decades by literally holding the Internet together and providing vital enhancement such as various address families like VPN (both L2VPN and L3VPN), Labeled Unicast, and IPv6. Another added advantage of BGP over IGP is its capability to provide extensive traffic control via policies. Given the need for scalability, extensibility, and versatility, it is not entirely surprising that early DCs chose BGP to be the protocol of choice. In fact, IETF has an RFC titled *Use of BGP for Routing in Large-Scale Data Centers* to outline and standardize the design and operation of data centers with BGP as the only routing protocol.[14]

The distributed DCs popping up all throughout the transport infrastructure, such as edge DCs and far-edge DCs, as covered in the previous chapters, are typically smaller in size than the central or regional DCs. In an effort to integrate these distributed DCs into IP transport and to create a uniform, single control plane throughout the network, IGP instead of BGP is starting to make inroads within these distributed DCs. Given the smaller size of these distributed DCs, IGP is usually able to handle the required scale. While the use of IGP within DCs (especially far-edge and edge DCs) continues to grow, overall, BGP remains the dominant routing protocol in DC environments.

Nevertheless, the use of Layer 3 routing raises some application- and mobility-related concerns. DCs host a lot of applications, and many of these applications may have multiple endpoints, typically spread across the data center fabric. In a lot of cases, these endpoints require L2 connectivity, which has to be ensured through the data center fabric, which now comprises a Layer 3 infrastructure. In this case, the DC network infrastructure must support a *Layer 2 stretch*, or a *Layer 2 overlay*, that extends L2 connectivity between the endpoint while utilizing the underlying Layer 3 networking infrastructure for actual traffic forwarding. *Virtual Extensible LAN (VXLAN)* and *Ethernet VPN (EVPN)* have emerged as the most commonly used Layer 2 overlay mechanisms to provide this L2 stretch and are covered in more detail in the next chapter. Before discussing these L2 overlay protocols and technologies, however, it will be helpful to understand various traffic flows that can exist within and across DCs, as well as between DCs and various domains in IP transport networks.

Traffic Flows in a Data Center

So far, this chapter has focused entirely on connectivity within the DC. While it is important that the applications in the DC can communicate with other applications in the DC, it is equally important that they also communicate with the outside network. For instance, in the case of a mobile network, in addition to the various 5GC functions communicating among them, they should be able to communicate with the mobile subscriber. Additionally, the DU in the far-edge DC must be able to communicate with the subscriber in the RAN as well as the CU in the edge DC. Figure 7-4 provides an overview of different types of traffic flows within and across DC boundaries.

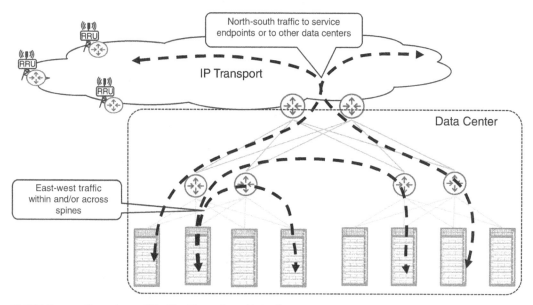

FIGURE 7-4   Overview of Traffic Flows in a Data Center

For these communications to happen effectively, VPN services should be established between various endpoints, whether in the local DC, remote DC, or in the IP transport. This presents some architectural challenges, as the VPN services required to provide this connectivity might traverse both the DC and the IP transport (or rather the xHaul network), which might differ in terms of technologies used to implement these networks. DCs predominantly use a BGP-based L3 infrastructure with a standardized (albeit DC-centric) protocol, such as VXLAN. In contrast, xHaul networks almost always use an IGP (IS-IS or OSPF) along with BGP-based L3 VPNs, or, more recently, Ethernet VPNs. Chapter 8, "Essential Technologies for 5G-Ready Networks: Transport Services," covers the motivation and significance of using VPN to provide transport services in greater detail.

VXLAN is a standards-based Layer 2 overlay technology for DCs defined in RFC 7348, *Virtual eXtensible Local Area Network (VXLAN): A Framework for Overlaying Virtualized Layer 2 Networks over Layer 3 Networks.*[15] VXLAN provides data encapsulation at Layer 2 through the use of a *virtual tunnel endpoint (VTEP)*, a router that encapsulates the original L2 frame within a VXLAN header. The

L2 VXLAN frame is then forwarded over the L3 network to the remote VTEP, which decapsulates the header and transmits the original frame to its destination. However, VXLAN is a data-plane-only technology that relies heavily on the flooding and MAC learning mechanisms, similar to a traditional L2 network, which, as mentioned many times, have severe adverse effects on the network. One of the major enhancements to the original VXLAN specification is the integration of the EVPN control plane with VXLAN, as specified in RFC 8365.[16] EVPN uses the BGP control plane to transmit routing information for L2 endpoints, enabling these endpoints to learn about other EVPN peers and forward L2 traffic using L3 routing information. When used in conjunction with VXLAN, EVPN provides the control plane and L2 endpoint discovery, while VXLAN provides data plane forwarding.

EVPN elegantly separates the control plane and data plane and is flexible in the choice of data plane encapsulations. When used in DCs, it is typically deployed with VXLAN for forwarding, while in an xHaul environment, EVPN is generally used with Segment Routing–based traffic forwarding. In addition to the flexible data plane, EVPN allows for both L2VPN and L3VPN functionality, making it useful in environments where both L2 and L3 VPN connectivity services might be desired. An example of this can include the connectivity between RU and DU, which is implemented as a L2VPN today, whereas DU-to-CU and CU-to-UPF are deployed as a Layer 3 VPN service. The use of EVPN in xHaul networks has been steadily growing, and with its symbiotic relationship with VXLAN, EVPN's use in 5G networks is expected to continue. Both VXLAN and EVPN are viable mechanisms to implement end-to-end services for 5G-ready networks and are discussed in detail in the next chapter.

Data Center Interconnect (DCI)

As covered in the previous section, east-west traffic (that is, the traffic that does not leave the DC) is the dominant traffic. However, there are also north-south traffic streams that do enter and exit the DC, whether this is to reach a service endpoint such as the mobile subscriber or to provide connectivity between various application endpoints that may reside in different DCs altogether. Some examples of this *inter-DC* connectivity include the traffic between the DU in a far-edge DC and the CU in an edge DC as well as traffic exchange between UPF and other functions of 5GC located in different DCs as part of CUPS implementation. Another example of such a traffic flow could be the flow of Voice over IP (VoIP) traffic that is transported between the CU in the edge DC and the IMS function, which is typically located in the central DC.

It should be reiterated here that CUPS does not automatically mean that UPF and other functions of the 5GC will be in different DCs; rather it allows this flexibility in an effort to enable mobile service providers either to offload mobile traffic off their network as close to the mobile subscriber as possible instead of transporting all the way to the central DC or to terminate the mobile traffic on a relevant application closer to the user as part of a uRLLC or MEC implementation. Whatever the case may be, data center architecture should accommodate traffic forwarding between multiple data centers. This inter-DC connectivity is called *Data Center Interconnect (DCI)* and is an integral part of overall network architecture and design.

DCI and Border Leaf

The terms *DCI* and *border leaf* are often used interchangeably since these functions are typically implemented on the same routers. However, strictly speaking, DCI refers to the functions and services required to connect a DC to other DCs, whereas border leaf is the device or function that connects a data center fabric to the rest of the transport network. A network architect must be cognizant of this subtle difference between the two terminologies, because although often implemented using the same devices and services, traffic requirements such as QoS or security might slightly differ between the two.

Typically, there are two dominant choices to implement DCI within a service provider environment: optical/DWDM or IP/MPLS-based packet networks. Both options are widely acceptable within the industry and used as appropriate. When selecting a DCI mechanism, a service provider should consider commonsense factors such as total traffic between the DC, distance limitations, and, obviously, the cost of the overall DCI solution. Purely optical solutions such as DWDM use dedicated fiber links to implement DCI between DCs and are ideal for scenarios where high amounts of data exchange is needed between data centers in different locations. It is a common solution for cloud providers that rely on huge amounts of data continually being exchanged between DC sites.

However, optical and WDM solutions require dedicated fiber connections and lack statistical multiplexing capabilities. All DCs require connectivity not only with other DCs but also to the service provider's IP transport network to ensure the application in the DC can communicate with the endpoints (for example, mobile subscriber) in the SP's access domain. This IP-transport-to-DC connectivity might just be a pair of leaf routers, sometimes called a *border leaf*, providing the interconnect between the IP network and DC spines. Depending on the size of the DC, in some cases, the spines themselves can act as the border leaf, connecting the data center fabric and the IP transport. The service provider, more often than not, uses the same routers that implement the border leaf functions to provide the DCI function as well. This helps keep the cost down by avoiding duplication of devices and connections, but it also utilizes the service provider's own IP transport network, resulting in extracting as much return on investment from the network as possible. For this to be feasible, the SP must own its own transport infrastructure connecting data centers in different locations. Use of the IP transport for DCI is also very popular in new architectures with far-edge and edge DCs integrated within the transport, unless the SP decides to use a cloud-based DC approach, as covered in the previous section. Generally, most service providers use a combination of DWDM and IP/MPLS-based connectivity to fulfill their DCI needs.

Orchestrating the Data Center Fabric

Design repeatability and ease of deployment are two of the most important and sought-after characteristics of any network deployment. Both of these characteristics contribute heavily toward an efficient and timely network rollout as well reducing the chances of encountering issues during large-scale deployment. This is even more true for DCs, given their scale and quantity in modern networks.

Clos fabric–based DC design solves the repeatability aspect of a design to a large extent. A network architect has to develop the architecture (routing design, QoS and security policies, high availability, and so on) just once using the defined topology, and new ToRs, leafs, or spines can be added to the fabric when needed. The design also acts as a blueprint for any new DC that needs to be spun up as part of the overall distributed DC model.

Ease of deployment does require additional planning as well the use of additional tools and applications. These applications are typically geared toward the automated orchestration of the data center fabric with as little human interaction as possible. Sensing the need and market opportunity, over the past several years, networking equipment manufacturers have intensified their orchestration and automation solution offerings. With mobile service providers regularly opting for multivendor networks, a lot of these tools focus on multivendor orchestration capabilities in addition to a vendor's own devices and solutions. Some of these tools may focus squarely on DC orchestration such as Cisco's *Data Center Network Manager (DCNM)* or Juniper's *Apstra System*, while others may be more general purpose such as *Network Services Orchestrator (NSO)* by Cisco and *NorthStar* by Juniper.

Multivendor capabilities are such an important part of today's automation and orchestration ecosystem that traditional networking equipment providers are creating, either in-house or through acquisition, semi-independent companies solely focused on generic automation and orchestration. Examples of this include *Tail-F, Blue Planet*, and *Nuage*—all of which are software-focused automation, orchestration, and management companies, but owned by Cisco, Ciena, and Nokia, respectively. Using such an arrangement allows these solutions to create the impression of a multivendor, generic solution instead of being focused on a particular vendor. This practice promotes solution neutrality to a certain extent and benefits the customers and networking industry in general.

Orchestration is the key for any networking solution and offers a quick, efficient DC deployment through the use of various automation and orchestration tools. Automation is a topic worthy of a publication of its own, and this book uses the concept of automation as it pertains to the network deployment and implementation. Note, however, that all automation and orchestration solutions rely heavily on a robust, repeatable, and extensible underlying architecture. Using a Clos fabric design with a uniform architecture across DCs (small, medium, or large) allows service providers to use orchestration solutions without the need to create custom automation for every single deployment.

Optimizing Compute Resources

With the massive use of the general-purpose COTS hardware in today's large-scale DCs, the efficient and optimal use of these hardware resources becomes an important consideration. The optimization is required for energy efficiency, application performance, and cost reduction. This section aims to outline the need for resource optimization as well as covers commonly used optimization techniques in data center environments.

Why Optimize?

The unprecedented growth of cheap computational power and the emergence of large DCs might create the impression that any computational challenge can be solved by installing faster central processing units (CPUs) and throwing in more computational resources at the task. Although this extensive approach results in a quick growth of computational power, it also inflates the cost and power required for such a solution. Moreover, certain types of computational tasks do not benefit from running on massively parallel systems, and while custom-designed application-specific integrated circuits (ASICs) and field-programmable gate arrays (FPGAs) can provide a viable solution in such cases, they lack flexibility when a change in algorithm is required. ASICs and FPGAs might outperform general-purpose CPUs in tasks they are designed for and can be energy efficient. Yet, in order to provide a reasonable level of flexibility, they are typically used as expansion modules while the general-purpose CPUs remain the main engine of today's commercially available server hardware.

In today's highly virtualized world, with its innumerable virtual machines, containers, and applications running on shared compute resources, the importance of optimizing the use of computational resources can hardly be overestimated. Due to the sheer number of servers running in a typical DC or in the whole MCN, any inefficiency in computational resource utilization results in significant wastage of power, cooling, and space—and, ultimately, money. Microprocessor and server manufacturers do recognize these challenges and offer a variety of features to increase the power efficiency of their solutions. Indeed, scaling down the clocking speed for idle or underutilized CPU cores, use of low-power modes for both CPU and memory (when not actively used), CPU dynamic voltage control, and other features help to reduce each individual server's power consumption. Nevertheless, these features can cause unintended consequences if implemented without proper consideration for the requirements of actual applications and virtual functions.

Common Optimization Techniques

Virtual functions running in today's DCs can have specific and diverse expectations on memory and disk access latency as well as available CPU cycles. Failure to satisfy these expectations might cause severe instabilities in code execution, and even result in an application crash. Such instabilities are extremely hard to troubleshoot, as they might happen in the absence of obvious signs of a system overload, such as high CPU load or lack of free memory resources. Optimizing the use of compute resources helps to prevent instabilities and avoid costly side effects of resource overprovisioning, while allowing for safely engaging power-saving features of modern computational hardware.

In simple terms, any application code execution relies on pulling data from memory, performing desired operations on it using CPU, and storing the result in memory again. Modern high-performance CPUs are based on extremely complex architectures featuring multiple cores, low-latency cache memory, and memory controllers on a single die. A few such CPUs can be installed in a typical server, hosting various VMs and applications, and while they provide plenty of computation resources, memory access is far from being simple on such systems.

A typical commercially available server usually supports multiple physical CPUs with plenty of memory slots. In these multi-CPU systems, all memory slots are divided into groups, with each group connected directly to only one physical CPU, referred to as a CPU package. A CPU designed for use in multi-CPU servers has its own memory controller performing read and write operations from/to the random-access memory (RAM) connected to it. At the time of this writing, server CPUs support up to two memory controllers on a die, each providing up to four channels of memory connections.[17] Multichannel memory access allows for parallelizing memory operations, and reading or writing more data at once without queuing requests from multiple CPU cores, thereby reducing memory access latency dramatically. However, operating systems (OSs) or hypervisors supporting multi-CPU systems allow any core on any CPU package to access all memory, connected to all CPU packages. Thus, it is entirely possible for a process to be executed by a core on one CPU package, while using data residing in memory connected to another CPU package. Server CPUs, supporting multi-CPU configurations, have special inter-CPU links to exchange data in such scenarios. These inter-CPU connections, however, have less bandwidth compared to that of memory controllers, and accessing memory resources connected to other CPU packages introduces significant latency. Such multi-CPU systems are called *non-uniform memory access (NUMA)* systems, reflecting the fact that access to local and remote memory resources is not uniform. In a NUMA system, each CPU package (and its connected memory banks) is called a *NUMA group*. Figure 7-5 shows a NUMA system consisting of two NUMA groups.

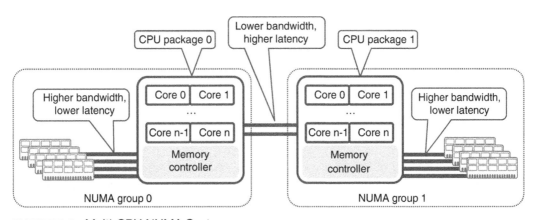

FIGURE 7-5 Multi-CPU NUMA System

Virtually all operating systems and hypervisors today support multi-CPU systems, and their CPU schedulers are designed to run effectively on NUMA systems. Nevertheless, OS and hypervisor schedulers have to find a balance between efficient load distribution of different processes across all available cores, and memory connectivity specifics in a NUMA system. The algorithms, employed by CPU schedulers, do well in many scenarios, but under certain conditions they might struggle to allocate resources optimally. For example, a guest OS running in a VM uses its own CPU scheduler to run multiple processes on virtual CPUs allocated to it by a hypervisor. The hypervisor, in turn, uses its own CPU scheduler to properly distribute the load from multiple VMs over all available CPU cores. Although the hypervisor's CPU scheduler is well aware of the NUMA system details it is running on and generally tries to allocate CPU and memory resources on the same CPU package, it might not always be able to do so, depending on the processing power demanded by other VMs. The guest OS could end up scheduling a process on one NUMA group while using memory resources from another. In such an undesirable scenario, a process can experience higher and sometimes unpredictable memory access latency, which can result in instabilities and process crashes.

Proper sizing of VMs can be considered a good practice to prevent such scenarios. A VM overprovisioned with virtual CPUs and memory resources that cannot be accommodated by a single CPU package will likely end up running on multiple CPU packages with the negative effects described previously. However, even a properly sized VM could still end up running on multiple physical CPU packages, depending on how loaded the system is and the number of other VMs running concurrently. Configuring *affinity values* for VM CPU resources, also known as *CPU pinning*, instructs the hypervisor or OS schedulers to use only specific physical CPU cores or packages to schedule tasks. This technique is very effective in preventing the scheduling of VM computations on different physical CPU packages. Depending on implementation, memory allocation may follow CPU assignments automatically or can be configured with an affinity value to stick to a certain CPU package as well, thereby avoiding unnecessary latency in accessing data in memory.

Besides multiple physical cores, modern CPUs also allow execution of multiple (usually two) *application threads* in parallel on each physical core, using the *Simultaneous Multi-Threading (SMT)* feature (Intel's implementation of SMT is called *HyperThreading*, or *HT*).[18] This feature presents a logical equivalent of a core to the operating system/hypervisor. Although actual operations are executed on a single physical core, in many scenarios it is beneficial to treat a single physical core as two logical cores and run more than one parallel application threads simultaneously. CPU schedulers in today's hypervisors allow operators to choose between treating SMT-enabled CPU cores as multiple logical ones and mapping the whole physical core to a VM's virtual CPU.

The use of FPGAs and ASICs in expansion cards can provide great benefits for faster and more energy efficient computational tasks. One example of such technology is the Stateless Offload (a.k.a. TCP Offload Engine), which takes the load of calculating TCP, UDP, and IP checksums off the CPU. Another example of offloading computationally intensive tasks to specialized FPGAs is Intel's FPGA-based hardware Layer 1 FEC accelerator. It can offload FEC calculations in 4G and 5G applications from the server's general-purpose CPU, thus facilitating the hosting of RAN components such as DU and CU on these commercially available servers.[19] In fact, all the resource-optimization techniques discussed are essential in product design for various 5GC functions or RAN nodes in an effort to provide an effective transition from hardware-based to virtual and cloud-native solutions for MCN.

Power efficiency requirements for edge and far-edge DCs further propelled the search for more efficient computational solutions to host DU and CU functions. In particular, far-edge DCs might have very strict constraints on power and cooling provisions while hosting computationally intensive

DUs. Use of graphics processing units (GPU) can provide vast floating-point calculation capacity for mMIMO and mmWave applications, while reducing power consumption in comparison to general-purpose CPUs. Major radio vendors and GPU manufacturers are already exploring these new possibilities for building energy-efficient and powerful DUs.[20]

The real-time baseband processing nature of the DU functions presents challenges for conventional computational systems. To solve this, chip manufacturer Intel has been promoting a reference architecture called FlexRAN that uses a combination of hardware enhancement (such as accelerator cards) and associated software stack for efficient and low latency processing of baseband traffic while using generic compute hardware[21] The FlexRAN architecture is based on Intel's x86 processor family and uses what is called a "lookaside" approach. In the lookaside approach, CPU performs the bulk of the functions while offloading some tasks to the hardware accelerator resulting in multiple data exchanges between the CPU and the accelerator. In other words, the CPU "looks aside" to the hardware accelerator when needed. Intel's FlexRAN has been the only choice for vRAN implementation so far. More recently, however, another approach referred to as "inline acceleration" has been introduced by ASIC manufacturers such as Qualcomm and Malinox. The inline acceleration approach hands off the traffic from CPU to ASIC only once, and relies on it to perform all the baseband data processing functions thus reducing dependency on the CPU[22]. Though this has been demonstrated using peripheral cards on x86 based compute systems, this is viewed as a possible shift from dependency on x86 based CPUs and Intel's FlexRAN architecture.

Summary

This chapter explored the fundamentals of DC networking as an essential building block of an end-to-end 5G mobile communication network.

This chapter covered the following DC-specific topics:

- Origins and evolution of large-scale DCs along with various DC models such as on-premises (on-prem) DCs, co-location DCs or co-location racks, managed hosting services, and public cloud

- The use of Clos-based fabric as a basic DC building block and the concepts of spine and leaf in a data center fabric

- The ongoing transitions from centralized to distributed and cloud-based DC deployment models

- Routing and switching technologies within a DC as well as traffic flows and connectivity mechanisms for inter-DC communication as well as connecting DCs to the IP transport network

- The importance of automation and orchestration of the data center fabric

- The importance of, and some of the commonly used optimization techniques for compute resources in the DCs used for MCN

The next chapter will dive further into the essential technologies and focus on service deployment for end-to-end (E2E) connectivity between various components of the mobile communication network. It will cover the protocols and technologies that enable E2E services across the MCN domains.

References

1. https://www.crn.com/news/data-center/microsoft-to-build-new-200m-data-center-as-azure-sales-soar (last visited: Mar 2022)

2. https://www.microsoft.com/en-us/research/wp-content/uploads/2009/06/2009-06-19-Data-Center-Tutorial-SIGMETRICS.pdf (last visited: Mar 2022)

3. https://www.ieee802.org/3/hssg/public/nov06/diminico_01_1106.pdf (last visited: Mar 2022)

4. Morgan Stanley Research, "Technology Eating the World—Top Trends Post COVID-19," https://advisor.morganstanley.com/the-irvin-and-bevack-group/documents/field/i/ir/irvin-and-bevack-group/12%20Top%20Tech%20Trends%20Post%20COVID-19%206%2017%202020.pdf (last visited: Mar 2022)

5. AT&T web hosting services, https://webhosting.att.com/ (last visited: Mar 2022)

6. Morgan Stanley Research, op. cit.

7. https://ia801901.us.archive.org/8/items/bstj32-2-406/bstj32-2-406_text.pdf (last visited: Mar 2022)

8. https://news.microsoft.com/innovation-stories/project-natick-underwater-datacenter/ (last visited: Mar 2022)

9. Caser Wu and Rajkumar Buyya, *Cloud Data Centers and Cost Modeling*, (Waltham, MA: Morgan Kaufmann), 2015

10. https://aws.amazon.com/wavelength/ (last visited: Mar 2022)

11. https://aws.amazon.com/outposts/ (last visited: Mar 2022)

12. https://azure.microsoft.com/en-us/overview/azure-stack/#overview

13. IEEE RFC 6326, "Transparent Interconnect of Lots of Links (TRILL) use of IS-IS"

14. IEEE RFC 7938, "Use of BGP for Routing in Large-Scale Data Centers"

15. IEEE RFC 7348, "A Framework for Overlaying Virtualized Layer 2 Networks over Layer 3 Networks"

16. IEEE RFC 8365, "A Network Virtualization Overlay Solution Using Ethernet VPN (EVPN)"

17. https://www.intel.com/content/www/us/en/products/docs/processors/xeon/3rd-gen-xeon-scalable-processors-brief.html (last visited: Mar 2022)

18. https://www.intel.com/content/www/us/en/gaming/resources/hyper-threading.html (last visited: Mar 2022)

19. https://builders.intel.com/docs/networkbuilders/virtual-ran-vran-with-hardware-acceleration.pdf (last visited: Mar 2022)

20. https://www.ericsson.com/en/blog/2020/2/virtualized-5g-ran-why-when-and-how (last visited: Mar 2022)

21. FlexRAN™ Reference Architecture for Wireless Access - https://www.intel.com/content/www/us/en/developer/topic-technology/edge-5g/tools/flexran.html (last visited: Mar 2022)

22. How to build high-performance 5G networks with vRAN and O-RAN? https://www.qualcomm.com/media/documents/files/how-to-build-high-performance-5g-networks-with-vran-and-o-ran.pdf, Slide 15 and 16 (last visited: Mar 2022)

Chapter **8**

Essential Technologies for 5G-Ready Networks: Transport Services

The mobile communication network's services are collectively implemented using functions spread across the RAN, xHaul, and mobile core domains. These functions seamlessly interact to implement the mobile service through connectivity provided by the xHaul network. In the early generations of mobile communications, a simple Layer 2 (L2) or circuit switched network was sufficient for back-hauling mobile traffic. But in the current and future generations of mobile communications network (MCN), the xHaul networks require the flexible, scalable, cost-effective, and operationally simple solutions provided through IP- and MPLS-based networks. For these xHaul networks to provide the connectivity expected of them, *transport network services*, or simply *transport services*, are implemented as an overlay using *virtual private networks (VPNs)*. These transport services are typically a subset of an end-to-end mobile service and have a vital role in the realization of services provided by the MCN. This chapter will explain the various technologies and methods used to implement the transport services for enabling a 5G network.

What's a 5G Transport Service?

It should be well understood by now that the components that make up a mobile service for an end consumer reside in multiple network domains. The RAN domain contains the radio-related equipment, where a mobile subscriber connects to the mobile provider's *network*. This equipment consists of antennas and baseband processing units that, by virtue of RAN decomposition, can be spread across multiple geographical locations (that is, the cell site, the far edge, and the edge DCs). The RAN devices must communicate with the 5GC functions, which are also likely to be spread over multiple data centers (DCs) through the introduction of CUPS. The 5GC provides subscriber authentication, registration, and connectivity to the data network (DN) and other required functions to enable *mobile services* for the end subscriber.

These mobile services would not be possible without a robust transport infrastructure, which in turn offers a *transport service*, enabling connectivity between mobility functions in different domains as well as within the same domain. Examples of interdomain transport services include connectivity between the centralized unit (CU) that is part of the RAN, and the user plane function (UPF) that is part of the 5GC. Intradomain service examples may include connectivity between the radio unit (RU) and distributed unit (DU) and between the DU and CU—all of which are in the RAN domain.

While the forwarding mechanism might vary with the network domain (for example, Segment Routing in xHaul, VXLAN in the DC), the overlay services almost always require some degree of isolation to allow multiple traffic types to be transported independently over the same underlying infrastructure. This traffic separation is provided by the use of a VPN that can be established entirely within the xHaul domain (for example, Xn for 5G and X2 for 4G interfaces between cell sites) or extended into different DCs in a 5G network with decomposed RAN. The next section elaborates on the type of VPN services used in the transport network to enable end-to-end mobile services.

VPN Services

The term *VPN* has different meanings for different groups of people; in general, a VPN is equated with interoffice connectivity or secure remote access. In a service provider environment, however, VPNs are virtually always synonymous with transport services aimed at providing separation between traffic from different source groups in an effort to transport them over a common underlying infrastructure. Figure 8-1 highlights the use of VPNs in a service provider environment, where traffic from different service types (such as residential, enterprise, and mobile) is transported over a single underlying infrastructure that provides a degree of separation. This separation ensures that each service type can receive differentiated treatment based on the agreement with the service provider.

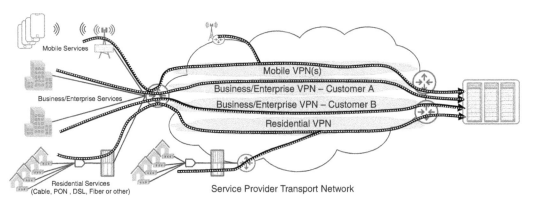

FIGURE 8-1   Service Isolation Using VPNs in Service Provider Networks

Using VPNs, the service provider can offer transport services for either Layer 3 (L3) or L2 traffic. When L3 traffic (IP) is transported over the service provider network, the service is called L3VPN, whereas L2VPN refers to a VPN service capable of transporting L2 frames. With Ethernet replacing older L2 technologies such as ATM and Frame Relay, *modern L2VPN* refers to the mechanism used to transport Ethernet traffic over an IP or MPLS transport *underlay*. Over the years, L2VPN technologies have been an area of extensive innovation. Traditionally, L2VPN services were implemented to provide an alternative to point-to-point leased lines, later evolving into multipoint Layer 2 technologies. More recently, *Ethernet VPN (EVPN)* has emerged as the de facto replacement for traditional L2VPN technologies such as *Ethernet over MPLS (EoMPLS)*. This section covers both the traditional L2VPN technologies as well as EVPN for L2 transport over an IP/MPLS-based infrastructure.

Traditional Layer 2 VPN Services

L2VPNs have been instrumental in providing mobile services in early MCNs. As covered in Chapter 2, "Anatomy of Mobile Communication Networks," and Chapter 3, "Mobile Networks Today," pre-4G mobile networks required connectivity only between base stations (that is, cell sites) and their controllers (base station controllers in the case of 2G or radio network controllers in 3G). These controllers typically resided in the central office (that is, a regional or central DC), and their connection to the cell sites was initially achieved through the use of Frame Relay over T1/E1 links. As the transport networking technologies evolved in the 1990s and early 2000s, ATM started competing with Frame Relay for this connectivity. By the time 4G started gaining traction, the de facto standardization of Ethernet and MPLS over IP as the transport technology of choice made L2VPNs over MPLS the dominant technology for mobile transport.

Point-to-point L2VPN continued to be the predominant connectivity mechanism from the cell sites to the central office; however, the use of X2 interfaces in 4G (that is, connections between cell sites) introduced point-to-multipoint communication into the mobile backhaul. While L3VPNs are better suited for multipoint connectivity and are preferred for mobile transport networks, L2VPNs are still used in certain cases. One such example is the connectivity between the RU and DU in the case of decomposed RAN deployments. At the time of this writing, almost all implementations of RU and DU require L2 connectivity, which is implemented using traditional L2VPN or, relatively newer, Ethernet VPN (EVPN). This section covers the technical fundamentals of implementing point-to-point and multipoint traditional L2VPNs, whereas the next section will cover EVPN.

> **Note**
>
> Even though the 3GPP and O-RAN Alliance specifications allow the use of either Ethernet (L2) or IP (L3) for connectivity between the RU and DU, virtually all current implementations of RU and DU use Ethernet (L2) connectivity through the fronthaul network, thus requiring L2VPN services in the fronthaul.
>
> Future implementations of RU and DU may transition to IP-based connectivity, making L3VPN a feasible option for fronthaul. Backhaul and midhaul already use L3VPN services, as specified in O-RAN's xHaul Packet Switched Architecture Specifications.

Point-to-Point L2VPN Services

Various different industry terminologies are used to describe the functionality provided by point-to-point L2VPN services. In the MEF ecosystems, point-to-point L2PVNs are called *Ethernet Line (E-Line)* services, whereas earlier IETF RFCs called this functionality *Pseudo-Wire Emulation Edge-to-Edge (PWE3)*, or simply a *pseudowire.*[1] The terms *virtual circuit (VC)* and *pseudowire* are also used interchangeably to define an L2VPN point-to-point circuit. Vendors also have been using their own terminologies to define the point-to-point L2VPN services. For instance, some Cisco implementations refer to point-to-point L2VPN as *Any Transport over MPLS (AToM),* signifying that in addition to Ethernet, other traffic types such as ATM and T1 could also be transported over an MPLS infrastructure.[2] Other vendors, such as Nokia and Huawei, use the more generic *Virtual Leased Line (VLL)* terminology to refer to point-to-point L2VPN.[3] Nokia further classifies its various L2VPN implementations as x*Pipe*, where *x* can be substituted for the traffic type being transported in the L2VPN. For instance, ePipe, aPipe, or iPipe would refer to Nokia's implementation of Ethernet, ATM, or IP transport over L2VPN, respectively.[4] More recently, the industry as a whole has embraced *virtual private wire services (VPWS)* as the standard terminology when referring to point-to-point L2VPN services.

Ethernet has been the dominant L2 transport technology, and MPLS has been the de facto forwarding mechanism in large service provider networks. With this context, it comes as no surprise that Ethernet over MPLS (EoMPLS) has been the most widely used point-to-point L2VPN technology for several years. Effectively, EoMPLS works by encapsulating an Ethernet L2 PDU within an MPLS label (called the *VPN label, Service label,* or *VC label*) and forwarding the traffic over the underlying MPLS infrastructure. This VC label is unique to each individual EoMPLS pseudowire and is used to uniquely identify VPWS circuits. The L2VPN packet is typically encapsulated within another MPLS label, called the *next-hop label* or *transport label*, which identifies the forwarding path. In other words, almost all L2VPN traffic contains at least *two* MPLS labels: the inner label (VC label) that identifies the L2VPN circuit, and the outer label (transport label) that identifies the label switched path the traffic should take in the MPLS network.

The VC labels remain unchanged between the service endpoints, while the transport label might change due to the nature of MPLS-based forwarding where a label swap can occur at intermediary nodes. When the traffic is received on the penultimate hop, the outer label might be removed due to the *penultimate hop popping (PHP)* behavior and the remaining frame is forwarded toward the destination provider edge (PE) router with the inner label exposed. At the destination PE, this VC label identifies the L2VPN circuit and the *attachment circuit* associated with it. The attachment circuit is simply an Ethernet interface connecting the end device to the PE router providing the EoMPLS functionality. The VC label is then removed and the original Ethernet payload is forwarded over the attachment circuit, thus completing the L2VPN. Figure 8-2 shows the use of these inner and outer labels in a VPWS service.

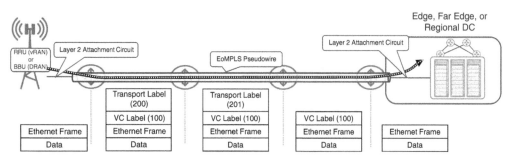

FIGURE 8-2   Ethernet over MPLS (EoMPLS) Forwarding

The VC labels are unique to each VPWS, and the PE devices on either end of the pseudowire are responsible for imposing these labels. Although these imposed labels don't have to match, both PE devices must be aware of each other's VC label in order for the EoMPLS pseudowire to be established. These VC labels can be configured statically on both PE devices or dynamically allocated and exchanged during the pseudowire setup process. Multiple competing IETF RFCs exist that define the protocols used for dynamic VC label allocation and propagation. One of the earlier standards, RFC 4906, prescribes the use of Label Distribution Protocol (LDP) to assign and distribute VC labels. LDP is already used to exchange transport labels between adjacent routers in MPLS-LDP environments. Because the endpoints of an EoMPLS PW typically are multiple hops away, RFC 4906 proposes a mechanism to establish a *Targeted LDP (T-LDP)* session between nonadjacent MPLS routers.[5] This T-LDP session is in addition to the already existing LDP sessions an MPLS-LDP-enabled router would establish with its directly connected neighbors. RFC 4906 was based on an IETF draft co-authored by Luca Martini of Level 3 Communications (later joined Cisco Systems), and as such the T-LDP-based EoMPLS is also commonly referred to as *draft-martini*.

The other mechanism for VC label exchange was documented in RFC 6624 and RFC 4761, both of which propose the use of Border Gateway Protocol (BGP) for L2VPN signaling and discovery.[6, 7] These RFCs enhance BGP by introducing a new *L2VPN address family* to exchange L2VPN information between the PE routers. Using this new address family, the MPLS PE routers could automatically discover and signal the establishment of L2 pseudowires. BGP-based L2VPN signaling and auto-discovery was first proposed by Juniper Network's Kireeti Kompella, and thus BGP-based L2VPN implementations were commonly called *draft-kompella*.

Cisco originally favored draft-martini, which popularized T-LDP-based EoMPLS implementations. Cisco later joined Juniper Networks in drafting the RFCs supporting BGP-based L2VPN auto-discovery and signaling mechanisms based on draft-kompella. Today, most if not all networking equipment manufacturers support both the draft-kompella and draft-martini implementations for L2VPN services.

The use of LDP in transport networks has been steadily declining over the past several years for many reasons (as discussed in Chapter 6, "Emerging Technologies for 5G-Ready Networks: Segment Routing") and being substituted with Segment Routing (SR). Because SR deprecates the use of LDP for transport label exchange, the VC label signaling can't happen over T-LDP and can only be exchanged using BGP, or configured statically. When using statically defined VC labels, the EoMPLS pseudowire is colloquially called *static pseudowire* and is supported by most networking equipment vendors.

Use of Q-in-Q for L2VPN

Using EoMPLS end-to-end requires the cell site routers (CSRs) to support MPLS-based forwarding. While an overwhelming majority of current CSRs support MPLS, there might be scenarios where a service provider chooses an L2-only CSR. In those cases, L2VPN tunneling through the access domain is provided by Q-in-Q, which encapsulates Ethernet frames (usually VLAN tagged) within another VLAN, called *Service VLAN* or *S-VLAN*.

In these cases, EoMPLS is implemented in the aggregation and core domains, which works in conjunction with Q-in-Q in the access domain to implement an end-to-end L2VPN. This scenario was briefly discussed previously in Figure 3-18 in Chapter 3. Nevertheless, today, Q-in-Q-based architecture for mobile transport is rarely, if ever, used due to the availability of low-cost, feature-rich, MPLS-capable CSRs and is mentioned here only for completeness.

Due to the simplicity, ease of deployment, and effectiveness of VPWS services, point-to-point L2VPNs are by far the most widely deployed L2VPN in service provider networks—mobile and otherwise. The VPWS service is always configured between two endpoints and, thus, traffic is not flooded to other devices as it would in a flat L2 network. As such, there is no need for MAC learning and address table lookups, saving precious memory space. VPWS services can be port-based (that is, all traffic from an attachment circuit is transported over the pseudowire) or VLAN-based, where every individual VLAN on the attachment circuit can be assigned its own VPWS pseudowire.

Point-to-point L2VPN services do have some drawbacks, however, particularly around scalability and redundancy of the pseudowires. In larger networks, with tens or hundreds of thousands of cell sites, the number of pseudowires required to provide connectivity from each cell site router to the central DC can push the scalability boundaries of the device(s) at the hub locations. The two endpoints of the pseudowire—the CSR and the terminating router, possibly a DCI or DC border leaf—represent single points of failure for the service. Cell sites typically rely on a single CSR, but, as a best practice, the router on the other end of the VPWS service is typically deployed in pairs.

By definition, a point-to-point pseudowire can only be established between the CSR and only *one* of the remote routers, raising redundancy concerns. To address this concern, EoMPLS allows the use of a *backup pseudowire*, where a CSR establishes a primary or an active pseudowire to one of the remote nodes, while at the same time establishing a backup pseudowire to the second one. In case of a primary node failure causing the active pseudowire to go down, the backup pseudowire assumes an active role and starts forwarding traffic, thus allowing service continuity. Figure 8-3 illustrates this concept of an active-backup pseudowire. While this solves the redundancy challenge, only one of two pseudowires can be used at any given time, thus reducing overall efficiency and scalability. Ethernet VPN, discussed later in this chapter, is one of the newer technologies that addresses this concern and offers an *All-Active multi-homing* solution for VPWS.

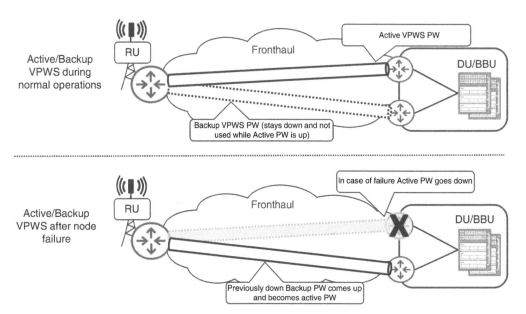

FIGURE 8-3   VPWS Redundancy Through Active-Backup Pseudowires

Multipoint L2VPN Services

Point-to-point L2VPN services are effective and easy to implement, but as previously indicated, these can present both device and architectural scale challenges should a large number of VPWS pseudowires converge on a single endpoint. Device scalability issues arise from the total number of discrete pseudowires the endpoint would need to support, whereas architectural scalability results from the network-wide resource usage, such as VLANs that might be required for each of those pseudowires. In some cases, it can be beneficial to terminate all the *spoke* pseudowires (that is, the pseudowires coming from multiple access locations) into a single *bridge domain* on the destination endpoint, thus creating a virtual hub-and-spoke topology.

A bridge domain is an indispensable element of any multipoint L2 service that represents a virtual construct within a PE router, providing L2 traffic-switching and MAC-learning functions. In simplistic terms, a bridge domain could be thought of as a mini-L2 switch within the PE router itself that provides traffic switching between its many *interfaces.* In the context of L2VPN, the interfaces associated with a bridge domain could be physical ports, Layer 2 subinterfaces, or pseudowires connecting to other PE devices. As such, a bridge domain provides traffic switching between L2 attachment circuits and pseudowires, as shown in Figure 8-4.

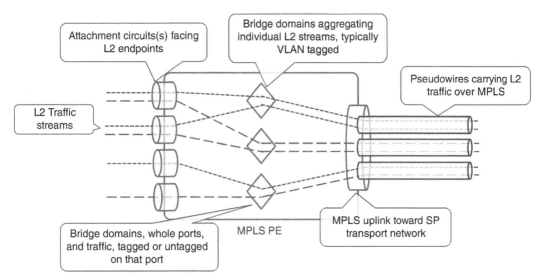

FIGURE 8-4   Bridge Domain Concepts

In a *point-to-multipoint* architecture, the bridge domain on the hub site router terminates pseudowires from multiple spoke routers—likely CSRs. While not decreasing the total number of pseudowires, the use of point-to-multipoint L2VPN simplifies the overall architecture by eliminating the need to maintain each pseudowire as a separate transport service. Additionally, terminating all the pseudowires on a single bridge domain on the hub site's router simplifies the configuration required at the hub by possibly eliminating the need for a separate L2 construct (typically a L2 sub-interface) for each pseudowire. The bridge domain performs MAC learning to ensure traffic from the attachment circuit is forwarded over the correct pseudowire, although any broadcast traffic, multicast traffic, and unicast traffic to a destination with an unknown MAC address (collectively called *BUM traffic*) from the attachment circuit are expected to be sent over all the pseudowires terminating on that bridge domain. This behavior is indeed required to ensure that equipment at the hub site can communicate with the access nodes on the other end of the pseudowires.

On the other hand, to ensure that traffic from spoke nodes does not get sent to other spoke nodes, split horizon functionality can be implemented on the hub site where multiple pseudowires are terminated. Split horizon, in this case, allows traffic from any of the PE devices (that is, a pseudowire) to be sent only to the attachment circuit and not to other pseudowires, thus significantly reducing traffic flooding over the point-to-multipoint services. Return traffic from the attachment circuit is forwarded to the pseudowire based on the MAC address learned on the bridge domain. Metro Ethernet Forum refers to this hub-and-spoke, point-to-multipoint L2VPN implementation as an *Ethernet Tree (E-Tree)*. Figure 8-5 shows a comparison between multiple VPWS and a single point-to-multipoint service.

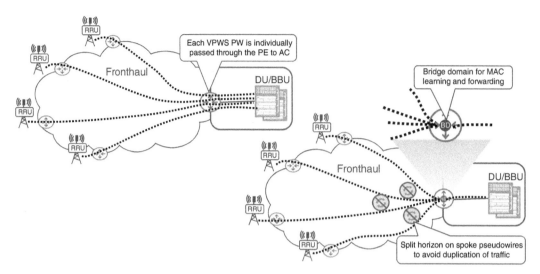

FIGURE 8-5   Point-to-Point and Point-to-Multipoint L2VPN Services

The E-Tree scenario outlined in Figure 8-5 is helpful where multiple spokes need to establish Layer 2 connections to a single hub site. This scenario is, however, not conducive to a truly multipoint communication where spokes would want to communicate with each other, in addition to the central locations. The any-to-any L2 connectivity, referred to as *Ethernet LAN (E-LAN)* by the Metro Ethernet Forum, was in fact a precursor to E-Tree. Multipoint E-LAN services have traditionally been implemented using *Virtual Private LAN Services (VPLS)*, originally defined in RFC 4761 and RFC 4762. The two RFCs define the use of Kompella and Martini draft-based mechanisms in establishing in the individual pseudowires that make up a VPLS-based multipoint service.

Strictly speaking, VPLS is not a technology but rather an architecture that relies on participating PE routers to establish a full mesh of individual pseudowires among them to exchange L2 traffic. These pseudowires can be established using T-LDP session (RFC 4762) or BGP (RFC 4761) and, depending on the vendor's implementation, are tied together through a combination of a *VPLS instance* and bridge domain. Juniper's implementation uses the term *VPLS Routing Instance*, whereas Cisco calls its VPLS instance a *Virtual Forwarding Interface (VFI)*. Whatever the case, each VPLS instance, configured on participating PE routers, identifies the network-wide multipoint L2VPN service and provides L2 traffic switching between PE routers and their respective attachment circuits. Because VPLS is typically implemented as a full-mesh architecture, loop avoidance becomes a key tenet of any viable VPLS implementation. As a rule of thumb, VPLS architecture, similar to E-Tree implementation (covered earlier), should not transmit traffic received from a PE (that is, from a pseudowire) to another PE (that is, to another pseudowire). Traffic from a pseudowire, even BUM traffic, should be forwarded only to an attachment circuit to avoid loops and traffic duplication within the L2VPN service. Typically, this behavior is the default implementation by major networking equipment vendors, but it does allow configuration tweaks to allow flexibility in design choices. One such design is the use of Hierarchical VPLS (H-VPLS), which circumvents the split-horizon rules to allow traffic to be passed between *select* pseudowires in an effort to create a more scalable multipoint L2VPN architecture.

While useful for multipoint L2 connectivity, the full-mesh implementation for VPLS results in an extremely high number of individual pseudowires in the network should the number of L2 endpoints grow beyond just a handful of PE devices. For instance, a six PE topology, such as that shown in Figure 8-6, requires 15 pseudowires to provide any-to-any full-mesh connectivity. Each of these 15 pseudowires have two endpoints (originating and terminating PE), and thus 30 configuration touchpoints. A network double its size (12 PE devices) would require more than four times as many (64) pseudowires, using the mathematical formula:

$$n*(n-1)/2$$

where n is the number of PE devices.

Given these calculations, it is fairly obvious that a network with dozens or tens of dozens of L2 endpoints could result in an unmanageable number of VPLS pseudowires for each VPLS instance. If multiple VPLS instances are required, the result is an unfathomable number of total pseudowires that will test the scalability limits of individual devices as well as the network as whole. Another challenge with full-mesh VPLS implementations is the introduction of new L2 nodes or PE devices in an existing VPLS instance. Introducing a new PE in an VPLS instance is a network-wide disruption, where configuration changes might be required on all the existing PE devices to support the new pseudowires that need to be implemented.

H-VPLS offers a flexible and scalable alternative to the full-mesh VPLS topology by creating a two-level hierarchy of pseudowires. The core or aggregation devices implement the full mesh of pseudowires, as is typically done in a traditional VPLS implementation. The endpoints, or rather their associated PE routers in the access domain, then use a *spoke pseudowire* to connect to their closest aggregation or core PE. As the typical number of core and aggregation PEs is substantially lower than access PE devices, H-VPLS delivers a more scalable architecture that requires a lower number of total pseudowires. Split-horizon rules have to be tweaked in H-VPLS deployments to allow traffic forwarding between the spoke and core pseudowires. Network architects must ensure a loop-free topology in an H-VPLS architecture through careful split-horizon planning between core and spoke pseudowire. Figure 8-6 explains this further by highlighting the reduced number of pseudowires in an H-VPLS environment compared to a traditional VPLS architecture.

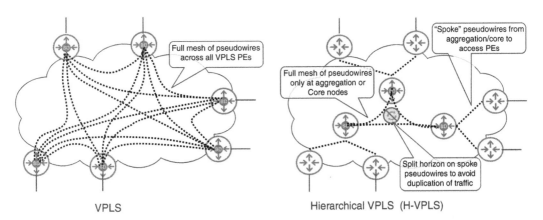

VPLS

Hierarchical VPLS (H-VPLS)

FIGURE 8-6   VPLS and Hierarchical VPLS (H-VPLS) Concepts

Multipoint L2VPN is an important tool in a network architect's arsenal, but its applicability in MCN has been steadily decreasing over the past several years. This is because more and more endpoints are becoming "IP aware," and thus most modern MCNs use Layer 3 VPNs as their primary transport mechanism. Pockets of MCNs, where RAN or mobile core devices might not be L3 aware, still rely on Layer 2 point-to-point or multipoint services, such as the RU-DU connectivity in the fronthaul, where L2 services are the only viable option currently. The rest of the xHaul transport uses L3VPNs, as also defined in the O-RAN's xHaul Packet Switched Architecture Specifications.[8]

Layer 3 VPN Services

Commonly referred to as *IP VPN* or *MPLS VPN*, L3VPN services are some of the most successful, if not *the* most successful, transport services over the past few decades. L3VPNs have universal applications in both the service provider and enterprise sectors to achieve traffic separation and connectivity between multiple sites. While L2VPN provides Layer 2 (primarily Ethernet) connectivity over an MPLS network, L3VPN offers Layer 3 (usually IP) connectivity. With IP being the primary connectivity mechanism for various MCN components, mobile service providers extensively use L3VPNs within and across each MCN domain to enable end-to-end mobile services.

MPLS-based L3VPN is not precisely a new technology. In fact, the earliest IETF draft outlining MPLS VPN methods and functions dates back to the year 1998, and it was adopted as RFC 2547 in 1999.[9] Since its introduction, MPLS VPN have gone through many updates defined in various RFCs, all aimed at enhancing its functionality and operations.

At its core, MPLS L3VPN enable a router to isolate and terminate a customer connection using a feature called *Virtual Routing and Forwarding (VRF)*. A VRF is a Layer 3 construct within the MPLS PE that creates a separate routing and forwarding table. An MPLS PE supports multiple VRFs, thus providing a number of discrete customers their own routing table, thus segregating each customer's routing. These VRF-specific routing tables are different from the *default* or *global* routing table and contain only the reachability information for specific VPNs. Each VRF also contains one or more interfaces, both physical and logical. Physical interfaces in the VRF are used to connect the provider's PE device to the customer equipment.

> ### What Does VRF Stand for Anyway?
>
> Although in the earlier L3VPN RFCs, a VRF was called *VPN Routing and Forwarding*, the industry has since moved to using the *Virtual Routing and Forwarding* terminology instead, and this shift is reflected in vendor documentation as well as later RFCs.

Traffic received on interfaces belonging to a VRF can either be routed only to other interfaces that are part of the same VRF or sent to the remote VPN destinations using the routes in the VRF routing table. The VRF-specific routes are exchanged between MPLS PEs using *Multi-Protocol BGPs (MP-BGP)*—a term given to a collection of extensions and features that allows BGP to carry reachability information for multiple address families, including VPNv4, VPNv6, L2VPN, and EVPN, as well as the global IPv4/IPv6 routes. The routes exchanged for VPN are different from regular IPv4 routes in the sense that these are 12-byte entities instead of a regular 4-byte IP address. The additional 8 bytes come from a field called *Route Distinguisher (RD)* that is appended to every IPv4 route in the VRF, making it a *VPN-IPv4* route, commonly called a *VPNv4* route.[10]

Route Distinguishers

Although first defined and used for MPLS L3VPN, Route Distinguishers have since been used for making routes unique in other address families, such as EVPN, as well.

RD values are defined by service providers and generally use an autonomous system number (ASN) as part of the naming convention. This, however, is just a popular approach for naming consistency, rather than being mandated by the standard bodies.

The use of a unique RD for each VRF unlocks the possibility of IP address overlap between the multiple VRFs. In fact, one of the key benefits of L3VPN is the possibility of using the same IP addresses in the global routing table as well as in one or more VRFs, allowing the VPN customers to use any IP addresses for their endpoints, including private IP addresses, without worrying about IP address overlap with other customers. An RD has no discernable value in the MPLS VPN ecosystem other than uniquely distinguishing VPNv4 routes across multiple VRFs. Although entirely symbolic in nature, the RDs are transmitted as part of VPNv4 routes using MP-BGP. Figure 8-7 shows the MPLS BGP L3VPN concept across an SP network.

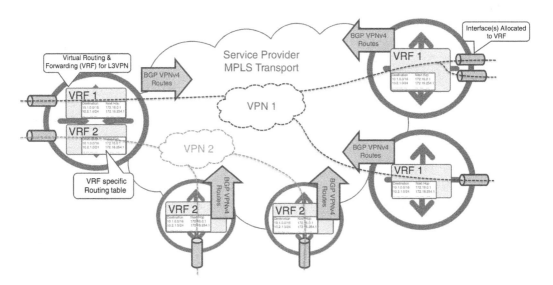

FIGURE 8-7   L3VPN Overview

Upon receiving the VPNv4 routes from remote MP-BGP peers, an MPLS PE populates its VRF-specific routing table based on the *Route Target (RT)*, an 8-byte field that determines the VPN membership of a route, and can also be used for route filtering between multiple VPN sites. RTs are configured upon VRF creation and are *exported* with a VPNv4 route. These RTs are carried to other PE devices using MP-BGP Extended BGP Communities defined in RFC 4360.[11] Upon receiving a VPNv4 route and its associated RT, the remote MPLS PE may choose to *import* the routes tagged with this RT into the VRF, thus populating the VRF-specific routing table. Multiple RTs, both for import and export, can be configured on a VRF and provide a simple yet powerful route-filtering mechanism in VPN-enabled networks.

Route Distinguishers vs. Route Targets

Networking professionals can sometimes find the concept of RD and RT confusing, maybe due to the somewhat similar naming convention. Both the RD and RT are assigned by the service provider implementing VPN services and have no significance outside their network.

In short, RDs are only used to allow possibly overlapping IP addresses across VRFs by making the *RD:IP* combination unique and preventing BGP speakers from comparing routes belonging to different VPNs.

RT, on the other hand, controls the distribution (that is, the import and export) of VPNv4 routes with an MPLS VPN.

Since its introduction in the late 1990s, MPLS-based L3VPNs have gone through a number of refinements and enhancements. One of the recent enhancements was the use of L3VPN with Segment Routing Traffic Engineering (SRTE) through route coloring and automated steering, as already discussed in Chapter 6. In fact, given the popularity and widespread use of MPLS-based L3VPNs, automated steering of L3VPN traffic into a Segment Routing policy was among the very first use cases to be implemented for SRTE.

L3VPNs are used extensively in today's mobile communication networks. These VPN services are implemented not only to provide connectivity between various MCN domains, but also to ensure traffic isolation between mobile, fixed access, enterprise, and other services. Almost all mobile networks offer multigenerational services, where 2G and 4G are the most commonly offered services, with some providers still offering 3G services as well. In these scenarios, a separate L3VPN is typically used for each mobile generation. VPN services are also used to implement logical interfaces defined by 3GPP for connectivity between mobile components. For instance, X2 (for 4G) and Xn (for 5G) interfaces require inter-cell-site (or rather inter-eNB or inter-gNB) connectivity, which is usually implemented by using L3VPN.

Route targets, among other route-filtering techniques, play an important role in ensuring VPNs provide an appropriate level of connectivity. For instance, when all cell sites are part of the same VPN, it creates scalability challenges. To reiterate, cell site routers are typically smaller, relatively lower-cost devices with limited memory and CPU resources. Learning the IP or VPN routes of *all* other cell sites (often tens of thousands of sites) on a single CSR creates a significant scalability challenge. Xn (or X2) connections are typically required only between adjacent cell sites for handovers and advanced antenna functions such as multi-radio or coordinated multipoint transmissions. Route targets can prove useful here by filtering unwanted routes across the VPN PE devices. In the case of MCN, each RAN domain (that is, the collection of RAN sites in close vicinity) can export VPN routes tagged with a route target unique to that domain. Neighboring RAN domains can then import only the route with the desired route targets (typically only the neighboring RAN domains and the packet core), thus providing built-in route filtering. Central VPN sites, such as those connecting the mobile core to the VPN service, will need to import routes tagged with RTs from all the RAN domains in order to ensure connectivity between the mobile core and cell sites. These could be a significant number of routes, but the networking devices at the central sites are high-end routers that do not suffer from the same scalability challenges as a typical CSR, and are able to support a much higher route scale. Figure 8-8 shows an example use of L3VPNs in an MCN.

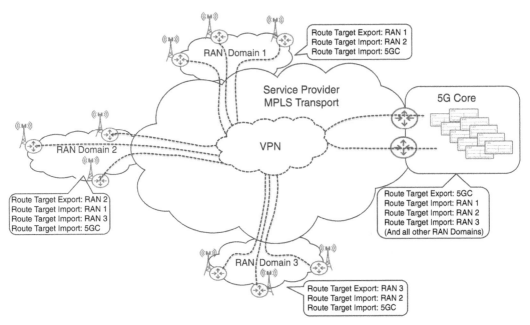

FIGURE 8-8   Route Targets Controlling VPN Route Distribution in an MCN

Ethernet VPN (EVPN)

The tremendous popularity and deployment success of both L2 and L3 VPN services over the last two decades did drive a lot of innovation and development work in both L2 and L3 technological camps. Although more and more end devices are steering away from L2-only connectivity and embracing the routable L3 approach, L2 services still play a vital role in modern MCNs and DCs. Indeed, not every communication flow can be easily retrofitted to use IP protocol stack, as this might require significant redesign of an end device's hardware and software. Besides, there is common perception that the use of L2 simplifies redundancy and mobility of a service. In fact, there is a degree of truth in such perception. Applications in geo-redundant DCs often rely on L2 for load mobility, as migrating an IP flow in the backend of a DC can be a challenging task due to services disruption caused by reconfiguring IP addressing and routing. While the use of L2 technologies might simplify applications' architecture, it usually does not reduce overall system complexity, but rather shifts it from applications to the network.

As discussed in the previous section of this chapter, L2VPN services do have their own set of challenges, such as scalability of MAC learning via a *flood-and-learn* approach and the lack of All-Active redundancy models, especially in point-to-point pseudowires. Ethernet VPN was introduced as an innovative solution to these challenges, as described in RFC 7432, *"BGP MPLS-Based Ethernet VPN."*[12]

EVPN Concepts

The EVPN solution aims at providing optimizations in the areas of MAC address learning, BUM traffic handling, endpoint connection redundancy, as well as provisioning and deployment simplification. While the primary focus of EVPN is to provide L2VPN services, it also has the capability to transport L3 traffic. Most EVPN improvements required rethinking of the control plane, and, as such, the procedures defined by the EVPN standard predominantly deal with the control plane mechanisms. Unsurprisingly, MP-BGP was selected as the basis for EVPN, reusing the same Address Family Identifier (AFI) of 25, used by L2VPN services, with the new Subsequent Address Family Identifier (SAFI) of 70 defined specifically for EVPN.

The major difference between EVPN and traditional L2VPN technology is the exchange of MAC addresses learned by PE devices via the control plane. MAC learning in EVPN no longer uses the simplistic yet poorly scalable flood-and-learn method, but rather uses BGP to exchange information about MAC reachability. In other words, EVPN introduces the concept of *routing of L2 packets* across the transport network to their ultimate destination. For this purpose, EVPN uses *Ethernet VPN Instance (EVI)*, *Ethernet Segment Identifier (ESI)*, and a number of *route types* along with various attributes exchanged via BGP.

In essence, an EVI is a single EVPN service across the service provider network and consists of *MAC-VRFs* across all PE routers participating in that service. Each MAC-VRF is an instantiation of an individual VPN on a PE device, where instead of IP routing information, the VRF is populated with MAC addresses. A MAC-VRF can be implemented as a bridge domain associated with an EVI and performs L2 switching between local attachment circuits and EVPN peers.

Within the EVI, each connection from the PE to the end device is called an *Ethernet segment*, which is the equivalent of an attachment circuit in traditional L2VPN services. The end device in this case can be a host, a server, switch of even a router, and is using EVPN for L2 connectivity. In the case of an MCN, the end device might be an RU, DU, or other mobility-related component.

An Ethernet segment is not necessarily a single Ethernet link; it can be a link aggregation group (LAG) that might even span different PE devices. In the latter case, the end device is multi-homed to two or more PE devices, and all links connecting the same end device are considered to be the same Ethernet segment. These multi-homed links can be operating in *Single-Active* (only one link used for forwarding, others being backup) or *All-Active* (all links forwarding simultaneously and load-balancing traffic) mode. Each Ethernet segment is represented by an Ethernet Segment Identifier (ESI), which is exchanged between PE devices providing multihoming. Different PE routers can discover that they are connected to the same Ethernet segment by examining the ESI exchanged in one of the EVPN BGP route types (Route Type 4). Figure 8-9 illustrates EVPN concepts, including the use of EVIs, Ethernet segments, and multihoming.

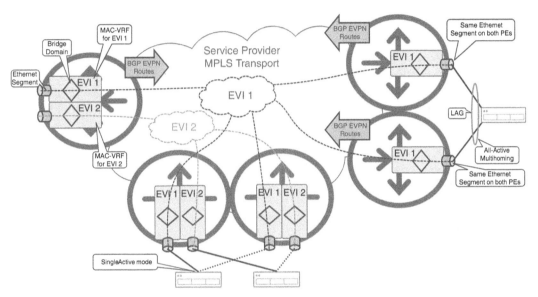

FIGURE 8-9 EVPN Concepts

EVPN Route Types

A number of EVPN BGP route types and special extended communities are used by EVPN PE devices to exchange information about EVPN instances, MAC addresses learned on Ethernet segments, labels, and other information required for EVPN operation. Five route types (1 through 5) have been standardized with a few more proposed by new IETF drafts at the time of this writing. These route types are covered here not in the order of their type number but rather based on their purpose.

EVPN Route Type 2

EVPN Route Type 2, or *MAC/IP Advertisement Route*, is the cornerstone of any multipoint EVPN service. PE devices use Type 2 routes to exchange information about learned as well as statically configured MAC addresses in their MAC-VRF. On each PE device, local MAC addresses are learned using the standard MAC learning process as L2 frames arrive on the Ethernet segment. As the MAC addresses are learned by the PE, it constructs a MAC/IP advertisement route and advertises it via BGP to other PE devices participating in the EVI, thus enabling *remote MAC learning*. This is in direct contrast to the traditional L2VPN approach where MAC addresses are learned via the data plane through the flood-and-learn approach. Each MAC/IP advertisement route relies on a set of route targets (RTs) to ensure remote PE devices import the route into the appropriate EVI. In a way similar to L3VPN, route distinguishers ensure uniqueness of BGP routes even if MAC/IP routes overlap in different EVIs. Interestingly enough, a MAC/IP advertisement route may carry the IP address of the end device as well; however, this information is used for ARP suppression rather than routing.

In a DC environment, especially with the use of virtual machines and containers, it is not uncommon for virtual entities to migrate to other servers within the same EVI, but connected to different PE devices. This results in their MAC address to be reachable from the new PE and thus requires every other PE in the network to learn about this MAC mobility. In order to support MAC mobility, a MAC/IP advertisement route relies on a *MAC Mobility extended community* defined specifically for this scenario. This extended community carries the sequence number, which is used to identify the latest version of the MAC/IP advertisement route and determine which PE should be used to deliver packets toward this MAC address.

EVPN Route Type 1

EVPN Route Type 1 is called *Ethernet Auto-Discovery (A-D) Route* and is advertised by PE routers per Ethernet segment and per EVI. Type 1 routes are used in fast convergence procedures and enable load balancing when end devices are multihomed to more than one PE device.

Indeed, without the A-D routes, the convergence can take substantially longer, as every MAC entry (learned using Type 2 routes) has to be individually timed out and replaced when an advertising PE fails. Instead, PE advertises an A-D route for an EVI/ESI along with its MAC/IP routes, thus creating a dependency between Type 2 and Type 1 routes. As a result, in the case of PE device or Ethernet segment failure causing a withdrawal of an A-D route, every MAC/IP route associated to that PE or Ethernet segment is withdrawn simultaneously. This process is also known as *massive MAC with-drawal*. This method is faster and more reliable than traditional L2VPN convergence, where a PE or attachment circuit failure simply means loss of traffic, and MAC entries are only updated via timeout or if traffic with the same MAC address is received through another path.

A-D routes are also fundamental for another EVPN key feature—*All-Active multihoming*. In an All-Active multihoming scenario, end devices connect to multiple PE routers, sharing the same EVI, and form a link aggregation group (LAG) spanning across these PE routers. The member links of the LAG are considered the same Ethernet segment by all participating PE devices and, thus, each PE advertises the A-D route for the common Ethernet segment. It is common for multihomed endpoints' MAC addresses to be learned and advertised by only one PE, even though endpoints are multihomed to multiple PE devices. When a remote PE receives Type 2 MAC/IP routes and Type 1 A-D routes for the same Ethernet segment, it aliases all PE devices advertising these A-D routes to the set of MAC/IP routes. Therefore, *aliasing* enables load balancing of traffic for these MAC addresses across all available PE devices. Figure 8-10 illustrates aliasing and massive MAC withdrawal concepts.

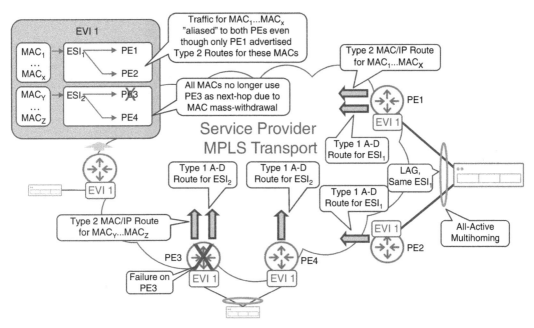

FIGURE 8-10   Aliasing and MAC Mass-Withdrawal in EVPN

When *Single-Active* multihoming is used, the traffic for learned MAC addresses is forwarded only to a preferred PE, also called a *Designated Forwarder* or *DF*. This is explained in detail later in this section. Other PE devices connected to the same Ethernet segment are used for forwarding only if the DF PE fails. Nevertheless, in the event of a single PE failure, it is not required to relearn all MAC/IP advertisement routes to start forwarding packets to backup PE devices. The aliasing of Type 2 MAC/IP routes to other PE devices via Type 1 A-D routes ensures faster switchover time in Single-Active multihoming scenarios as well. The desired redundancy mode used in multihoming (that is, single-active or all-active) is signaled by a flag in the *ESI label extended community* attached to an A-D route.

EVPN Route Type 4

EVPN Route Type 4 is an *Ethernet segment route* and is used for selection of a DF for the Ethernet segment in multihomed scenarios to avoid BUM traffic duplication toward an endpoint. When a BUM frame is transmitted over the network, every PE that is part of the same EVI receives a copy of it. Without a special mechanism, all PE devices would forward a copy of this BUM frame toward connected endpoints. This could result in a multihomed endpoint receiving multiple copies of the same BUM frame. To avoid this problem, PE devices on the same Ethernet segment select a single DF PE for their Ethernet segment. By exchanging Ethernet segment routes, PE devices discover common Ethernet segment connections and independently run a deterministic algorithm to identify which PE becomes a DF for a given Ethernet segment. Only the DF PE sends a copy of the BUM frames received from the network to the Ethernet segment, thus ensuring no duplicated frames on end devices. This behavior is shown on Figure 8-11.

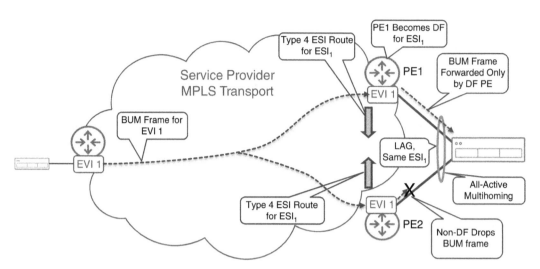

FIGURE 8-11   Designated Forwarder PE in EVPN

Although the introduction of DF PE solves the problem of BUM traffic duplication on the multi-homed Ethernet segments, it does so only for BUM frames received *from the network*. The duplication problem can still occur in the reverse direction, when a BUM frame is received *from a multihomed end device* on an Ethernet segment. The hashing mechanism on the end device itself determines which PE would receive this BUM frame, and it can be either a DF PE or a non-DF PE.

If this BUM frame is received on the DF PE, it is then forwarded to all other PE devices sharing the same EVI over the MPLS network. Any non-DF PE connected to this Ethernet segment would also receive a copy of this BUM frame through the MPLS network. These PE devices will never forward it back to the same Ethernet segment because the non-DF PE is not allowed to forward any BUM frames received from the network to the Ethernet segment. No duplication occurs in this scenario.

In the second scenario, the BUM frame is received from a multihomed end device by a non-DF PE. Similar to the first scenario, the receiving PE (non-DF PE in this case) forwards this BUM frame over MPLS network to all other PE devices, but it inserts an additional label to identify the Ethernet segment it was received from. This label is advertised in the Type 1 A-D routes. When the BUM frame circles back over the MPLS network to the DF PE for the same Ethernet segment, the DF PE identifies the Ethernet segment via this label and never forwards it back the Ethernet segment, thus preventing frame echo. This is how EVPN implements split horizon. This mechanism applies only to DF PE devices connected to the originating Ethernet segment. The remote DF PE devices, connected to other Ethernet segments, follow the process shown in the Figure 8-11 and ignore the Ethernet segment identifier label.

EVPN Route Type 3

EVPN Route Type 3 is called the *Inclusive Multicast Ethernet Tag* route and provides a mechanism for PE devices to signal their interest in receiving BUM traffic for EVI as well as the required replication method. These replication methods could include an ingress PE performing the replication or the network itself implementing the replication via one of the multicast protocols (mLDP, PIM, and so on). By using Type 3 routes, remote PE devices may request *ingress replication* of BUM traffic at the originating PE or use already established point-to-multipoint trees in the network. With ingress replication, the source PE receiving a BUM frame from an end device would replicate and send a copy of this frame to all other PE devices sharing the same EVI. Although this mechanism is simple and does not require additional network-wide configuration to support multicast or other multipoint communication mechanisms between PE devices, ingress replication can be challenging for PE devices in large-scale EVPN networks. In those environments, the use of point-to-multipoint replication trees between the PE devices can dramatically reduce replication load on the ingress PE, as well as increase bandwidth utilization efficiency. However, the responsibilities of constructing and maintaining replication trees fall on the network and require network architects to consider use of appropriate protocols and replication tree design.

EVPN Route Type 5

The *IP Prefix Advertisement* route, or EVPN Route Type 5, was an enhancement introduced via RFC 9136, "IP Prefix Advertisement in EVPN," since the original EVPN RFC 7432 defines only four Route types.[13] Although Type 2 MAC/IP routes can exchange IP information, the IPs in these routes are always linked to MAC addresses. Due to this linkage, the Type 2 routes cannot be effectively used for pure L3 reachability information, which may be needed in some scenarios. In those scenarios, EVPN instances use *Integrated Routing and Bridging (IRB)*, which allows both L2 and L3 connectivity. For these scenarios, a Type 5 EVPN route can be used to advertise just the IP subnet, without linking it to any specific MAC address. In other words, the Type 5 route enhances EVPN to offer VPN connectivity at L3.

In a simple case, traffic for a prefix advertised by a Type 5 route can be forwarded to the advertising PE using the label included in the Type 5 route. However, there are some advanced use cases, where a Type 5 route can be recursively resolved to a next-hop PE using either a Type 1 A-D route or Type 2 MAC/IP route. A combination of Type 5 and either Type 1 or Type 2 route in EVPN provides flexibility to link IP prefixes advertised in Type 5 routes with MAC information contained in Type 2 routes or directly with Ethernet segments via Type 1 routes.

Typically, a Layer 3 VRF is created on a PE router when a Type 5 route is used to advertise an IP prefix untied from MAC addresses. This Layer 3 VRF is paired with a bridge domain in a MAC-VRF via IRB interface configuration. Although it is entirely possible to use EVPN Type 5 routes to exchange Layer 3 routing information in a similar way as L3VPNs, it is not always feasible to replace L3VPN services with EVPN. At the time of this writing, EVPN is still an emerging technology, and feature parity with L3VPN is yet to be achieved. O-RAN Alliance recommends the use of both L3VPN (in midhaul and backhaul) and EVPN (in fronthaul) technologies in xHaul networks.

EVPN VPWS

The procedures, route types, and extended communities defined in RFC 7432 for Ethernet VPN services are mostly concerned with the routing of L2 frames over MPLS networks and enabling effective multipoint services. Nevertheless, point-to-point services, or pseudowires, are also supported by RFC 7432. Strictly speaking, a pair of Type 1 A-D EVPN routes exchanged between two PE devices for a common EVI is sufficient to establish a virtual private wire service (VPWS) between two Ethernet segments. Even Type 2 MAC/IP routes are not necessary for traffic forwarding, as MAC learning is not needed for point-to-point connections. Any frame received on one PE should be forwarded to the remote PE.

Legacy point-to-point L2VPN implementations allowed only two PE devices and used the terminologies such as dual-active, active-active, or active-backup pseudowires. IETF RFC 8214, "Virtual Private Wire Service Support in Ethernet VPN," describes the procedures and tools to apply robust All-Active or Single-Active EVPN redundancy, high availability, and load balancing mechanisms to the EVPN VPWS service.[14] The term *All-Active* was carefully chosen by the EVPN working group to reflect the capability to allow two or more PE devices for redundancy and high availability on either end of the VPWS service.

This RFC for VPWS defines an additional extended community to be propagated by Type 1 A-D EVPN routes. When multiple PE routers are attached to the same Ethernet segment and configured in *Single-Active redundancy mode*, they run a Designated Forwarder election. Unlike regular EVPN service, this process in EVPN VPWS results in electing a *primary-selected PE* for the Ethernet segment, a *backup-selected PE*, and others—if more than two PE devices are connected to the same Ethernet segment. The result of this election process is signaled via special flags in a newly defined BGP extended community. Remote PE devices then send pseudowire traffic to the primary-selected PE in all cases, except when a failure is detected. If the Type 1 A-D route for the primary-selected PE is withdrawn, the traffic is forwarded to the backup-selected PE. The Single-Active EVPN VPWS mechanism effectively re-creates the legacy active/backup pseudowire redundancy method described in the point-to-point L2VPN section.

All-Active redundancy mode is where EVPN VPWS provides innovative and effective redundancy mechanism when compared with traditional point-to-point L2VPN services. When configured for All-Active redundancy, PE routers connected to the same Ethernet segment do not elect a DF; instead, all the active PE devices set their respective flag in the BGP extended community attached to the Type 1 A-D route, indicating each of them is the primary PE. The remote PE can now perform flow-based load balancing to all active PE devices serving the same Ethernet segment. Figure 8-12 shows the use of EVPN VPWS with All-Active multihoming redundancy for eCPRI traffic transport between the RU and DU, as also recommended by the O-RAN Alliance specifications.[15]

Although the original EVPN standard describes only the MPLS-based forwarding plane, the EVPN VPWS RFC also mentions the *virtual eXtensible local area network (VXLAN)* as a forwarding mechanism alternative to MPLS. In fact, the EVPN control plane is becoming increasingly common in most VXLAN implementations.

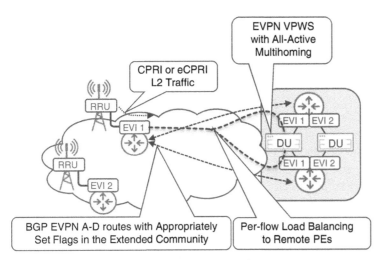

FIGURE 8-12 EVPN Point-to-Point Service

VXLAN

In parallel to EVPN development, network architects were also trying to solve the challenges of L2 connectivity in the growing DC, as was mentioned in previous chapter. Proliferation of virtualization techniques pushed the number of individual MAC addresses in a typical DC far beyond the numbers of physical servers. Within a typical server, multiple tenants or virtual machines (VMs) use their own MAC addresses, which exacerbated the already serious scalability challenge for the L2-based DC networks of the time. The use of 802.1Q VLAN tagging offered temporary relief by providing flow isolation across DC tenants, but the number of VLANs required to support the growing number of DC tenants greatly exceeded the hard limit of 4096 VLANs in a single-tagged 802.1Q frame. Moreover, purely Layer 2 connectivity models had to rely on Spanning Tree Protocol families to prevent L2 loops from occurring in the networks. An idea of creating an overlay network for L2 services by encapsulating them into a special header and transporting it over the underlying L3 transport network was proposed to solve these challenges. This solution became standardized as RFC 7348 and is known today as *virtual eXtensible local area network (VXLAN)*.

In simple terms, VXLAN creates a multitude of non-overlapping overlay networks on the same IP-based underlay transport. VXLAN expands traditional VLANs to 16 million separate instances by using a 24-bit *VXLAN network identifier (VNI)* in its header. VNI is akin to an EVPN instance and effectively creates isolation for MAC addresses and VLANs used by different tenants not involved in direct communications. Besides the VNI, the VXLAN header contains flags and fields reserved for future use. An L2 frame received from an end device is appended with a VXLAN header and is then transported using a UDP datagram over an IP-based transport.

In order to perform all necessary encapsulations and decapsulations, edge network devices implement a *VXLAN tunnel endpoint (VTEP)*. Typically, a single VTEP serves multiple VNIs originating or terminating on the single edge network device. VTEPs can also be implemented as a software function inside the hypervisor, providing VXLAN services directly to the hosted VMs, without the use of dedicated networking hardware.

The original VXLAN RFC mainly focuses on data plane forwarding and does not explicitly discuss control plane mechanisms. L2 frames for remote MAC addresses are encapsulated with an appropriate VXLAN header and sent toward a remote VTEP based on its IP address. Early VXLAN implementations required all VTEPs for the same VNI to be explicitly configured with each other's IP addresses. This lack of a proper control plane defined in the VXLAN standard as well as the flood-and-learn approach significantly limited the scalability of the VXLAN solution. To remedy this, the network equipment vendors attempted to create custom automation tools for VXLAN deployment and management in large DC environments. Examples of such tools include Cisco's Virtual Topology System (VTS) and Arista's CloudVision eXchange (CVX).[16, 17] Figure 8-13 illustrates the concepts of VXLAN.

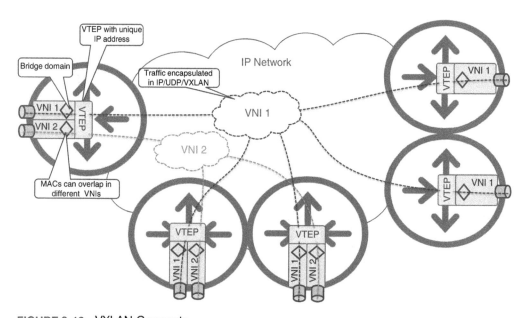

FIGURE 8-13   VXLAN Concepts

For BUM frames, two main options were defined:

■ The use of multicast for replication in the underlying transport network

■ Ingress replication of BUM frames and unicast delivery to all concerned remote VTEPs

Due to the lack of a control plane, BUM frame delivery is critical in the VXLAN's flood-and-learn-based MAC-learning mechanism. The directly connected VTEP learns the MAC addresses of connected endpoints using a standard approach—by examining the source MAC addresses of L2 frames and populating the local MAC table. At the same time, for traffic forwarding, a lookup of the destination MAC address is performed in the local MAC table. If the destination is unknown, or a frame is sent to the multicast or broadcast MAC address, it is treated as a BUM frame and sent to all other VTEPs for the same VNI. Once this is received, the remote VTEP would learn the MAC addresses of the source, update its own MAC table, and use this information to unicast the return traffic to the originating VTEP.

While this process seems like basic Layer 2 switching, the critical difference in VXLAN is the *routing* of the encapsulated L2 frames over an IP underlay. With IP as the underlying transport, IP routing protocols could be used between Layer 3 switches implementing VTEPs and thus provide all the benefits of a robust Layer 3 transport, such as ECMP, L3 loop avoidance, and more.

Whereas VXLAN standards mostly cover data plane functionality, EVPN provides a comprehensive control plane for transporting Layer 2 frames over an MPLS-enabled forwarding plane. As both these technologies were being developed mostly in parallel, the networking industry quickly turned to augment the VXLAN solution with a BGP-based EVPN control plane. The standardization efforts to use EVPN as a control plane for forwarding planes other than MPLS resulted in IETF RFC 8365, "A Network Virtualization Overlay Solution Using Ethernet VPN (EVPN)."[18] Although some EVPN-defined procedures and the use of messages and flags were adjusted to support non-MPLS forwarding planes, the main concepts, route types, and procedures remained mostly intact. When used with VXLAN, label fields in EVPN messages exchange information about VXLAN network identifiers, and VTEP IP addresses are used instead of PE addresses.

Today, Segment Routing MPLS-based DCs are growing in popularity, but many existing DCs still use VXLAN as their forwarding technology. By introducing scalable MAC-learning procedures via the EVPN control plane, VTEP auto-discovery and support of All-Active multihoming scenarios, in combination with VXLAN and EVPN, can offer the same level of service as MPLS-based EVPN.

Transport Services Across MCN

In addition to the commonly used VPN technologies discussed in this chapter, a plethora of networking technologies and connectivity protocols can be used to provide transport services. Some of these technologies include L2TPv3, GRE, DMVPN (which uses multipoint-GRE), Generic Network Virtualization Encapsulation (GENEVE), Network Virtualization using Generic Routing Encapsulation (NVGRE), and Overlay Transport Virtualization (OTV); however, they are virtually never used as the primary connectivity mechanism in an MCN. There might be a few outlier scenarios and use cases where some of these technologies may be applicable (such as L2TPv3 for L2 connectivity over a non-MPLS IP-only underlay, or GRE to provide Layer 3 overlay), but overall such instances are few and far between. Virtually all modern networks use a combination of overlay technologies discussed in this chapter—L2VPN VPWS, L3VPN, EVPN, and VXLAN—in various MCN domains. The choice of the VPN protocol used is dependent on product support, feature richness, deployment simplicity, and sometimes based on golf course discussions between organizational leaders.

Unless L2 connectivity is required explicitly by the endpoint(s), MPLS L3VPNs are the preferred connectivity mechanism within an MCN. As mentioned previously, one such example is the explicit use of L2VPN for RU and DU connectivity through the fronthaul, which is typically provided through traditional VPWS or EVPN VPWS-based pseudowires. In contrast, L3VPN is preferred for midhaul and backhaul as well as for management connectivity across all xHaul domains, as specified in the O-RAN Packet Switched xHaul Architecture specifications.[19]

As mentioned previously in Chapter 5, "5G Fundamentals," the O-RAN architecture defines four planes of operations for any modern-day MCN:

- The management plane (M-Plane), which provides RU management functions such as software maintenance and fault management

- The control plane (C-Plane), which is used for control messaging regarding RF resource allocation for functions such as scheduling, multi-radio coordination, beamforming, and so on

- The user plane (U-Plane), which carries the actual mobile user data

- The synchronization plane (S-Plane), which provides timing and synchronization between RAN components

Transport network connectivity for all these planes of operations is provided by the VPN technologies described throughout this chapter.

A separate L3VPN instance is used for M-Plane connectivity to ensure management traffic is kept separate from other traffic on the network. C-Plane traffic and U-Plane traffic are closely related, as they both pertain to mobile user traffic. As such, they may have their own separate VPN instances or share a VPN instance with separation provided by using different IP subnets, depending on the RAN vendor implementation. The VPN instance for end-to-end C-Plane and U-Plane is composed of VPWS (traditional EoMPLS based or EVPN based) in the fronthaul and L3VPN in the midhaul and backhaul. This could change to end-to-end L3VPN-based C- and U-Planes if the RU and DU start supporting L3 connectivity in the future. Figure 8-14 illustrates the VPN services and their implementation.

While traffic from other planes uses VPN overlay for transport, S-Plane is implemented natively as part of the transport infrastructure. This is due to the nature of synchronization traffic, where better accuracy could be achieved if transport network elements (that is, routers) along the traffic path participate in the synchronization process. The next chapter will discuss the details of timing and synchronization as well as its importance and implementation in the 5G networks.

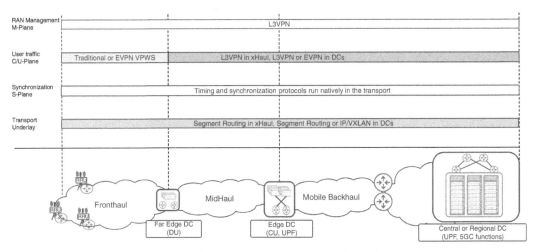

FIGURE 8-14 Transport Services Across Various Planes of Operations

Summary

This chapter focused on transport services that are essential for establishing end-to-end connectivity within an MCN.

The following technologies and services were discussed in this chapter:

- Components of an end-to-end 5G transport service

- The use of virtual private networks (VPNs) in a service provider environment and their relevance to enable mobile services in an MCN

- Point-to-point Layer 2 VPN services and their applications, benefits, and limitations

- The use of Multipoint Layer 2 VPN services such as Virtual Private LAN Service (VPLS), Hierarchical VPLS (H-VPLS), and the MEF services

- An overview of BGP-based Layer 3 VPNs and their benefits over traditional Layer 2 VPNs in an MCN

- The drivers for Ethernet VPN (EVPN), its operations, and its applicability for transport services, providing flexible, scalable, and versatile VPN services for Layer 2 and Layer 3 connectivity

- The use of Virtual eXtensible LAN (VXLAN) in data centers, its lack of a control plane, and its augmentation with EVPN to provide a flexible MAC-learning mechanism, thus providing an effective Layer 2 overlay using an IP underlay

- The use of L2VPN, L3VPN, and EVPN to implement O-RAN-specified management, control, and user planes in an MCN

The synchronization plane (S-Plane), unlike the M-, C-, and U-Planes, does not use the VPN services defined in this chapter. Instead, the S-Plane is implemented through additional protocols running natively on the underlying transport infrastructure. Chapter 9, "Essential Technologies for 5G-Ready Networks: Timing and Synchronization," will focus on the concepts of timing, synchronization, and clocking, which are important to understand in an effort to implement S-Plane and, subsequently, mobile services.

References

1. IETF RFC 3985, "Pseudo Wire Emulation Edge-to-Edge (PWE3) Architecture"

2. "Any Transport over MPLS (AToM)," https://www.cisco.com/c/en/us/products/ios-nx-os-software/any-transport-over-multiprotocol-label-switching-atom/index.html (last visited: Mar 2022)

3. Huawei virtual leased lines overview, https://support.huawei.com/enterprise/en/doc/EDOC1000178321/3e8aae35/overview-of-vll (last visited: Mar 2022)

4. Nokia virtual leased line services, https://documentation.nokia.com/html/0_add-h-f/93-0076-10-01/7750_SR_OS_Services_Guide/services_VLL-Intro.html (last visited: Mar 2022)

5. IETF RFC 4906, "Transport of Layer 2 Frames Over MPLS"

6. IETF RFC 6624, "Layer 2 Virtual Private Networks Using BGP for Auto-Discovery and Signaling"

7. IETF RFC 4761, "Virtual Private LAN Service (VPLS) Using BGP for Auto-Discovery and Signaling"

8. O-RAN Xhaul Packet Switched Architectures and Solutions

9. IETF RFC 2547, "BGP/MPLS VPNs"

10. Ibid.

11. IETF RFC 4360, "BGP Extended Communities Attributes"

12. IETF RFC 7432, "BGP MPLS-Based Ethernet VPN"

13. IETF RFC 9136, "IP Prefix Advertisement in Ethernet VPN (EVPN)," https://datatracker.ietf.org/doc/draft-ietf-bess-evpn-prefix-advertisement (last visited: Mar 2022)

14. IETF RFC 8214, "Virtual Private Wire Service Support in Ethernet VPN"

15. O-RAN, op. cit.

16. "Cisco Virtual Topology System," https://www.cisco.com/c/en/us/products/cloud-systems-management/virtual-topology-system/index.html (last visited: Mar 2022)

17. Arista's CloudVision solution, https://www.arista.com/en/cg-cv/cv-introduction-to-cloudvision (last visited: Mar 2022)

18. IETF RFC 8365, "A Network Virtualization Overlay Solution Using Ethernet VPN (EVPN)"

19. O-RAN, op. cit.

Chapter 9

Essential Technologies for 5G-Ready Networks: Timing and Synchronization

Although not always front and center, synchronization has always been deeply intertwined with network communications. The role of synchronization was far more pervasive in the earlier transport networks that utilized technologies such as time-division multiplexing (TDM) circuits, which relied heavily on both ends of the link to coordinate the transmission of data. The easiest way to achieve this coordination is to use a common *timing reference,* acting as the synchronization source, delivered to the communicating parties. This reference signal is in addition to the user traffic, much like a coxswain in modern-day rowboat competitions. The coxswain is the person at the end of the rowboat who keeps the rowers' actions synchronized to ensure maximum efficiency, but he does not contribute to the actual rowing capacity. In the absence of a coxswain synchronizing the rowers' actions, it's entirely possible for paddles to get out of sync and break the momentum. Similarly, in a transport network in the absence of a reference timing signal, both the transmitter and receiver could get out of sync, resulting in transmission errors.

The need for synchronization is more pronounced in full-duplex scenarios where communication could be happening over a shared transmission medium. If the two ends are not synchronized with regard to their transmission slots, both sides could start transmission at the same time, thus causing collisions. Similarly, last-mile access technologies such as passive optical network (PON), cable, and digital subscriber line (DSL) require strict synchronization between the customer-premises equipment (CPE) and the controller in the central office. All these last-mile technologies use TDM principles, where each CPE is assigned a timeslot for transmission, and unless the CPEs are synchronized with their respective controllers, the transmission of data will not be successful. In all of these cases, the synchronization mechanisms (that is, the reference signal) are built into the protocol itself, typically through a constant stream of bits and embedded special cues that keep the endpoints in sync.

Carrying synchronization information within the transport protocol or communication medium itself might not always be practical in all cases. Sure enough, last-mile multi-access technologies do require this continuous synchronization, but most modern transport technologies forgo this option in an effort to increase efficiency and simplicity, with Ethernet being one example. Ethernet, by principle, uses an on-demand transmission method in the sense that it transmits bits on the line only when there is actual data to be sent. This means that there are gaps between frames, which are essentially silence on the wire. Ethernet uses this to improve link utilization through statistical multiplexing and simplify hardware implementation by eliminating the complex mapping of data in discrete timeslots, as was the case with TDM. However, this lack of constant synchronization also introduces some challenges. First of all, in absence of a TDM-like coordinated timeslot, it is possible that devices on either end of a connection might start transmitting at the same time, resulting in a collision on the wire. Ethernet uses the well-known mechanisms such as Carrier Sense Multiple Access (CSMA) to remedy this situation. Second, as stated earlier, the receiving node must be ready to receive the frames sent by the transmitting node. The Ethernet preamble, which is 7 bytes of alternating zeros and ones, followed by the 1-byte Start of Frame Delimiter (SFD) inserted before the actual frame, helps the receiver *temporarily synchronize its internal clock* to the bitstream on the wire, thereby ensuring successful communication. Figure 9-1 illustrates the difference between the two approaches, aimed at synchronizing the transmitter and receiver on a given transmission medium.

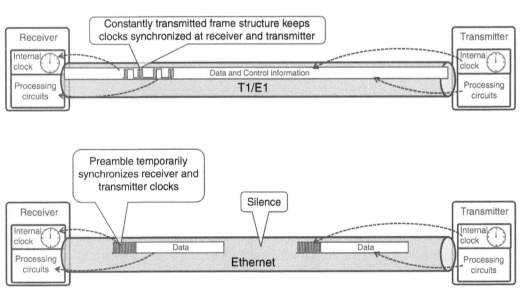

FIGURE 9-1   Synchronizing Transmitter and Receiver on a Transmission Medium

Synchronization, therefore, is a key component of any communication network, and a mobile communication network (MCN) is no exception. In an MCN, in addition to the underlying transport network equipment synchronizing its interfaces for successful transmission of raw data, components of the RAN domain require additional synchronization for RF functions. The remote radio unit (RRU), responsible for RF signal generation, relies heavily on continuous instructions from the baseband unit (BBU), or the distributed unit (DU) in a decomposed RAN architecture, as to when and how to transmit RF signals. In a typical D-RAN environment the collocated RRU and BBU communicate using the Common Public Radio Interface (CPRI) that carries the synchronization information—in addition to the control and user data. However, in a 5G decomposed RAN deployment, the BBU, or rather the DU, may be geographically separated from the RU, relying on the fronthaul network to provide connectivity. This fronthaul network maybe a CPRI Fronthaul (that is, WDM-based Fronthaul carrying CPRI over fiber) or Packetized Fronthaul (that is, carrying RoE or eCPRI). The nature of packetized fronthaul networks is radically different from the constant bitrate (CBR) nature of the CPRI in a D-RAN environment. Such fronthaul traffic might experience unpredictable latency and jitter; hence, the RU and DU cannot rely on the embedded synchronization information in packetized CPRI traffic for synchronizing their clocks. To remedy this, the packetized fronthaul network must provide timing and synchronization to the RU and DU to ensure continued mobile network operation.

The rest of this chapter will focus on the various aspects of synchronization, including the type of synchronization as well as its application and propagation in 5G networks.

Types of Synchronization

Considering time and synchronization as a singular monolithic entity is a common misconception. A closer look at transport networks paints a more intricate picture of the various aspects that need to be coordinated. The synchronization of transport network equipment is made up of more than just the *time of day (ToD),* which is probably the only interpretation of *time* in everyday life. The ToD refers to an exact moment in the regular 24-hour daily cycle and is aligned with the planetary time, maintained at both the global and individual government levels through the use of highly accurate atomic clocks. The concept of planetary time and atomic clocks is covered later in this chapter. Synchronizing the ToD across devices in a given network is an important aspect of ongoing operations. If all the devices in the network are aware of the ToD, event logging with timestamping can be used to correlate and trouble-shoot problems in the network.

Nevertheless, in addition to the ToD, mobile communication networks also require *frequency* and *phase* synchronization. For someone new to timing and synchronization topics, the concepts of frequency and phase might be hard to grasp, and, as such, this section will try to use everyday examples to convey these concepts before delving deeper into frequency, phase, and time of day synchronization in mobile networks.

To understand these concepts, consider the example of two identical, fully operational clocks. As these clocks are identical, it can be safely assumed that both clocks will be ticking every second at the same speed; hence, these clocks are considered to be in frequency sync with each other. However, if these clocks do not *tick* at the exact same moment, they will not be considered *phase synchronized* or *phase aligned.* If one of the clocks starts running faster or slower due to an internal error or external param-eters, its perspective of what constitutes 1 second will change. In other words, the *frequency* at which this clock ticks will change. Should this happen, the frequency synchronization between the two clocks will be lost, and their phases cannot be aligned either. Sure enough, on a linear timescale, and assuming both clocks stay operational, it is possible that the two clocks may start their *second* at the exact same moment, thus providing a singular, momentary instance of accidental phase alignment. However, because they now operate on separate frequencies, this phase alignment will be a one-off, accidental event with no meaningful significance.

The public transportation system could be another example that showcases the extent to which frequency and phase are interrelated. The schedules of buses and trains in modern public transport systems are carefully synchronized to provide riders the benefit of switching between the two transport mediums as quickly as possible. Consider the case of a central station that acts as an exchange point between a particular bus and a train route used by a substantial number of riders. If this specific bus and train arrive at the station every 55 minutes and stay there for another 5 minutes, their *frequencies* are considered to be synchronized. Suppose the bus always arrives 30 minutes past the hour, but the train arrives at the top of every hour; the riders who need to switch between the two will have to wait for an extended period of time. However, if both the train and bus routes are synchronized such that they both arrive at the top of the hour and stay for 5 minutes, this allows the riders to switch between the two without wasting any time. Now, the bus and train routes are not only frequency synchronized (arriving every 55 minutes and staying at the station for 5 minutes), they are also *phase synchronized*, as they both arrive and leave at the exact same time—that is, at the top of the hour. Thus, by aligning both frequency and phase, the public transportation network introduces efficiency in its system.

The 5-minute wait time between the bus or train arriving and departing also serves as a *buffer* should their arrival frequencies get temporarily out of sync, thus impacting their phase alignment as well. It could be a result of additional traffic on the road, unexpected road closures forcing the bus to take longer routes, or simply encountering too many traffic lights, resulting in the bus getting delayed and potentially losing its alignment and synchronization with the train. If these factors result in a cumulative delay of less than 5 minutes, there is still a possibility that riders will be able to switch between the bus and train in a timely fashion. Hence, the 5 minutes constitute the total *time error budget* (that is, either the bus or the train could be misaligned with each other for up to a maximum of 5 minutes without a major impact). Should the delays exceed 5 minutes, the system suffers performance degradation. In other words, the time error budget is the maximum *inaccuracy* a system can handle, before the *time errors* start impacting the overall operation of the system.

In short, *frequency* refers to a cyclical event at a predetermined interval, and frequency synchronization between two or more entities ensures that all entities perform the desired function at the same intervals. Examples of frequency synchronization in a mobile communication network include the internal oscillators of the RAN equipment (such as the RRU) oscillating at a predetermined interval, thus generating a predetermined frequency. On the other hand, *phase* refers to an event starting at a precise time, and *phase alignment* or *phase synchronization* refers to multiple frequency aligned entities starting the said event at precisely the same moment in time. An example of phase alignment in mobile communication networks can be a TDD-based system where the base station and mobile handsets must be in agreement on when a timeslot starts. Figure 9-2 outlines the concepts of frequency and phase synchronization.

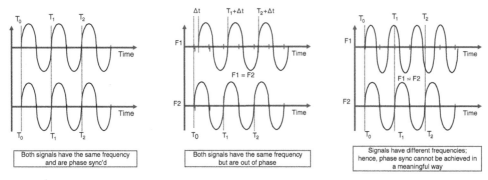

FIGURE 9-2   Frequency and Phase Synchronization

Similar to how the 5-minute wait time acts as a measure of time error budget in the train and bus example, frequency, phase, and ToD have their own measure of time error budgets as well. The time error for ToD is perhaps the easiest to understand and envision. A second is universally considered to be the standard measure of time, as it refers to an exact moment in the 24-hour daily cycle. A ToD synchronization error is usually measured in seconds or milliseconds. The unit of measure for phase synchronization errors is similar to ToD in terms of base unit but differs significantly in terms of granularity. Whereas the ToD is measured in seconds or milliseconds, phase synchronization and its errors are measured in sub-microseconds or nanoseconds. The unit of measure for frequency sync errors is *parts per million (ppm)* or *parts per billion (ppb)*. Here, *parts* refers to an individual frequency cycle, and *ppm* or *ppb* refers to an inaccuracy in a frequency cycle over the stated range. For instance, 10 *ppm* refers to an allowance of gaining or losing 10 cycles every 1 million iterations. Likewise, a 10 *ppb* allowance is the equivalent of gaining or losing 10 cycles every 1 billion iterations.

Why Synchronization Is Important in 5G

Undoubtedly, modern radio communication systems provide the convenience of being connected to the network without rigid constraints of tethering wires. Radio waves easily propagate in every direction and can cover large areas. However, the flip side of this is the interference of signals from multiple transmitters, making it hard and sometimes impossible to receive a transmission reliably without taking special measures. Chapter 1, "A Peek at the Past," and Chapter 2, "Anatomy of Mobile Communication Networks," briefly introduced the phenomenon of interference, along with various approaches to manage it in earlier mobile communication networks. The easiest of these was to use different frequencies in neighboring cells, thus greatly reducing the potential for signal interference. Unfortunately, this approach is unsustainable, as the usable frequency ranges for MCN are quite narrow. Rapidly increasing demand for bandwidth pushed later generations of mobile communication networks to use more sophisticated ways to share the transmission media (that is, radio waves).

As explained in Chapter 3, "Mobile Networks Today," and Chapter 5, "5G Fundamentals," LTE and 5G NR use Orthogonal Frequency-Division Multiple Access (OFDMA) with its 15KHz subcarriers. The use of narrow subcarriers imposes strict requirements on the frequency accuracy used in both base station radios and mobile devices. High frequency accuracy is crucial for keeping adjacent subcarriers free from interference. The 3GPP specification requires 5G NR frequency accuracy on the air interface to be in the range of ±0.1 ppm for local area and medium-range base stations and ±0.05 ppm for wide area base stations.[1]

Modern electronic equipment uses high-quality crystal oscillators to generate stable frequencies; however, crystal oscillators are susceptible to the fluctuations of environmental parameters such as temperature, pressure, and humidity as well as other factors such as power voltage instabilities. Although it does not completely eliminate the frequency drift, the use of specialized *temperature-compensated crystal oscillators (TCXO)* in the radio and processing equipment of the MCN reduces the effects of these fluctuations. Combined with an externally provided, highly stable reference frequency signal, the required frequency accuracy can be achieved at the base station. The accuracy of the reference frequency signal provided by the network should be substantially better than the required 50 ppb (±0.05 ppm in 3GPP documents) for the LTE and 5G networks, as explained in the ITU-T G.8261/Y.1361 recommendation, and many documents suggest the frequency reference provided by the network should have an accuracy of better than 16 ppb.[2] A similar approach is used in the mobile device, where the carrier frequency generation circuit is corrected using the frequency extracted from the base station's signal for higher accuracy. Frequency division duplex–based (FDD-based) mobile systems, as discussed in Chapter 2, require frequency synchronization for continued operations.

Phase synchronization, or rather time alignment, is another crucial signal transmission parameter in MCN. The term *phase synchronization* might be confusing for architects not very familiar with the synchronization aspect of mobile networks. The concept of phase here is used to describe the start of a radio frame. In TDD-based transmission systems, where both the base station and mobile device use the same frequency for upstream and downstream transmissions, the alignment of timeslots between the two is critical, and therefore phase synchronization is essential.

Additionally, when two neighboring cells use the same frequency bands, it is crucial to coordinate the usage of OFDM resource blocks between these cells. Coordination between the cells ensures that overlapping OFDM resource blocks are not used to transmit data for the subscribers at the edges of the cells, where interference can cause transmission errors. In simple terms, the neighboring cells coordinate which resource blocks are used and which are left for the other cell to use. In a perfectly aligned transmission between the cells, the resource block used by one cell is matched by the void or unused blocks by the other. This allows the sharing of resource blocks between the two receivers residing in the proximity of the cell edge. If the phase alignment is not achieved between the neighboring cells, the resource blocks used in both cells start overlapping, causing transmission errors, as shown in Figure 9-3.

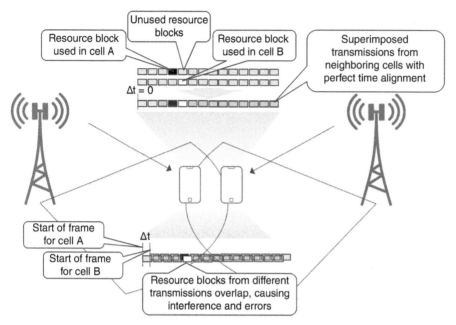

FIGURE 9-3   Intercell Interference and Synchronization

The required precision of time alignment between multiple neighboring cells is dependent on functionality implemented at the cell sites. 5G NR allows intercell time deviation of $\pm1.5\mu s$ with $\pm1\mu s$ budget allowed for network transport. This budget also allows the use of coordinated multipoint (CoMP) transmission. However, advanced antenna features impose even more demanding requirements. For instance, carrier aggregation in 5G NR imposes the tight 260ns maximum absolute error for intra-band allocations. The time alignment tolerance for multi-radio MIMO transmission is even tighter, with a whooping 65ns maximum error.[3]

Collectively, these strict requirements imposed by advanced radio functions, scalable spectrum utilization, and reliable connectivity make it even more important for ToD, frequency, and phase in a 5G deployment to be highly synchronized. This is achieved by ensuring that highly reliable and uniform clock sources are used to acquire timing information across the 5G network, and when that's not possible or feasible, then the MCN is able to accurately carry this timing information across. The next two sections discuss these topics in further detail.

Synchronization Sources and Clock Types

Broadly speaking, a clock is a device that counts cycles of a periodic event. Of course, such a clock does not necessarily keep time in seconds or minutes but rather in measures of periodic event cycles. By selecting the *appropriate* periodic event and denominator for the cycle count, a clock can produce meaningful timing signals for the desired application. Similar to how mechanical clocks use pendulums or weights attached to a spring, commonly referred to as *oscillators*, electronic equipment relies on circuits generating a periodic change in voltage or current. Although a rudimentary oscillator circuit made of resistors, capacitors, and inductors can do the job of generating the desired frequency, it lacks the accuracy to qualify as a useful reference. Clearly, the accuracy of an oscillator depends on its components' precision. Nevertheless, it is usually not feasible to increase the precision of a simple oscillator's components as another, more practical approach became popular in the electronics industry in the previous century.

By far the most popular way to build a simple yet accurate electronic clock is to use quartz crystal oscillators in its frequency-generating circuit. Voltage applied to the tiny slice of quartz in such an oscillator creates mechanical stress. When this voltage is removed, the dissipating stress creates electricity. This process would then repeat at the resonant frequency of this quartz slice until all initial energy is dissipated in the form of heat. However, if the signal is amplified and applied back to the crystal, a stable constant frequency can be produced. The resonant frequency of a quartz crystal oscillator depends on the shape and size of the slice of quartz, and it can easily be manufactured today with great precision. For example, virtually every electronic wristwatch today uses a quartz crystal oscillator manufactured with the resonance of 32,768Hz. The sine wave cycles are then counted, and the circuit provides a pulse every 32,768 cycles, precisely at each 1 second interval—that is, a *1 pulse-per-second (1PPS)* signal. The accuracy of clocks using quartz crystal oscillators is typically in the range of 10 to 100 ppm, which equates to roughly 1 to 10 seconds per day. This time drift may be acceptable for common wristwatch use but may be catastrophic for automated processes and other applications that rely on much more accurate timekeeping.

Besides the manufacturing precision, other factors affect the accuracy of a quartz crystal oscillator. Temperature fluctuations and power voltage fluctuations are among the usual suspects. Luckily, these factors can be compensated for, and more sophisticated *temperature-compensated crystal oscillator (TCXO)* and *oven-controlled crystal oscillator (OCXO)* can provide substantially more accurate frequency sources. The accuracy of an OCXO can be as good as 1 ppb, which translates to a drift of roughly 1 second in 30 years.

For clock designs with even higher accuracy, a different physical phenomenon is used as the source of a periodic signal. Although the underlying physics of this phenomenon is quite complex, suffice it to say that all atoms transition between internal states of a so-called hyperfine structure (that is, energy levels split due to the composition of an atom itself). These transitions have very specific resonant frequencies, which are known and can be measured with great precision. Because the atoms' resonant frequencies are used in lieu of oscillators, a clock using this phenomenon is generally called an *atomic clock*. The resonant frequency of cesium atoms used in atomic clocks is 9192631770 Hz.[4] The measured resonant frequency is not used directly by the atomic clock but rather to discipline quartz oscillators, which are still used to generate the actual frequency for the clock's counting circuits. Cesium atomic clocks are some of the most accurate clocks and can maintain an accuracy of better than 1 second over 100 million years. The International Bureau of Weights and Measures relies on the combined output of more than 400 cesium atomic clocks spread across the globe to maintain accurate time. This is considered the ultimate planetary clock and is referred to as *Coordinated Universal Time*, or *UTC*.[5]

Cesium atomic clocks are ultra-accurate, but they have bulky designs and high costs. For many practical applications, the accuracy of cesium clocks is not needed, and rubidium atomic clocks can commonly be used instead of cesium-based devices. Rubidium atoms are used to build much more compact and cheaper atomic clocks; however, their precision is lower than that of a cesium clock by a few orders of magnitude. Rubidium atomic clocks have an accuracy sufficient for most practical purposes and can maintain time accuracy within 1 second over 30,000 years. Due to their portability, rubidium clocks are commonly used as *reference clocks* in the telecom industry, military applications, and in the satellites of many countries' *global navigation satellite systems (GNSSs)*.

GNSSs are well known for the great convenience they provide in everyday navigation. Aircrafts, ships, cars, and even pedestrians routinely use navigation apps on their computers and mobile devices. These apps calculate the current position of a user based on the difference of timing signals received from multiple GNSS satellites. A few countries and unions have developed and launched their own version of GNSS, such as the United States' *Global Positioning System (GPS)*, the European Union's *Galileo*, Russia's *Global Navigation Satellite System (GLONASS)*, and China's *BeiDou*. Although Japan's *Quasi-Zenith Satellite System (QZSS)* and the *Indian Regional Navigation Satellite System (IRNSS)* are also systems designed for satellite navigation and provide accurate time, they are regional systems designed to augment the GPS system for their respective regions.

Although navigation can be perceived as the main purpose of any global navigation satellite systems, these systems are also used to provide accurate time reference (called *timer transfer*) for many applications, including mobile communication networks. The GNSS signals encode both frequency and phase as well as ToD information, along with the information about each satellite's orbit. In fact, the major goal of all GNSS satellites is to maintain accurate time and transmit it to the consumers on Earth's surface and in the air. Satellite transmissions can cover large areas effectively and are ideal for the distribution of a reference timing signal.

As mentioned earlier, due to their good accuracy and portability, GNSS satellites use rubidium clocks. Satellites' clocks are also periodically synchronized with each other as well as with the terrestrial atomic clock sources to maintain the highest accuracy of the time signals necessary for navigation calculations and providing a timing reference to surface receivers, as shown in Figure 9-4.

Interestingly enough, due to Earth's gravity, the clock on a satellite runs a notch faster compared to the same clock on the ground. The navigation apps routinely calculate necessary corrections to account for this phenomenon, called gravitation time dilation and explained by Einstein's theory of General Relativity.

Normally, GNSSs provide timing signals with very high accuracy. For example, more than 95% of the time, the time transfer function of a GPS system has a time error of less than 30 nanoseconds.[6] Additional errors could be introduced by the processing circuit of a GNSS receiver, and most GPS clock receivers used in the telecom industry can provide time reference with an error of less than 100 nanoseconds to the time reference signal consumers.

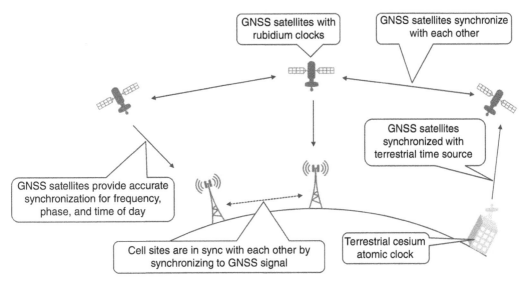

FIGURE 9-4   Synchronization in GNSS

Implementing Timing in Mobile Networks

So far, this chapter has discussed various concepts about time, its synchronization, and its importance in 5G transport networks. As mentioned earlier, network timing is not a monolith but rather is composed of frequency, phase, and time of day—all of which have to work in unison to provide timing and synchronization for various scenarios. Generally speaking, basic FDD-based mobile networks require only frequency synchronization, whereas TDD-based mobile networks require strict phase synchronization. However, most multi-radio transmissions and intercell interference coordination (ICIC) scenarios—whether FDD or TDD based—also require strict phase synchronization.[7] As previously mentioned, phase and frequency are interrelated; hence, it is always considered a best practice to implement both phase and frequency synchronization in mobile networks. ToD is important for all networks due to its use for correlating events and failures using logs with accurate timestamps.

In a traditional D-RAN implementation, the CPRI between the co-located RU and BBU is responsible for carrying the synchronization information. The RU has to be in constant sync with the BBU since the DU component of the BBU provides the necessary instructions to the RU to perform RF functions. In this case, the synchronization traffic usually remains confined to the cell site location; however, the instructions provided by the DU components of the BBU often require synchronization with neighboring cell sites' BBUs for use cases such as ICIC implementations. If all the cell sites directly acquire their timing signal from a highly reliable, common, and accurate source such as atomic clocks in the GNSS-based satellites, the BBUs will be considered in sync with each other and thus the mobile transport network will not be explicitly required to distribute timing and synchronization information. In this case, the satellite-based timing signal is acquired directly at the BBUs using a

GNSS antenna, and any required timing information is provided to the RU through the CPRI. There is no need to acquire or distribute the timing signal to the CSR, thus removing any dependencies with respect to the timing interfaces or protocols supported on the CSR. This is the exact deployment model for a large number of existing mobile deployments today and is shown in Figure 9-5.

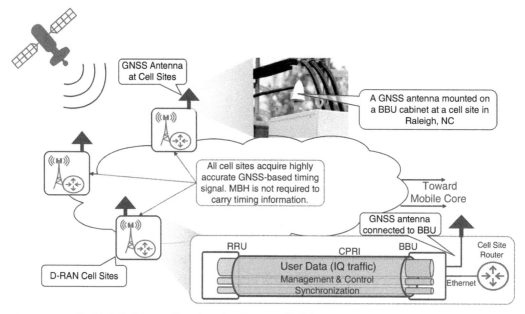

FIGURE 9-5   D-RAN Cell Sites Synchronization via GNSS

In cases where GNSS signals might not be acquired at every cell site, the mobile backhaul would need to distribute a synchronization reference across the cell sites. One of the primary reasons for such a scenario could be security concerns, stemming from the fact that different GNSSs are controlled by individual governments. For instance, the Galileo-based GNSSs became operational in 2016, and prior to that, if a Europe-based service provider wanted to avoid using GPS, GLONASS, or BeiDou satellites, it would have to implement terrestrial timing signal acquisition and transport mechanisms.[8] Additionally, with the gradual move toward a decomposed RAN architecture comprising sometimes geographically distanced RUs and DUs, the fronthaul now has to *always* transport timing information between the cell site and far-edge DCs, even though the rest of the mobile transport may not have to be aware of, or even carry, the timing information. Hence, it can be concluded that while distributing timing and sync information using transport networks was optional in the pre-5G networks, it is absolutely mandatory for a 5G transport network to implement the capabilities of distributing timing and synchronization information to cell sites, as demonstrated in Figure 9-6.

The packetized fronthaul network relies on packet-based transport protocols that are asynchronous in nature (for example, Ethernet), which cannot be used as is to distribute timing information. In order to reliably transport timing information across this packetized fronthaul, additional mechanisms are required to distribute frequency, phase, and ToD information. These mechanisms are *Synchronous Ethernet (SyncE)* for frequency synchronization and accuracy, *Precision Time Protocol (PTP)* for phase alignment, and *Network Time Protocol (NTP)* for ToD synchronization.

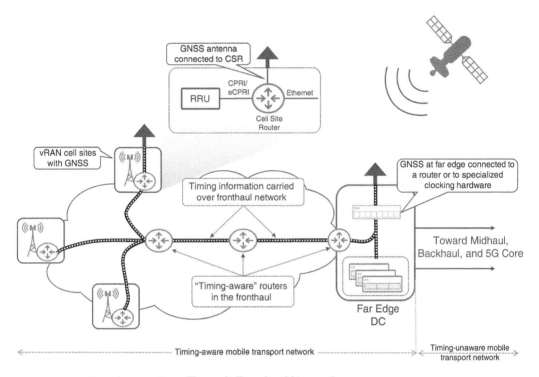

FIGURE 9-6   Distributing Time Through Fronthaul Network

The rest of this chapter will cover how the reference timing signal is acquired, packetized, and propagated through the mobile transport networks.

Acquiring and Propagating Timing in the Mobile Transport Network

Over the past several years, the use of GNSS has emerged as an effective and cheap mechanism to distribute the reference timing signal in mobile communication networks. Using an antenna, the network device(s) would acquire the satellite signal from one of the GNSS constellations—GPS, Galileo, GLONASS, or BeiDou. This device can be a router or other specialized clocking devices from a vendor that specializes in timing and clocking devices, such as Microsemi.[9] The GNSS-based timing signal is a single composite signal that carries ToD, frequency, and phase information from the atomic clock aboard the GNSS satellites in Earth's orbit. The network device receiving the GNSS is considered a *primary reference clock (PRC)* if it acquires only the frequency signal or a *primary reference timing clock (PRTC)* if it acquires the frequency, phase, and ToD signal. The PRTC then distributes the phase, frequency, and ToD reference to the rest of the packet network using PTP, SyncE, and NTP.

The GNSS antenna requires a clear, unobstructed view of the sky, which in some cases limits the places where a GNSS signal can be acquired in mobile transport networks. It might be beneficial to acquire the GNSS signal at a more central location such as a far-edge or edge DC and propagate it down to the cell sites. However, in a lot of cases, the mobile service provider does not own the far-edge or edge DC and, as part of its lease agreements, might not have access to the roof for GNSS antenna installation. In these cases, the GNSS antenna could be installed at the cell sites and the timing signal distributed to the rest of the mobile network. Acquiring GNSS at multiple cell site locations also allows for timing signal redundancy; that is, in the case of a GNSS reception problem on one site, another site could take over and be used as the reference clocks.

Considerations for GNSS Antenna Installation

GNSS antenna installation is a bit more involved process than simply mounting a piece of hardware on the roof. Many factors impact the quality and accuracy of the timing signal acquired through satellites. Apart from requiring an unobstructed view of the sky, the installation must also take into account the propagation delay of the signal from the antenna to the actual device where the signal is being processed. This delay is directly proportional to the length of the cable. As such, at the time of GPS antenna installation, the length of the cable from the antenna to the receiver is carefully measured, and the receiving device is configured with a "cable delay compensation" value. As a general rule of thumb, 5ns compensation should be configured for every meter of cable length.[10]

GNSS antenna installers would need to perform a site survey to determine an optimal location where the antenna could be placed. The survey takes into account things such as a clean mounting surface, with no metal or other material that may shield the GNSS signal, and tall trees that may block the view of the horizon. The distance from the install location to the equipment is also measured to calculate the cable delay compensation values. It is highly recommended to use a professional company that specializes in GNSS antenna installation.

While very common and easy to use, GNSS signals are susceptible to jamming as well as spoofing. Technological advances have made devices that can jam GNSS easily accessible. While an individual with malicious intent can access GNSS jammers and jam signals within a few kilometers, disrupting mobile services in the process, the major concern for national governments is the use of jamming technologies by foreign governments or their proxies. Given the importance of satellite-based navigation and timing systems, most governments treat GNSS jamming as a threat to their national security and are taking actions to safeguard the system. For instance, the U.S. Department of Homeland Security (DHS) considers GPS (the U.S. version of GNSS) a "single point of failure for critical infrastructure."[11] Recognizing the importance of an alternate to GPS, the U.S. Congress passed a bill called *National Timing Resilience and Security Act of 2018* in December of 2018 aimed at creating a terrestrial-based alternative to GPS in order to solve any problems that may arise from GPS signal jamming. Similar efforts are underway in other geographies as well.

In mobile communication networks, the service providers sometimes use anti-jamming equipment at their GNSS receivers in order to mitigate efforts to jam the GPS signal. Another approach is the use of a terrestrial frequency clock to provide a reliable source of frequency sync in case of a GNSS failure. If phase is fully aligned throughout the network, an accurate frequency signal can keep phase in sync for an extended period of time in case of a GNSS failure.

Most modern cell site routers are equipped with a specialized interface that can be connected to a GNSS antenna, acquire the signal, and propagate it to the rest of the network. Depending on the vendor implementation, the routers might also have the input interfaces to acquire the reference signal for phase, frequency, and ToD individually. Acquiring each timing component individually typically requires a specialized device at the premises that can act as the PRC or PRTC and provide individual frequency, phase, and ToD references to the router. The reference signal for frequency is acquired through a 10MHz input interface, which can be connected to a frequency source that provides a highly accurate 10MHz frequency for the networking device to align its internal clock to. Older systems used a *Building Integrated Timing Supply (BITS)* interface for frequency acquisition, but today BITS is seldom if ever used. Phase alignment is achieved by using a 1PPS (sometimes also called PPS) interface. As the name suggests, the 1PPS interface provides a sharp pulse that marks the start of a second and thus allows the router (or other device) to align its phase to the start edge of the pulse. The duration of this pulse is slightly less than 1 second, and the start of the second is marked by the start of the pulse.

Most networking equipment has the capability for both these options. Figure 9-7 shows the front panel of Cisco and Juniper routers with interfaces for both GNSS signal and individual frequency, phase, and ToD alignment.[12, 13]

Once the timing signal is acquired, it needs to be propagated throughout the rest of the network to distribute the frequency, phase, and ToD information. The rest of this section will discuss the various protocols and design models used to efficiently and accurately distribute timing information through the mobile transport network.

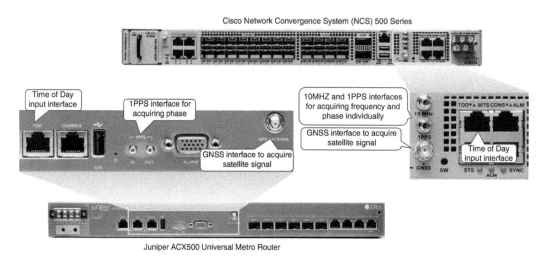

FIGURE 9-7   Front Panels of Cisco and Juniper Routers with Timing Acquisition Interfaces

Synchronous Ethernet (SyncE)

The proliferation of Ethernet beyond its original application area of local area networks (LANs) into the territory of traditional long-haul SONET/SDH transport helped keep the cost of higher-speed wide area network (WAN) interfaces in check. Although circuit-emulation services over packet-based networks allowed for connecting islands of traditional TDM networks over Ethernet, synchronization between the two sides of an emulated circuit required additional considerations. ITU-T defined an architecture and procedures, known as *Synchronous Ethernet (SyncE)*, to propagate a synchronization signal over a packet-based network. The synchronization model of SyncE is designed to be compatible with that of SONET/SDH and, by design, can only provide frequency synchronization and information about the clock quality. The following few ITU-T standards define SyncE architecture and operation:

- **G.8261:** Timing and synchronization aspects in packet networks

- **G.8262:** Timing characteristics of a synchronous equipment slave clock

- **G.8264:** Distribution of timing information through packet networks

As mentioned earlier, the Ethernet interface synchronizes its receiver to the bitstream on the wire only for the duration of a frame sent by the remote node. In fact, this temporary synchronization can be used for frequency propagation between SyncE-capable devices. For such a synchronization propagation method to be effective, a SyncE-capable device should have a good oscillator to keep the frequency generator of its clock from drifting when synchronization from a better clock is not available. When such a condition happens, where a device loses its reference signal, the device is said to be operating in *holdover* mode.

Clock accuracy used in a typical Ethernet device is quite low (around ±100 ppm). SyncE-capable devices require clocks with ±4.6 ppm accuracy or better, as per the G.8261 standard.[14] Additionally, the clock on SyncE-capable devices can be locked to an external signal.

The frequency generator of a SyncE-capable device can be locked to a frequency signal extracted by the specialized Ethernet physical layer circuit from the bitstream received on the interface. Sync-E-capable devices constantly send a reference signal on the Ethernet interface. This signal does not interfere with actual packet transmission but is incorporated into it. The edges of the signal on the wire, or in the optical fiber, are used as a reference for the SyncE-capable device's frequency generator. The internal clock is then used to synchronize all signal edges of the transmitted Ethernet frames, thereby providing a frequency reference for downstream SyncE-capable devices.

In SyncE applications, the source of a highly accurate frequency signal such as an atomic clock is referred to as a *primary reference clock (PRC)*. When the internal clock of a SyncE-capable device is locked to a PRC via a timing acquisition interface, it becomes the source of frequency synchronization for other SyncE-capable devices. The frequency synchronization is propagated *hop by hop* through the SyncE-enabled network from the PRC-connected SyncE-capable devices to the downstream devices and eventually to the ultimate consumers of frequency synchronization. Figure 9-8 shows the mechanism of frequency (clocking) recovery from the signal edges of an Ethernet frame and sourcing of the frequency synchronization for the downstream hop-by-hop propagation.

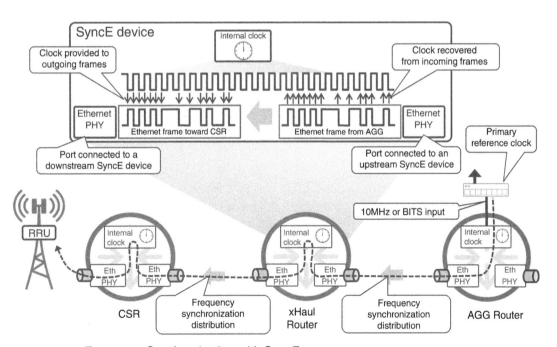

FIGURE 9-8 Frequency Synchronization with SyncE

SyncE-capable devices can be explicitly configured with the synchronization hierarchy or can automatically identify it based on the exchange of messages in the *Ethernet Synchronization Messaging Channel (ESMC)* defined by ITU-T G.8264.[15] This messaging channel is created by exchanging frames with EtherType set to 0x8809 and is required for compatibility with SONET/SDH synchronization models. ESMC channels carry a Quality Level (QL) indicator for the clock, which is in essence a value representing the clock position in the hierarchy (that is, how far the clock is from the PRC and the operational status of the clock). QL values are exchanged between SyncE-enabled devices and used to identify upstream and downstream ports in the synchronization hierarchy.

Although it requires hardware enhancements, SyncE architecture is very effective in propagating frequency synchronization, but it cannot propagate phase or ToD information. While NTP continued to be used for ToD propagation, Precision Time Protocol (PTP) was defined to transport phase synchronization information in modern networks supporting mobile communication and other applications.

Precision Time Protocol

Communication networks have used Network Time Protocol (NTP, discussed later in this section) since the 1980s to distribute timing information (more specifically the ToD). Its accuracy, or rather the lack thereof, however, left a lot to be desired for most modern applications. These applications, such as mobile communications, require much stricter accuracy (typically, to the tune of sub-microseconds), whereas NTP provides accuracy in the magnitude of multiple milliseconds at best.[16]

As discussed earlier, one of the ways to provide accurate timing information to relevant devices is the use of GNSS on all devices, thus acquiring a common reference time from a satellite-based atomic clock. However, it might not always be feasible, or even possible, to set up a GNSS antenna next to every device that needs phase alignment. Common reasons for not being able to implement GNSS everywhere could be excessive cost, lack of a suitable location for antenna placement, unfavorable locations, and national security concerns, among others. In short, the existing timing transport protocol fell short of the required features, and the only viable alternative of providing an atomic clock input everywhere was not realistic.

Precision Time Protocol (PTP), often called *IEEE 1588 PTP* after the IEEE specification that defines the protocol, fills this gap by not only providing sub-microsecond accuracy but also the convenience and cost-effectiveness of acquiring the timing reference at a few select locations and distributing it through the packet network. The first implementation of PTP, called PTPv1, was based on the IEEE 1588-2002 specification, where 2002 refers to the year the specification was published. The specification was revised in 2008 and again in 2019 to provide enhancements such as improved accuracy and precision. The implementation of IEEE 1588-2008 is called PTPv2, whereas IEEE 1588-2019 is referred to as PTP v2.1.

PTP Versions Compatibility

PTPv2 is not compatible with PTPv1, but this is not an issue as PTPv1 is rarely if ever used. PTPv2.1 is backward compatible with PTPv2.

PTP Operation Overview

From PTP's perspective, any device participating in timing distribution is considered a *clock*. This includes not only the atomic clock that generates the reference timing signal but all the routers in the transport network that process PTP packets as well. A PTP-based timing distribution network employs a *multi-level master-slave clock hierarchy*, where each clock may be a slave for its upstream master clock and simultaneously act as a master to its downstream clock(s). The interface on the master clock, toward a slave clock, is referred to as a *master port*. Correspondingly, the interface on the slave clock toward the master is called a *slave port*. The master port is responsible for providing timing information to its corresponding slave port. These are not physical ports but rather logical PTP constructs that provide their intended functions using a physical interface. In most cases, the master and slave PTP functions reside on directly connected devices. This is, however, not the only mode of PTP operations, as covered in the PTP deployment profiles later in this chapter.

> **Note**
>
> Use of the terms *master* and *slave* is only in association with the official terminology used in industry specifications and standards and in no way diminishes Pearson's commitment to promoting diversity, equity, and inclusion and challenging, countering, and/or combating bias and stereotyping in the global population of the learners we serve.

PTP uses two-way communication to exchange a series of *messages* between the master and slave ports. These messages can be broadly classified in two categories: event messages and general messages. An *event message* carries actual timing information and should be treated as priority data due to its time-sensitive nature. By contrast, a general message carries non-real-time information to support various PTP operations. An example of a general message is the *announce* message, which, as the name suggests, *announces* the capability and quality of the clock source. For instance, a master port may send periodic announce messages to its corresponding slave port that contain information such as clock accuracy and the number of hops it is away from the clock source, among other information. The announce messages are used to select the best master clock based on the PRTC and build a master-slave hierarchy through the network using the *Best Master Clock Algorithm (BMCA)* defined by IEEE 1588. Here are some of the other relevant PTP messages that help distribute time through the network:

- **Sync:** An event message from the master port to slave port, informing it of the master time. The sync message is timestamped at the egress master port.

- **Follow_Up:** An optional event message that carries the timestamp for the sync message if the original sync message is not timestamped at egress.

- **Delay_Req:** A message from the slave port to master port to calculate the transit time between the master and slave ports.

- **Delay_Resp:** The master port's response to delay_req, informing the slave port of the time delay_req was received.

Best Master Clock Algorithm (BMCA)

PTP uses the Best Master Clock Algorithm to define the hierarchy of master and slave clocks in the timing distribution network. It first helps select a *grandmaster*, which acts as the source of timing information in the network and then builds a master-slave hierarchy. Grandmaster clocks are covered later in the "PTP Clocks" section.

The grandmaster is chosen using a set of criteria defined in the BMCA. These criteria include a list of characteristics such as a clock's priority, device class, its relationship to the PRTC, and so on. In case of a failure on the selected grandmaster, BMCA automatically selects the next grandmaster using its list of criteria.

Figure 9-9 shows a basic event messages exchange between master and slave ports to distribute timing information. The *sync* message is initiated by the master port with egress timestamp either included or carried in the *follow_up* message, depending on the vendor implementation. Accurate timestamping of a sync message at the last possible instant as the message is leaving the master clock is critical for time calculation. However, recording the exact time the message leaves the interface *and* stamping it on the outgoing packet simultaneously may present technical challenges. To alleviate this, PTP specifications allow a two-step process, where the timestamp is recorded locally at the master when the sync message is transmitted but is sent to the slave in a subsequent follow_up message. When the sync message (or the follow_up message) is received at the slave port, the slave clock becomes aware of not only the reference time at the master but also the time at which the sync message is sent (called t1) and the time at which the sync is received (called t2). However, t1 is marked relative to the master's internal clock, while t2 is marked relative to the slave's internal clock, which may have drifted away from the master. Thus, if the slave wants to synchronize its internal clock, it must be aware of the transit time between the two. This is accomplished by the slave sending a *delay_req* message to the master, which then responds with a *delay_res* message. The timestamp on the delay_req transmission is called t3, whereas t4 is the time when the delay_req is received at the master. The master clock notifies the slave of the receive time (that is, t4, using the delay_res message).

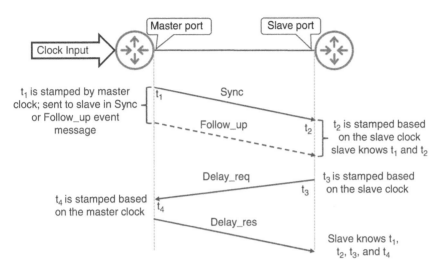

FIGURE 9-9 PTP Sync and Delay Messages Between Master and Slave Ports

In order to achieve time synchronization with its master, the slave clock must calculate how much its internal clock has drifted from the master—a value defined as *offsetFromMaster* by IEEE 1588. Once this offsetFromMaster value is calculated, the slave clock uses it to adjust its internal clock and achieve synchronization with the master clock. The offsetFromMaster is calculated using the two data sets known by the slave clock: t2 and t1, and t3 and t4. In an ideal scenario, with a transmission delay of 0 between the master and slave clocks, the values t1 and t2 should be identical, even though they are timestamped using the master and slave clocks, respectively. In this scenario, any deviation between the two timestamps could only mean that the two clocks are not synchronized; whatever the difference is between the two timestamps should be added (if t1 > t2) or removed (if t2 > t1) from the slave clock. However, every real-world scenario incurs some transit time, however miniscule, between the master and slave clocks. Using the *meanPathDelay*, which could only be calculated by averaging the timestamp difference for transit time in both directions, gives a fairly accurate picture of the actual offset between the master and slave clocks. IEEE 1588 specifications define the logic and process of calculating this offset in greater detail, but it eventually comes down to the following equation:[17]

$$offsetFromMaster = (t_2 - t_1 + t_3 - t_4) / 2$$

Figure 9-10 outlines three scenarios and their respective calculations for measuring the offsetFrom-Master. The first scenario assumes the master and slave clocks are in perfect synchronization and thus the offsetFromMaster is 0. The other two scenarios assume that the slave clock is either ahead of or lagging behind the master clock by a value of 1µsec. Although the transit time stays constant at 2µsec in all scenarios, the timestamping in scenarios 2 and 3 is impacted by this inaccuracy. However, in each of these three scenarios, the preceding equation calculates the offsetFromMaster correctly. Once calculated, the offsetFromMaster is used to adjust the slave clock and maintain its synchronization with the upstream master clock, as also shown in the figure.

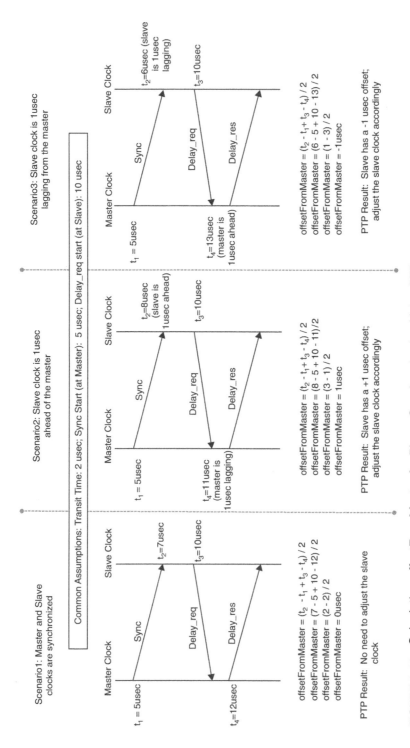

FIGURE 9-10   Calculating offsetFromMaster for Phase Synchronization Using PTP

As seen in all the example scenarios in Figure 9-10, PTP relies heavily on the assumption that the forward and reverse paths between master and slave clocks are symmetrical. In timing distribution networks, this property of equal path in either direction is referred to as *path symmetry*. However, if there is any *path asymmetry* between the master and slave clocks (that is, the transit time from master to slave and from slave to master differs), the offset calculation will be skewed and will eventually lead to time synchronization errors. Thus, any transit difference due to asymmetry must be taken into account by PTP during the offset calculation. The asymmetry in transit times could result from a few different factors but is usually due to the difference in cable lengths between transmit and receive ports. Just a minor asymmetry in the length of cable in either direction, sometimes introduced simply by leaving a few extra feet of slack in one strand of fiber, could lead to different transit times between the master and slave clocks in either direction. Even with transceivers using a single strand of fiber for transmit and receive, the chromatic dispersion properties of different wavelengths may cause light to travel at different speeds in either direction. This can potentially result in asymmetry of message travel time between master and slave. The actual transit time difference in both directions could be miniscule, but for a protocol like PTP, where accuracy requirements are in the sub-microseconds, even a small and otherwise negligible discrepancy in transit time between the master and slave clocks could negatively impact PTP accuracy. To remedy any possible problems, path asymmetry must be measured at the time of network deployment and accounted for as part of PTP configuration. Various test equipment vendors provide specialized tools to measure network asymmetry. As long as the network asymmetry is measured, accounted for, and remains unchanged, PTP will continue to operate correctly and provide time synchronization using the packet network.

PTP Clocks

As mentioned in the previous section, any network device participating in PTP operation is considered a clock. It is already mentioned in the previous section that the GNSS-based atomic clock provides the reference timing signal to a PRTC. From PTP's perspective, the PRTC that provides reference time to the packet networks is called a *grandmaster*. Sometimes the terms *grandmaster* and *PRTC* are used interchangeably, as the two functions are often embedded on the same device in the network. However, there is a clear distinction between the two. A PRTC refers to the source for frequency, phase, and ToD, whereas a grandmaster is a PTP function where packetized timing information is originated.

For distributing timing information from the PRTC to the rest of the devices in a packetized timing distribution network, IEEE 1588 defines various types of network clocks:

- Ordinary clock (OC)
- Boundary clock (BC)
- Transparent clock (TC)

An ordinary clock, or OC, is a device that has only one PTP-speaking interface toward the packet-based timing distribution network. Given that PTP networks are usually linear in nature—that is, PTP messages flow from a source (grandmaster or PRTC) to a destination (a timing consumer)—an OC can only be a source or a destination. In other words, an OC is either a grandmaster that distributes timing reference to the network (that is, an OC grandmaster) or a consumer of the timing information from the network (that is, an endpoint). A boundary clock, or BC, on the other hand, is a device with multiple PTP-speaking ports. A BC is simultaneously a master for its downstream slave clocks and a slave to its upstream master.

A transparent clock, or TC, does not explicitly participate in the PTP process, although it allows PTP messages to *transparently* pass through it. IEEE 1588 defines two different types of transparent clocks—an end-to-end TC and a peer-to-peer TC—although only the end-to-end TC is used in telecommunications networks.[18] An end-to-end TC records the *residence* time of a PTP message (that is, the time it takes for the packetized PTP message to enter and exit the TC). This information is added to the *correctionField* in the PTP header of the sync or follow_up message transiting through the TC. The correctionField helps inform the master and slave clocks of any *additional* time incurred while transiting the TC. This effectively eliminates the transit time introduced while the packet is forwarded through the TC.

Figure 9-11 shows a PTP-based timing distribution network with different types of clock and ports.

PTP Deployment, Performance, and Profiles

IEEE has defined the mechanics of the Precision Time Protocol in IEEE 1588 specification with a lot of choices and flexibility for vendor-specific implementations to carry timing information with a very high degree of accuracy. To keep up with the continuously changing landscape, IEEE also revised the specification in the years 2008 and 2019. IEEE, however, by its nature, focuses primarily on research and development as well as the inner details of the protocol itself rather than an end-to-end architecture. Deploying a timing distribution network using PTP, on the other hand, requires a high degree of planning and use of an appropriate network architecture to meet various constraints such as interoperability with older deployments and performance of various types of PTP clocks.

The *International Telecommunication Union Telecommunication Standardization Sector (ITU-T)* fills that much-needed gap through a series specification and profile definitions aimed at standardizing various aspects of a packet-based timing distribution network. This helps in creating a more cohesive end-to-end deployment model from a network timing perspective, and it also provides a set of expectations for devices participating in the timing processing and distribution. While many different standards are defined by ITU-T for packetized timing networks, this section focuses on the following critical aspects of design and deployment of 5G-ready mobile transport networks:

- Reference points in a time and phase synchronization network (ITU-T G.8271)

- Performance characteristics of various PTP clocks (ITU-T G.8272 and G.8273)

- Deployment profiles for packet-based time and phase distribution (ITU-T G.8265 and G.8275)

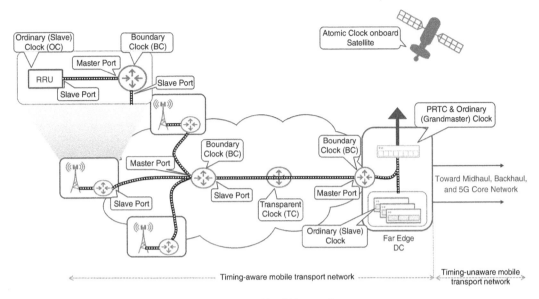

FIGURE 9-11   PTP Clock and Port Types in xHaul Network

ITU-T specifications use a different set of terminologies than what is defined by IEEE 1588 PTP for various clock types. The PTP grandmaster (GM) is called a *Telecom Grandmaster (T-GM)* in ITU-T terminology and has the same purpose as a PTP GM. However, a T-GM allows more than one master port, whereas a PTP GM was considered an ordinary clock (OC) with a single PTP-speaking port. Similarly, a PTP boundary clock (BC) is called *Telecom Boundary Clock (T-BC)*, a PTP transparent clock (TC) is called a *Telecom Transparent Clock (T-TC)*, and an ordinary slave clock is called a *Telecom Timing Slave Clock (T-TSC)* in ITU-T terminology. From a mobile xHaul perspective, an RU or a DU could be considered a T-TSC as also shown in the O-RAN Alliance's Synchronization Architecture and Solution Specification.[19] From here on, this chapter will primarily use the ITU-T defined clock terminologies because a lot of deployment-related specification, such as O-RAN Alliance's Synchronization Architecture and Solution Specification, uses the same ITU-T terminology.

Reference Points in a Time and Phase Synchronization Network

Formally titled *Time and Phase Synchronization Aspects of Telecommunication Networks*, the ITU-T G8271 specification defines various reference points and their characteristics for a packetized timing distribution network. These reference points, referred to as *A* through *E*, span the whole network from the time source to its ultimate destination and everything in between. The G.8271 specification uses the concept of *time error* budget, which is the maximum inaccuracy allowed at various reference points in the timing distribution network.

The G.8271 reference points are defined from the perspective of time distribution, *not* from the packet network's perspective. In fact, the G.8271 reference model views the packet network transport as a monolith, a singular black box, where the timing signal enters through the T-GM and exits just as it's ready to be provided to the end application. Following are the reference points defined by the G.8271 specification and the error budgets allowed within each:

- **Reference point A:** This is the demarcation at the PRTC and T-GM boundary. The total error budget allowed at the PRTC is ±100 nanoseconds (that is, the PRTC can drift up to a maximum of 100 nanoseconds from the global planetary time).

- **Reference point B:** This refers to the demarcation between the T-GM and the rest of the packet network. G.8271 specs do not define a time error budget for T-GM, but since PRTC and T-GM are implemented together in most implementations, vendors and operators consider the ±100ns deviation for both the PRTC and T-GM combined.

- **Reference point C:** The packet network between the T-GM and the last T-TSC before handing over the timing signal to the end application. The total TE budget allowed for the packet network is ±200 nanoseconds, irrespective of the number of T-BCs used.

- **Reference points D & E:** These reference points correspond with the end application in the ITU-T specification. While ITU-T distinguishes between the T-TSC and end application as two separate entities, telecommunication networks oftentimes refer to the end application as a *clock*. For instance, the O-RAN timing specification refers to the O-RU as a T-TSC. Additionally, reference point D is optional and only used when the end application further provides the clock to another end application, as shown in Figure 9-12.

ITU-T G.8271 also defines maximum time error budgets for various failure scenarios such as PRTC failure and short-term or long-term GNSS service interruptions. In most failure scenarios, the maximum end-to-end time error from the PRTC to the end application, as defined by ITU-T G.8271, should not exceed 1.5μsec, or 1500 nanoseconds. This 1.5μsec value is inclusive of the usual ±200 nanosecond budget for a packet network resulting from T-BC or T-TSC inaccuracies, as well as any errors resulting from path asymmetry and clocks entering holdover state due to GNSS or PRTC failures. The maximum total time error expected at reference point C is 1.1μsec, or 1100 nanoseconds, and includes up to 380 ns of path asymmetry and 250 ns inaccuracy that may be introduced in case of PRTC failure. The maximum time error allowed for the end application is 150 nanoseconds. Figure 9-12 provides a graphical representation of these reference points and their respective time error budget.

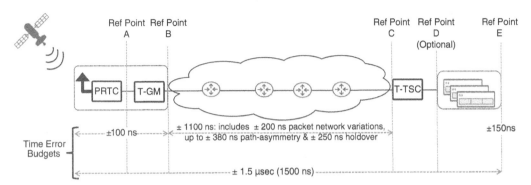

FIGURE 9-12 G.8271 Defined Time and Phase Synchronization Reference Points and Error Budgets

Performance Characteristics of Various PTP Clocks

As stated previously, the packetized timing distribution network is made up of ordinary clocks (OCs) and a boundary clock (BC). These clocks implement the PTP functions to distribute timing information, but they inevitably introduce time errors due to the strict timestamping requirements imposed by PTP. As such, the total time error introduced in the packet network is the combination of the total number of clocks used in the topology *and* the time error introduced by each one. The commutative value of the time error introduced by all the clocks in the packet network cannot exceed ±200 nanoseconds, as specified by ITU-T G.8271 specification and mentioned in the earlier section.

The time error accumulates while PTP propagates timing over the packet network, but it is not a constant value. ITU-T G.2860, aptly named "*Definitions and terminology for synchronization in packet networks*," indeed defines a few different types of time errors that a PTP clock may introduce in a PTP-based timing distribution network. Here are some of the noteworthy error types:

- **Maximum absolute time error (max |TE|):** This is the maximum error allowed by a clock. Under normal circumstances, a clock should be well below the max time error and closer to a constant time error (cTE).

- **Constant time error (cTE):** cTE refers to the *mean* of time error experienced by the clock over time. ITU-T G.8260 defines cTE as an *average* of the various time-error measurements over a given period of time. A device's cTE is often considered an indicator of its quality and accuracy.

- **Dynamic time error (dTE):** Similar to how jitter is used to define the variation of latency in packet networks, dTE is a measure of variation in the time error introduced by the clock. A higher dTE value often indicates stability issues in the clock implementation and/or operation.

Since the introduction of PTP in 2002, network equipment manufacturers have been constantly improving their PTP-enabled devices. But the reality is that most of the functions required for PTP—a good quality internal oscillator, capability of real-time recording and timestamping of sync messages, and so on—are hardware-based functions. Any meaningful leap in the quality of PTP handling and accuracy requires updated hardware. At the time of this writing, ITU-T has defined four classifications of PTP-supporting devices based on their accuracy in handling PTP functions. These classifications are Class A, B, C, and D.

Class A represents the first generation of PTP-supported hardware and is the least accurate with higher allowance of time error budgets. *Class B* represents an upgraded hardware with better performance than Class A hardware, and *Class C* offers even better PTP performance than Class B. Class D hardware is expected to surpass the capabilities of Class C PTP devices, but it is not yet available for mobile communication networks. Almost all network equipment providers support Class C timing on their mobile networking equipment portfolio.

ITU-T G.8273.2 defines the time error allowance for Class A, B, and C PTP hardware, as seen in Table 9-1. Specification for Class D is still being finalized at the time of this writing.[20]

TABLE 9-1   Permissible Time Error for Class A, B, C, and D PTP Clocks

T-BC/T-TSC Class	Permissible max|TE|	Permissible cTE Range
Class A	100 nanoseconds	±50 nanoseconds
Class B	70 nanoseconds	±20 nanoseconds
Class C	30 nanoseconds	±10 nanoseconds
Class D	Not yet defined	Not yet defined

The classification of a PTP device plays an important role in building a packetized timing distribution network. Recall that, as shown in Figure 9-12, ITU G.8271 specification allows a total time error of ±200 nanoseconds for the packet network irrespective of the number of T-BCs used. For example, when using Class A PTP devices, with a cTE of ±50 nanoseconds, the network topology is limited to a maximum of only 4 PTP-aware devices before the time error budget exceeds the ±200 nanosecond threshold. Conversely, using a Class B or Class C device allows a maximum of 10 or 20 devices, respectively.

As the PTP clock classification is hardware dependent, a software-only upgrade will *not* convert a Class B timing device into Class C. Converting an existing device class (for example, Class B to Class C) requires a forklift upgrade; as such, service providers must take into account a device's timing class while choosing the appropriate hardware for their 5G network deployments. Class C (or above when available) timing-capable devices are recommended for 5G fronthaul deployments.

PTP Deployment Profiles

In addition to defining network reference points and device accuracy classifications, ITU-T also provides several timing deployment profiles. The primary purpose of these deployment profiles is to establish a baseline reference design for both brown field and green field deployments. These deployment models are necessary for the industry, as service providers have a huge preexisting install base made up of devices that may not be capable of transmitting time with the precision required by

PTP. ITU-T G.8275, "Architecture and requirements for packet-based time and phase distribution," defines two primary deployment profiles:

- **ITU-T G.8275.1:** Precision Time Protocol telecom profile for phase/time synchronization with full timing support from the network

- **ITU-T G.8275.2:** Precision Time Protocol telecom profile for time/phase synchronization with partial timing support from the network

The profiles' names are pretty self-explanatory: the ITU-T G.8275.1 deployment profile requires full PTP support from every device in the packet network. In this profile, every transit node (that is, router) must support the T-BC function and be responsible for generating sync and delay_req messages for PTP operations. G.8275.1 is aimed at new deployments where service providers have the option to deploy network equipment with full PTP support. It is the recommended deployment profile for 5G xHaul networks and results in the best possible timing synchronization using PTP.

Conversely, G.8275.2 is aimed at scenarios where PTP needs to be deployed over an existing infrastructure composed of both PTP-speaking and non-PTP-speaking devices, thus creating a *Partial Timing Support (PTS)* network. In other words, G.8275.2 allows the use of non-T-TBC and non-T-TSC devices in the timing distribution network. This deployment profile allows the service providers the flexibility to deploy phase and time synchronization in their existing network without having to build a brand-new PTP-capable transport. Using G.8275.2, mobile service providers may place a few T-BC-capable devices in their existing infrastructure and enable PTP-based timing and phase distribution. The T-BC connecting the non-PTP-aware and PTP-aware parts of the network is called T-BC-P (T-BC with Partial Timing Support). It must be noted that while it is permissible to use the G.8275.2 deployment profile, the PTS nature of this profile usually results in a lower accuracy compared to the G.8275.1 profile.

Both deployment profiles mentioned allow multiple Telecom Grandmasters (T-GM) to be deployed in the network. This means that the timing reference signal may be acquired at multiple locations in the network and distributed throughout the packet transport. When the G.8275.2 profile is used, it may be possible that T-GMs reside in two separate timing networks connected by a non-PTP-speaking network in the middle. This could be a common scenario in 5G networks where a service provider may have deployed a T-GM in its core or aggregation network and now wants to deploy a 5G-capable xHaul network with T-GM at multiple cell sites. Should such a scenario happen, a feature called *Assisted Partial Timing Support (APTS)* can be used to ensure the Core T-GM stays synchronized with the Edge T-GM, while both serve as a PRTC/T-GM for their respective networks. In other words, APTS is used to *calibrate* the PTP signal between the Core and Edge T-GMS, using GNSS as a reference, thus creating a more robust and accurate timing distribution network, even with a G.8275.2 profile.

Figure 9-13 shows the various ITU-T G.8275 deployment profiles.

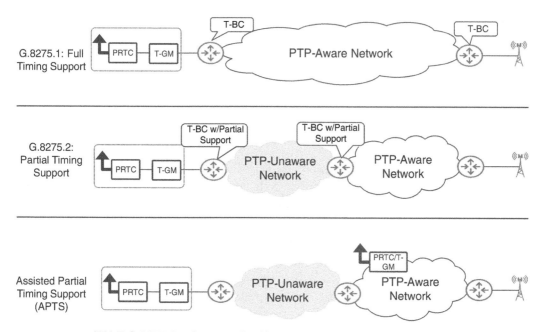

FIGURE 9-13   ITU-T G.8275 Deployment Profiles

Network Time Protocol

Because both NTP and PTP carry timing information over a packetized network infrastructure, a question that network architects often ask themselves is, "Should PTP replace NTP in my network?" The answer to this question is a resounding *NO!* for a variety of reasons.

NTP has been a widely used timing distribution protocol in communication networks over the past several decades. It has gone through several enhancements over the years to make the protocol more robust and efficient. Not only does NTP have widespread support across vendors and device types, but it is also a lightweight protocol when compared to PTP and does not require expensive hardware. Although the accuracy provided by NTP is magnitudes lower than that of PTP, it is sufficient for its proposed application—that is, to carry the ToD information, accurate in the order of milliseconds. The primary application for ToD in a network is event tracking, where routers and other network devices use the ToD learned through NTP to timestamp the system log (*syslog*) messages. These syslog messages are used to report a wide range of events such as user login/logoff, configuration changes, protocol-level events, alarms, errors, warnings, and so on. Network management systems make use of this stamping to correlate various events in the network. Given NTP's widespread use in the networking industry, its (mostly) well-understood nature, and a plethora of reputable sources that cover NTP extensively, this book will not go into the details of NTP operations.

It is expected that NTP will continue to be used for ToD synchronization between network devices for the foreseeable future due to its widespread support across almost all network devices. At the same time, PTP and SyncE will be used to distribute phase and frequency synchronization in 5G-ready mobile xHaul networks.

Summary

During the design phase of a mobile transport network, there is usually a lot of focus on topics such as routing, forwarding, quality of service, and VPN services. Timing and synchronization design and deployment discussions for mobile services have traditionally been an afterthought at best, and justifiably so for the most part.

This chapter explored the importance of distributing timing and synchronization through mobile communication networks. It also examined the reasons why timing and synchronization were considered optional for previous generations of mobile transport networks but is mandatory for next-generation 5G mobile networks. Additionally, this chapter also covers the following topics:

- Basic concepts of time and synchronization

- Various types of synchronization, such as frequency, phase, and time of day (ToD) synchronization and their relationship to each other

- The various sources of clocks and why atomic clocks provide the highest level of accuracy for providing a reference timing signal

- The use of the global navigation satellite system (GNSS) and how it can be used to distribute high-quality, accurate time reference to mobile transport networks

- The use of Synchronous Ethernet (SyncE) to distribute frequency synchronization across packet networks

- Precision Time Protocol (PTP) operations, clock types, reference network, and deployment profiles to distribute phase synchronization through a packet-based mobile transport network

- The use of Network Time Protocol (NTP) for distributing ToD synchronization and why NTP cannot replace PTP in mobile networks for the foreseeable future

Timing and synchronization are the final building blocks discussed in this book for designing and deploying 5G-ready mobile transport networks. The next chapter will focus on combining all the essential technologies needed to build a mobile communication network—RAN decomposition and virtualization, 5G Core, mobile xHaul transport, Segment Routing–based transport underlay, data center networking, VPN services, and time synchronization—and how to use these individual technologies to create a cohesive, end-to-end 5G network design.

References

1. 3GPP Technical Specification 38.104, "NR; Base Station (BS) radio transmission and reception," https://www.3gpp.org/ (last visited: Mar 2022)

2. ITU-T G.8261, "Timing and synchronization aspects in packet networks," https://www.itu.int/ (last visited: Mar 2022)

3. 3GPP Technical Specification 38.104, op, cit.

4. National Institute of Standards and Technology (NIST) F1 Cesium Fountain Atomic Clock, https://www.nist.gov/ (last visited: Mar 2022)

5. Bureau International des Poids et Mesures (BIPM): Time Department, https://www.bipm.org/en/home (last visited: Mar 2022)

6. GPS Accuracy, https://www.gps.gov/ (last visited: Mar 2022)

7. "5G is all in the timing," Ericsson, https://www.ericsson.com/ (last visited: Mar 2022)

8. Galileo Initial Services, https://www.euspa.europa.eu/ (last visited: Mar 2022)

9. Microsemi, https://www.microsemi.com/ (last visited: Mar 2022)

10. "Configuring the Global Navigation Satellite System," Cisco, https://www.cisco.com/ (last visited: Mar 2022)

11. "Resilient Navigation and Timing Foundation," https://rntfnd.org (last visited: Mar 2022)

12. Cisco NCS540 front panel, https://www.cisco.com/ (last visited: Mar 2022)

13. Juniper ACX500 front panel, https://www.juniper.net (last visited: Mar 2022)

14. Rec. ITU-T G.8261.1, "Packet delay variation network limits applicable to packet-based methods (Frequency synchronization)," https://www.itu.int/ (last visited: November 2021)

15. ITU-T G.8264, "Distribution of timing information through packet networks," https://www.itu.int/ (last visited: Mar 2022)

16. RFC 1059, "Network Time Protocol (Version 1) Specification and Implementation," https://www.ieee.org/ (last visited: Mar 2022)

17. Dennis Hagarty, Shahid Ajmeri, and Anshul Tanwar, *Synchronizing 5G Mobile Networks* (Hoboken, NJ: Cisco Press, 2021).

18. Ibid.

19. O-RAN Synchronization Architecture and Solution Specification 1.0, https://www.o-ran.org/specifications (last visited: Mar 2022)

20. ITU-T G.8273.2, "Timing characteristics of telecom boundary clocks and telecom time slave clocks for use with full timing support from the network," https://www.itu.int/ (last visited: Mar 2022)

Chapter | **10**

Designing and Implementing 5G Network Architecture

The last few chapters have gone over network technologies used to build a 5G mobile network. Prior to that, the history and evolution of mobile communication networks (MCNs) were extensively covered. This chapter will merge these topics, focusing on the implementation of the 5G transport network through the application of these essential networking technologies. The chapter will go over various design criteria and architectural considerations that are critical to any such network's design. It will also touch upon the interpretation of the mobile system requirements that the network needs to support, the selection process for the transport network devices, topology design considerations, and choosing the right features and services.

5G Architecture Recap

Before diving deeper into this design and architecture discussion, it will be helpful to recap key 5G innovations and their influence on the transport network. Here are some of the highlights of the 5G MCN:

- **5G Mobile Core:**
    - The mobile core in 5G (5GC) is highly granular, with a focus on functions rather than devices. Its cloud-native nature makes it well-suited to be hosted on public cloud environments as well as mobile providers' private data centers.

    - 5G accelerated the adoption of CUPS for the mobile core, which truly separates the user and control planes, thus allowing the option to move the user plane closer to the network edge. The infrastructure availability, signal flow, peering points, and device placement now have to accommodate this separation of the data plane.

- **5G RAN:**

    - 5G NR features new capabilities such as massive MIMO and beamforming.

    - The utilization of higher frequency ranges results in smaller coverage zones and hence densification of the radio deployments, thus creating new connectivity challenges.

    - The use of wider bands offers increased connection speed to end users. Collectively, the denser deployment footprint and faster available speeds directly translate into higher-bandwidth requirement in the transport network.

    - The decomposition and virtualization of the previously co-located RAN components has resulted in an ongoing architectural transformation toward what is commonly known as a vRAN architecture.

    - Hosting these RAN functions at far-edge and edge DCs has strong implications for transport network design.

- **5G Mobile Transport:**

    - This RAN decomposition has also resulted in the evolution from backhaul to xHaul, creating a new market opportunity through the use of midhaul and packetized fronthaul networks.

    - The choice of lower-layer split (LLS) and higher-layer split (HLS) options has a direct impact on fronthaul and midhaul network designs as well as equipment selection.

    - The fronthaul network *must* provide timing and synchronization information to the packetized transport between RU-DU.

    - The O-RAN architecture and its advocacy toward open interfaces have opened up market segments, which were once dominated by a select number of vendors, to many new entrants.

Figure 10-1 summarizes this 5G MCN architecture as well as the O-RAN-defined planes of operation—that is, control (C-Plane), management (M-plane), user (U-plane), and synchronization (S-Plane). As the figure shows, the pieces of decomposed RAN (RU, DU, and CU) are spread across the xHaul (fronthaul, midhaul, and backhaul) networks. Each one of these xHaul networks has its own constraints when it comes to bandwidth, latency, and device capabilities, which determine their individual design aspects such as the type of devices that can be used and the physical topology. These constraints and design criteria will be discussed in detail later in this chapter. As depicted in the figure, the transport network integrates and provides connectivity for different planes of operations spanning the far-edge, edge, and regional data centers that host the mobile functions. The location, sizing, and even the existence of these DCs depend on the RAN and 5GC deployment model used. The figure also reflects the control and user plane separation of the 5GC as well as the offloading of user traffic closer to the mobile subscriber through distributed peering or processed by MEC applications.

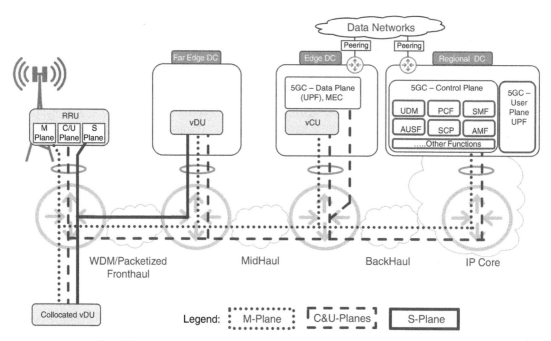

FIGURE 10-1 5G MCN

A parallel yet independent evolution was taking place in the transport technologies that has also shaped mobile communication networks. The development of these new protocols and technologies, such as Segment Routing (SR), Ethernet VPN (EVPN), Software-Defined Networking (SDN), and Network Functions Virtualization (NFV), were fueled primarily by the desire to reduce operational and capital costs, simplify design, achieve deployment agility through automation, and improve efficiency. Although it was not 5G driven, the resulting transport evolution brought by these technologies directly benefits 5G (and even pre-5G) mobile networks, and hence they become essential technologies for building a 5G MCN. A transport network equipped with these (r)evolutionary technologies could now realize the promise of new 5G services. The subsequent sections in this chapter will focus on the design and architecture of the 5G transport network using these technologies.

5G Fronthaul Considerations

The introduction of fronthaul in RAN is perhaps the single most disruptive aspect of next-generation mobile transport networks. Fronthaul was first introduced with Centralized RAN in 4G LTE, but its adoption has been accelerated by the ever-increasing number of 5G deployments.

Decomposed RAN also introduced the concept of a midhaul network to support the HLS option defined by 3GPP. The design requirements of a midhaul are somewhat similar to existing backhaul networks, albeit a bit stricter in terms of latency budgets, and demand higher bandwidths when compared to a traditional backhaul. Network architects, by and large, can draw on their backhaul design experience to create a suitable midhaul network design. Fronthaul networks, on the other hand, require meticulous planning to accommodate the strict requirements resulting from the variety of LLS choices available for the mobile networks. This section aims to highlight various design aspects critical to creating an efficient and functional fronthaul network.

Packetized or WDM Fronthaul Transport?

When Centralized RAN was first introduced, Common Public Radio Interface (CPRI) was a foreign concept for the networking industry. Routers did not support CPRI interfaces and therefore initial fronthaul deployments used wavelength-division multiplexing (WDM)–based optical transport to extend CPRI from cell sites to the C-RAN hub. The use of WDM for CPRI transport might have been necessary in those early fronthaul networks, but with networking equipment vendors starting to implement IEEE's Radio over Ethernet (RoE) and O-RAN Alliance's Fronthaul Gateway (FHGW) functions, there are now options to implement a multipurpose, stat-mux-capable, packet-based fronthaul. Additionally, the introduction of evolved CPRI (eCPRI) using O-RAN's 7-2x or eCPRI Forum's 7-2 split enables the RUs and DUs to communicate using Ethernet-based transport. The end result in all these scenarios is a packet-based fronthaul that benefits from traditional routing and switching technologies.

As mobile service providers embark on their RAN transformation journey, they will continue to support existing 4G LTE fronthaul networks, simultaneously looking to deploy 5G networks based on LLS Option 8 or Option 7-x. With eCPRI-enabled RUs and DUs, the use of a packetized fronthaul is a no-brainer; however, with LLS Option 8 and for existing WDM-based fronthaul networks, the transport networking team is faced with a simple yet powerful question with far-reaching consequences: should the fronthaul continue to be a special-purpose, exclusive, CPRI-only network, or should it be a general-purpose packetized fronthaul network that could benefit from the flexibility and benefits of an IP-based network? Usually, this choice boils down to the networking team deciding whether to use WDM or a packet-based (Ethernet, PON, and so on) network for fronthaul connectivity between cell sites and the far-edge data center. Both the approaches have their own set of benefits and challenges: WDM offers a simple, easy implementation choice, but is limited in general-purpose usability and management capabilities. On the other hand, packetized CPRI transport offers flexible design, uniform architecture across all xHaul domains, and stat-mux capabilities but requires additional functions such as Radio over Ethernet (RoE) or FHGW, which might not be available on all routers. Also, higher CPRI rate options might not be considered "router friendly" due to their high data rate. For instance, CPRI Rate Option 10 is a 24.33Gbps bitstream, thus mandating the use of 25Gbps, or higher, Ethernet interfaces for the CSR uplink. Current cell site routers typically use 1Gbps interfaces toward the BBU and 10Gbps uplinks. However, newer cell site routers (CSRs) are starting to use 25, 40, and 100Gbps interfaces to accommodate higher bandwidths expected of 5G networks.

Service providers will make this decision based on their own calculus, but Table 10-1 aims to provide network architects with a brief overview of the two contrasting approaches that can be used in fronthaul networks.

TABLE 10-1   WDM vs. Packetized Fronthaul Networks

	WDM-based Fronthaul	Packetized Fronthaul
Fiber Use	Requires P2P dark fiber from each site to hub or requires Add Drop Multiplexer (ADM) at every site to provide rings or daisy-chained topologies.	Inherently supports flexible topologies such as rings and partial mesh.
Statistical Multiplexing	Has to be designed based on peak capacity required by the cell sites. Further, service is dedicated to the mobile network only, hence no statistical multiplexing.	Statistical multiplexing capabilities are inherent, and the Fronthaul network can be used to carry other services' traffic, if so desired.
Redundancy	Optical layer redundancy - typically more expensive to deploy.	Topology based (e.g., rings) as well as protocol based (e.g., fast reroute).
Operations and Management	Passive WDM (typically used in fronthaul) has no monitoring and remote management capabilities. Active WDM, which is not cost-effective, provides limited monitoring capabilities still not well-suited for automation and operational monitoring.	Data collection, programmability, and automation capabilities are built into virtually all routers, including CSRs, thus facilitating operations and maintenance using existing network management tools.
Scalability	Dedicated lambdas per site potentially result in inefficient fiber utilization, resulting in increased cost for higher scale.	Stat-mux offers a better utilization of the overall network capacity.
Optics Flexibility and Maintenance	Use of colored optics presents a challenge, where colors on either end of a CPRI circuit need to match. Any changes in optics have to be implemented on both ends. Spares have to be maintained for every colored optic used. Tunable optics and active WDM could be used to mitigate this, but it drives the costs higher.	Generic gray optics are used at cell sites and pre-aggregation nodes, making maintenance, spares management, and replacement simpler.
Value-Added Features	Limited applicability and harder to implement due to the dedicated nature of lambdas.	Myriad of IP-based features and functions such as network programmability, transport network slicing support, traffic engineering, and more.
Cost	Higher total cost of ownership.[1]	Cost-effective in most scenarios.
Technical Expertise	Limited number of trained staff.	Reuse of existing backhaul and IP expertise.

Table 10-1 clearly shows the technical benefits of the packetized fronthaul over a pure optical-based one. While engineers can be wooed with the technical elegance of a proposed solution, more often than not, the final decision comes down to the total cost of ownership (TCO), including both the capital expense (CAPEX) and operational expense (OPEX) for the proposed solution. Every deployment scenario has its own variables, and research has shown packetized fronthaul to be between 13 and 65% more cost-efficient over various optical-only solutions.[2] Nonetheless, network architects must perform a detailed comparison of both the cost and technical capabilities of optical/WDM and packetized fronthaul solutions to choose the best option for their deployment scenario. It is expected that service providers would mix-and-match both the optical and packet-based fronthaul in their network based on fiber availability and preexisting deployments.

Fronthaul Bandwidth Considerations

Bandwidth is one of the two foremost technical considerations (the other one being latency) that dictates much of the design choices for a packetized fronthaul network. The term *bandwidth* has different meanings for mobility and network architects. Mobility architects use this term to refer to the RF bandwidth (that is, how much frequency spectrum is available). In contrast, for network architects, bandwidth refers to the bitrate of the underlying transport networks. This section refers to the latter definition of bandwidth and the considerations to accurately estimate the fronthaul network's requirements.

Network bandwidth requirements and estimations for a mobile backhaul network in a traditional D-RAN deployment are fairly straightforward, where the network bandwidth is a function of the number of baseband units (BBUs) at the cell site and the Ethernet bitrate sent from each of the BBU to the CSR. Because all the baseband processing has been performed by the BBU, the network bandwidth requirements are not astronomically high—typically just a few hundred megabits per second from each BBU. This is why virtually all existing BBUs use a 1Gbps Ethernet interface to connect to the CSR. The uplink from the CSR toward the backhaul could either be a 1G or 10G interface, with newer deployments using 10G or higher uplink interfaces for future proofing.

On the other hand, estimating network bandwidth for the fronthaul is neither that simple nor straightforward. As the bulk of baseband processing happens off the cell site, the network bandwidth required from each cell site becomes a function of the RF characteristics, the LLS option used, and the CPRI transport mechanism (that is, RoE for Split Option 8 or eCPRI in case of Split Option 7.x).

There are many RF characteristics that directly impact the network bandwidth utilization in the fronthaul. 5G, as well as some 4G LTE deployments, makes use of wider RF channels that provide a higher data rate to end user, thereby resulting in higher network bandwidth utilization. Additionally, the 5G NR advanced antenna functions seek to maximize the RF bandwidth through features such as mMIMO, beamforming, carrier aggregation, multi-radio transmission, and others. Any effort to extract higher air interface speeds has a direct correlation with bandwidth requirements in the fronthaul network. Thus, the total bandwidth requirement for packetized fronthaul must take into account the following:

- The total number of CPRI and eCPRI interfaces from all RUs at the cell site

- The individual CPRI rate option used (for LLS Option 8) or the estimated network bandwidth for each eCPRI stream (for LLS Option 7-x)

- The choice of packetizing mechanism to transport CPRI over the packet fronthaul network, if LLS Option 8 is used

The total number of CPRI and/or eCPRI interfaces from RUs to the CSR is determined by the number of sectors at the cell site and the number of frequency carriers in each of these sectors. Although the exact number of these interfaces will depend on RF configuration and RAN equipment vendor implementation, a fair estimate of the total number of interfaces is to assume one CPRI or eCPRI interface per carrier per sector for any given cell site. For instance, a cell site with three sectors and four carriers will typically result in a total of 12 CPRI or eCPRI interfaces from RUs to the CSR. The aggregate bandwidth of these 12 interfaces will be the *total uplink bandwidth* required from the cell site toward the fronthaul network, and will be influenced by the LLS option used.

LLS Option 8, a common split option used in both 4G LTE and some 5G deployments, results in a constant bitrate CPRI stream of uncompressed RF data from each the RUs at the cell site. In this case, the CPRI traffic is an always-on, peak-data-rate bitstream from the RU based on its RF characteristics. Hence, the average data rate for each CPRI interface, in this case, is actually the maximum data rate, which is the derivative of the aforementioned RF characteristics. Unlike other types of network traffic, CPRI traffic cannot be queued, policed, shaped, or otherwise dropped to avoid or manage network congestion. Hence, network architects must plan the fronthaul network to accommodate the cumulative maximum bandwidth from all the CPRI interfaces from all of the cell sites. For Split Option 8, the CPRI packetizing mechanism also plays a role in fronthaul network bandwidth calculations. As previously mentioned in Chapter 5, "5G Fundamentals," RoE Type 0 (structure-agnostic tunneling mode) actually slightly increases the bandwidth to accommodate Ethernet headers, as CPRI traffic is tunneled using Ethernet frames. On the other hand, RoE Type 1 (structure-agnostic line-code-aware mode) provides up to 20% bandwidth savings due to the 8B10B line-coding being removed and reapplied on CSR and the far-edge DC's aggregation node in either direction. However, RoE Type 1 might raise interop concerns between the network and the RAN equipment vendor, also previously discussed in Chapter 5. Any service provider looking to use RoE Type 1 must perform extensive interoperability testing between the RAN and networking components of the fronthaul network before production deployment as well as ensure this interop continues across subsequent software releases.

The use of LLS Option 7-x, on the other hand, results in a bandwidth-efficient fronthaul network, as eCPRI allows statistical multiplexing where the bandwidth consumption is based on actual mobile endpoint usage instead of maximum constant bitrate, as is the case with CPRI. With LLS Option 7-x and eCPRI, mobile service providers can plan the fronthaul network bandwidth requirements by analyzing and/or estimating actual network usage. One of the dimensioning principles for fronthaul networks often cited is "one peak and two averages" (that is, in a three-sector cell site, fronthaul network bandwidth can be estimated by using peak bandwidth for one sector and average bandwidth for the remaining two).[3]

With the introduction of fronthaul networks, almost all RAN and network equipment vendors have developed their own fronthaul bandwidth calculators. Network architects in mobile service providers looking to design 5G fronthaul networks must ask their respective equipment vendors to share estimated bandwidth expectations for each radio antenna and RU based on their specific RF parameters and LLS options.

Impact of Lower-Layer Split on Fronthaul Transport

The choice of LLS option has profound implications on the fronthaul network planning, design, and implementation. As previously discussed, CPRI can either be transported over dedicated fiber links using WDM or sent over packetized fronthaul networks. When using a packet-based fronthaul network, the split option as well as the choice of packetizing technology directly impacts the traffic behaviors, bandwidth needs, as well as the choice of routers to be used at both the cell site and the far-edge data center.

For instance, the use of Split Option 8 requires a specialized CPRI interface on the CSR as well as appropriate packetizing mechanisms such as IEEE 1914.3 RoE or Fronthaul Gateway functionality. The choice of CPRI packetizing mechanism (RoE or FHGW) also defines the network design aspects, such as a two-box bookended solution (that is, RoE mapper and demapper functions) or a one-box CPRI to eCPRI conversion (FHGW). In contrast, Split Options 7-2 and 7-2x both use eCPRI that relies on Ethernet-based framing. Hence, when planning the fronthaul network, the network architecture team must take into consideration the effects of various LLS options, as summarized in Table 10-2.

TABLE 10-2   Lower-Layer Splits and Their Impact on Fronthaul Networks

	Lower-Layer Split Option 8					LLS Option 7-2	LLS Option 7-2x
	WDM	RoE Type 0	RoE Type 1	RoE Type 2	FHGW		
Standardization Body	NA	IEEE	IEEE	IEEE	O-RAN	eCPRI Forum	O-RAN
Transport Type	WDM	Packet	Packet	Packet	Packet	Packet	Packet
CSR to RU Interface	Layer 1	CPRI	CPRI	CPRI	CPRI	Ethernet	Ethernet
Bookended Solution	N/A	Yes	Yes	Yes	No	N/A	N/A
CSR CPRI Awareness	N/A	None	Line code aware	Full CPRI aware	Full CPRI aware	N/A	N/A
RAN-Network Interop Requirement	N/A	PoC Only	Yes	Extensive	Extensive	N/A	N/A
Bandwidth Saving over CPRI	N/A	None	20% (rate 1–7)	High	High	High	High
Stat-mux	No	Limited	Limited	Yes	Yes	Yes	Yes

Latency Considerations

Another critical aspect of the fronthaul network design is the strict latency budget between the RU and the DU. Latency has not been a pressing concern in traditional mobile backhaul networks because all baseband processing was performed at the cell sites. With geographically separated RU and DU, the baseband processing responsibilities are now divided between the cell site and the far-edge DC. The strict latency requirements between the RU and DU arise from the delicate nature of RF processing, which requires near-real-time communication between the two.

While the RAN equipment (that is, the DU and RU) vendors should provide the exact latency tolerance for their products, 3GPP and the O-RAN Alliance have also defined guidelines for maximum allowed latency between the RU and DU. The latency budget allocated to the transport network is 100 usec or less for most cases.[4] In other words, network architects must ensure their network designs and topologies adhere to a one-way latency of less than 100 usec between the DU (possibly located at the far-edge DC) and the RU at the cell site.

Fronthaul network latency is a function of the following:

■ Physical distance between RU (that is, cell site) and DU (that is, far-edge DC). Every kilometer of fiber adds approximately 4.9 usec of latency.

■ Transit time for a packet to pass through the CSR and the far-edge DC aggregation router, or WDM equipment in non-packet-based fronthaul.

■ Number of intermediate routers in the fronthaul topology.

Considering the preceding defined factors, a network architect can estimate the total latency incurred in a given fronthaul network using the following equation:

Total Fronthaul Network Latency $= (L_F * 4.9) + T_{CSR} + T_{Agg} + (n * T_{IR})$

where:

L_F = Length of fiber in kilometers

T_{CSR} = Packet transit time through CSR in usec

T_{Agg} = Packet transit time through far-edge DC aggregation router in usec

n = Number of intermediate routers in the fronthaul network topology

T_{IR} = Packet transit time through the intermediate router in the fronthaul network in usec

Note that the equation calls for calculating the transit time of a packet through the CSR and far-edge DC aggregation router separately from other transit nodes. The reason for this is to accommodate special processing and handling of CPRI traffic at the ingress or egress of these devices, which is different from simply transporting Ethernet frames through a router. The processing required on these devices is based on the LLS option and the features used on the network devices to transport traffic between the RU and DU. For instance, in the case of Split Option 8, the CSR must packetize the CPRI stream using either an RoE mapper or the FHGW function. If RoE is being used, the packetized CPRI traffic must be converted back into CPRI bitstream on the far-edge DC aggregation router using the RoE demapper function. Both the mapper and demapper functions will add extra latency due to the processing performed on the routers. The same is true when using FHGW functionality on the CSR. Although when using FHGW functions, the far-edge DC aggregation router does not require any demapping function because the FHGW performs the CPRI-to-eCPRI conversion. As mentioned in Chapter 5, the FGHW functionality can be vendor-specific (that is, requires RU and DU from the same vendor), or could be implemented as defined by the O-RAN Alliance specifications.[5] In this case, the transit time of the packet through the DC aggregation router could be similar to any other transit nodes, as no specialized processing is being performed. Figure 10-2 showcases various scenarios and combinations that could impact latency in a fronthaul transport network.

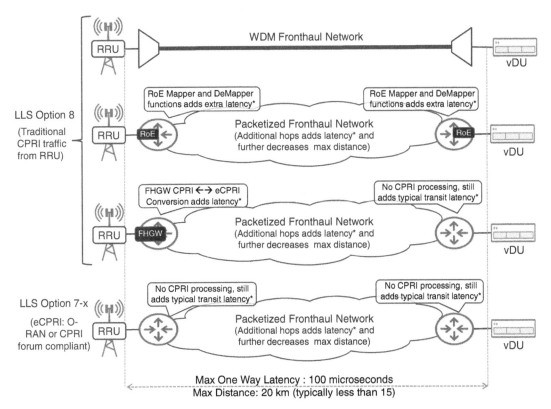

FIGURE 10-2 Latency Considerations for Various Packetized Fronthaul Transport Scenarios

In order to accurately estimate the fronthaul network latency, the network architects must ask the fronthaul network equipment vendor(s) to provide transit latency data for their products with regard to each scenario shown in Figure 10-2. Transit latency for fronthaul routers is dependent on network vendor implementation. In order to provide the lowest possible latency for CPRI/eCPRI traffic through their routers, many network equipment manufacturers are opting to implement *IEEE Time Sensitive Networking (TSN)* profiles, on top of existing features and functions necessary for mobile communication networks.[6] These TSN profiles are a set of specifications defined by the IEEE TSN technology group focused on providing deterministic services through IEEE 802 networks and establishing guidelines for guaranteed packet transport, low packet loss, and predictable latency, among others. At the time of this writing, the TSN technology group has standardized two profiles, with several others in development. Here are the two TSN profiles that have been standardized:[7]

- **802.1BA:** Audio/Video Bridging (AVB) Systems

- **802.1CM:** Time-Sensitive Networking for Fronthaul

The other profiles under consideration include TSN for industrial automation, service provider networks, aerospace communications, and automotive in-vehicle communications, among others.

IEEE 802.1CM, "TSN for Fronthaul," overlaps significantly with 3GPP and O-RAN specifications defining aspects of the fronthaul network, such as the use of different LLS options, CPRI and eCPRI transport over an IEEE 802 network, and the use of PTP for timing and synchronization, among others. Additionally, 802.1CM tackles the issue of low latency and deterministic packet transport for fronthaul networks by defining two sub-profiles:[8]

- **IEEE 802.1CM Profile A:** Defines prioritization of CPRI IQ data over other fronthaul and non-fronthaul traffic. It also calls for the use of strict priority queuing for fronthaul traffic. Most, if not all, existing routers support QoS features defined in 802.1CM profile A.

- **IEEE 802.1CM Profile B:** Defines the use of 802.1Qbu, "Frame Preemption," in addition to strict priority queuing. Networking equipment vendors are starting to support Profile B in their fronthaul product offerings.

The TSN specification for 802.1Qbu strives for the highest priority traffic (for example, CPRI or eCPRI) to spend *no time* in the input or output queues on the fronthaul routers. Whenever possible, network architects should opt for 802.1Qbu-enabled fronthaul routers to ensure that CPRI or eCPRI traffic is promptly processed and forwarded by preempting any non-fronthaul traffic. The resulting latency savings, however miniscule, could allow for slightly more distance between the cell site and the far-edge DC, thus making the far-edge DC placement and selection process a little more flexible.

Selecting a Far-Edge DC Location

A critically important yet sometimes overlooked aspect of fronthaul network design is the selection of a suitable far-edge DC location, sometimes also called a C-RAN hub site. In some cases, the mobile service provider may choose to use an existing cell site, likely to be a macrocell site, as a far-edge DC for its downstream cell sites. In most cases, this makes a lot of sense, as many of these macrocell sites already have the infrastructure necessary to support a small far-edge DC deployment. In other scenarios, it might be more practical to set up a new site for far-edge DC instead of repurposing an existing macrocell location. Whatever the case may be, the following baseline conditions must be met for any location to act as a far-edge DC:

- The proposed location must not be more than 20km fiber-length away from its downstream cell sites.

- The proposed location must have adequate fiber infrastructure to connect to downstream cell sites as well as to the edge or regional DC.

- The proposed location should have sufficient real estate, power, and cooling capacity to accommodate compute and networking equipment required to provide services to its downstream cell sites.

It is important to note that there are no simple and direct answers for a far-edge DC site selection. It is rather a function of technical constraints (such as latency budget limitations between the RU and DU) that defines logistical constraints such as the distance between the far-edge DC and cell site. The physical network topology might also introduce additional latency, as discussed in the previous section, which reduces the 20km distance limitation for fronthaul networks.

Depending on the size of the far-edge DC and the number of cell sites to which it provides services, this location could be a traditional shelter with redundant power supplies, cooling equipment, and racks to mount compute and storage devices for hosting virtualized DUs as well as networking equipment such as aggregation nodes. This could also be a small location without a shelter but a few outdoor cabinets to host a small number of computing devices with built-in storage. Service providers would typically have both these types of far-edge DC sites in their network infrastructure.

If any of the previously defined conditions for a proposed site(s) cannot be met, the mobile service provider should find another site to act as the far-edge DC for its downstream cell sites. If this is not possible, then the provider should consider using a deployment model where the RU and DU are co-located at the cell site.

xHaul Transport Technology Choices

A mobile transport network is only as good as its underlying transport technology, and, as such, the choice of an appropriate transport technology is a key consideration for xHaul design and deployment. Chapter 3, "Mobile Networks Today," covered a host of technologies that can be used for mobile transport. Traditionally, backhaul networks have used a combination of all the technologies covered in Chapter 3—Ethernet, WDM, PON, cable, DSL, microwave, and, in remote and hard-to-reach places, satellite. All of these technologies are perfectly capable of backhauling mobile traffic, and oftentimes the choice of the transport technology boils down to cost-effectiveness and the service provider's level of comfort with the chosen option.

Cost-effectiveness is an ever-relevant factor of any viable network design. However, the evolution of a mobile backhaul to mobile xHaul demands reexamining the technical characteristics of a given transport technology to ensure it can fulfill the strict, heretofore unseen requirements of a mobile fronthaul network. Network architects designing 5G xHaul networks must carefully consider the technical attributes of various transport technologies to gauge their suitability for fronthaul, midhaul, and backhaul domains. Every service provider's deployment scenario is different; therefore, Table 10-3 lists various technical characteristics of transport technologies as well as their suitability for different xHaul domains to help network architects make informed decisions about their xHaul design.

TABLE 10-3   Transport Technologies and Their Applicability to xHaul Domains

Transport Tech	Attributes and Characteristics					Suitable For:		
	BW	Latency	Stability	Design Flexibility	Cost	FH	MH	BH
Ethernet	High	Depends on the number of nodes and fiber length	High	High	Med	Yes	Yes	Yes
WDM	High		High	Med	High	Yes	Yes	Yes
PON	High[1]		High	Med	Med	Possible[2]	Yes	Yes
DOCSIS	Med[1]		High	Med	Med	Limited[2]	Yes	Yes
DSL	Med[1]		Med	Med	Med	Limited[2]	Yes	Yes
Microwave	Med	Med	Med	High	Low	Limited[2]	Yes	Yes
Satellite	Low	High	Low	Low	Low[3]	No	Yes	Yes

[1]Dependent on the technology flavor (for example, NGPON offers higher bandwidth than traditional GPON). Similarly, newer flavors of DOCSIS and DSL should be used.

[2]Topology dependent, as these are shared-access technologies. A higher number of devices on a shared connection could result in inadequate bandwidth for fronthaul needs.

[3]Excludes the cost of launching satellites into orbit.

Virtually all mobile service providers have built, and will continue to build, xHaul networks that rely on a combination of transport technologies shown in Table 10-3. The exact combination of technologies used will be based on the service provider's policies, level of expertise, tooling capabilities, preexisting infrastructure, and, of course, the total cost of ownership.

Designing the Mobile Transport Network

Designing a 5G mobile transport network goes well beyond just transport technology choices. The network architecture team must take into consideration a lot of varying factors such as physical network topology, the placement of the RAN and 5GC components as well as their impact on existing mobile networks, end-to-end quality of service, and even the selection of appropriate network devices for a particular role. This section goes beyond just the fronthaul design considerations and aims to take a look at various design aspects for an end-to-end mobile transport network.

Physical Topology Considerations

The topological considerations of a network are often dictated by the choice of underlying transport technology. While technologies like Ethernet allow flexibility and a variety of choices in terms of topological design enabling network architects to build redundancy into their topologies, other technologies such as PON, cable, and DSL offer only the possibility of a point-to-point or point-to-multipoint topology, thus limiting the options available for network design and architecture planning. When multi-access technologies like PON, DSL, and cable are used as the transport underlay for mobile transport, the primary topological consideration is to ensure adequate bandwidth for fronthaul, midhaul, and backhaul deployments by limiting the number of access nodes on the shared topology. Fiber-based mobile transport, however, has the flexibility to deploy different topology options such as *rings* and *point-to-point network fabric*.

Ring-based xHaul Networks

Rings have been the topology of choice for most wired networks spanning a large geographical area. They are cost-effective, provide potential for load balancing across multiple paths, and have built-in redundancy mechanisms where traffic could be rerouted in case of link or node failure. Access nodes (or cell site routers in case of an MCN) in a ring topology are generally terminated on a pair of aggregation or pre-aggregation nodes to ensure not only path redundancy but also aggregation node redundancy. Because a fiber ring typically serves a larger geographical area, aggregation node redundancy becomes an important aspect of any ring design since an aggregation node failure has the potential to impact a large number of subscribers. Ring topologies, by far, make the largest number of wired mobile backhaul deployments and will continue to be an important aspect of any xHaul network implementation for 5G transport networks. However, with new requirements regarding latency and bandwidth, network architects must reexamine some of the finer details of a ring-based mobile transport network for their applicability to 5G xHaul networks. One such aspect is the number of devices in a fiber ring and its impact on latency and bandwidth.

Mobile service providers have commonly been connecting up to 10 cell sites, sometimes more, in a single fiber ring. This practice worked pretty well for mobile backhaul, as such a ring would provide connectivity for cell sites over a moderately large geographical area while staying within the maximum latency and bandwidth requirements from all of the cell sites combined. The same practice of roughly 10 cell sites per ring would actually work well with midhaul networks as well. Because the bulk of the baseband processing has already been done at the DU, the latency and bandwidth requirements in a midhaul network are not that drastically different from mobile backhaul. As a reminder, both backhaul and midhaul can tolerate a few milliseconds of latency, which allows for a moderate number of network devices as well as larger distances when compared to fronthaul's 100-usec one-way latency.

The strict latency and high-bandwidth requirements of a fronthaul network means that network architects must look at the number of devices as well as the distance between those devices in a ring more critically. Every CSR in the ring adds transit latency as well as contributes to the total accumulated bandwidth for the entire ring network. Under normal circumstances, traffic on the ring is balanced across both directions, but given the time-sensitive and lossless nature of the CPRI/eCPRI traffic on the fronthaul, service providers must plan for the worst-case scenario and consider the traffic behavior in case of a failure on the ring. As Figure 10-3 shows, for a 10-node ring, with each cell site 1 km apart and ~10-usec transit latency for each device, the latency requirement of 100 usec from every cell site to the far-edge DC could still be met. However, in case of a failure on the ring, traffic from a cell site would need to take the longer path to the aggregation node. The accumulated transit and path latency could push some sites over the 100-usec threshold, thus creating scenarios where RU–DU communication would become unstable, resulting in loss of service to a large number of mobile subscribers. There is also a potential for congestion if the accumulated bandwidth from all cell sites exceeds the interface capacity of the uplink interfaces on the CSRs.

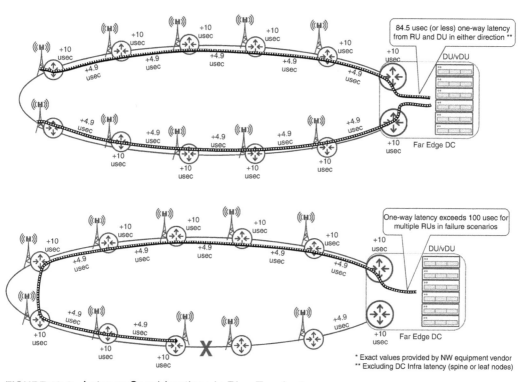

FIGURE 10-3   Latency Considerations in Ring Topologies

With these restrictions, a lot of service providers are moving to smaller fiber rings (typically five cell sites or less) and lower fiber distances to ensure latency budgets and total bandwidth stay within the required thresholds. In some cases, mobile service providers are also moving toward an Ethernet fabric-based fronthaul network, with direct links from cell sites to the far-edge DC, in order to satisfy the strict bandwidth and latency requirements imposed by lower-layer splits between the RU and DU.

Ethernet Network Fabric for xHaul

Point-to-point hub-and-spoke fiber connectivity has long been the gold standard of a wired network. It offers unparalleled flexibility and potentially unlimited bandwidth, albeit at a higher capital expense resulting from both added equipment (such as additional transceivers and ports on aggregating switches) and the cost of laying fiber over a larger geographical area. However, point-to-point hub-and-spoke network fabrics have been a mainstay of data center networks, offering a repeatable, resilient, and horizontally scalable architecture through a spine-leaf design.

Mobile service providers are warming up to the idea of point-to-point links between cell sites and the far-edge DC, in large part due to the bandwidth and latency limitations imposed by fronthaul networks, although midhaul and backhaul networks may also make use of such a topology. The result is a fabric-like Ethernet xHaul topology that is somewhat similar to a data center fabric, where the leafs are the CSRs and the spines are the pre-aggregation or aggregation routers at the DC sites. There is, however, one notable exception between a DC and xHaul network fabric's composition: a leaf node in a DC fabric is multihomed to two or more spines, whereas a cell site router in an xHaul network fabric is usually single-homed to one aggregation node. This lack of redundancy can be attributed to the cost of laying multiple fibers from the cell site to the data center. The single-homed connection from the cell site does present a single point of failure for a cell site, where a fiber cut could result in the potential loss of service for all mobile subscribers serviced by that cell site. However, an effective RF design using an overlap of coverage and speed bands can mitigate against complete service failure. Sure enough, some subscribers may face degraded service, but with an umbrella coverage band, the service failure would not be absolute.

The lack of any intermediary transit devices maximizes the distance between cell sites and the DC while ensuring the bandwidth requirements are met for xHaul deployments. The cost of fiber deployment is still a limiting factor, and thus point-to-point fiber links are used between cell sites and the DC only when absolutely necessary. Fronthaul is the primary use case for deploying an Ethernet fabric, rather than a ring network, when possible. The densification of cell sites in 5G, coupled with a potentially large number of far-edge DCs, results in scenarios where fronthaul cell sites might be relatively closer to their respective far-edge DCs. The outcome is a relatively lower cost to run the fiber to an individual cell site, making fabric-based fronthaul networks more feasible. It is expected that mobile transport networks would be composed of both ring and point-to-point topologies in most cases, as shown in Figure 10-4. Other transport mechanisms such as microwave, PON, satellite, and so on would also coexist with fiber-based network topologies.

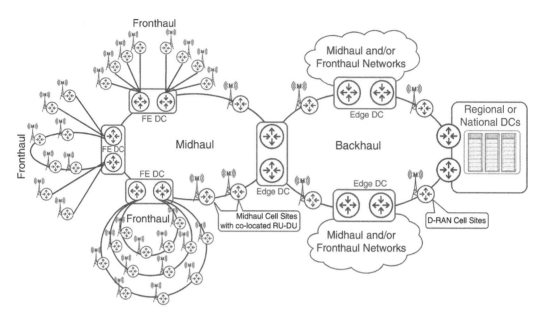

FIGURE 10-4   Topological Choices in a Wired xHaul Network

vRAN Deployment Scenarios

As has been discussed over the past few chapters, the location of the decomposed RAN components (that is, the RU, DU, and CU) determine the nature of the xHaul network and whether it should be considered a fronthaul, midhaul, or backhaul—each one with its own requirements and design considerations. The potential placement combinations of these RAN functions and the resulting xHaul domains have already been covered in Chapter 5 (refer to Figure 5-12). Nevertheless, mobile service providers looking to deploy a vRAN architecture for 5G must also consider the possibility of a preexisting 4G or 3G network infrastructure that will continue to coexist with the newer 5G deployments. Many mobile network operators are grappling with adequately defining the use cases and scenarios they will need to support in their next-generation xHaul network. Therefore, network operators in the O-RAN Alliance, in an effort to provide leadership and guidance, documented a few xHaul scenarios pertinent to a typical 5G deployment.[9]

Figure 10-5 documents several such xHaul scenarios an operator can deploy based on their existing infrastructure and future 5G vRAN plans.

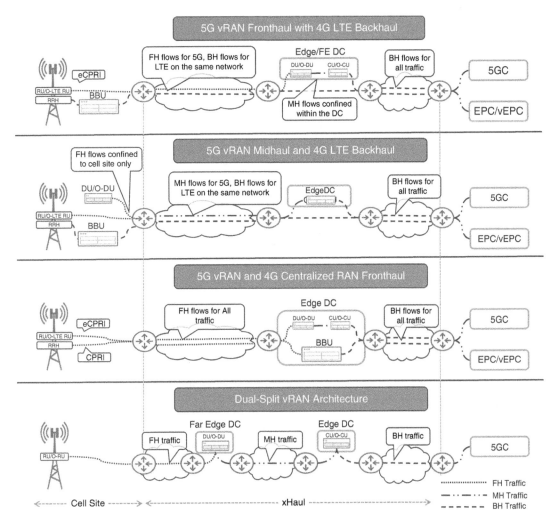

FIGURE 10-5   Commonly Used vRAN and xHaul Deployment Scenarios

As Figure 10-5 illustrates, the packet network connecting the cell site router to the rest of the mobile transport can serve as a fronthaul, midhaul, and/or backhaul simultaneously, depending on the RAN functions used and their respective placements. Network architects must take into account this multi-purpose aspect of an xHaul network domain, where a router at the cell site might act as fronthaul CSR for 5G deployment but also as a backhaul CSR for 4G LTE services. In these scenarios, the CSR must be able to provide preferential treatment to the fronthaul traffic, irrespective of which generation RU the traffic might be coming from. The preferential treatment can include priority queuing, guaranteed bandwidth, and the use of TSN-enabled ports to allow frame preemption if available.

The User Plane Function (UPF) moving closer to the subscriber edge is another aspect of designing an efficient xHaul network. Because UPF provides actual connectivity between the subscriber traffic and external data networks, the placement of UPF is heavily dependent on the peering availability at the installation location. While not a function of 5G transformation per se, the evolution and availability of peering points across the xHaul network play a critical role in creating an efficient 5G network.

Peering Considerations

Peering with data networks, such as the Internet or private intranets, has been a pivotal component of any service provider network. The job of a service provider, including mobile service provider, is to connect its subscribers to the content hosted on various data networks. Traditionally, service providers have been limited by the availability of Internet peering exchange locations, forcing them to extend their network presence to those locations. Prior to the widespread use of cloud providers, most of the content was scattered all over numerous smaller networks, and hence robust and diverse connectivity with other networks and transit service providers was of great importance. All consumer traffic and content have to be hauled back and forth from these peering locations (typically on the other end of the service provider network) to the far edges of the network, thereby forcing the buildout of high-capacity IP aggregation and IP core network. The very name *mobile backhaul*, as mentioned before, was a consequence of this characteristic of hauling traffic from the cell sites all the way to the peering points.

Bringing Content Closer to the Subscriber

In an effort to decentralize traffic flows and reduce content delivery times, web service providers offer caching solutions to be placed right in the service provider's networks, closer to its subscribers. Such caching solutions in many cases are presented to the service provider's network as a *connection* to the web service provider's network and use eBGP peering with them. In other words, the peering with the major traffic attraction points can be placed anywhere in the service provider's network. Typically, a number of separate instances of caching solutions are placed right in the service provider's network, bringing content very close to the edge of its network, creating peering points within the service provider's edge. Some well-known web and content providers offering caching solutions are Akamai, Google, and Netflix, among others.

In addition to traditional peering providers such as Equinix expanding their reach, the past several years have also seen the emergence of special-purpose cloud and web providers offering attractive and cost-effective solutions for hosting content, applications, and other resources typically accessed by the subscribers of mobile and traditional service providers. Today, the bigger part of overall Internet traffic originates or terminates in the autonomous systems of these web service providers, such as Amazon,

Google, and Microsoft. These cloud and web service providers own some of the largest networks on the planet, spanning multiple countries and continents. Their unprecedented size and reach have afforded them the capability to establish peering points at many locations, sometimes bringing their presence into service providers' networks. Given the sea-change in the availability of distributed peering locations, mobile service providers now can benefit from these diverse and plentiful peering locations. By establishing distributed peering across multiple locations in their network, mobile service providers can now offload traffic from their network closer to the subscribers. Peering design is considered an essential part of an xHaul architecture and allows the mobile service provider to use public cloud to augment its own network. The use of public cloud for 5G MCN is further discussed later in this chapter.

End-to-End QoS Design

Quality of service (QoS) has been an integral part of any effective network design, and MCNs are no exception. Through QoS, a network administrator can mark certain traffic with a defined priority level through IP precedence or DSCP, MPLS EXP, or class of service (CoS, a.k.a. 802.1P bit). Multiple congestion management and avoidance techniques can then be used to ensure target SLAs are met by preferring high-priority traffic in oversubscribed or congested networks. Some of the QoS mechanisms include ingress policing, shaping, bandwidth guarantee, and priority queuing.

Priority Queueing vs. Frame Preemption in TSN

QoS mechanisms ensure that different classes of traffic are processed by the router based on their priority. For instance, Priority Queuing (PQ), also known as Low Latency Queuing (LLQ), ensures that certain classes of traffic are processed before others and, as such, spend a minimal amount of time in the input and output queues. LLQ and PQ are essential features for real-time video, voice, and gaming.

The Time Sensitive Networking (TSN) specification 802.1Qbu strives for the highest priority traffic (for example, CPRI or eCPRI) to spend *no time* in the input and output queues. It enables CPRI traffic to preempt any existing frames from processing, thus ensuring fast and continuous traffic forwarding. This is different from PQ, where a packet might still have to wait in the queue if another packet is being processed or forwarded. 802.1Qbu allows the highest priority traffic to *bump* the current packets in favor of higher priority traffic.

As discussed in Chapter 5, the fundamental difference between 5G and 4G LTE QoS is how it is applied to bearers. While 4G relies on assigning QoS on a per-bearer basis, 5G allows flow classification within bearers and, as such, offers a granular end-to-end QoS mechanism. 3GPP defined a wide list of 5QIs for a range of services such as conversational voice and video, gaming, V2X messaging, non-conversational video, mission-critical data, and signaling, among many others—each with its own intended network characteristics, such as bandwidth guarantee, maximum packet delay budget (that is, latency), acceptable packet loss, and so on. Both the RAN and 5GC domains use 5QI and QFI markers in a flow to offer QoS for different types of services. Generally speaking, the 5QI profiles defined by 3GPP can be classified in two major categories, similar to previous generations:

- **Guaranteed bitrate (GBR):** Flows that require some sort of guaranteed bandwidth. These could either be delay-critical or non-delay-critical GBR flows.

- **Non-guaranteed bitrate (non-GBR):** Flows that do not require any bandwidth guarantee across the MCN.

5G QoS Markers

The QoS classification markers such as 5QI, QFI, and QCI were previously discussed in Chapter 5. A list of all standardized services, their respective 5GQI values, and associated characteristics is documented in 3GPP technical specification TS 23.501, titled "System architecture for the 5G System."[10]

The 5QI and QFI (as well as QCI for 4G LTE) have great utility in RAN and the mobile core domain, but networking equipment is generally oblivious to these parameters. The routers and switches that make up the transport network rely on IP, MPLS, or Layer 2 (Ethernet/VLAN) based markings to implement QoS. As such, network architects must create a mapping between the 3GPP-defined QoS marking and their transport networking counterpart, which can then be used to define per-hop behaviors (PHBs) for different traffic types. It should be noted that 3GPP defines a plethora of 5QI values—much more than its IP networking counterparts. One way to overcome this imbalance is to group similar types of traffic into a common QoS profile with the same transport networking QoS markings (that is, the same MPLS EXP or 802.1p values for multiple traffic types). These groupings can be based on individual characteristics such as low-latency traffic, traffic that requires guaranteed bandwidth, or traffic that is more flexible on latency and bandwidth. Once the types of traffic are grouped together, the network architecture team can create a complete QoS policy for each different class of service, which includes per-hop behavior like policing, shaping, bandwidth guarantees, maximum time a packet can spend in queue, and whether a packet should be dropped for avoiding or managing congestion. Table 10-4 presents some sample mapping a mobile service provider could use, where groups of traffic from different 5QI values are bundled into a common profile along with their MPLS EXP, IP DSCP, or 802.1P mappings and relevant QoS characteristics. The IP or VLAN-based QoS markings should be imposed by the RU or the 5GC functions when sending traffic to the transport network. It must be stressed that this is a sample QoS profile, and every mobile service provider should look at their own traffic types, network requirements, and service level agreements to create a detailed QoS table.

TABLE 10-4 Sample QoS Schema for MCN

Traffic Class*	5QI	Transport Markings (CoS/EXP/ DSCP)	Forwarding Behavior	BW Allocation ***	Drop Probability	Queue Depth
Conversational Voice	1		Realtime Expedited Forwarding (that is, Priority Queuing)	50	None	5 msec
Conversational Video (Live)	2	5/5/46				
Real-time Gaming	3					
Non-real-time Video	4	4/4/36	Assured Forwarding	40	None	20 msec
OAM	—	4/4/10				
IMS Signaling	5	6/6/32	Assured Forwarding	5	None	50 msec
Network Control	—	6/6/48				
Data High Priority	6	2/2/18	Assured Forwarding**	55	Low	50 msec
Non GBR Video	7	2/2/20			Med	50 msec
Data Reg Priority	8	2/2/22			High	50 msec
Data Low Priority	9	2/2/14			High	50 msec
Data – Scavenger	—	0/0/0	Best Effort	0	High	50 msec

* Not all traffic classes shown.

** Classified as non-GBR by 3GPP. Service providers can use oversubscription on these traffic types.

*** Total bandwidth exceeds 100% since Priority Queue bandwidth is not counted in the total, as it can take bandwidth away from other classes when needed. Non-PQ classes add up to 100% of the *remaining* bandwidth after PQ requirements are met.

Selecting the Right Network Device

Mobile communication networks are generally spread over larger graphical areas spanning entire cities, states, provinces, or, in a lot of cases, entire countries. Needless to say, the underlying transport network that supports these MCNs also spans hundreds or, in some cases, thousands of kilometers. Networks as large and diverse as mobile transport require appropriate network devices at every layer of their infrastructure. The choice of these devices is guided by many different factors, such as their intended role in the network, the location in which they will be placed, the scale they need to support, and obviously the features and functions they need to perform. This section aims to highlight some key factors that network architecture teams must consider when selecting devices for mobile transport networks.

Environmental and Placement Considerations

Routers for mobile networks come in various shapes and sizes depending on their intended placement and function. IP aggregation and core devices are usually placed in well-developed structures such as a point of presence, a local DC, or a regional DC. These devices can also be larger in size, sometimes half a rack size or more. Due to the number of subscribers served by an aggregation or core node, these devices should also have built-in redundancy to ensure a single failure does not bring down the whole router. The typically larger size provides ample space for multiple control modules (sometimes called *route processors* or *route engines*), power supplies, fan trays, and, of course, dozens, if not hundreds, of high-speed interfaces. Given that these large routers are usually placed in well-built structures with controlled environments, they are not required to be environmentally hardened to the extent where they need to withstand extreme temperatures and outdoor conditions.

For access nodes, such as CSRs, their size and environmental tolerance are important consideration factors for any deployment planning. While each deployment is different, CSRs are expected to be placed in one of the three types of locations typical of a vast majority of cell sites. First is a cell site with a well-built shelter, right at the cell site or a short distance away, with ample space for power and cooling equipment as well as potentially space for multiple racks where the CSR and other equipment can be mounted. This type of location could also act as a far-edge DC for downstream cell sites. Another common deployment location is a cell tower with a few cabinets at the base of the tower that provide some degree of protection from the environment but is constrained in the space available for the CSR and other equipment. The last one is a new but growing trend, where 5G cellular antennas are mounted on a standalone pole or street light, with limited or no space underneath.[11, 12] Figure 10-6 shows examples of each of these cell site deployment types.

FIGURE 10-6   Environmental Protection at Cell Sites

The CSRs must be able to accommodate the requirements for the type of cell site they are being deployed at. In cases where the CSR will be installed in the cabinet or a rack in the shelter, environmental requirements are somewhat relaxed, but the CSR must meet the physical size requirements to fit in the cabinet or shelf. Service providers prefer the CSR to be a compact device, able to fit the 19-inch-wide rack commonly used at the cell sites, rather than the 21-inch ETSI racks that are more common in point-of-presence and central DCs. The CSR is also preferred to be *1 rack unit* in height. A *rack unit* is a measure of the *regions* a rack is divided into. Depending on the height, a typical 19-inch rack may have up to 45 rack units, with each one about 1.75 inches in height. A 1-rack-unit CSR leaves a lot of space on the rack that could be used to mount other equipment such as BBUs in D-RAN deployments or DUs in case of a decomposed vRAN design with co-located RU and DUs. By comparison, the aggregation or IP core routers can span multiple rack units, some as high as 18 or 20 rack units or more.

The growing popularity of small cells with street lights being turned into cell towers and antennas being mounted on standalone poles adds another set of constraints for the CSR placement. In these cases, the overall dimensions as well as environmental hardiness become key selection criteria for an appropriate CSR. If the router is to be installed directly on the antenna post out in the open, it must be compact in size and must be appropriately weatherproofed. A vast majority of these deployments require the CSR to adhere to relevant ingress protection (IP) ratings, such as IP65, which protects the complying node from dust and low-pressure water jets such as rain.[13] Another important aspect of an outdoor-capable CSR is its size and weight. As seen in Figure 10-6, some of the newer cell towers might be deployed with a net-zero ground footprint, which means that all the equipment, including the CSR, has to be placed within an enclosure in the streetlamp or mounted on the pole. Hiding the equipment in such an enclosure or placing it several feet above the ground also reduces the chances of vandalism. Bulkier gear might not fit in the limited space on the street light enclosure, and a heavier CSR that needs to be pole-mounted might require additional consideration such as aerial lifts and teams of people to install such a device, thereby increasing the costs and timelines of deployment. Limiting the size and weight of the outdoor CSR can allow a mobile service provider to expedite the cell site rollout at a lower cost.

In many cases, the size and weight of a router are considered table stakes to determine whether a device could act as a CSR for a given 5G deployment. Once a proposed CSR meets the guidelines of dimensions and environmental hardiness, network architects must closely examine the features supported, or planned to be supported in the near future. The availability of software and hardware features is equally as important as environmental factors, if not more so.

Timing and Synchronization Support

The previous chapter covered the importance of timing and synchronization in a fronthaul network. The devices used in these 4G or 5G fronthaul networks (the CSR and far-edge DC aggregation nodes) must support time of day as well as phase and frequency acquisition and distribution. In other words, the fronthaul routers must support PTP, SyncE, and NTP.

To ensure the highest degree of accuracy and precision in distributing timing and synchronization information through the fronthaul network, it is highly recommended to use a Class-C or higher PTP device where possible. As mentioned in the previous chapter, the accuracy ratings of a PTP device (that is, Class A, Class B, Class C, or Class D) are a function of device's hardware components rather than software implementation, and, as such, the decision to use fronthaul devices that support appropriate timing and synchronization functions must be made at the time of deployment. Certain value-added features and software functions (usually vendor implementation specific) could be added to the device's operating system at a later time, but failure to appropriately select a Class C or higher device at the onset of network deployment could lead to costly forklift-upgrades in the future if timing accuracy and precision between the RU and DU become a problem.

Additionally, when possible, fronthaul networks should be designed using the G.8275-1 Telecom Profile, where every router acts as a boundary clock (BC), thus ensuring the highest level of accuracy when distributing timing information. This means that all devices in the fronthaul network (even intermediary ones) must support the PTP BC functions. Today, virtually all routers designed for 5G mobile transport networks support PTP BC functionality.

Other deployment profiles such as G.8275-2 and Assisted Partial Timing Support (APTS) could still be used if any intermediary devices do not support BC functionality. These scenarios are more prevalent in cases where preexisting network devices not capable of timing distribution are used to carry fronthaul traffic. However, the use of these devices can add to the inaccuracies in timing distribution, thus causing potential connectivity issues down the line.

Supported Interface Types

5G is promising exponential bandwidth growth with the unlocking of new, higher-capacity RF spectrum and advanced antenna features such as mMIMO, multi-radio transmissions, and beamforming. Many of the cell sites are expected to be multiple radio access technologies (multi-RAT); that is, in addition to the new 5G services and traffic, they would continue to support earlier services and traffic from earlier cellular generations.

All this translates into higher bandwidth demands on the network, and the network architecture team must ensure there are enough 100Gbps interfaces, or even 400Gbps interfaces, to provide adequate capacity for new and existing cellular service. Fronthaul is an especially bandwidth-hungry xHaul domain, where the use of LLS options, particularly Option 8, further exacerbates the need for higher-bandwidth interfaces. As previously mentioned, network architects must work with the RAN team to determine the total capacity required at every cell site and determine appropriate interfaces. The network topology (for example, Ethernet rings or a wired cell site aggregating multiple microwave cell sites) also plays a role in choosing the appropriate interfaces.

Bandwidth and higher capacity interfaces are not the only considerations a sound network design needs to take into account, however. At every cell site, the RAN components connect to a CSR. This connection between the RAN and the CSR have traditionally been an Ethernet link, but the use of an LLS option in a decomposed RAN environment adds a degree of variability to this long-standing practice. If the LLS option results in an eCPRI (typically Option 7-2 or 7-2x) from the RU, this link between the RU and DU could continue to be an Ethernet link. But if LLS Option 8 is used, the connection between the RU and CSR will be CPRI, and the CSR must be able to terminate the CPRI link. Hence, a fronthaul CSR, expected to be deployed in a scenario where Split Option 8 is used, must have CPRI port(s) to terminate the connection from a Split Option 8 RU. As previously mentioned, this CSR would then implement RoE or FHGW functions to transport packetized CPRI traffic over the fronthaul network. When using RoE, the far-edge DC aggregation node should reciprocate this setup by accepting the packetized CPRI traffic from the fronthaul, convert it back to CPRI, and send it to the DU (or the BBU). Therefore, the far-edge DC aggregation node, in this case, not only needs to have CPRI ports to connect to the DUs, but must also ensure it has the port density required to connect all the DUs required to serve the cell sites. This is a fronthaul-only consideration, and only when Split Option 8 is used. Midhaul and backhaul CSRs and aggregation nodes require only Ethernet interfaces.

Figure 10-7 provides a decision tree to help network architects understand the types of interfaces required on a CSR based on their xHaul placement and LLS option used. Networking equipment vendors are starting to provide both CPRI and Ethernet interfaces in their newer fronthaul CSR and FE DC aggregation node offerings. Although this type of deployment is expected to be fairly limited—either 4G LTE Centralized RAN or 5G RUs with Split Option 8—it is absolutely critical that xHaul networking design take this niche requirement into consideration if needed.

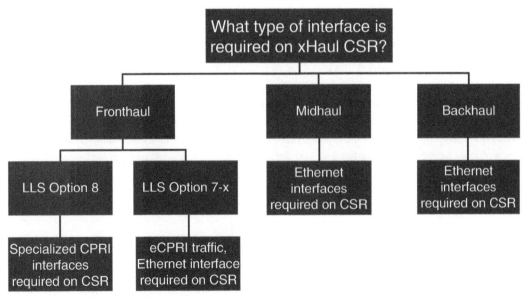

FIGURE 10-7 Selecting the Right Interface on CSR

Planning for Scale

At the time of this writing, 5G deployments are still in their infancy, and yet every indication is that 5G isn't going to be anything like its predecessors as far as the scale is concerned. Whether it's cell site densification, higher bandwidth requirements for eMBB, the use of multi-access edge compute (MEC), or an increase in the number of devices connected to the Internet through mMTC services, the growth of cellular networks and the devices served by them is expected to be exponential. Network architects must ensure that the underlying transport networks responsible for carrying 5G traffic for all these multiple traffic types can scale to match the 5G growth expectations.

Network scalability is essentially a function of ensuring appropriate scale at every level of the network—the CSR, the core and aggregation nodes, as well as the use of a *scalable* architecture to stitch all xHaul domains together. There are many dimensions to a network's scale, focusing on things like routing table scale to accommodate higher number of devices, port density, software resources such as VPN instances, MPLS label space, access control lists, and other miscellaneous features and functions.

As the mobile networks continue to grow in size through cell site densification and addition of new xHaul domains (midhaul and fronthaul), routing scalability both from an architecture standpoint and from an individual device's standpoint becomes an important characteristic of a sound network design. Routing architecture scaling can be achieved through Seamless MPLS and BGP Labeled Unicast (BGP-LU), previously discussed in Chapter 3, where network architects can optimize and scale the routing design by ensuring that only the host routes are advertised into BGP-LU and imported across discrete routing domains as needed. Routing design scaling and simplification mechanisms are also discussed later in this chapter, but network device selection for an MCN must ensure the nodes chosen for various roles are capable of the routing table scale required in a large network.

Some of the major roles a network device plays in a 5G MCN are cell site router, pre-aggregation or aggregation node at the far-edge or edge DC, IP core router, data center interconnect, and peering router, among others. As mentioned in the previous section, most of the routers in an MCN, with the exception of the CSR, are typically larger devices that should have adequate resources to handle the required scale. Appropriate architectural decisions are critical to ensure that CSRs maintain the delicate balance of low cost yet a functional end-to-end design. Some of these scale and network simplification techniques to allow this are discussed in the sections that follow.

Adequate Feature Richness

The networking landscape is undergoing rapid changes. Its traditional role is undergoing an unprecedented disruption after the introduction of software-defined networking and increasingly intelligent applications that demand visibility deep into the network. Networking devices today must support a multitude of software features and functions to provide a level of *network abstraction* that enables higher-layer application to not only interact with but also control the network. Notably, these features are not entirely related to MCN but are essential in supporting various transformative aspects of next-generation networks such as orchestration and closed-loop automation.

Network architects must be cognizant of the holistic direction the networking industry in general, and their organization in particular, is heading toward with regard to automation, network programmability, orchestration, and other transformations. For example, if one of the goals is to move toward a software-defined transport allowing applications like Path Computation Element (PCE) to control traffic flows, the router should support appropriate protocols such as the Path Computation Element Communication Protocol (PCEP) for external applications to dictate the traffic path based on a certain set of constraints defined by said application. Another example could be the use of automated orchestration, where routers should support APIs to allow external applications to connect to and make desired configuration changes. The network devices might also be required to provide an adequate level of visibility into operations and events. As such, they should support features like telemetry in lieu of, or in addition to, traditional SNMP and syslog support. It's important to note that a lot of these features and functions are not *directly* related to fundamental operations of an MCN, but these value-added features are becoming increasingly important to simplify network operations and enable mobile service providers to operate networks at an unprecedented scale.

Routing Design Simplification

While 5G itself is complex, the routing in the transport network should not be. The 5G mobile communication network's comprehensive improvements are tightly coupled with the new level of decentralization and decomposition of its previously monolithic parts. The flip side of the flexibility and power of decentralized MCN is its complexity and strong dependence on highly sophisticated transport networks, especially with introduction of new domains. Traffic patterns and communication flows in 5G MCN are even more intricate and demanding. The routing design simplification becomes paramount to ensure the 5G transport network does not become too complicated to operate.

Chapter 3 covered some of the complexities of mobile backhaul and core networks. A large number of cell sites, common in MCNs, do not align well with cost-efficiency requirements for individual CSRs to support simple network designs. The network designers are forced to split xHaul networks into numerous smaller routing domains to stay within typical CSR scale constraints. Without redistribution of routes between domains, which causes scalability challenges on CSRs, it is not easy to maintain an end-to-end label switched path (LSP). The use of BGP labeled unicast solves the problem of providing MPLS LSP, but it poses many questions such as what to do with next-hop path attributes, where to put route reflectors, and how to keep the number of BGP-LU routes under control. BGP-LU-based designs, standardized as Seamless MPLS, have become the de facto standard in mobile transport networks. Nevertheless, it is notoriously complex and operationally expensive.

Segment Routing brings a new set of tools to enable end-to-end services over mobile transport network. In order to take advantage of cost-effective platforms at the cell sites, xHaul networks continue to rely on multiple IGP domains. At the same time, SR features, such as Segment Routing Traffic Engineering and On-Demand Next Hop, allow mobile service providers to ditch BGP-LU designs in favor of simpler and cleaner SR-enabled transport networks, while offering the necessary MPLS LSPs to establish services over multidomain xHaul networks. This section discusses some of the techniques used to simplify routing in mobile transport network.

Designing Multidomain IGP for 5G Transport

Radio densification and larger coverage areas of 5G MCN significantly increase the number of nodes in transport networks, compared to the previous generation of mobile networks. The question is not if the network should be segmented into multiple IGP domains but rather how big those domains should be and where to place domain boundaries. The main driver for introducing IGP domains is the desire to contain number of routes on CSRs. Many architects use a rule of thumb to limit the number of CSRs in a single domain below a few hundred or even a few dozen. Although it is not uncommon to have thousands of nodes per IGP domain in SP networks, the SPF recalculation churn can put a significant strain on a cost-effective CSR and is therefore not ideal.

Naturally, the most direct approach in defining IGP domain boundaries is to use the network's topological features. For instance, in ring-based topologies, the nodes aggregating multiple CSR rings can become domain border routers and divide the network into separate domains. With fabric-like topologies, splitting the network into routing domains can be less straightforward. In this case, one possible approach is to select clusters of cell sites residing next to each other and expect to have a significant number of handoffs. Ideally, CSRs in such cell sites should be connected to the same aggregation nodes so they can participate in the same IGP domain. This principle of natural boundaries applies to both D-RAN and Centralized RAN deployment scenarios. In fact, the hard distance limitations of RU-DU communications create another potential for IGP domain separation in fronthaul networks. With no communication expected between RUs in different clusters, it is logical to divide fronthaul networks into multiple IGP domains based on RU-DU clustering. Figure 10-8 shows a possible routing domain segmentation scenario.

The choice of IGP can also influence the layout, the size, and the number of domains. In a typical service provider network, the choice of IGP is usually narrowed down to OSPF and IS-IS. Although both OSPF and IS-IS are capable of supporting modern mobile transport networks, many operators lean toward IS-IS because it is independent of IP and, unlike OSPF, can exchange IPv4 and IPv6 reachability information simultaneously.

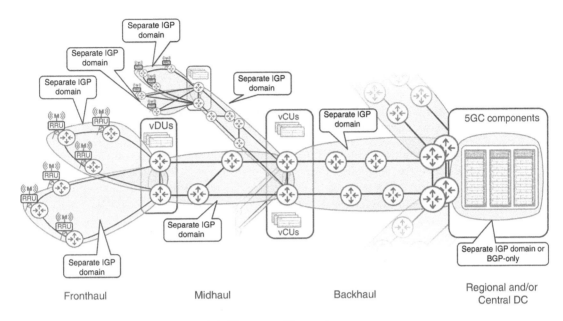

FIGURE 10-8   IGP Domains in Mobile Transport Network

IPv6 in OSPF and IS-IS

IPv6 support is becoming increasingly essential due to the increased number of devices in transport networks. Networks running OSPF for IPv4 cannot just enable another address family. Another version of the protocol, OSPFv3, has to run in parallel with OSPFv2 to exchange IPv6 reachability information. Although the use of the IPv4 address family was proposed by IETF RFC 5838 for OSPFv3, not many major network operating systems currently support this functionality.[14]

Unlike OSPF, IS-IS does not rely on IP to form and maintain adjacencies and can thus exchange both IPv4 and IPv6. Moreover, it can offer multiple or single topology calculations for different address families, which provides extra flexibility for network architects.

Many approaches can be taken to split the mobile transport network into multiple IGP domains, but here are the two that are by far the most popular:

- Use of IGP's multi-area capabilities
- Use of separate IGP instances for different IGP domains

Strictly speaking, the use of separate IGP instances, in the latter approach, is only required on boundary routers interconnecting multiple IGP domains. The CSR routers themselves are not ever required to support multiple IGP instances, as they participate in only one IGP instance. Therefore, the choice of the boundary routers becomes critical for the IGP multidomain design. Depending on the number of domains interconnected by these border routers, the number of required IGP instances can be significant and could become the limiting factor. If such a design is implemented, it is important to consult with the routing platform vendors to confirm the supported number of IGP instances.

The use of multi-area capabilities of an IGP protocol introduces its own set of constraints and implications. The most notable is the requirement to connect all IGP areas to some kind of a backbone area—Area 0 in OSPF and Level 2 area in IS-IS. In other words, it is impossible to create a multi-area IGP design with ABRs connecting non-backbone or Level 1 areas to other non-backbone or L1 areas. This might compel architects to combine multiple, otherwise independent, non-backbone or L1 areas into a single bigger area, thus negating the whole point of routing domain segmentation. Besides, OSPF and IS-IS also have slightly different concepts of areas, which can result in additional design constraints, depending on the IGP of choice. In OSPF, areas cannot overlap and have to be connected to a backbone area via area border routers (ABRs), while IS-IS allows routers to establish both Level 1 and Level 2 adjacencies with the same neighbor, creating an overlap of L1 and L2 areas. This IS-IS behavior comes in handy when L1 routers in a ring topology connect to an L2 aggregation. Without L1 adjacency closing the ring, IS-IS preference for intra-area routes can result in suboptimal routing in some failure scenarios. Such designs are sometimes referred to as *open rings*. Besides providing suboptimal routing, open rings also introduce implications for rapid restoration scenarios.

The original OSPF specification RFC 2328 dictated that an interface can belong to only one area, thus making it difficult to use OSPF in such scenarios. The use of multi-area adjacencies (added to OSPF in RFC 5185) on ABRs connecting non-backbone rings to backbone areas allows for great design simplification while keeping traffic flows optimal. Figure 10-9 shows the potential for suboptimal routing in ring topologies, common in mobile transport networks, as well as the desired behavior.

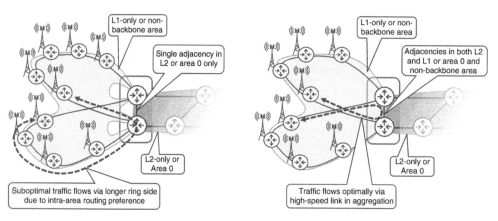

FIGURE 10-9   Suboptimal and Desired Traffic Flows Due to IGP Intra-area Route Preference

Another aspect of using multi-area IGP designs is the route leaking from L1 into L2 areas in IS-IS and from non-backbone to backbone areas in OSPF by default. Oftentimes, such route leaking is not desirable, as it causes scalability issues in L2 or backbone areas of IGP. Both IS-IS and OSPF offer mechanisms to override the default behavior and filter routing information from being leaked between areas.

Although disabling route leaking between IGP domains is beneficial for stability and scalability, some limited number of routes still needs to be injected into IGP domains to provide connectivity between CSRs and centralized components of transport infrastructure, such as Path Computation Element (PCE) for use with Segment Routing Traffic Engineering (SR-TE). The next section covers PCE placement and reachability implications.

Simplification with Segment Routing

Besides basic reachability inside IGP domains, OSPF and IS-IS can be also used to exchange information required to build MPLS LSPs. MPLS is the de facto transport standard in today's MCN for end-to-end VPN services. For the purpose of building an end-to-end LSP, mobile transport network uses a combination of LDP and RSVP protocols with BGP-LU. Segment Routing can greatly simplify MPLS designs by eliminating the need for LDP and RSVP protocols, and, with the use of SR-TE and automated steering, even BGP-LU can be removed from the network.

By the virtue of Segment Routing IGP extensions, loopback prefixes and adjacencies between routers within each IGP domain can obtain their respective MPLS labels (that is, *segment ID*, or *SID*). Synchronization between MPLS and IP forwarding planes occurs automatically and no longer requires additional features, further simplifying transport designs. On top of providing basic MPLS forwarding information within each routing domain, SR also enables Topology Independent Loop-Free Alternate (TI-LFA) for traffic protection, thus providing rapid restoration functionality to replace commonly used RSVP-TE FRR. All these essential features of MPLS transport can be provided in SR-enabled IGP domains without the need for more advanced SR-TE, which can be helpful in brownfield deployments for transitioning from traditional Seamless MPLS architectures to more robust SR-based architectures.

Strictly speaking, SR-enabled IGP domains can support seamless architecture with BGP-LU communicated end-to-end LSPs, just like LDP-enabled domains. Nevertheless, BGP-LU can be eliminated from the transport network too. Instead, SR-based end-to-end LSPs can be programmed on CSRs with the help of automation, statically, or by offloading the interdomain path calculation to a path computation element (PCE). In other words, SR-TE policy is used to provide end-to-end LSPs instead of BGP-LU. Attaching color extended community to VPN routes triggers automated steering of VPN traffic into the respective SR-TE policies on headends, as explained in Chapter 6, "Emerging Technologies for 5G-Ready Networks: Segment Routing." In fact, a number of different SR-TE policies toward the same destination can be instantiated at CSRs to provide different traffic types with the respective class of service.

Although paths for SR-TE policies can be calculated dynamically on the CSR itself, this requires full knowledge of link-state databases in all IGP domains along the path. While possible, this defeats the purpose of splitting the network into multiple routing domains. Instead, it is more practical to offload path computation to the PCE.

In order to calculate an end-to-end path across multiple routing domains, the PCE needs to create a representation of a combined topology of all these domains. Collection of link-state information is normally performed on routing domain border routers or ABRs and transported to the PCE via the BGP Link State address family. In turn, PCEs can establish BGP-LS peering directly across domains, or leverage the existing route reflector hierarchy, to exchange the topology database, thus creating an end-to-end network view. Once the PCE learns the topology and all attributes associated with links and nodes, it can effectively solve the optimal path calculation problem and provide its clients with lists of SIDs representing SR-TE policy paths across the network. In fact, the PCE can even stitch together different autonomous systems with the use of BGP Egress Peering Engineering (EPE) SIDs. This is also one of the recommended scaling mechanisms as defined in the O-RAN xHaul Packet Switched Architecture Specification.[15] Figure 10-10 illustrates an example of SR-TE policies stitching together multiple IGP domains and ASNs.

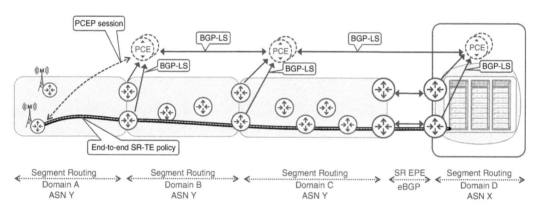

FIGURE 10-10   SR-TE Policies Across Multiple Routing Domains

Although BGP-LU can be eliminated from the transport network, BGP is still required to transport VPN routes as well as remote PE loopback reachability in order to satisfy the BGP next-hop validation rule. Besides, there is an additional requirement of planning, pre-programming, and maintaining SR-TE policies on CSRs. This can be further simplified with the use of On-Demand Next-Hop functionality. On-Demand Next-Hop triggers the instantiation of SR-TE policies automatically upon reception of BGP routes with appropriate color extended communities. SR-TE policies are instantiated only when triggering routes are present, and they are torn down when the routes are withdrawn, thus saving precious CSR resources. Depending on the vendor implementation, On-Demand Next-Hop may even relax the BGP requirement for having reachable next hops for VPN routes and reduce the amount of routing information on CSR to the bare minimum.

Path Computation Element Placement and Scale

A PCE removes the burden of knowing the whole network topology from the CSR by offering its services for SRTE policies' path calculation. Although each PCE needs to know and maintain the topology knowledge, it doesn't mean that a PCE should collect and keep the whole network's topology in its entirety. In fact, a typical network implementing SR-TE will likely to have a number of PCEs sprinkled over different routing domains. There is no requirement to have a single centralized unit, and each PCE can serve devices in only a few or even a single routing domain. Moreover, it is sufficient for such a PCE to learn and maintain link-state information only for the routing domains along SR-TE policies' paths it is anticipated to calculate. Figure 10-11 illustrates the scenario where some PCEs require full topology information, whereas others require only partial topology information based on the SR-TE policies they need to implement. This scenario is closer to the real-world deployment where some PCEs on the far edge might have partial topology information as they calculate the SR-TE policy path from access domain to the regional or national DC only. On the other hand, the PCEs in the IP core might be required to calculate the SR-TE policy path to multiple access regions and, as such, would require a broader view of the topology.

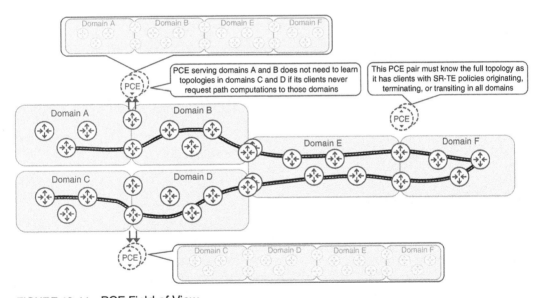

FIGURE 10-11   PCE Field of View

Being a critical part of the transport infrastructure, PCEs are usually deployed in pairs to provide adequate redundancy. Depending on the number of PCE clients in a routing domain and the number of SR-TE policies per client, a single domain might have multiple PCE pairs to distribute the load of path computation requests. For smaller networks, a single pair of PCEs may be shared across multiple domains. Because a PCE communicates with its clients over TCP-based Path Computation Element Protocol (PCEP), a route toward the PCE must be injected into its serving IGP domains or can be shared with CSRs using BGP. In turn, the PCE should know how to reach its clients, and a respective summary route has to be provided for the PCE. Also, the PCE must learn the link-state topology information in multiple domains. As mentioned earlier in this section and in Chapter 6, this can be done by originating BGP-LS routes from the routing domain boundary routers or the ABRs. The BGP-LS information can then be delivered over existing BGP hierarchy and consumed by the PCE. Figure 10-12 shows an example of this design.

Placing the PCE strategically and properly setting it up to learn multidomain link-state topology information is essential for efficient and stable network operation. However, there is another important aspect of the Segment Routing network that is critical to ensure end-to-end communication without disruptions: the segment IDs (SIDs) must be properly allocated and assigned throughout the whole network.

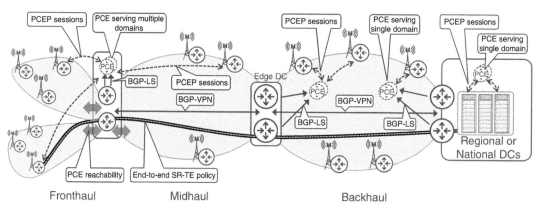

FIGURE 10-12   PCE Placement Across Various Routing Domains

Defining SIDs and SRGB

Segment Routing extensions can be enabled in a network via a simple configuration knob, but unlike the LDP or RSVP protocols, MPLS labels (that is, SIDs) used in SR for forwarding traffic to specific prefixes are globally significant. Due to this feature, Segment Routing requires explicit allocation of prefix segment IDs and, as such, needs an SID allocation plan, just like an IP addressing plan is required to properly assign IP addresses on interfaces. In fact, prefix SIDs are usually derived in some ways from the IP prefix they are representing.

The composition of SR MPLS labels for prefixes (prefix SIDs) was discussed in Chapter 6 and can be summarized as follows: An index value, assigned to a loopback interface's prefix, is added to the base value, representing the start of the Segment Routing Global Block (SRGB). The resulting value is used as an MPLS label and is installed in the forwarding table of upstream routers. Because SRGB has direct impact on SR MPLS label composition, the recommended best practice is to use the same SRGB block throughout the whole network and avoid any label inconsistencies.

The SR Prefix SID space is limited by the SRGB range, and although current SR implementations allow adjustment of SRGB from its default value, it is still limited by the supported MPLS label space. The hard limit for the number of MPLS labels is dictated by the standards and cannot exceed roughly 1 million labels. This number can be significantly lower, depending on the platform's capabilities, which is usually the case for cost-effective CSR platforms. Besides, some label space should be set aside for VPN service labels, for dynamic label allocations of adjacency SIDs, and other special purposes. The size of available and supported MPLS label space is one of the key factors in deciding the method for allocating prefix SIDs throughout the network.

Prefix SIDs can be allocated either contiguously for the whole network or per IGP domain. With contiguous allocation, every prefix SID is unique in the whole network, which makes it trouble-shooting and planning friendly. On the other hand, the overall number of prefix SIDs allocated in the whole network cannot exceed the size of SRGB and therefore limits the number of SR-enabled devices within the network.

The second approach for allocating prefix SIDs on a per-IGP basis is free of this limitation and can be used in networks of any size. In simple terms, prefix SIDs are reused in different IGP domains and are no longer required to be unique outside of their IGP domains. Nevertheless, an important consideration for this prefix SID allocation method is that it can be reused only in networks that are at least one domain apart. In other words, prefix SIDs should not overlap in adjacent IGP domains or in domains that share ABRs. Indeed, border routers connecting different IGP domains should be able to correctly forward MPLS packets into respective IGP domains based on prefix SID. One of the effective ways to avoid such overlaps is to allocate ranges of prefix SIDs for different IGP domains and reuse ranges in non-adjacent IGP domains. This approach is suggested in IETF RFC 8604 for ultra-large networks.[16] Figure 10-13 illustrates an example of SRGB and SID allocation for different IGP domains.

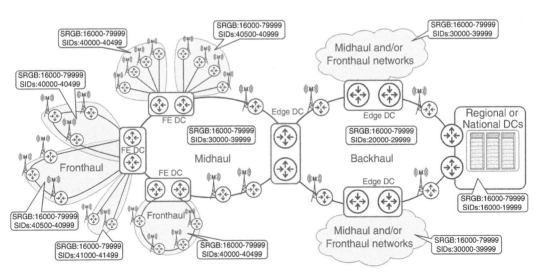

FIGURE 10-13   Example of SRGB and SID Allocation in Mobile Transport Network

Although many vendors support very large SRGB ranges today, it is important to leave enough label space for other protocols as well (for example, EVPNs and L3VPNs that use MPLS labels to identify services).

Transport Services for 5G MCN

The functions implementing 5G mobile service use various protocols and interface types to communicate while the traffic is carried over IP-based xHaul and core networks. The user data traffic carried by the fronthaul network is either CPRI encapsulated using RoE (if Split Option 8 is used) or eCPRI (based on eCPRI forum or O-RAN). When CPRI is used, the control traffic, user data, and timing information are all carried within the CPRI stream. However, as mentioned in Chapter 5, eCPRI carries only user-plane traffic, referred to as U-plane. Though this U-plane traffic is the dominant traffic type in the fronthaul, there is also control traffic, management traffic, and synchronization traffic. These are referred to by O-RAN as C-Plane, M-Plane, and S-Plane, respectively, as described in previous chapters.

In the midhaul network, the control and data traffic exchanged between the DU and CU is encapsulated using the F1 User Plane Interface (F1-U) and F1 Control Plane Interface (F1-C). The DU and CU communicate using IP-based protocols; the F1-U uses GTP-U/UDP on top of IP, while the F1-C uses Stream Control Transmission Protocol (SCTP) as the transport layer over IP.

Stream Control Transmission Protocol (SCTP)

SCTP is a transport layer protocol defined in RFC 4960. Although not as popular as TCP and UDP, which are widely known and used in the networking world, SCTP provides certain advantages over TCP while still using a connection-oriented approach and congestion control using rate adaptation. However, in contrast to TCP, SCTP is stream oriented. This means that it can handle multiple streams between endpoints. Additionally, SCTP has the capability to simultaneously use multiple source and destination IP addresses, thus allowing for multihoming of the traffic stream and making it more fault tolerant. Despite its advantages, SCTP has relatively fewer implementations because it was a late entrant compared to TCP and UDP. It is also not as "firewall friendly" due to its multihoming and stream-oriented design.

The NG interfaces defined between the CU and the 5GC traverse over the backhaul and IP core networks. By definition, the NG interface communication relies on IP connectivity. Figure 10-14 summarizes these interfaces as well as planes of operation across the transport network.

As mentioned earlier, MPLS-based L2 and L3 VPNs are used to seamlessly connect the mobile functions over the transport network.

The fronthaul router connecting to the RU would need to cater to the C, U, M, and S planes. The RU is expected to tag each of these traffic streams with its own VLAN tag, thus allowing the fronthaul device to treat them differently. Because the RU-DU communication typically requires Layer 2 connectivity, a single or separate L2VPN can be used to transport C- and U-plane traffic between them. Depending on the implementation, this might be a point-to-point VPWS or point-to-multipoint L2VPN service using a bridge domain. EVPN is the preferred protocol of choice for this, although legacy L2VPN (EoMPLS or H-VPLS) can be used instead. The pros and cons of this choice were discussed in detail in Chapter 8, "Essential Technologies for 5G-Ready Networks: Transport Services." In cases where the RU and DU support Layer 3 communication, L3VPN can be used for the C and U planes. The M plane typically also uses L3VPN, while achieving segregation through the use of a separate VRF. This VRF is configured on the far-edge, edge, and regional DCs, making them part of an L3VPN instance that provides M-plane connectivity between the various mobility functions. The S plane is usually transported natively over the xHaul network because it allows quick and easy consumption of timing information at each boundary clock.

Maximum Transmission Unit (MTU) Recommendation

The C- and U-plane traffic is usually packaged into jumbo Ethernet frames (9000 Bytes Payload) to reduce overhead. To avoid fragmentation of this traffic, larger MTU values should be used across the mobile transport network. In contrast, the S- and M-plane traffic usually does not exceed 1500 bytes.

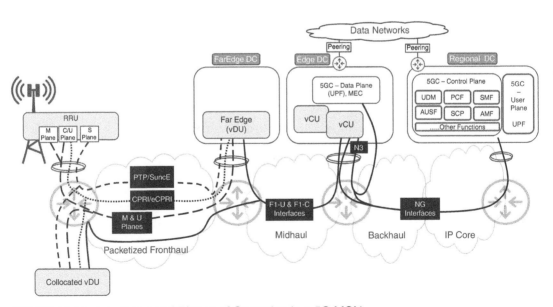

FIGURE 10-14   Interfaces and Planes of Operation in a 5G MCN

The C- and U-plane VPNs terminate at the DU, and a separate L3VPN is used to carry F1-U and F1-C traffic between the DU and CU. To reemphasize, the user and control traffic may or may not share the L3VPN VRF. From the CU toward the 5GC, the same L3VPN can be extended to carry the NG interfaces or a new set of L3VPNs can be used. The choice to use the same or separate L3VPN might come down to a design discussion between the network architecture and operations teams. The contributing factors for choosing one design over the other could be due to operational, administrative, or scalability concerns. This L3VPN might be terminating on a UPF hosted on the same edge DC as the CU, a UPF at other locations, or 5GC-Control functions at the regional DC.

Figure 10-15 captures these details about the various VPNs used to provide connectivity service by the IP-based transport to the mobile functions.

Taking MCN to the Cloud

Historically, mobile service providers—just like data service providers—have deployed their own or leased their network infrastructure. The mobile service providers have the added cost of procuring the spectrum band, which has its own big price tag. Collectively, the high capital expense associated with all this presents a barrier to entry for new providers. Even if the initial investment is secured, the management and operations of such a network require a large team of varying expertise and skill levels. Over the recent years, service providers (both data and mobile) have been facing the challenge of flat revenues, while the bandwidth and capacity requirements have been going up exponentially. Thus, service providers have been trying to optimize their operational cost through use of automation, increased utilization of existing gear, as well as other cost reduction measures. These have helped their bottom line but the absence of substantial revenue growth severely limits new investment and capital expense on infrastructure upgrades. Mobile service providers, both existing and new, have therefore been exploring the options to reduce those cost barriers. Indeed, this was one of the key driving factors behind O-RAN, where virtualization and open interfaces are expected to significantly reduce equipment and operational costs through the use of commercial off-the-shelf (COTS) hardware and foster competition between new and existing RAN equipment vendors.

The benefits for incumbent mobile service providers are obvious, because they can upgrade the equipment while leveraging the same fiber infrastructure, data center facilities, and existing points of presence. They would still need to add or repurpose radio bands and deploy new cell sites, but those are relatively affordable compared to deploying an entire infrastructure. For new entrants with limited or no existing infrastructure, it is therefore cost prohibitive to enter this business and build from scratch. To work around this challenge, two popular approaches have emerged in the recent years. Both approaches heavily leverage the vRAN architecture, SBA-based 5GC with containerized components, and the cloud-native nature of the mobile functions The primary difference between the two approaches is who owns the cloud infrastructure.

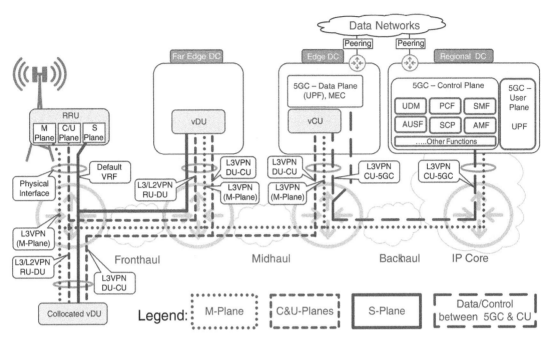

FIGURE 10-15 Transport Services in a 5G MCN

Privately Owned Cloud Infrastructure

The first of these approaches relies on the cost reduction achieved by building the mobile network through the use of containerized networking functions (CNFs) from various vendors and running them on top of COTS hardware owned by the provider. For connectivity across the MCN domains, the incumbent providers using this approach might use their existing infrastructure whereas the new entrants may deploy new infrastructure, lease dark fiber, or buy connectivity services from other service providers—also called *alternative access vendors (AAVs)*. Examples of AAV services include point-to-point or point-to-multipoint Metro Ethernet services such as E-LINE, E-Tree, and E-LAN, or MPLS-based L3VPN services. The data center equipment (placed at shared or fully owned sites), radio sites, and spectrum make up the bulk of cost for the mobile provider. This approach fully utilizes the benefits of the Open vRAN deployment model, cloud-native mobile core, and NFV principles. Japan's Rakuten Mobile is widely regarded as the first such mobile provider and is credited for being the first fully virtualized mobile provider.[17]

The primary challenge in this approach is the integration of the hardware and software from multiple vendors and overcoming interoperability issues. However, use of non-proprietary and open interfaces is a step toward overcoming this challenge. Rakuten is reportedly utilizing technology from 18 different vendors such as Altiostar (DU), Ciena (Optical), Cisco (data center), NEC (radio), Robin.io (orchestration), Intel (compute), and so on.[18] Some of the functions are implemented using multiple vendors.

The use of cloud-native architecture made it possible to achieve dynamic scalability without performance degradation,[19] and using this approach, Rakuten, despite being a new mobile service provider,
was able to quickly become one of the largest mobile service providers on the island. It was able to
achieve this while saving capital expense by 40% compared to traditional deployment, and reports
an operational expense that is 30% lower compared to legacy mobile network operators.[20] Another
consideration here, when using AAV, is to ensure that stringent requirements of 5G communication
are met. This includes requirements for bandwidth, latency, quality of service, and so on. Fronthaul
requirements are the strictest, but other parts of the MCN have certain expectations from the transport
network as well. The choice of AAV should consider the service level agreements (SLAs) offered, to
ensure these requirements are met. Figure 10-16 presents a pictorial view of this approach of using
privately owned NFV infrastructure for providing mobile services.

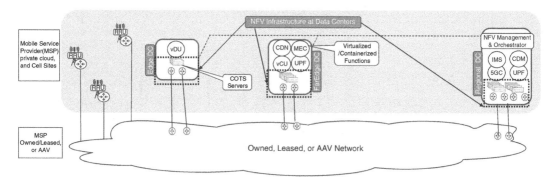

FIGURE 10-16   MCN Using Privately Owned NFV Infrastructure

Even though this approach suits greenfield deployments, the obvious reduction in expense through
the use of NFV, cloud-native components, and vRAN architecture makes this attractive to incumbent
mobile providers as well. Brownfield deployments, therefore, are also headed in this direction in the
process of transitioning to 5G. The cost benefit is even higher for these incumbent providers since the
connectivity infrastructure is already in place and existing DC locations can be utilized in addition to
new ones, as needed.

Building a 5G Network in the Public Cloud

The second approach takes a different direction; it still uses CNF from multiple vendors, but it leverages
public cloud infrastructure to host cloud-native 5G functions. Public cloud provides a very attractive
option with its exponential growth and availability, diversity of capabilities, high degree of resilience,
reduction in cost of leasing, and powerful automation capabilities. Using the cloud provider's infrastructure for the DC and transport means that the mobile service provider does not need to be concerned
with deploying, owning, or maintaining hardware for a big chunk of its network. Scalability of the
architecture is easily possible due to the (seemingly) infinite resources available in the public cloud.

Orchestration and automation capabilities offer a "cherry on top" to this already feasible option. In fact, many mobile vendors are starting to ensure that their CNFs/VNFs are compatible with the public cloud orchestration and ensure that these functions run smoothly on the public cloud.[21]

Being cloud native, the functions of 5GC and even the vRAN are ready and a good fit for the public cloud. Not every component of the mobile network can be moved to the public cloud, however. Obviously, the antenna and RU are on that list, as they need to be physical hardware. As it's not realistic to expect the public cloud provider to meet the strict distance requirements and latency constraints of the fronthaul network, the far-edge DC may not be a candidate for public cloud either. In some cases, even the edge DC may need to be privately hosted if the peering point to the public cloud does not happen to be available within a reasonable distance. This approach therefore results in a hybrid cloud environment hosting the 5G functions. An example of such a deployment is U.S.-based Dish Network. Despite being a new entrant, Dish aims at becoming a nationwide service provider and is pioneering an architecture using the public cloud to host 5G Core and RAN functions whenever possible.[22] Far-edge DCs hosting DUs are typically Dish-owned, leased, or managed rack-space, thus creating a hybrid cloud environment.[23] Such a hybrid environment might still benefit from a uniform and common set of tools for orchestration and management. In other words, the privately hosted servers may be managed by, and integrated with, the public cloud provider's orchestration and monitoring tools thus creating a consistent management layer for this hybrid cloud. AWS Output and GCP Anthos are examples of such service offerings. Figure 10-17 presents a pictorial view of this approach of using a hybrid cloud for creating a 5G MCN.

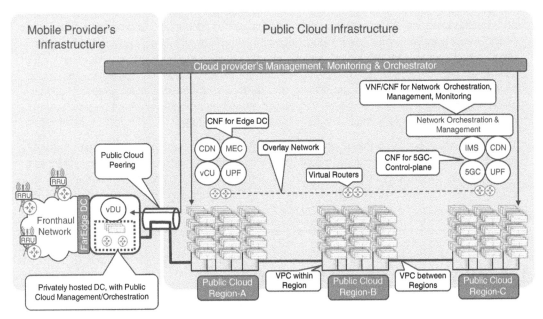

FIGURE 10-17   Use of Hybrid Cloud for 5G MCN

It is important to note that leveraging the public cloud for a portion of the mobile network is not limited to hosting just the VNF/CNF. These functions need to be connected using network-level services, as emphasized earlier in this chapter. Even though public cloud offers networking capabilities, referred to as *virtual private cloud (VPC)* or *virtual network (VNET)*, these might not be sufficient to create a large end-to-end network that could replace the transport network and services needed for an MCN. To overcome this, virtual routers (hosted on the same public cloud) can be used to form an overlay network on top of the public cloud infrastructure, and thus use Infrastructure as a Service (IaaS) offerings of the public cloud.[24] This overlay network could then be used to deploy network services and VPNs as described the section "Transport Services for 5G MCN," earlier in the chapter. It is worth mentioning here that while the MANO and automation capabilities of the public cloud work with the VNF/CNF, running this hybrid network's DC, another layer of orchestration, monitoring, management, and automation may be needed to use for the network devices, routing, and services.

Not only does this approach almost eliminate the capital expenses (as there is very little infrastructure that needs to be deployed), it also reduces the operational costs. The additional benefits of a public cloud infrastructure, such as hardened common orchestrator, scalability, no need for hardware lifecycle management and maintenance, and so on, offer added benefits to this approach.

Is Network Design Still Needed for Hybrid Cloud 5G Deployments?

Irrespective of which model is deployed by the 5G mobile service provider, networking-level design and architecture are must-haves. While this requirement is obvious when the networks and mobile functions are privately owned, when it comes to public cloud hosting, there is a strong misconception about networking becoming irrelevant. After all, public cloud environments boast simple, easy, and rapid deployment of network functions and services. That might be true for simplistic networks with basic services (for example, a simple scalable web hosting service with a load balancer, secure firewall, and threat prevention). When it comes to sophisticated networks that would be needed to build an end-to-end mobile service, however, there is more effort required than just spinning up a few network functions.

The proper applications of these functions and stitching them together to complete an end-to-end service requires capabilities that cloud services might be lacking, thus creating the need for an overlay network. In addition, fine tuning of the services' and functions' parameters for efficiency, design and tweaking of various network-level configurations, addressing security concerns, and end-to-end service delivery require deep networking knowledge and experience.

Automation in 5G Networks

A design involving high levels of scale and multiple protocol stacks might be cumbersome for humans to implement—and complex to maintain—but automation provides a means to break these barriers. Additionally, automation eliminates human error, thus bringing accuracy in addition to efficiency. In a nutshell, automation makes provisioning, maintaining, managing, troubleshooting, and even remediation fast, easy, and efficient. Network architects therefore should not be hesitant to use automation but rather leverage it to achieve complex, scaled-up, repetitive network workflows.

When it comes to mobility components, 5GC and RAN functions are implemented with a cloud-native approach. As stated earlier in Chapter 5, cloud-native implementations are incomplete and meaningless without relevant automation and orchestration. The deployment, lifecycle management, scaling, upgrading, interconnecting, and provisioning of these functions are expected to be completely automated in a 5G deployment. O-RAN defines real-time and non-real-time RAN intelligent controllers (RICs) to take care of this and many other automated tasks in a 5G MCN. Similarly, use of automation at the transport layer is expected—both at the device level, such as zero-touch deployment, and for cross-network domains, such as the use of PCE to deploy SRTE policy.

5G MCN therefore relies heavily on automation and orchestration at every level—whether it's the mobile core, the RAN components, or the cross-domain transport network. Collectively, these automation mechanisms need to jive well to meet 5G's expectations. The resulting cost saving from such automation is exactly what the goal behind virtualization, containerization, and hardware disaggregation had been. Mobile service providers utilizing automation claim to be able to provision a 5G cell site in just a few minutes—a feat that previously would have taken hours, if not days.[25]

It must be highlighted that the benefits of automation are only truly meaningful when scale and repetition are involved. In a low-scale deployment, or for tasks that only need to be done once, the effort required to automate outweighs the benefits. Hence, the decision to automate requires some consideration and thought toward the cost to automate.

Even though public cloud platforms are perceived to be strong and mature in their automation capabilities, those automation frameworks generally cover only instantiation, basic connectivity, and lifecycle management of virtualized or containerized functions and services. However, this is just a fraction of the overall automation requirement. Network devices' configuration management, service level assurance, and network-wide monitoring are equally critical and essential for an efficient MCN.

Device-Level Automation

Device-level automation can be considered a combination of automated deployment of the network device, the provisioning of services on it, and ongoing operations involving the said device. The idea of automated deployment of hardware, colloquially referred to as *zero-touch deployment (ZTD)*, is not new in the server and compute world. However, network devices have started to implement this capability only recently. Through the use of ZTD capabilities, a network device is expected to be able to discover a software repository, download and install a predetermined network operating system, and provision itself by downloading and parsing the production configuration. ZTD ensures that all of this can take place without human intervention, save for connecting the physical links and device powerup. Depending on the nature of ZTD implementation, a network designer might not need to take any special measures. If the server hosting the image and configurations is accessible using the public

Internet, the networking devices might be able to use local Wi-Fi service, Bluetooth connectivity to a device with Internet access, or even a mobile network to reach those servers. On the other hand, if the image-hosting servers are reachable only via the intranet of the service provider (which is often the case), network boot methods such as *iPreboot eXecution Environment (iPXE)* can be used, which involves use of *Dynamic Host Configuration Protocol (DHCP)*. In such cases, the network designer might need to provision DHCP relays as well as take extra measures to block off rogue DHCP requests.

For ongoing operations and management of the devices through automation, the network devices should be application friendly and provide an interface to applications and programs through the use of APIs. Some examples of protocols used for network device configuration management are Netconf and Google Network Management Interface (gNMI). These typically rely on configuration and data-modeling techniques such as YANG as well as data encapsulation methods such as Google Remote Procedure Call (gRPC), eXtensible Markup Language (XML), and Java Script Object Notation (JSON). Details of these protocols and technologies, however, are beyond the scope of this book.

Cross-Domain Automation

While device-level automation is important, it is only a small subset of automatable workflows. In a network as large as an MCN, cross-domain automation is equally if not more important, and it complements the device-level automation. Each transport network domain should be able to support automation within it, as well as cohesively with other domains. The most prominent example of use of such automation in 5G MCN is the implementation of network slicing.

Network slicing is not limited to an individual MCN domain. To establish an E2E network slice; RAN, 5GC, and transport network must implement slicing functions within their domain, which collectively comprise an end-to-end *Network Slice Instance (NSI)*. The domain-specific slice is called a *Network Slice Subnet Instance (NSSI)* and would require an over-arching slice controller to identify individual NSSIs as part of an end-to-end NSI. There could be 1:1, N:1, or 1:N mapping between NSSIs in each domain. For instances, multiple RAN slices could be mapped to a single transport network slice, or vice versa. Without a viable cross-domain controller, relying on automated *Network Slicing Template (NST)* that can instantiate and tear down slices within each domain, stitching them together as and when required, network slicing will be impossible to implement in an 5G MCN. This is but one example of the importance of cross-domain automation. CI/CD and DevOps models, which are quickly becoming mainstream, rely heavily on cross-domain automation to keep networks running smoothly at scale with minimal or no human intervention.

Closed-Loop Automation: Assess, Automate, Reassess

Automation's role is not limited to predetermined tasks and functions. In fact, the use of closed-loop automation (where monitoring and analytics are used in conjunction with automation) offers a very compelling use case. This could offer self-managed, self-optimizing, and self-healing networks. Figure 10-18 provides a pictorial view of the key ingredients of a closed-loop automation flow.

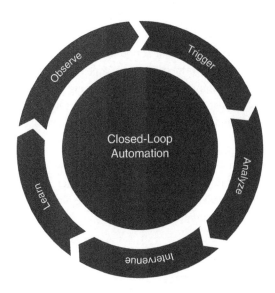

FIGURE 10-18 Key Ingredients of Closed-Loop Automation

Each one of the key ingredients shown in the figure performs functions and actions critical to closed-loop automation, with the basic idea of such a system revolving around the following capabilities:

- **Observe and monitor**: The state of the network devices, interfaces, mobile functions, amount of traffic, resource utilization, and so on can be observed in various ways. For network devices, the design process should consider the use of both the traditional methods and protocols such as Simple Network Management Protocol (SNMP), NetFlow, and device logs, as well as use of network telemetry techniques that have been gaining popularity lately. Monitoring of cloud-native components also needs to be part of the automation design strategy, and it is typically done through use of keepalives and health stats (CPU utilization, memory consumption, and so on) of the individual functions. Tools that are part of NFV's management and orchestration (MANO) block perform this monitoring for the CNF and VNF.

- **Trigger**: Observation leads to knowledge of triggers, which stand out as an anomaly or change in state of a monitored parameter. This change might be benign, or it might be detrimental to the network or virtual functions. A closed-loop automation design should be able to identify and detect these triggers.

- **Analyze**: To determine the nature of the anomaly, and to determine the appropriate reactive step, if needed, it is critical to analyze the information from the trigger. Preexisting anomaly signatures and repositories of known problems and solutions may be used for this purpose and are expected to be an implicit part of any closed-loop automation strategy. By matching against these signatures, a closed-loop automation system can accurately determine the nature of the trigger and the corrective action (if any) that can be taken.

■ **Intervene**: If analysis has led to the conclusion that there is need for action to correct, remediate, or resolve the root cause, then intervention can be performed. This could be of a very diverse nature. For example, in a network the intervention might involve provisioning a new SR-TE policy, deploying a new service, or even actions at a lower level such as restarting a device or process. Protocols such as gNMI, Netconf, and simple command-line interfaces may be used for this.

■ **Learn**: A closed-loop automation system can work well using existing signatures. However, such a design should ideally make use of machine learning (ML) and artificial intelligence (AI) capabilities and hence should be continuously learning, adapting, and improving the observation, trigger, and analysis capabilities, thus closing the automation loop.

Deciphering 5G Mobile Requirements

The first step toward building a viable transport network capable of supporting 5G services is to accurately understand the RAN and mobile core language. The network planning and architecture team must be well-versed in 5G jargon and able to translate that into specific requirements a network should meet. The network architecture team must be willing to step outside of their comfort zone (that is, routing and switching) and able to engage in conversation with various other 5G teams. Those conversations should involve direct but meaningful questions that help the network architects to plot out the foundation of a 5G transport network design. The following conversation is just an example how the networking team can interact with the RAN, mobile core, and deployment teams to extract and decipher these requirements. The network team is represented by NW, whereas the RAN, deployment, and mobile core teams are represented by the RAN, DEP, and MC abbreviations, respectively.

RAN	We have recently purchased a new chunk of C-band and mmWave spectrum. We are planning to put this spectrum to use shortly by deploying 4000 new 5G cell sites, as well as repurpose the existing macrocells. Can you plan your network to support this?	
	Wonderful news, but this gives us almost no information to make our decisions. Do you mind if we ask some follow-up questions?	NW
RAN	Sure, what do you want to know?	
	Can you provide us with a breakdown on the sites about how many sectors and carriers will be on each one?	NW
RAN	Seventy percent of the sites are macrocells, with three sectors, four carriers each. Remaining are single-sector, single-carrier small cells.	

	So, for the macrocells, it will be 12 interfaces coming from the RUs, one interface per sector per carrier? And only one interface on small cells?	NW
RAN	Correct!	
	Are these all D-RAN sites?	NW
RAN	No, we are moving away from D-RAN. Almost all new sites will be O-RAN compliant vRAN sites. Some will be non-O-RAN sites but still use vRAN architecture.	
	Oh, so most will be 7-2x eCPRI from RUs, so we are all good, as these will be Ethernet based. Can you tell us what split options are used for non O-RAN sites?	NW
RAN	They will be Split Option 8 for LLs and Option 2 for HLS.	
	Oh, that's a bit of a problem, as we will have to terminate CPRI on CSRs. Fortunately, we do have network vendors that have RoE functionality implemented on their CSR and enough uplink bandwidth to accommodate the number of radios on the site. We just need to make sure our topology does not get overloaded by multiples of these sites in the same ring.	NW
	Are there any advance antenna features that might affect the bandwidth requirements?	NW
RAN	Yes, absolutely! We will use 32×32 massive MIMO in most cases.	
	That's great, but how many transmit and receive layers?	NW
RAN	It will be 4T4R in most cases.	
	So, we are looking at four times the max network bandwidth for these sites. We'll make sure the network interfaces and topology can handle this, but we will need more details on the exact bandwidth for each of the eCPRI and CPRI interfaces. Can you ask the RAN equipment vendor to use their BW calculators based on the channel width, modulation techniques, and other parameters?	NW
RAN	Alright, we will get exact CPRI rate options for each Split 8 RU. We will get the average and peak bandwidth expectations for each eCPRI interface.	
	That will help a lot with network bandwidth dimensioning.	NW
	Based on the information, this seems to be a dual-split vRAN scenario. Where do you plan to place your DUs—at each cell site, or pool them at the far far-edge DC?	NW
RAN	A mix of both actually. DUs for suburban and rural areas would be at cell sites, but for urban areas we are looking to pool DUs at macrocell sites acting as far-edge DCs. Also, CUs will be pooled at Edge DC sites.	
	So there will be a mix of fronthaul, midhaul, and backhaul networks. We need to get some information from the deployment team about prospective cell sites as well as far-edge and edge DCs.	NW
DEP	We have compiled a list of sites with adequate power and space availability to act as far-edge and edge DCs.	
	Wonderful, what do the distances between the cell sites and their respective far-edge DCs look like?	NW

DEP	Not that much, between 5 and 25 kilometers.	
	We cannot go to 25 kilometers. For every site above 15-kilometer distance, we need to find a new far-edge location.	NW
DEP	Why? We have used far longer distances in 4G deployments and never had any issues.	
	True, but those were all backhaul deployments, so distance was not a limiting factor. In fronthaul, the RU-DU distances cannot exceed 20 kilometers in the best-case scenario due to strict latency requirements. We need to keep it under 15 kilometers to accommodate any latency introduced by the transport nodes.	NW
DEP	That's a problem, but we will see what we can do. Maybe some sites need to be upgraded to far-edge DCs to accommodate this.	
	Another question: do you plan to install a GNSS receiver at every cell site?	NW
DEP	No, just a handful of cell sites and all the far-edge DC sites.	
	That's fine. We just need to ensure that every FE DC has it so that timing information can be propagated to every cell site. We need to use Class-C PTP devices in the fronthaul anyway to ensure accuracy and precision.	NW
	Given all the new spectrum and antenna functions, we expect much higher bandwidth in the xHaul network. Should we plan to haul everything back to the regional DC for offloading to the Internet, as before?	NW
MC	No. We want to offload the traffic from our network as soon as possible. So, we are implementing CUPS and bringing 5GC closer to the subscribers. Most of the UPFs will be collocated with the CUs in the edge DC.	
	That would help. Now only the midhaul will need to carry higher bandwidth traffic, but it will still be lower than the fronthaul, as all baseband processing is done by the DUs at the far-edge DC or at the cell sites. We would need peering at edge DCs in addition to regional and national DCs.	NW
MC	Yes.	
	Anything else you think the network team should know?	NW
MC	Given that everyone is moving to the cloud, we will run some 5GC workloads in the public cloud as well.	
	That is interesting. We will need to find out more from the cloud provider how we can build our VPN services and other network functions on top of their infrastructure.	NW
	We believe we have enough information for now to start planning transport services for the new mobile offering.	NW

The preceding communication exchange is highly hypothetical; however, it outlines the importance of the RAN and 5GC knowledge a network architect must possess to accurately extract required information from the RAN and mobile core teams. Once the network architects acquire enough information, they can start network planning and finalize underlying transport technologies, topologies, protocols, and services to fulfill the 5G MCN promise.

Summary

As highlighted in earlier chapters, in a 5G MCN, the mobile system components such as RAN and 5GC are much more tightly coupled with the transport network than ever before. Hence, not only is it crucial for transport network architects to work closely and understand those mobile communication domains, but they also have to understand the requirements imposed by those domains when designing the transport network. Network control points, in most 5G deployments, are moving towards the RAN, and, as such, network architects must be able to carry on intelligent conversation with the RAN team in order to extract actionable intelligence to build effective 5G transport networks. The 5GC move toward SBA and CUPS adds an additional layer of complexity that the network architects need to deal with.

A typical network design for data networking is predominantly focused on bandwidth, high availability, and services; however, the network design in an MCN has to put additional focus on environmental constraints, latency and distance, and physical characteristics, among other factors. All of the following design and selection criteria were discussed in this chapter:

- Fronthaul design considerations, including the impact of the lower-layer split option, viable fronthaul transport technologies, and the importance of a far-edge DC location

- Physical topology, distributed peering, and QoS design for an end-to-end xHaul network

- Commonly used vRAN deployment scenarios and the coexistence of previous mobile generations in 5G

- Selecting the right network device based on varying factors for fronthaul, midhaul, and backhaul networks

- Approaches to simplify routing design in Seamless MPLS and PCE-based deployment architectures

- The nature and composition of transport network services to interconnect different xHaul and 5GC domains

- The growing role of public clouds in creating 5G MCN and how this is driving architectural innovation across public clouds and private service provider infrastructures

- The importance of programmability and automation in deploying, operating, and managing the new 5G MCNs

This chapter concluded by amalgamating a network architecture's knowledge of mobile networks with that of the new innovations in transport networks. A hypothetical conversation was used to demonstrate how a transport network architect can decipher the RAN and 5GC requirements and start designing the 5G mobile communication network.

References

1. Viktor Skogman, "Building efficient fronthaul networks using packet technologies," https://www.ericsson.com/en/blog/2020/4/building-efficient-fronthaul-networks-using-packet-technologies (last visited: March 2022)

2. Peter Fetterolf, "An Economic Comparison of Fronthaul Architectures for 5G Networks," https://www.cisco.com/c/dam/en/us/solutions/collateral/service-provider/mobile-internet/acg-fronthaul-architectures-for-5g-networks.pdf (last visited: March 2022)

3. https://www.ciscolive.com/c/dam/r/ciscolive/us/docs/2021/pdf/BRKSPG-2065.pdf

4. O-RAN Xhaul Transport Requirements 1.0, November 2020 (O-RAN.WG9.XTRP-REQ-v01.00), https://www.o-ran.org/specifications

5. O-RAN Hardware Reference Design Specification for Fronthaul Gateway 2.0, July 2021 (O-RAN.WG7.FHGW-HRD.0-v02.00), https://www.o-ran.org/specifications

6. "Cisco NCS 540 Fronthaul Router Portfolio At-a-Glance," https://www.cisco.com/c/en/us/products/collateral/routers/network-convergence-system-540-series-routers/at-a-glance-c45-743315.html (last visited: March 2022)

7. IEEE 802.1, "Time-Sensitive Networking (TSN) Task Group," https://1.ieee802.org/tsn/ (last visited: March 2022)

8. IEEE 802.1CM, "Time-Sensitive Networking for Fronthaul," https://www.ieee802.org/1/files/public/docs2018/cm-farkas-overview-0718-v01.pdf (last visited: March 2022)

9. O-RAN Xhaul Packet Switched Architectures and Solutions 2.0, July 2021 (O-RAN.WG9.XPSAAS-v02.00), https://www.o-ran.org/specifications

10. 3GPP TS 23.501, "System architecture for the 5G System"

11. Mobility Solutions, Infrastructure, & Sustainability Committee, City of Dallas, "Deployment Update of Small Cell Network Nodes," https://dallascityhall.com/government/Council%20Meeting%20Documents/msis_3_deployment-update-of-small-cell-network-nodes_combined_051319.pdf (last visited: March 2022)

12. City of Fairfax, Virginia, "Small Cell Antennas & Wireless Facilities," https://www.fairfaxva.gov/government/public-works/small-cell-antennas-wireless-facilities (last visited: March 2022)

13. ANSI/IEC 60529-2020, "Degrees of Protection Provided by Enclosures (IP Code) (Identical National Adoption)," https://www.nema.org/docs/default-source/about-us-document-library/ansi-iec_60529-2020-contents-and-scopef0908377-f8db-4395-8aaa-97331d276fef.pdf (last visited: March 2022)

14. IETF RFC 5838, "Support of Address Families in OSPFv3"

15. O-RAN Xhaul Packet Switched Architectures and Solutions 2.0, July 2021 (O-RAN.WG9. XPSAAS-v02.00), https://www.o-ran.org/specifications

16. IETF RFC 8604, "Interconnecting Millions of Endpoints with Segment Routing"

17. Rakuten Mobile and Rakuten Communications Platform New Initiatives, http://global.rakuten.com/corp/investors/assets/doc/documents/20Q2_Mobile_E.pdf (last visited: March 2022)

18. Caroline Gabriel, "Rakuten close to deploying the first 5G cloud-native vRAN," https://re-thinkresearch.biz/articles/rakuten-close-to-deploying-the-first-5g-cloud-native-vran-2/ (last visited: March 2022)

19. Rakuten Mobile and Rakuten Communications Platform New Initiatives, http://global.rakuten.com/corp/investors/assets/doc/documents/20Q2_Mobile_E.pdf (last visited: March 2022)

20. Ibid.

21. Diana Goovaerts, "Nokia teams with Google Cloud on 5G core, edge," https://www.mobile-worldlive.com/featured-content/top-three/nokia-teams-with-google-cloud-on-5g-core-edge (last visited: March 2022)

22. https://telecomstechnews.com/news/2021/nov/17/cisco-and-dish-establish-multi-layered-agreement-to-accelerate-5g-services-deployment/ (last visited: March 2022)

23. https://www.netmanias.com/en/?m=view&id=oneshot&no=15098 (last visited: March 2022)

24. Ryan Daws, "AWS Private 5G helps enterprises to deploy and scale their own networks," https://telecomstechnews.com/news/2021/dec/01/aws-private-5g-helps-enterprises-deploy-scale-own-networks/ (last visited: March 2022)

25. GSMA Association, "Altiostar and Rakuten Mobile Demonstrate Success Across Performance and Scalability for Open RAN Network," https://www.gsma.com/membership/resources/altiostar-and-rakuten-mobile-demonstrate-success-across-performance-and-scalability-for-open-ran-network/ (last visited: March 2022)

Afterword: Beyond 5G

The ink is barely dry on the 5G specifications and its adoption still nascent, yet industry insiders are already abuzz with the possibilities 6G will bring. The transition from 4G LTE to 5G is not a one-time flip-of-a-switch transformation but rather a journey composed of gradual enhancements and upgrades to cellular capabilities, new service offerings, and a shift toward cloud-native architectures. This gradual transition is in line with all the previous cellular generational transitions and will continue to be the model for the future. Similar to how IMT-2020 specifications, defined in 2015, became the foundational standard for 5G, IMT-2030, expected around the year 2025, would lay the foundation for services that will define the next era of cellular services—6G.

Mobile operators and service providers have steadily been putting the newly acquired RF spectrum into service, while deploying vRAN architectures, xHaul transport, and cloud-native 5G Core. At the same time, members of academia, industry groups, government-led institutions, and equipment vendors are hard at work advancing the cellular technology further. Some of the preliminary concepts at the forefront of 6G development are the accelerated use of artificial intelligence (AI), machine learning (ML), the possibility of a new human–machine interface, and, of course, additional bandwidth through higher-frequency RF spectrum.

Increased bandwidth usage has been a consistently common factor across all mobile generations, and the trend is expected to continue, even accelerate, in 6G with the continued adoption of bandwidth-intensive applications. 5G unlocked new sub-7GHz and mmWave spectrum in the 24–52GHz range, and research is ongoing to unlock an even higher spectrum in the 100GHz–10THz range, generally referred to as terahertz (THz) frequencies. The challenge associated with THz frequencies is their signal propagation properties—similar to the mmWave spectrum. Not only is it more difficult for THz frequency waves to penetrate buildings and structures, they are also more easily impacted by the slightest weather anomalies. Research is ongoing to gauge the commercial viability of THz frequency ranges for cellular use as well as new and innovative antenna designs to overcome some of the obstacles associated with such a high frequency range spectrum.

However, higher speeds and bandwidth availability are usually a means to an end—in this case to support new service offerings. What these new services are going to be in 6G are anyone's guess at this point in time, but industry experts agree that 6G will further blur the lines between the human, physical, digital, and virtual worlds. Previous cellular generations had been underscored by multimedia and, to some extent, immersive content, but future cellular generations will be defined by the fusion of these different "worlds" and the extrasensory experiences resulting from this fusion. Sure enough, the augmented reality (AR), virtual reality (VR), and mixed reality (MR) applications (collectively called XR) will continue to grow and thrive, but experts also theorize the use of a new human–machine interface, where humans interact with their environment and other users through sensory and haptic messaging. Whether this new human–machine interface will be in the form of wearable tech, smart body implants, embedded devices in one's environment, a combination of all these, or something entirely different is yet to be seen. It is, however, abundantly evident that such an interface will use massive amounts of data and require ultra-low response time, while maintaining mobility, signifying the continued importance of Multi-access Edge Compute (MEC).

This new framework of multiple infused worlds, referred by some as the metaverse, will create digital societies for people to interact in this new environment. The concept of the metaverse, however, has far reaching real-life applications beyond just leisure and entertainment. It provides an environment free from spatial or temporal constraints that can be used to simulate and monitor physical world activities in a virtual world. Coupled with advancement in AI, ML, and automation, this metaverse can be used to analyze, predict, and solve problems before they manifest in the physical world. Next-generation industrial operations are expected to go beyond simple automation and use these new capabilities in a wireless environment, potentially powered by private 6G to create safe and effective environments that usher in a new era of productivity.

If history is any indication, 6G will fulfill a lot of the promises of 5G and will make some of its own. The research and standardization work for 6G is still in the early stages, but both industry players as well as governments around the globe are looking to influence the standardization effort with ideas of their own. 5G (and 4G before that) have definitively proven the ever-growing importance of mobile telecommunication, and the technology leaders of 6G will undoubtedly hold the proverbial keys to the kingdom in an ever-changing geo-political landscape.

So what does this mean for the network architects? 5G will dominate the mobile landscape the next few years. 6G is still in its infancy and will need years to become a subject of broad interest. For a network architect, however, the trajectory has already been set for supporting the subsequent mobile generations. Besides the introduction of new networking protocols as well as the design challenges associated with vRAN and mobile core decomposition, network architects must acquire additional skill sets to design cellular networks over both private and public cloud environments. The increased scale of deployment as well as time-to-market pressures will also demand expert knowledge of automation and deployment tools such as Kubernetes and Ansible. In short, the network architects of the future will be required to bring the cutting-edge network technologies into the very fabric of cloud environments. These are the skills this book has focused on and will be necessary for any network architect over the next decade.

Index

Symbols

I

U

Photo by marvent/Shutterstock

VIDEO TRAINING FOR THE **IT PROFESSIONAL**

LEARN QUICKLY
Learn a new technology in just hours. Video training can teach more in less time, and material is generally easier to absorb and remember.

WATCH AND LEARN
Instructors demonstrate concepts so you see technology in action.

TEST YOURSELF
Our Complete Video Courses offer self-assessment quizzes throughout.

CONVENIENT
Most videos are streaming with an option to download lessons for offline viewing.

Learn more, browse our store, and watch free, sample lessons at
informit.com/video

Save 50%* off the list price of video courses with discount code **VIDBOB**